Islamic Philosophy and the Crisis of Modernity

SUNY SERIES IN THE THOUGHT AND LEGACY OF LEO STRAUSS

KENNETH HART GREEN, EDITOR

Islamic Philosophy and the Crisis of Modernity

Leo Strauss's Relationship with al-Fārābī, Avicenna, and Averroes

Georges Tamer

Translated by Ezra Tzfadya

SUNY PRESS

Cover Credit: Wikimedia.org, "Leo_Strauss_USA_1939.jpg"
Published by State University of New York Press, Albany

Printed in the United States of America

Original version "Islamische Philosophie und die Krise der Moderne: Das Verhältnis von Leo Strauss zu Alfarabi, Avicenna und Averroes" by Georges Tamer (Brill, 2001), ISBN 9789004120297. © BRILL, all rights reserved. This English translation was published by arrangement with BRILL.

The transliteration of Arabic and Hebrew words follows the transliteration rules of the Library of Congress.

For information, contact State University of New York Press, Albany, NY
www.sunypress.edu

Library of Congress Cataloging-in-Publication Data
Names: Tamer, Georges, author.
Title: Islamic philosophy and the crisis of modernity : Leo Strauss's relationship with al-Farabi, Avicenna, and Averroes / Georges Tamer ; translated by Ezra Tzfadya.
Other titles: Islamische Philosophie und die Krise der Moderne. English
Description: Albany : State University of New York Press, 2024. | Series: Suny series in the thought and legacy of Leo Strauss | Includes bibliographical references and index. | Translated from German.
Identifiers: LCCN 2024012208 | ISBN 9798855800111 (hardcover) | ISBN 9798855800135 (ebook)
Subjects: LCSH: Islamic philosophy. | Fārābī. | Avicenna, 980-1037. | Averroës, 1126-1198. | Strauss, Leo. | Political science--Philosophy.
Classification: LCC B741 .T3513 2024 | DDC 181/.07--dc23/eng/20240814
LC record available at https://lccn.loc.gov/2024012208

10 9 8 7 6 5 4 3 2 1

Dedicated to the Memory of Marie
and Nicolas Tamer

CONTENTS

Translator's Foreword **ix**

Acknowledgments **xiii**

Introduction to the Translation **xv**

Introduction to the Original Text 1

Chapter One: On the Genesis of Leo Strauss's Thought:
Spinoza and Averroes 25

Chapter Two: Discovery and Change 39

Chapter Three: The Fruits of Change 55

Chapter Four: Crisis and Prophecy 79

Chapter Five: Reason, Religion, and Social Order 105

Chapter Six: Leo Strauss, al-Fārābī, and the
Primacy of Political Philosophy 133

Epilogue 171

Appendix: Arabic Texts and the Texts of
Islamic Philosophers Viewed by Strauss **187**

Notes **191**

Bibliography **269**

Index **307**

TRANSLATOR'S FOREWORD

This text was first published in 2001 amid the political tumult of 9/11, the Second Intifada, and increasing tensions between Muslims and non-Muslims in western and central Europe. Polemical discourses emerged surrounding Islamic fundamentalism, with Samuel Huntington's "clash of civilizations" narrative imposed upon the relationship between Islam and the West. These polemics inspired renewed academic interest in questions of Carl Schmitt's political theology pertaining to public religion and political demarcations made by statespersons and public intellectuals between "friends and enemies." Additionally, the medieval tradition of Islamic philosophy rooted in the rational powers of human reason also began to receive increased attention from scholars in the humanities and religious leaders concerned with interreligious dialogue. The tradition of Islamic philosophy could serve as an internal Islamic antidote that could make Islam commensurable with the democratic demands of Rawlsian public reason in the Western public sphere. Using the resources of this Greek-inspired Islamic philosophical tradition, scholars could thereby push back against arguments that Islam was not solely a religion of legalist theocracy but also a religion concerned with human autonomy and philosophic reason. Islam, like the modern West, draws on Plato and Aristotle to promote democracy. Islam could and should be a friend and not an enemy. Leo Strauss, this book argues, was a nuanced critic of Schmitt uniquely attuned to questions of both modern public religion and political theology while being immersed in the philosophical traditions of Hellenic antiquity and medieval Judeo-Islamic civilization. Indeed, *Islamische Philosophie und die Krise der Moderne* foresaw the explosion of studies on Strauss that ensured in the subsequent two decades partially as a response to the developments described above.

Currently, in the early 2020s, "the West" itself is once again facing a crisis of democracy. Populist forces of nationalism and "Judeo-Christian" theocratic fundamentalism are on the rise, increasingly voted into power through democratic structures whose democratic values they are often keen on undermining in favor of a majoritarian "will of the people." The explosion of digital communications technologies over the past two decades was originally perceived as heralding an era of globalized democratic political mobilization, as reflected in the Islamic world by the Arab Spring and in the West by the twice-elected Obama coalition and deepened European Union integration. Yet the "crisis of modernity" identified by Strauss in his early texts of the 1920s and 1930s, texts written in the shadow of nationalism, populism, and fascism, appears to have returned. Strauss seems to offer intellectual resources in our age for the following two interlocking questions: How can democratically committed elites successfully "manage" diverse democracies in the public sphere through political philosophy and/or ideology such that antidemocratic populism does not take control over the powerful apparatus of the nation-state? And how can moral values be epistemically imprinted on the populace through a close coordination of the religious and political spheres? In a contemporary era torn between the poles of postmodern secularism keen on dispensing with universal morality in favor of a nebulously defined consensual ethics and populist forms of nationalism and fundamentalism that worship revelation-based morality and/or the power of politics to enable the "will of the people," these questions assume outsize importance for political philosophers and theorists. As Strauss might argue, the answers to these questions are to be found through a careful reading of the philosophies of medieval Jewish sages such as Maimonides and Judah Halevi, along with Islamic greats such as al-Fārābī, Averroes, and Avicenna. Taken together, the study of these figures could ultimately unlock the political power of the original sages: Plato and Socrates.

Thus, a translation of Georges Tamer's philosophically erudite and philologically rigorous book emerges as a necessary contribution to and intervention into the current scholarship on Strauss. Unlike many studies, it neither worships Strauss nor attempts to negate the power and value of his most important insights. Tamer, a notable scholar of Islamic philosophy with a command of classical Arabic that far exceeded Strauss's abilities, highlights the philological, and in turn conceptual, errors and distortions of Strauss's scholarship on Islamic sources. Yet he also appreciates the normative power of the ideas emerging from both "correct" and "error-prone" readings (some proved by Tamer to be deliberate!) and their relevance to Strauss's larger philosophical project: How can one ensconce the ideas of past masters in a continuous yet often hidden tradition of political philosophy operating between the poles of reason and revelation? And how can such masters be rendered relevant for the "crisis of modernity" ensuing from the secular transformations of the European Enlightenment?

This was an incredibly difficult text to translate due to its philosophical depth and the necessary command it required of both German and Arabic. I wish to thank Professor Tamer for his patient mentorship in seeing this project to its completion and his chair of oriental philology and Islamic studies at the University of Erlangen – Nürnberg for funding the translation. My gratitude goes to Professor Kenneth Hart Green and Dr. Michael Rinella of SUNY Press for the extended deadlines, editorial support, and recognition of the immense intellectual value of this translation. And a special thanks goes to Mr. Yaaqub Kutterer of the University of Erlangen – Nürnberg for his careful and crucial editorial efforts. I would finally like to acknowledge both the Allen and Joan Bildner Center for the Study of Jewish Life at Rutgers in New Brunswick, New Jersey, where I am serving in the spring term of 2023 as the Norman and Syril Reitman Visiting Scholar in Jewish Studies, and Indiana University's Center for the Study of the Middle East, where I have served as a senior fellow since 2021.

— Ezra Tzfadya

The Upper West Side

January 2023

ACKNOWLEDGMENTS

In the last two decades following the publication of my book *Islamische Philosophie und die Krise der Moderne: Das Verhältnis von Leo Strauss zu Alfarabi, Avicenna und Averroes*, I have had the opportunity to constructively engage with various other scholars interested in the thought of Leo Strauss. I have had productive conversations with Professors Clemens Kauffmann (d. 2020), Harald Bluhm, Charles Butterworth, John P. McCormick, and Rasoul Namazi. However, the scholar with whom I have shared the most intensive engagement with Strauss is Dr. Thomas Meyer. Dr. Meyer has greatly expanded my knowledge of Strauss's early years in Kirchhain, Germany. He exposed me to materials from the Strauss archive that demonstrate the close connection of Strauss's intellectual development with his engagement with medieval Muslim sources. These insights have confirmed many of the research results presented in this book. I thank him and my other colleagues immensely for their insights.

I would like to thank Dr. Ezra Tzfadya for translating this book. I would also like to offer my sincere thanks to Professor Kenneth Hart Green for accepting this book in his series at SUNY Press. His patience following an extended delay in submission of the manuscript is much appreciated. My gratitude extends to Dr. Michael Rinella at SUNY Press for his patient supervision of this project. This book should have been published much earlier, but exceptional circumstances such as the COVID-19 pandemic and various career developments delayed its completion.

— Georges Tamer

INTRODUCTION TO THE TRANSLATION

Twenty years after its publication in German, this book has now been translated into English. However, its subject matter has lost none of its relevance. The importance of medieval Muslim philosophers, and of al-Fārābī in particular, for the thought of Leo Strauss and the development of his philosophy has gained traction, as recent studies of his thought show.[1] Additionally, Strauss's importance for the study of Islamic philosophy in the twentieth century remains uncontested. Strauss, along with his colleagues and students, is responsible not only for the scholarship on philosophers such as al-Fārābī, Avicenna, and Averroes but also for the publication and translation of al-Fārābī's works, which previously existed only in manuscript form. Such an effort has led to the development of a productive discourse and an explosion of scholarly circles around medieval Islamic philosophy (and especially al-Fārābī). Nevertheless, the relationship of medieval Muslim philosophy to Strauss's thought remains to be explored.[2]

The studies included in this book reveal the way Strauss dealt with the philosophy of Averroes, Avicenna, and, most importantly, al-Fārābī. The book begins with his work on Spinoza and proceeds to examine his later oeuvre. It reveals the impact of those ideas emerging largely from these earlier works on his overall approach to political philosophy. Using a methodological combination of primary-source-based philology and intellectual history, I critique the relative strengths and weaknesses of Strauss's engagement with medieval Islamic philosophy.

In this introduction to the English translation of this book, I would like to summarize Strauss's overall approach to the Muslim philosophers rather than delve into the content developed in the following chapters. Leo Strauss discovered the importance of Averroes for Spinoza's critique of religion and notion of the state early in his career. Through the nineteenth century, this Andalusian philosopher was vitally important for intellectual efforts in Europe aimed at achieving a separation between church and state. His ideas made an enormous impact upon Strauss's evolution from a young man growing up in an Orthodox Jewish milieu to a philosopher who adhered to "atheism out of honesty."[3] Thus, Strauss's engagement with Averroes continued beyond his book on Spinoza.[4] A statement by Avicenna, even if misinterpreted, led Strauss to an intensive engagement with religion within the framework of Platonic political philosophy. This topic should be regarded as his lifelong preoccupation. From

Avicenna's statement onward, Strauss understood religion as law. His critique of the Enlightenment focused on its perceived expulsion of religion from the public sphere. It prompted him to engage with medieval Islamic philosophy as a useful vehicle for articulating the "political-theological problem" latent in Spinoza. This effort would consume his entire career.

The hidden conceptual allusions in Avicenna's pronouncement gave Strauss a decisive motivation to return to Plato.[5] However, the use of Platonic thought to ground the law of revelation and prophecy was something Strauss discovered in al-Fārābī. It was in al-Fārābī's works that Strauss found the guidance he was looking for in order to link prophecy and religious law to Plato.[6] Indeed, it is at the philosophical intersection of al-Fārābī and Plato that Strauss's peculiar interpretive power reveals itself in particular sharpness. He interprets al-Fārābī's writings on Plato in such a way that the tenth-century Muslim philosopher becomes what Strauss considers a "true" Platonist, one who correctly understood Platonic philosophy and thus identified Islam as the realization of the Platonic ideal state and Plato's *Laws* as the basis for the philosophical interpretation of Islamic sharia. Moreover, Strauss made al-Fārābī an atheist and an esoteric philosopher who invented Platonic speeches. Strauss appears to have personal motives for this move. Al-Fārābī, whom Strauss portrays as an atheist, allows for Maimonides, specifically the Maimonides of *Dalālat al-Ḥāʾirīn* (Guide for the Perplexed), to be considered an infidel philosopher without compromising his esteemed position in Jewish intellectual history. Strauss — as a former Orthodox Jew — needed a philosophical justification for his own atheism. The al-Fārābī, and subsequently the Maimonides, he fashioned together provided him with such a justification.

However, in his interpretation of al-Fārābī's writings on Plato, Strauss ignored historical facts, for example, by tacitly assuming that al-Fārābī knew Plato's writings, especially the *Laws*, in their entirety, which is not at all consistent with the history of the transmission of the Platonic dialogues into Arabic.[7] Strauss thus fashioned al-Fārābī in his own image and made him his primary point of reference in treating religion as an indispensable factor of social order, which, according to Strauss, is used by philosophers so that they can pursue philosophy as a relentless search for truth without exposing themselves to censure or persecution by the society whose stability they threaten with their irreligious project of inquiry.[8]

In the following chapters, I present a detailed, philologically rigorous, and source-based criticism of both Strauss's interpretation of al-Fārābī, Avicenna, and Averroes and his own understanding of Islamic philosophy. In this introduction, I intend to deal only with the scholarship on Strauss that has emerged since the publication of my book, especially those studies critical of my own conclusions. Unfortunately, I do not have space here to discuss all Straussian interpretations of medieval Islamic philosophy, which have percolated in the last few decades.[9]

I begin by discussing the philosophical-historical question of the extent to which the fact that Avicenna, admittedly without knowing it, referred to a pseudo-Platonic Book of Laws when he spoke of Plato's treatment of prophecy and religious law in two "Books of Laws" would shake the philosophical-historical foundations of Strauss's own interpretation of religion within a Platonic-political framework.[10]

Avicenna's claim regarding the treatment of prophecy and religious law in Plato's *Laws* became seminal for Leo Strauss, as mentioned above. It brought about a key change in his understanding of medieval Islamic and Jewish philosophy: Strauss now attributed to the Muslim philosophers the view that religious law has its counterpart in the Greek nomos and, thus, that the sharia is an essentially political phenomenon. This view was not one of mere philosophical-historical significance for Strauss. Rather, he adopted it himself and attempted to interpret religion purely politically within the framework of a "Platonizing political philosophy."[11] Those familiar with Strauss are well aware of the impact this Avicennian view had on his philosophical activity; the standard interpretation is that, under this influence, Strauss considered and attempted to explain the conflict between philosophy and revealed religion in the same way as the conflict between Plato and the poets.

In my investigation of a pseudo-Platonic *Book of Laws* (*Kitāb an-Nawāmīs li-Aflāṭūn*), I uncovered significant similarities with Avicenna's thought. Together with the *Nomoi*, which Plato is known to have authored, Avicenna evidently considered the spurious *Book of Laws* to be similarly genuine; consequently, the Platonic thought of which he was aware and that he considered suitable for the treatment of prophecy and religious law was not pure and unadulterated. Indeed, it was not identical in every instance with Plato's philosophy. In general, the extent to which Avicenna and other Muslim philosophers were familiar with Plato's actual works has yet to be fully fleshed out, for the Arabs apparently were only familiar with incomplete Platonic dialogues, which they derived from fragments and commentaries in most cases translated from Syriac.[12] This form of textual corruption led to a unique understanding of Plato in the medieval Arab world, thereby compelling us to better understand Avicenna's relationship with Plato.[13] It must lead us to carefully study the concepts he used in this context. Strauss does not do this, although he claims that his hermeneutics is characterized by a return to the history of philosophy in order to understand past philosophers as they understood themselves.[14]

Following the publication of my book, I made an outstanding discovery. Strauss knew early of the existence of the pseudo-Platonic book *Kitāb an-Nawāmīs li-Aflāṭūn*! The book is held in the University of Leiden's manuscript collection 169 Golius (cat. cod. or. III, 307). The mostly legible manuscript consists of forty folios. As reflected in the Leiden library records, Strauss borrowed it from Leiden through the Prussian State Library in Berlin from July 29, 1931, until August 3, 1932.[15] Thus, he knew that the Arabic *Kitāb an-Nawāmīs li-Aflāṭūn* and its mix of Greek and Islamic ideas was not composed by Plato. In the entry on the Bodleian manuscript of the same pseudo-Platonic book in Sachau and Ethé's 1889 catalog, p. 873, no. 1422, the translation of the work into Arabic is attributed to Ḥunayn ibn Isḥāq (d. 873/4 CE) or Abū ʿAlī Ibn Miskawayh (d. 1030 CE). However, this is also incorrect, as the book is not a translation from Greek but rather an Arabic forgery. Strauss was surely aware of these details. The fact that this manuscript was in his possession for an entire year proves that he definitely knew that a second Book of Laws was ascribed to Plato, which included the treatment of prophecy and sharia, was circulating in the lifetime of Avicenna, and was known to him. The Arabic text of the pseudo-Platonic *Kitāb an-Nawāmīs* with a translation and commentary will be available soon.[16]

Strauss may have ordered the manuscript from Leiden and studied it in the Prussian State Library after discovering Avicenna's statement on prophecy and law in his *Treatise on the Divisions of the Rational Sciences* in 1929 to 1930.[17] He must have discovered that this text differed significantly from Plato's *Laws* and was in fact an Islamic forgery. Nevertheless, he concealed the results of his research. In order to reconstruct the crucial passage of Avicenna's treatise according to his own interests, he acquired a manuscript from Gotha.[18] In this manuscript, one of the two books of the *Laws* is erroneously attributed to Aristotle.

Strauss should have interpreted Avicenna's ideas with a greater degree of care and circumspection. Strauss did not do that. An acknowledgment that Avicenna's statement on prophecy and religious law did not solely rely on Plato's *Nomoi* but was also falsely based on an Arabo-Islamic forgery would have weakened his attempted philosophical-historical Platonization of medieval Islamic and Jewish philosophy. Much of Avicenna's "Platonic" depictions of prophecy and religious law does not actually come from Plato himself but rather from the work of an unknown author or authors most likely from the tenth century.[19]

Therefore, my critique of Leo Strauss is not based solely on the historical fact that Muslim philosophers did not have access to Plato's *Laws*, as Rasoul Namazi accuses me of doing.[20] It is also guided by the certain knowledge that, in addition to the version of the *Nomoi* (which was summarized by al-Fārābī), Avicenna knew of a pseudo-Platonic text called *Plato's Laws* (*Kitāb an-Nawāmīs li-Aflāṭūn*), in which religious law (*sharīʿa*) is clearly and unmistakably differentiated from politics (*siyāsa*). This is precisely the work Avicenna was referring to when he referred to the treatment of prophecy (*nubuwwa*) and religious law (*sharīʿa*) in two "Books of the Laws," a fact that Strauss conveniently occludes. This fact stands in diametric opposition to Strauss's claim that the Muslim philosophers understood Muhammad, and Maimonides understood Moses to be a "Philosopher/Legislator," which "presupposes an idea that can be traced back to the Platonic Republic."[21]

Thus, Strauss did not merely misunderstand Avicenna, a fact I had assumed to be true in 2001. Instead, he self-consciously misrepresented certain ideas developed by Avicenna in a manner that served his purposes despite his own self-proclaimed hermeneutic imperative to understand philosophers as they understood themselves. Was it perhaps the discovery of this pseudo-Platonic work that prompted Strauss in *Philosophy and Law* to reconstruct Avicenna's argument using the Gotha manuscript instead of the printed text? In the printed version, Avicenna refers to two "Books of the Laws" (*nawāmīs*) without mentioning their authors. In the manuscript from Gotha used by Strauss, these books are explicitly attributed to Plato and Aristotle.[22] By identifying proper authorship in this manner, Strauss could tie Avicenna to Plato's *Laws*. Could this perhaps explain the fact that Strauss, in the quotation at the beginning of his last book, *The Argument and the Action of Plato's "Laws,"* simply omits the part of Avicenna's statement that is problematic for his own purposes?[23]

As far as I can see, Strauss never claimed that Aristotle wrote a Book of Laws. Such a title cannot even be found in Aristotelian or pseudo-Aristotelian Arabic translations. However, based on a misleading remark by Muhsin Mahdi, Rasoul Namazi tries to justify Strauss's error without much success. He connects Avicenna's statement about two books on the Laws to Diogenes Laertius's list of Aristotelian works, in which a summary of Plato's *Laws* and "Four [sic] books of Laws" are attributed to Aristotle.[24] Namazi ignores the fact that Diogenes Laertius's *Vitae philosophorum* could never have been known by Avicenna, as the work was never translated into Arabic.[25] In a problematic way, Namazi himself indirectly admits in a footnote that this work was not available in Arabic.[26] Nevertheless, Namazi does not abandon his efforts to rescue Strauss's interpretive moves and claims that the end of Aristotle's *Nicomachean Ethics* (1181b12ff.), which was available in Arabic translation,[27] "seems to promise a discussion of nomoi and legislation in another writing of his."[28]

Any informed reader of Aristotle's oeuvre knows that the end of the *Ethics* offers a transition into his *Politics*. But neither in the original Greek nor in the Arabic translation does Aristotle announce a subsequent book on the Laws, as Namazi, in good Straussian spirit, would have his readers believe. Thus, Namazi writes that

> it is true that Plato's Laws is not about, in Islamic terms, prophecy and sharīʿa, but it is not difficult to see how Muslim thinkers could have seen an overlap between the Platonic depiction of Zeus – Minos – Dorian laws and the Islamic idea of Allah – Muhammad – sharīʿa. In other words, the idea of a divine lawgiver, his messenger or a bringer of divine laws, and his detailed laws regulating different aspects of political society, is easily transferable from Plato's Greek context to a Muslim context; this can clearly be seen in Ibn Miskawayh's reading of the *Nicomachean Ethics*.[29]

The overlap of Greek and Islamic conceptions of divine law giving through a messenger (as promoted by Strauss and Namazi) does not appear in the work of Muslim philosophers of any relevance. As the fifth chapter of this book makes clear, neither al-Fārābī nor his successors equate the Islamic sharia with the Greek nomos. Ibn Miskawayh, whom Namazi attempts to use for a justification of his claim, does not help him accomplish this task. In the citation of his book *Tahdhīb al-akhlāq*, Ibn Miskawayh writes, "Maʿnā n-nāmūs fī lughtihi [Aristotle] as-siyāsa wa-t-tadbīr wa-mā ashbaha dhālik" ("In his [Arsitotle's] language, the law [*nāmūs*] means leadership [*siyāsa*], management [*tadbīr*], and all that resembles this"). On the basis of this, Namazi ascribes the following to Aristotle: "The highest law [*nāmūs*] is from God (blessed and exalted is He!), the ruler is a second law on His behalf, and money is a third law. The law of God [*nāmūs allāh*] (exalted is He!), i.e., the Law [*sharīʿa*], is the model for all the other laws."[30] Contrary to Namazi's interpretation, Ibn Miskawayh's proposed hierarchy of laws emphasizes the special rank of the sharia as the highest law in light of its divine origin, a designation that no Muslim philosopher ever gave to the laws described in Plato's *Nomoi*. We shall return to this point in chapter five of this book.[31]

Furthermore, Rasoul Namazi accuses me of mixing Strauss's personal views on religion with his interpretation of the historical conception of religion in the works of Muslim philosophers, Maimonides, and many other thinkers "as an instrument of political control."[32] But is it not a general problem of objective research on Strauss that it is almost impossible to distinguish between his own opinions and his interpretation of the scholars examined in his work? In this introduction, I cannot deal with this core hermeneutical issue exhaustively, in view of how much has been written on this topic out of substantive, polemical, and apologetic motives. Suffice it to say that Strauss made a conscious decision to embed his own philosophical views within the interpretation of other authors' works. He used interpretation as a means of philosophizing. Therefore, it is an almost insurmountable challenge to cleanly separate Strauss's views from those he interpreted, as Strauss himself did not desire such an approach.[33] He wanted his readers to consistently question whether he himself was using the same esoteric-exoteric "art of writing" that he attributed to his exalted idols, such as Maimonides and al-Fārābī. Leo Strauss did not provide the keys to unlock the hermeneutic interpretation of his own works.

Namazi comments on my interpretive position as follows: "Strauss finds an esoteric teaching according to which religion is only a salutary myth in the writings of Plato and Alfarabi; but neither of these thinkers spoke on this subject exoterically and in public."[34] Yet one must ask how Strauss could possibly arrive at this understanding when centuries or even millennia separate him from these philosophers. Indeed, these thinkers never expressed an opinion on these same matters. Is it not Strauss's own conception of religion that he projects onto al-Fārābī and Plato? He was able to accomplish this task through his hermeneutic method of "reading between the lines" in order to derive from the texts views that are not articulated by the authors in question themselves. Therefore, one must assume that these opinions are his own, even if he derives them "esoterically" from others. Is this the probable reason why Strauss chose to philosophize by means of interpretation, so that he could covertly express his true views in an esoteric way? Regarding Maimonides, Strauss writes to his friend Jacob Klein that it is "very difficult" to prove that Maimonides denied that "the ideal legislator must be a prophet [. . .] since he discusses the questions in exegetical form."[35] This is a hermeneutical imperative that he obviously applied to his own interpretations.[36] A similar dynamic is at work with Strauss's atheism. He attributes it to the medieval philosophers in order to neutralize his own atheism.

It is not that I would accuse Strauss of any anachronism for using historical views of antiquity and the Middle Ages to deal with contemporary problems of political philosophy.[37] He chose to "go to school" under the tutelage of Maimonides and the Muslim philosophers of the Middle Ages in order to find a solution for the crisis of modernity, namely the "theological-political" problem he famously articulated in *Philosophy and Law*. In light of Avicenna's intentionally misinterpreted statement, he presented these philosophers as Platonists who knew exactly how to create a Platonic template for philosophically positing religion as the chief organ of political order. He made this jump in order to enable philosophy to fully dispense with religion, an achievement that Enlightenment was unable to deliver. For unlike the thinkers of the European Enlightenment, the Muslim philosophers and Maimonides, as Strauss interpreted them, did not publicly dismiss religion in their writings and, for political reasons, did not question its didactic and social significance. However, his view of these philosophers is based on the fundamental insinuation that they considered the "credibility of revelation" to be "highly doubtful."[38]

My critique of Leo Strauss's interpretation of Islamic philosophy in the Middle Ages as an essentially political philosophy, in which the Muslim philosophers and Maimonides expressed their true views in an esoteric way so as not to endanger philosophical life, was not at all intended to defend a connection between philosophy and politics.[39] I do not question at all that the most important task of philosophy is the search for rational knowledge. It is precisely philosophy's own claim to rationality that leads it to voluntarily bring rational findings to bear in conversation with other sciences, thereby making philosophy relevant to society. Philosophy, in my opinion, does not consist of "a morally or religiously inspired engagement with the imperative of 'doing good deeds.'"[40] Precisely the opposite is the case. Philosophy should consist of a rationally demonstrable form of Enlightenment that is discursively pursued in order to enlighten society. This is how Socrates, as Plato conveyed him to posterity, understood and practiced philosophy. Philosophy is not to be practiced only within a small, secret circle of philosophers. It is not naive to see philosophy, by virtue of its rational imperative, as a permanent discursive corrective to society. A fundamental and unbridgeable gap between philosophy and society that threatened the livelihood of philosophers was simply not present in the historical context of al-Fārābī, Avicenna, and Averroes, as Strauss claimed. None of them were in danger due to their philosophical views, not even Maimonides. Maimonides and his family were forced to leave Andalusia during his childhood due to the oppression of the Jews under the Almohad dynasty, which required Jews to convert. Maimonides was still a child at the time. He developed his philosophy and Jewish scholarship primarily in Egypt under the Ayyubids, another Islamic dynasty that cultivated religious tolerance.

Philosophers are not always targets of persecution in every society in which they find themselves, so they need only esoteric forms of writing to protect themselves from the masses, as Leo Strauss propagated. This includes the Islamic-majority societies in which al-Fārābī, Avicenna, und Averroes lived, which were characterized by intellectual plurality expressed in a variety of philosophical, theological, and legal currents and doctrines. In many Islamic contexts, there was room for thinkers like Ibn ar-Rāwandī (d. 860 or shortly after 912) and Abū Bakr ar-Rāzī (d. 925 or 935), who openly expressed atheistic views and denied prophecy without legal repercussions.[41] The philosophic poet Abū l-ʿAlāʾ al-Maʿarrī (d. 1057) could express critical views on religion in his poems, views that gave him the reputation of an unbelieving sceptic. He also wrote a prose work in Arabic that was given the moniker Abū l-ʿAlāʾs Qurʾān by the literary critics of his age.[42] He was never subject to persecution.[43] The heterodox Dahriyya (or Dahrīs) were materialists who believed in the eternity of the world and denied prophecy, the Last Day, and the afterlife. Their beliefs did not prevent them from openly participating in public theological debates until the end of the Abbasid era.[44] Another example against ascribing a broad structural hostility to philosophy by medieval Islamic-majority societies is the rich translation movement in which a broad cross-section of the scholarly elite translated philosophical texts from Greek and Syriac into Arabic from the eighth to the tenth centuries, a movement that was supported by broad strata of early Abbasid society.[45] Additionally, the biographies of al-Kindī, al-Fārābī, Avicenna, Ibn Bāja, Ibn Ṭufayl, and Averroes all include sponsorship by various rulers and aristocrats. Al-Fārābī's Neoplatonic theory of emanation, which concerned the origins of the world and all things temporal, was expressed openly even though it stood in diametric opposition to Qurʾānic teachings.[46] Of course, some theologians accused these thinkers of heresy, but this was simply part and parcel of intellectual discourses at various junctures across the geographic and historical breadth of the Islamic world. Therefore, it is completely false to construe Islamic societies in terms of a structural animus toward philosophy, as Strauss would have it.[47]

The gap between philosophy and society claimed by Strauss is for him intrinsically linked to the contradiction between reason and revelation, Jerusalem and Athens. Of course, reason and revelation are different from one another. Reason can only be based on rational justification for objects of knowledge. Revelation, on the other hand, is an object of faith. Philosophers seek rational justification for revelation when they accept it as a historical possibility. Faith and knowledge are engaged in a rich interactive discourse within Islamic philosophy, which is no less intense and fruitful than any similar discourse in Judaism and Christianity (or any European or Middle Eastern discourse stemming from the Greek tradition) dealing with the same topic.[48]

Faith and knowledge are in a productive constellation that encompasses not only metaphysical questions but also secular issues of human life. Strauss was seemingly uninterested in the question of God's existence, most likely because he believed that this question was to be posed solely within the realm of faith. For political reasons, he considered revelation irrefutable, because only religions of revelation can act as factors of social order and, for this reason, function as instruments of the political philosophy propagated by Strauss.

In his unpublished Deakin University dissertation, "Leo Strauss and Islam," Daniel Townsend engages in an effective critique of Strauss. Central to Townsend's critique is the claim that Strauss was essentially a Nietzschean who "has a political project that relates, at base, to the revivification of religion. [. . .] *Strauss distorts ancient and medieval philosophy to comport with this project*" (36, italics in the original). However, Townsend does claim, "Contrary to Tamer's reading, I argue that Strauss did not simply *misunderstand* aspects of medieval Islamic philosophy; rather, Strauss appears to have *deliberately misread* prior thinkers as part of a philosophical-political project, a project with Nietzschean foundations" (36, italics in the original). Nevertheless, it seems that Townsend has made this evaluation solely based on the English-language summary at the end of my original book. Unfortunately, he does not seem able to read German.[49]

Starting from his basic thesis that Strauss is in complete agreement with Nietzsche in his critique of modernity, Townsend evaluates Strauss's interpretations of the medieval and ancient writings of philosophy as deliberately undertaken distortions by a "political theorist living in a Western democracy" who covertly sought to reject this political system (44). He seemingly applied a hermeneutical device derived from Nietzsche in order to rigorously interpret the medieval Muslim philosophers. Strauss, according to Townsend, is an atheist who seeks to subordinate religion for the purposes of philosophy. Like Nietzsche, Strauss exoterically advocates religion while esoterically denying the possibility of revelation.[50]

Townsend completely rejects Strauss's interpretation of al-Fārābī, a critical move that I cannot elucidate here. The radicality of his critique of Strauss is similar to the radicality of Strauss's followers who, in new studies, do not bring forth new insights but rather repeat or expound the theses of the guru, as Joshua Parens's latest book has perfectly demonstrated.[51]

However, Strauss's work deserves to be taken seriously; this means examining the theses he presents through careful analysis not only of his own texts but of those he interpreted. The question of whether Strauss utilizes the exoteric-esoteric hermeneutic method he ascribes to medieval and ancient Greek thinkers in order to articulate his own normative aims is of a secondary nature. The question of esoteric writing cannot be dealt with by objective hermeneutical means that seek to produce rationally justified results. This question can only lead to speculation.

It is my hope that this book will make a constructive and nonpolarizing contribution to the understanding of Leo Strauss's treatment of medieval Islamic philosophy. It is hoped that it will join the many excellent studies that Strauss has inspired, both on his own work and on the work of those who inspired him.

Introduction to the Original Text

Leo Strauss emerges as a truly unique thinker of the twentieth century. This professor of political philosophy wrote his doctoral thesis on epistemological problems in the thought of Jacobi and wrote his first book on Spinoza's critique of religion. His hermeneutical method demanded that past philosophers be understood today in the same way they understood themselves. But his interest lay in a forgotten art of writing based on identifying exoteric and esoteric layers in texts, through which the true views of their authors could remain hidden rather than revealed. Strauss did not produce any work that can be considered systematic. Instead, he produced a series of careful interpretive works that captured the history of political ideas as an uninterrupted chain of thought stretching from Socrates to Nietzsche.[1] This interpreter of texts makes it abundantly clear, though, that these thinkers' most important views are those that shape their individual understanding of the truth, and that are therefore developed exclusively in private.

Leo Strauss had many faces, a fact that led to divergent interpretations and presentations of his work. Strauss's own affirmation of the necessity of esoteric writing has led to much confusion among his own interpreters. Indeed, the controversies among Strauss's own most important students in America surrounding his intellectual legacy following his death in 1973 point toward this dynamic. The nature of Strauss's work as well as his mode of teaching has led Strauss's critics to accuse him of creating a sectarian cult of philosophers while concealing nihilistic ideas behind the guise of esoteric writing. Both Strauss's admirers and critics, the former promoting the "true" Strauss and the latter discrediting his ideas, have a bone to pick with his manner of philosophizing. Obviously, Strauss has succeeded by having his interpreters approach his works in the same way that he approached the works of great philosophers, namely by claiming to uncover the many layers in his writings.

In recent years, there has been a growing body of scholarship on various dimensions of Strauss's thought.[2] Yet interest in Strauss's work in his native Germany[3] has only recently begun among political scientists and philosophers.[4] In the literature of a chiefly philosophical character, three main trends have emerged. The first sees Strauss as primarily a Jewish philosopher, for whom Jewish thought stands at the heart of his oeuvre. Another perspective identifies Strauss as a Platonist keen on reorienting contemporary political philosophy to

Socrates. Finally, a third trend portrays Strauss as an esoteric who sought to hide socially dangerous ideas behind grandiose and mysterious masks.

One aspect of Leo Strauss's philosophizing has not been sufficiently taken into account: namely, Strauss's relationship with the Muslim philosophers of the Middle Ages, through his treatment of al-Fārābī (870 to 950), Avicenna (980 to 1037), and Averroes (1126 to 1198). This gap persists even though Strauss studied the works of these philosophers extensively in the early and middle stages of his career.[5] Indeed, Strauss's inquiries into Spinoza's critique of religion reveal that the genesis of his thought lay in an intense engagement with Averroes. The theological-political problem that Strauss derived from Spinoza and thereafter retained as the conceptual fulcrum of his entire oeuvre retains unmistakable ideas from Averroes. These ideas pertain to the depiction of Spinoza's relationship with religion, biblical criticism, and statecraft. His engagement with Avicenna's text *The Divisions of the Rational Sciences* augured a substantive change in Strauss's thought. Subsequently, he conceived of religion on the basis of revelation, that is, in terms of a law delivered to the masses by a prophet.[6] Leo Strauss's mode of philosophizing should therefore be seen against the background of the idea, which he attributed to Avicenna, that prophecy and religious law could be explained philosophically with the help of Plato. Furthermore, Strauss became aware of the fact that Avicenna's reference to Plato would have not been possible without the previous commentaries and philosophic works of his predecessor al-Fārābī. Strauss holds al-Fārābī to be the founder of a medieval, largely Platonic tradition of post-revelation in the Islamic context. He viewed himself as beholden to this tradition.

This work will examine Leo Strauss's relationship with these Muslim philosophers. Since al-Fārābī had the strongest impact on Strauss's thought, I will focus on his influence. In this introduction, I will lay out the dominant trends in the research on Strauss and the positions of the interpreters who are most relevant to the focus of my inquiry.

Leo Strauss as a Jewish Philosopher

To characterize Strauss as a Jewish philosopher is to place his engagement with Jewish ideas and issues as a lifelong academic raison d'être. Most important for this interpretation is Strauss's deep debt to Maimonides. It is without doubt that Maimonides is a central figure in Strauss's work. His interest in Maimonides lasted over three decades and was primarily centered upon his philosophical magnum opus, *The Guide of the Perplexed*.[7] From the inception of Strauss's creative output, Maimonides was a guidepost in navigating the clash between

Jewish rationalist and orthodox thinkers. He relied on Maimonides for the conceptual tools with which to engage both streams of thought critically.

Those interpreters who would like to posit Strauss as primarily a Jewish philosopher believe that Strauss's interpretation of Maimonides should be considered central for both his specifically "Jewish" thought and his project of philosophizing more broadly. Kenneth Hart Green is the first interpreter who devoted an entire monograph to Strauss's Jewish thought.[8] Green's interpretation is guided by the conviction that Leo Strauss's Jewish thought, represented by his return to Maimonides, is key to understanding his oeuvre as a whole.[9] This return to Maimonides occurred in three stages that correspond to his "key works."[10]

The first stage begins with his exploration of Spinoza, in which Strauss reveals Maimonides to be a deeper thinker than Spinoza. In this study, Strauss pays primary attention to theological questions such as revelation, creation and prophecy as he demonstrates the weaknesses in Spinoza's critique of Maimonides. While treating Spinoza's critique of religion, Strauss seems to question Judaism as a revealed religion just as little as he questions rational philosophy, instead regarding both as prerequisites for his thought, allowing himself to be guided accordingly by the "philosophical theologian" Maimonides.[11]

The second stage of Strauss's return to Maimonides, as presented by Green, occurs in Strauss's book *Philosophy and Law*, a book that offered a new understanding of Maimonides's Jewish thought, in which Maimonides's prophetology[12] was rendered capable of answering lingering critical questions. Strauss notes that prophetology provided Maimonides with a unique and penetrating philosophical approach to biblical religion and enabled him, through a political approach to philosophy, to design a worldview that did justice to the importance of religion in the life of a society.[13] He thereby saw Maimonides's philosophical achievement not primarily in its scientific qualities but rather in its political character.[14] The "Straussian" Strauss, namely the lawyer of the biblical and Platonic traditions as harmonized in Maimonides, begins to appear at this point.[15]

According to Green, the third stage in the return to Maimonides lies in Strauss's decision to return to premodern philosophy.[16] Central to this decision is Strauss's conviction that Maimonides largely hid his true opinions behind the literary structure of the *Guide*. Following Strauss's discovery of this art of esoteric philosophic writing, he elevates esoteric writing to a universal typology of philosophizing in the premodern period.[17] In *Persecution and the Art of Writing* and the subsequent interpretations of Plato, Xenophon, and Machiavelli, Strauss brings the paradigm of "noble rhetoric" into modern philosophical discourse.

His esoteric mode of philosophizing was derived from the Maimonidean categorical imperative that philosophers should disguise the truth.[18]
Green concludes that Strauss's understanding of Maimonides as presented in *Persecution and the Art of Writing* deepens during this period and remains "fundamental" for him. This enables Strauss to better pursue his long-standing engagement with reason and revelation. Against the backdrop of this particular harmonization of reason and revelation, Strauss is able to create a connection with Plato. According to Green, Strauss's positioning is not purely Platonic as it emerges in light of a deepening conflict between the Bible and the philosophers. Maimonides occupies a middle position in the history of philosophy between the arch-rivals Averroes and Thomas Aquinas, thereby making him appealing to Strauss.[19]

Two other volumes also contribute to the school of thought that posits Strauss's thought as primarily Jewish.[20] These works attempt to root Strauss's Jewish intellectual identity in a demonstrable dichotomy between Athens and Jerusalem. According to Hillel Fradkin, Strauss's writings on medieval philosophy do not merely possess a historical character but also touch on contemporary questions regarding the position of rationalism in Judaism.[21] However, Fradkin demonstrates in a later work that Strauss's engagement with Maimonides served less to illuminate the enormous conceptual difficulties in this figure's oeuvre than to bring the reader to follow Maimonides's mode of philosophizing and to think with him (rather than to understand him).[22]

Another interpretation of Strauss's relationship to Maimonides highlights the fact that his interest in medieval philosophers was of a political nature. Alfred Ivry observed that Strauss presented Maimonides as a political figure even in his earliest works, where the significance of prophecy was posited more as a question of politics rather than of metaphysics. Strauss deals at no point with Maimonides's metaphysics. Instead, he argues that both Maimonides and other medieval philosophers posited revealed law as the core object of political philosophy, thereby relegating the "nonpolitical" dimensions of revelation to a secondary role. Inasmuch as the various roles of the prophet are already identified and elucidated across the breadth of medieval Islamic philosophy, Strauss embeds Maimonides's views squarely within the philosophical context of al-Fārābī and Avicenna.[23]

These interpretations agree that Strauss's long-standing engagement with Maimonides and other Jewish figures lies at the heart of his philosophical work. This seems justified, especially in light of the fact that Strauss was born into a Jewish family and that, as a young academic, he dealt with religious and political issues relevant to the Jewish context of the Weimar Republic.[24] His initial works include enthusiastic newspaper articles regarding Jewish political and religious questions.[25] As a young researcher he endeavored to rehabilitate Spinoza in the eyes of Judaism's intellectual gatekeepers and thereafter remained focused on Jewish political questions, perhaps as a result of events that took place in Nazi Germany.[26] One could assume that Strauss, just like Hermann Cohen (with whom he engaged both at the beginning and end of his career), was keen on positing the religion of his forefathers as a "religion of reason" in order to buttress and shield the connection between reason and revelation from the attacks of relativists who sought to divide them.[27] Apparently this compelled Strauss to engage with the philosophy of Maimonides, who belonged to the medieval tradition of Judeo-Islamic philosophy written in Arabic under the influence of his Muslim predecessors, particularly al-Fārābī.[28] However, Strauss's interest in Islamic philosophy was not only based on the historical situation in which the medieval Jewish philosophers — first and foremost Maimonides, whom Strauss used to demonstrate the presence of reason in Judaism — themselves emerged in the context of Islamic philosophy and made use of Arabic and its conceptual vocabulary in their philosophical activity. Much more important was the situation in which the relationship between reason and revelation, which remained the central problem of Strauss's philosophizing, was first treated by the Islamic philosophers of the Middle Ages and subsequently became an important aspect of their philosophical activity. The return to Maimonides appeared to Strauss as "a return to the standards of human achievement," namely to the accomplishments of human reason that he found so very present in Maimonides's thought.[29] This return is not religiously motivated, even if such a reading seems plausible given their common religious affiliation with Judaism. It thereby appears that in this context one must speak of Strauss's "Jewish interests," which would not necessarily lead to treating him as an exclusively Jewish thinker.[30]

Another nuanced interpretation of Strauss's relationship to Judaism can be found in the thought of Steven Smith. According to Smith, Strauss is only interested in Judaism when it illustrates a more generalized "theological-political problem."[31] Because this problem is not only Jewish but also central to Christianity and Islam, there is no reason to claim that Strauss was interested specifically in Judaism. Furthermore, Smith criticizes the depiction of Strauss as a Jewish thinker who contributed to Jewish political thought, as he questions the very definition of such a body of thought as "Jewish."[32] From the beginning, Strauss dealt with the existence of the Jewish community within a liberal society and realized that assimilation could come at the cost of Jewish identity. The great contribution of Strauss's works lies in their novel thematization of the struggle between the universal and the particular, thereby positing "the Jewish question" in the Weimar Republic as a version of the more general question of the universal, social, and political problems of integrating "the Other."[33]

As will be demonstrated over the course of this work, Strauss left the traditional interpretation of medieval philosophy at the end of his early phase and charted a new path through a politically oriented interpretation of Jewish and Islamic philosophy. The starting point for this new interpretation was Maimonides's teaching on prophecy. For Strauss, the crux of the problem lay in the connection between the intellect and the imagination for the emergence of the prophetic act. On the one hand, Maimonides viewed the imagination as an obstacle to reason. On the other hand, he ascribed to the prophet a perfected combination of intellect and imagination. A further difficulty lay in the fact that the power of imagination is characterized not only by the function of representing transcendental truths but also by the baser capacity to divine the future. The two capacities appear to be incommensurate. Strauss recognized that the difficulties in Maimonides's philosophy could only be solved by engaging with the political philosophy of al-Fārābī, who recognized that prophecy constituted the unification of theoretical and practical perfection, with the different functions of the imaginative capacity interpreted in the framework of founding and leading an ideal state. Strauss thus discovered the deep connection between Maimonides and al-Fārābī, as well as the possibility of understanding Maimonides's obscure remarks on prophecy more clearly in the light of Fārābī's arguments.

Leo Strauss recognizes that the "political science" of Maimonides is derived from that of al-Fārābī and can only be justified and explained from it. He also sees that the link between the medieval Muslim and Jewish philosophers, on the one hand, and Plato, on the other, can be established only through al-Fārābī's philosophy. Strauss takes his cue from al-Fārābī's interpretations of Plato, through which he may have simultaneously found his own path to Plato. While Maimonides provides Strauss with the map, as Green metaphorically puts it,[34] al-Fārābī's work is Strauss's path to Plato.[35]

However, it is difficult to sustain such an interpretation of the relationship between Strauss, on the one hand, and Maimonides and al-Fārābī, on the other, in light of one matter. It is a biographical fact that Strauss learned of al-Fārābī after studying Maimonides. This leads most of the interpreters to conclude that Strauss's interest in al-Fārābī emerged from his stronger interest in Maimonides.[36] Against this approach, I will advance the thesis that Strauss's turn to al-Fārābī, which occurred through the reception of Maimonides, represented a turning point in his own interpretation of Maimonides. Strauss understood the dependence of the Maimonidean philosophy on al-Fārābī's philosophy. This led him to turn to the "second teacher" — as al-Fārābī has traditionally been considered — as the highest philosophical authority in the medieval era after Aristotle, and then to seek the theoretical foundations of Maimonides's political philosophy in the thought of al-Fārābī. Strauss's philosophical interest in Maimonides would have run dry had he not engaged with al-Fārābī. The chief themes of his treatment of Maimonides — namely, prophecy, political science, and the doctrine of Divine Providence — are not to be understood apart from al-Fārābī's teaching. With a curious vehemence, Strauss elevates Maimonides's recommendation to study the works of al-Fārābī in three different places.[37] He enthusiastically called for academics to search for al-Fārābī's texts and reconstruct them, an appeal that brought together scholars of Arabic, Judaism, philosophy, and history. One could conclude that Strauss's interest in al-Fārābī lay in the intrinsic worth of al-Fārābī's thought rather than in its utility for the study of Maimonides. It could therefore be said that Strauss loved Maimonides in his heart while revering al-Fārābī philosophically.[38]

The unique place that Maimonides occupied in Strauss's work is biographically and bibliographically strengthened by the fact that his treatment of Maimonides, unlike that of any other figure, persists across the substantive and chronological breadth of his oeuvre.[39] But it is also accurate to say that Strauss was engaged in interpreting al-Fārābī in all three phases of his career as well. With the exception of a single essay, "Eine vermißte Schrift Fārābī's," in the works Strauss produced during the first period (which can be said to extend until his immigration to the United States in 1938), al-Fārābī and Maimonides appear side by side.[40] Strauss could therefore obviously not interpret the latter without interpreting the former. In the second period (which can be said to extend from 1938 to 1954), the two figures begin to be treated separately. Maimonides's *Guide* would become Strauss's most beloved text due to its esoteric form of writing, in his view. However, Strauss curiously mentions al-Fārābī's name next to Plato. The important study of "entirely self-explanatory declarations,"[41] "Farabi's *Plato*," belongs to the middle of this period and would be considered a second source from which the esoteric art of writing could be understood.[42] Finally, the study "How Farabi Read Plato's *Laws*," which emerged in the third period (which could be said to extend from 1954 until his death), connects to the paramount importance of Plato's *Laws* for Strauss's perennial interest in the political-theological problem. Al-Fārābī's work on the *Laws* carried enormous importance for Strauss's understanding of this Platonic book, which is the subject of his last book,[43] as well as for his attempt to philosophically conceive a religion of revelation.[44]

Rest assured that I am not attempting to replace Maimonides with al-Fārābī at the pinnacle of those philosophers who influenced Strauss. In my attempt to rectify the gap in the previous research regarding the importance of al-Fārābī for Strauss, I am far from underestimating the importance of Maimonides's philosophy for Strauss's philosophic efforts. I am only concerned with emphasizing the relevance of al-Fārābī for Strauss without minimizing the authentic worth of Maimonidean philosophy. Those interpretations that wish to place the sole figure of Maimonides at the center of Strauss's work are justified so long as they recognize room for al-Fārābī's presence in that relationship. Strauss himself leaves his attentive readers aware of the central role of al-Fārābī for the development of his own thought. Readers of the seminal collection of ten essays gathered by Strauss in *What Is Political Philosophy?* — a collection that according to Joseph Cropsey (a longtime friend, colleague, and research assistant of Leo Strauss) should be considered a microcosm of his entire oeuvre[45] — will note that the essays on al-Fārābī and Maimonides are placed one after the other at the heart of the book.[46] Thus, given Strauss's emphasis upon al-Fārābī's influence on Maimonides, along with the incredible impact of al-Fārābī's interpretation of Plato on Strauss's own thought, the role of al-Fārābī should be given more attention. The attempt to prioritize Maimonides's importance for Strauss over al-Fārābī's due to the number of texts dedicated to one over the other is not convincing. Strauss himself emphasized the fact that the quantity of literary ink spilled on one author over another issues no judgment regarding a philosopher's assessment of philosophical merit.

Leo Strauss as a Platonic Political Philosopher

Those interpretations that posit Strauss as a primarily Jewish figure view Maimonides as his "hero."[47] In contrast to this approach, those interpretations that primarily emphasize the importance of Platonic political philosophy for Strauss's intellectual identity view Socrates as the main heroic figure surrounding the question of justice.[48] This interpretation posits Strauss as a historian of political philosophy whose return to Socrates is prompted by the contemporary intellectual crisis and the potential for finding a path out of this crisis.[49]

Thomas Pangle is one of the most important protagonists in this school of Strauss interpretation.[50] He assumes that Strauss was interested in the philosophical works of the past not out of pure historical interest. Instead, Strauss was prompted to engage with these works in order to discover the necessary preconditions for authentic philosophizing in an age characterized by intellectual decay even while core philosophical questions regarding human life remained the same.[51] In this regard, the reliance of modern rationalism on classical forms was formulated in terms of the need to know the same answers that Socrates had divined. Therefore, philosophy itself owed the justification of its existence to this figure.[52]

According to this line of interpretation, Leo Strauss's Platonic political philosophy was based on a new understanding of Plato's teachings in which the articulation of ideas could arise from their connection to the affairs of persons. This articulation would emerge from the human soul. In this fashion, Strauss clears a path for the identification of "unchanged ideas" with "the fundamental and permanent problems" of human existence, presenting Plato's ideas as an expression of the human need for the virtues that are very often missing in human life.[53]

In this context as well, Plato's *Laws* is accorded a special position in Strauss's thought whereby Strauss prefers this work to the *Republic*. For Strauss, the *Laws* constitutes not only Plato's "most political work" but rather "his only political work."[54] The justification for this claim lies in the fact that this work encourages the search for the best type of political regime through the investigation of past esteemed political orders, without behaving like a statesperson or lawgiver. Strauss identifies the reluctance of the theoretical philosopher to engage with political philosophy in Plato's paradigmatic depiction of the Socratic way of life. But the philosopher needs to be pushed to turn his analytical gaze to human affairs and to ask questions about what is just and noble in the context of the political community.[55] Pangle further emphasizes that Strauss documents a "Socratic turn" in Plato, which consists of Socrates adapting to society, even if only in appearance. The mature, Platonic Socrates declares himself aligned with the moral-religious norms of the society in which he lives and puts his more regular theoretical analytic gaze and moralistic preaching on the back burner. For Socrates, this transition did not change his convictions but rather constituted a new method to educate potential philosophers amongst the citizens of the city without coming into conflict with existing political and religious authorities.[56] This new form of Socratic political philosophy identified by Strauss required the mastery and deployment of a new art of communication. In this context, public and private rhetoric were to be differentiated. This results in Platonic political philosophy assuming the character of a philosophy that would consider the nature of all things, including the affairs of humankind. It would conduct such an inquiry in an explicitly political fashion.[57]

An important characteristic of Leo Strauss's Platonic political philosophy thereby emerges from such a mode of reading, namely that philosophical skepticism and modes of reading exist in an unavoidable confrontation between open and critical philosophic thinking and society. This conflict comes most stridently to the fore in the clash between philosophers and the bearers of religious tradition: the poets alongside the authorized interpreters of sacred texts. The conflict revolves chiefly around the question of whether reason is able to lead humanity without supernatural inspiration. This question, which Strauss, following Spinoza, identifies as a political-theological problem, can be traced back to its origins in Socrates, insofar as it is a moral problem. Strauss was aware that the Bible and ancient Greece were concerned with conceptual questions about miracles, revelation, and prophecy. Nevertheless, he learned from Avicenna that ancient thought and the religion of revelation were of comparable value. From al-Fārābī and Maimonides, Strauss learned that the law-giving prophet could rule in the name of divine authority through their rhetorical and poetic skills. Although Strauss was not unaware of the differences between the Bible and the Greek poets, he considered these differences secondary. Strauss posited the conflict between reason and revelation as a continuation of the fierce conflict between philosophy and the poets in antiquity.[58]

Allan Bloom grounded the primacy of Strauss's Platonism in the fact that for Strauss, the entirety of human existence resembles a Platonic cave. All men begin and end their lives as prisoners within the context of their respective era's authorities. Only through radical questioning can man find a way out of the cave of tradition.[59] Bloom reconstructed the arc of Strauss's thought that began with Spinoza and continued through Maimonides and the Muslim philosophers before arriving at antiquity. He notes that Strauss discovered the forgotten art of esoteric writing in medieval philosophers and from this discovery extrapolated the overarching themes of "Ancients and Moderns" and "Athens and Jerusalem," which dominated his efforts until the end of his career. From these philosophers, Strauss learned that Plato was the original teacher of the philosophical doctrine of prophecy, which inspired Strauss's own intensive study of his work.[60]

As I previously noted, Bloom identified three phases of Strauss's intellectual development. The first is the "pre-Straussian" Strauss as manifested in the books *Die Religionskritik Spinozas*, *Philosophie und Gesetz*, and *The Political Philosophy of Thomas Hobbes*. These books identify the historical premises of modern philosophizing. In this phase, Strauss was familiar with the Epicurean critique of religion and not the Platonic one. He sought a vantage point outside of modernity in order to criticize it. But he was not fully successful in this endeavor. In the second phase, Strauss discovered esoteric forms of writing as reflected in the books *Persecution and the Art of Writing*, *On Tyranny*, and *Natural Right and History*. While the first book elucidates a more general thesis regarding esoteric writing through the interpretation of earlier sources, the final book synthetically presents Strauss's interest in an ahistorical history of philosophy. The third phase is characterized by Strauss's dispensing with the methodologies and categories of modern research and completely surrendering to free and often enigmatic interpretation of works by Machiavelli, Aristophanes, Xenophon, and Plato. These interpretations showcase "the authentic, the great Strauss to which all the rest is only prolegomena."[61]

Laurence Lampert, in his analysis of Strauss's relation to Nietzsche, presents Strauss as a "philosophic laborer" whose primary task was to present Platonic political philosophy to modernity. However, his version of Platonic philosophy was fully under Nietzsche's influence beyond morality.[62] Strauss's work presents a form of philosophical return whose starting point consists of a deep disappointment in modern Enlightenment and proceeds through the Islamic and Jewish Middle Ages to Plato. In this act of return, Strauss finds answers to the problem of modernity. Lampert reconstructs Strauss's backward-going path and argues that his interpretation of the *Politeia* presents the core of his Platonic political philosophy. Strauss had, namely, found in this work the principles of the Platonic enlightenment as well as the politics of philosophy valid in all times, which consisted, on the one hand, in understanding the hierarchy of human and natural things and, on the other hand, in placing the autonomous human achievements in the service of philosophy as well as in establishing the close connection between philosophy and politics.[63] In his commentary on Plato's *Nomoi*, Strauss allows us to observe a Platonic "civic minded" form of law giving. Lampert considers the Platonic Socrates to be a "revolutionary theologian" who points us to "rational Gods." Strauss's Platonic political philosophy presents itself as a permanent solution for the political problem of philosophy, a defense of philosophy that styles itself as the most noble way of living in the world. In this fashion, Strauss distances himself from those issues that are not taken to lie at the heart of human existence. According to Lampert's analysis, Strauss's skeptical interpretation of Platonic political philosophy resembles Nietzsche's mode of reading Plato. In this fashion, Strauss opens the door to a new reading of the history of political philosophy.[64]

Susan Orr, who primarily follows the interpretive path of Harry Jaffa in her comprehensive commentary on Strauss's *Jerusalem and Athens*, argues against pulling Strauss too far from the pole of Jerusalem in the direction of Athens.[65] According to her, Strauss's interest in medieval Islamic and Jewish philosophy can be traced to the fact that in contrast to classical Greek poetry, the concept of revelation in medieval theology could be considered a worthy rival to philosophy.[66] Strauss was convinced of the rationality of his own religion as well as the necessity of revelation. Nevertheless, he hid his true commitments, thereby "lulling the atheists to sleep."[67] Orr evaluates Strauss's emphasis on the medieval conception of religion as a law that is revealed yet still characterized by rationality as an indication of Strauss's affinity toward revealed religion. His identification of these philosophers as nonbelievers is not addressed by Orr.[68] Her research is predicated on the opinion that reason and revelation are ranked equally in Strauss's thought. Thus, she leaves the question open as to whether Strauss was a "careful nihilist" or a "reluctant believer."[69]

Heinrich Meier places Strauss's confrontation with Heidegger's radical historicism at the center of his own interpretation. Heidegger's thesis that human thought, understanding, and action are historical is interpreted by Meier as a "historical point of departure" for Strauss's interpretive endeavor.[70] In his depiction of Strauss's position, Meier rejects the previous interpretative positions I have just presented as they pertain to Strauss's philosophic identity. He states, first, that Strauss must not be confused "with the protagonist of a 'Jewish philosophy' [. . .] which, like a 'Christian philosophy,' he himself recognized as — here agreeing with Heidegger — a square circle [lit. "wooden iron"]." He rejects the notion that Strauss's years-long preoccupation with the problem of Socrates was "an expression of a romantic yearning for the Greek polis or the sign of a political position calling for a return to antique conceptions of citizens' virtues." Finally, Meier rejects the characterization of Strauss's recovery of esoteric writing as essentially Talmudic or connected to "hidden Kabbalistic sources." Instead, Meier sets a boundary between religious-esoteric forms of writing and the kind of esoteric writing rediscovered by Strauss.[71]

Meier, in his interpretation of Strauss as the most consequential political philosopher of the 20th century, sought to push back against those who would claim that Strauss was not a political philosopher, given the lack of any systematic philosophic work attributable to him. Instead, the fact that Strauss primarily produced interpretations of past philosophers is a confirmation of Strauss's own philosophical value. Strauss's view that we today find ourselves in a "second cave" located just under Plato's "natural cave" of deficient understanding, lends legitimacy to Meier's own proclivity for historical interpretations of past philosophy. Insofar as the roots of modern thought are to be found outside of the modern era and are obscured by multiple layers of tradition, there emerges the imperative to clear away these layers so that modernity might be critically understood and reconstructed. Indeed, the philosopher must "become a good historian should he wish to remain a true philosopher."[72] Historical interpretation thereby becomes a cover for philosophical intentions, and, according to Meier, Strauss's thought moves from the interpretation of philosophical texts to the opinions of their respective authors. This method of double esoteric-exoteric writing plays a key role in this form of interpretation. It is not only necessary in order to "recognize the historical context in which these works were produced," but rather it establishes a relationship between hermeneutics and political philosophy, as part of which this same method presents the causes of the philosophers' double form of writing: both the persecution of the philosophers and above all "the irreconcilable tension between the political community and philosophy." This careful mode of philosophical expression becomes a synonym for political philosophy, a necessary reflection on "politics, philosophy and the nature of philosophers." Furthermore, Meier concludes that Strauss's path from the history of philosophy to the intentions of those philosophers he chooses to interpret is simultaneously a "movement from history to the nature" of the philosophers. This movement consists of a transhistorical dialogue between related natures dealing "with essentially the same philosophical problems."[73]

With this point, Meier emphasizes that Strauss's work distinguishes between the philosopher's intention and the philosopher's contribution to the history of philosophy. Strauss "concluded with reference to al-Fārābī" that what constitutes an "original" or "personal" contribution of a philosopher is significantly less important than their private, individual, and originally true understanding of a necessarily anonymous truth. This is also applicable to Strauss's own engagement with the philosophers of the past.[74]

Clemens Kauffman's introduction to Strauss's political philosophy was primarily inspired by Heinrich Meier.[75] Like Meier, Kauffman posits Strauss's work as belonging to the field of political philosophy whose origins could be traced to the historical conditions of the Weimar Republic and a confrontation with Heidegger's understanding of history. Following an overview of the American and German reception of Strauss, Kauffman attempts to justify Strauss's political philosophy by focusing on the possibility for the emergence of such a philosophy in the context of the crisis of modernity and its implications for the concept of the political. Through a depiction of Strauss's views regarding the relationship between philosophy and revelation, the double form of writing, and a historically open understanding of philosophy, Kauffmann attempts to demonstrate the necessity of Straussian political philosophy. He interprets Strauss's preoccupation with the problem of Socrates as a retrieval of the origins of political philosophy, which strives for a conception of a natural, that is to say, classical, hierarchical order of the powers of the soul (with justice at the top) in modern political-philosophical discourse.[76]

Kauffmann's portrayal of Strauss does not engage critically with Strauss's philosophy. This could be related to the essential nature of an introduction. Yet, given the breadth of the themes treated, it would have been welcome. Indeed, Kauffmann is insistent in this work that Strauss be freed from his reputation as both a "Jewish philosopher" and a "historian of ideas." He also crucially points to al-Fārābī's influence on Strauss's pursuit of both a reconciliation between philosophy and tradition and the double form of writing in its connection with the philosophers' relationship between the intellectual elite on the one hand and the masses on the other.[77]

The interpretations sketched here present a strong connection between Strauss's political philosophy and classical Platonic philosophy. However, the extreme accentuation of this connection leads to the neglect of other important connections inherent to his thought. Revelation as well as the related "theological-political problem" are highly relativized in this depiction, leading (as we see in the interpretation of Pangle) to their conceptual occlusion in the comprehensive assessment of Strauss's oeuvre. The focus on Socrates leads to a near-disappearance of the figure of the prophet and thereby to a one-sided reading of Strauss's works. Additionally, Allan Bloom's interpretation almost completely neglects Strauss's treatment of medieval Jewish and Islamic prophetology. Despite its importance for Strauss's turn to Plato, Bloom discusses neither Strauss's reasons for engaging in a conceptual study of prophecy nor the results of this engagement. Bloom falsely interprets the "big" themes of Strauss's work such as the controversy between Athens and Jerusalem as emerging from the discovery of esoteric writing, thereby ignoring important dimensions of Strauss's reception of medieval Muslim and Jewish philosophy. This is even more disappointing due to Bloom's enthusiastic declaration at this end of his own work that "I believe our generation may well be judged by the next generation according to how we judged Leo Strauss."[78]

Meier's work has loomed large in the German-language rediscovery of Leo Strauss. Meier posits Strauss as a political philosopher who emphasizes the tension between society and philosophy by differentiating between the "outward" contribution of that thinker to the history of philosophy and that thinker's "actual" intellectual intentions. Therefore, Strauss characterizes this form of philosophizing as a political philosophy not only because it explores political themes but also because it constitutes a politics of philosophy that considers those social and political conditions that may have led the author to conceal what they believed to be true. However, Meier's justification of Strauss's interpretive-historical orientation does not pay sufficient attention to the paradoxical character of this enterprise. Such a paradox is characterized by a philosophical investigation that takes the form of a historical interpretation that is primarily fixated on the conditions of persecution while rejecting any form of historicism, a modus operandi that inevitably leads to the neglect of the historical conditions under which philosophical thought develops. Moreover, this form of philosophizing, which fixates on the true intentions of a philosopher, runs the risk of never being able to make this often-invoked intention unambiguously clear. Intentions inherently do not lend themselves to clear interpretations, whether these intentions belong to those living in the present or (especially) to those no longer with us. Other time periods and other cultural circumstances problematize the recovery of hidden intentions. These difficulties remain totally obscured in Meier's interpretation. This gives the impression that he is committed to an already-fully-formed "dialogue among absentees." Meier insists on distilling "an oeuvre as a fully articulated whole based on a constitutive core."[79] Yet how can such a constitutive core of a particular thinker be distilled by a scholar when it is based primarily on deciphering the intentions of a figure who himself is deciphering the intentions of other past thinkers? At this point, it must be critically asked how to ensure that what is declared to be the intention of the interpreted philosopher in fact constitutes it and is not merely an opinion projected by the interpreter onto the past philosopher.

Leo Strauss as an Esoteric

The characterization of Strauss as a Jewish as well as Platonic philosopher is in both cases connected to his substantive orientation to issues and figures within the history of philosophy. In contrast to this approach, identifying Strauss as an esoteric would emphasize both his methodology and the content of his philosophizing, teaching, and interpretive endeavors. Strauss's work is inextricably linked by many with esoteric-exoteric writing.

Strauss seems to have developed early the view that the medieval philosophers could not fully express their true views due to religious and political persecution. Instead, they would construct their philosophy behind veiled formulations that could only be truly understood by a few.[80] Strauss first dealt with the exoteric dimensions of Lessing's twofold formulations in a posthumously published text from 1939. Two years later, he focused even more intently on the differentiation between exoteric and esoteric knowledge. The methodological details he presents in *Persecution and the Art of Writing* are then consequentially applied to interpretations of Maimonides's *Guide of the Perplexed*, Halevi's *Kuzari*, and Spinoza's *Political-Theological Treatise*.[81] The conviction that philosophers could express their true opinions without fear of potential or real political or religious persecution through a double form of writing that appealed to the highly sophisticated interpreter accompanied Strauss's interpretations of works by Machiavelli, al-Fārābī, Plato, and Xenophon. The esoteric-exoteric double meaning of philosophical writing became an identifying feature of Straussian hermeneutics. Since Strauss left no systematic treatise, but only interpretative studies, his own work is also under the verdict of the esoteric-exoteric distinction.

The claim that Strauss himself was mainly an esoteric writer can be summarized in the following fashion:

> Strauss largely followed the principle of communicating his true views orally, which meant that he let only a few insiders among his students know what he actually thought about religion, politics, and morality. Therefore, Strauss's true ideas are to be found less in his own works and more in the works of his students.
>
> Simultaneously, Strauss had a significant impact on his students, which resulted in the development of an academic cult of personality that was later perpetuated by his followers.
>
> Nevertheless, the Straussians have offered different interpretations of core themes in Strauss's work, each claiming to have understood Strauss correctly due to their reliance on orally communicated thoughts. Access to the true teachings of Strauss through his students is therefore difficult.[82]
>
> Strauss's claim that great thinkers have written their texts in a dual form in which an exoteric façade of understandable ideas hide an esoteric truth is deployed by his interpreters onto Strauss's own work. Strauss is said to be hiding dangerous political views behind the interpretations of various other philosophical works.
>
> Strauss's mode of interpretation is primarily concerned with the literary construction and external form of a given work. This mode of analysis can be criticized in terms of a puzzling insistence on remaining bound to a text's surface meaning without offering interpretations based on argument supported by relevant content. Consequently, the philosophical returns of such an approach are incommensurate with the philological heavy lifting involved. Strauss's work is deceptive in that it offers the reader a philosophical rind without any corresponding core.

Myles F. Burnyeat is one of Strauss's most vehement critics. He produced a sharp and compact critique in his review of the *Studies in Platonic Political Philosophy*. There, Burnyeat attacks Strauss's esoteric thought both in general and especially where it concerns Plato. This has led prominent Straussians to consolidate a united front against him.[83] Burnyeat's critique is composed of two parts. First, it is oriented against Strauss's method of teaching. Second, it relates to those interpretations and ideas that emerged from his classroom.

Critique of Strauss's Method of Teaching

Burnyeat's critique assumes that the immense effect Strauss had in America was based not in the extraordinary strength of his arguments but rather on the loyalty and naiveté of the students under his spell.[84] His very thin interpretation of "old books" impressed them given his positing of such books as having been written for young philosophers such as themselves. Strauss the teacher led his "disciples" to a work only after obliterating other interpretations. He convinced them that previous interpretations were captive products of modernity from which his students needed to free themselves in order to enter the realm of ancient wisdom. The old masters whom Strauss presented to his students were made to agree with the Straussian principle that an author must be understood the way he himself wanted to be understood without any text being considered "simply true."

Burnyeat's critique draws predominantly on the testimonies of Strauss's students. Strauss did not encourage his students to engage critically with the works they studied and thereby to gain an active understanding of them. Instead, he "commanded" them to relegate their own capacity of judgment to a secondary place behind the authority of past philosophers. In truth, these students were not following the authority of the examined texts but rather the authority of their powerful teacher. In this fashion, they became beholden to Strauss's interpretation of the texts. To enter the world of Strauss's ideas required the sacrifice of one's own critical judgment.[85]

Critique of Strauss's Ideas

Building on this critique of Strauss's teaching method, Burnyeat proceeds to engage in a broader critique of Strauss's ideas based primarily on Strauss's esotericism.[86] On this point, Burnyeat zeroes in on the central differentiation between the "gentlemen" and the philosopher. The gentlemen come from well-off families and are therefore in the position to engage in the philosophic endeavor. In an atmosphere far from the education of the masses, the philosopher is concerned with sharing his ideas as well as imparting lessons about the "limits of politics." The philosopher is a politically wise man who takes the responsibility of educating the gentlemen upon his shoulders. Instead of engaging in politics himself, he conveys to his students the impossibility of a perfectly just society. Strauss, according to Burnyeat, is so fixated on the themes of political philosophy that he becomes paranoid of any abstract form of argumentation that could put his own expertise as a philosopher into question. Insofar as exegesis replaces argumentation in Strauss's work, justified doubts emerge regarding his philosophical capacities.

Furthermore, Burnyeat criticizes Strauss for projecting the form of esoteric writing he finds in Maimonides onto major figures in every age such as Xenophon, Descartes, Machiavelli, Hobbes, and Locke, as well as onto other, minor ones. Strauss applies the instructions Maimonides left behind in the twelfth century for the discovery of esoteric ideas to texts composed in vastly different historical circumstances and political conditions. Burnyeat agrees with Strauss that in the Middle Ages, due to the dominant tensions between adherents of reason and revelation, esoteric dissimulation was necessary. However, Strauss projects this tension onto antiquity as well as the present in order to place philosophers under a fictitious threat of persecution that is not historically verifiable and thereby unjustly universalizes the necessity of writing "between the lines."[87] Burnyeat's chief bone of contention is that Strauss did not convincingly present evidence for Plato's secret teachings, teachings that needed a medieval art of interpretation in order to be revealed. Therefore, Strauss's undertaking is shown to be a vicious circle.[88]

Following his treatment of Strauss's interpretation of Plato's political philosophy, Burnyeat concludes that Strauss's model for commentary on Platonic dialogues seeks to confirm that the dialogic form of writing aims at allowing different meanings to be conveyed simultaneously to different readers. For this reason, Burnyeat claims that Strauss could argue that Plato advocated (through manipulated paraphrasing) the idea that a just state based on gender equality and absolute communism would be perverse. Strauss's mishandling of Platonic political philosophy was intimately tied to his esotericism inasmuch as such an esotericism paved the way for the entry of his (mis)interpretations into modern politics. The danger for international politics is clear when one thinks of Strauss's denial of equal justice and his "Platonic" view that it would be "just" to help one's friend and hurt one's enemy.[89]

Shadia Drury, in opposition to Burnyeat, identifies the reasons for Strauss's success not mainly in the establishment of a cult of personality but rather in the understandable seductiveness and arresting quality of his teachings.[90] Strauss, in Drury's eyes, is not a historian of ideas but rather primarily a philosopher with a unique and confusing bundle of ideas that he does not clearly explicate, instead using the history of thought as a vehicle to express them.[91] As a consequence, Drury attempts to put Strauss's own political ideas at the center of her inquiry. Drury explains that the esoteric art of writing that Strauss ascribes to his interpreted authors is neither a hermeneutic to be employed for writing a history of political thought nor a method for evading persecution.[92] Instead, it aims to conceal philosophical ideas that imperil the stability of the social order.[93] Thus,

Drury's engagement with Strauss's ideas is first and foremost an engagement with his esotericism.[94]

Drury's critical depiction of Strauss's esoteric philosophy begins with the observation that it was first the Muslim philosophers of the Middle Ages, and most notably al-Fārābī, who, according to Strauss, alerted him to the disharmony between philosophy and the world as well as the "precariousness" of the philosopher's worldly position. Afterward, Strauss started to ascribe an esoteric art of writing to the philosophers of antiquity as the key to ancient wisdom. Their revival was his primary project, a project that not only explained the reasons for the decline of Western modernity but was also intended to have far-reaching political consequences.[95]

According to Drury, Strauss's esoteric philosophy contains a specific understanding of the nature of philosophy and its relationship to the world, and as a result it presents philosophical ideas as a danger to the political order. To the extent that these ideas come into conflict with the social order, they endanger the very lives of these philosophers. In fear for both their own safety and the security of society, they keep their opinions secret. Strauss's philosophy posits an insurmountable chasm between the wise men and the masses, one which no manner of explanation or enlightenment could ever bridge in order to bring the former's philosophical truth to the latter. This truth consists in denying the existence of God and other theological dogmas. In addition, according to this reading, only philosophers can establish and lead the best political regime, a regime in which they do not serve as rulers but rather form an alliance with those who rule.[96] According to Strauss, the ancient philosophers hid these views with "noble lies." This constitutes the primary distinction between these thinkers and philosophers of modernity who gave up hiding their opinions in favor of public presentation. Strauss's return to philosophers of yore is simultaneously an appropriation of their esoteric philosophy. He also hides his own opinions behind the interpretation of their ideas.[97]

Strauss's esoteric art of writing, according to Drury, is tied to his own political philosophy, which Strauss himself describes as a "political treatment of philosophy" aimed at overcoming the "maladies of modernity." The crisis of modernity, he argues, arose primarily because the possibility of harmful philosophical beliefs, better concealed in the interest of the stability of the social order, was denied. The most important political idea that Strauss believed was harming the political order consisted of the negation of God and his divine punitive wrath. For Strauss, esoteric philosophy figures primarily as a cloak for his own atheism and as a corrective to the open enmity that Machiavelli displayed toward religion.[98] According to Drury, Strauss's turn from the crisis of modernity to esoteric philosophy occurred under the influence of Nietzsche. For Strauss, the method of esoteric writing and its hidden content are most clearly seen in al-Fārābī, especially in his commentaries on Plato. However, Strauss uses Machiavelli as a megaphone for his esoteric ideas.[99]

Commenting on Strauss's remark that people write in the way they read,[100] James Andrew Kent characterizes Strauss as an esoteric author who himself wishes to be understood esoterically.[101] Kent puts esotericism at the core of his stringent and provocative critique, in the course of which he compares aspects of Strauss's thought with thinkers such as Louis Althusser, Karl Marx, Richard Rorty, Friedrich Schiller, Friedrich Nietzsche, Paul de Man, Walter Benjamin, and Harold Bloom. In the first part of his work, Kent engages in an immanent critique of Strauss's political theory that he terms a "Straussian reading of Strauss." In the second part of his work, Kent discusses Strauss's theory of reading and interpreting.

Kent distinguishes between exoteric and esoteric teachings within Strauss's political philosophy. According to the exoteric teachings, political affairs are discussed in a way that is considered relevant to political life, with inquiry into what things are necessary for the political. The political philosopher must decide to what end fixed, universal moral standards are necessary or, on the other hand, whether he is interested in esoteric truth more than he is in any other form of political order.[102] Kent is on the same line as Drury at this point, seeing esoteric truth as grounded in the mutual conflict of philosophy and society. In this conception, political philosophy emerges as "a kind of writing that expresses necessary untruths; it is the exoteric aspect of philosophic writing, the socially useful teaching, [. . .] the exoteric writing of philosophic texts [. . .]. It is essentially a protective shell of salutary untruths."[103]

Kent goes on to accuse Strauss of advocating a philosophy oriented toward the restoration of a class society, in which philosophers form a parasite class and can philosophize poshly at the expense of society. With this move, Strauss degrades political philosophy to a form of opinion journalism that seeks to preserve the philosophers' privileged position in society. Relying on Althusser's critique of ideology, Kent classifies Strauss's thought as "ideological" in that esoteric writing serves to guide the qualified few to engage with philosophy, while the exoteric teachings serve to fill the minds of the many with ideas that should cement the stability of society. Strauss's political philosophy contributes to the construction and reestablishment of dominant ideologies. These ideologies, as Marx argued, are an expression of the dominant material relations that ensure the domination of a particular class.[104] Strauss argues for the concealment of philosophical positions and the associated dissemination of "noble lies" for the purposes of preserving the "vulgar" masses within a cocoon of philosophical ignorance. Kent believes that Strauss uses esoteric philosophy in order to preserve the social status quo for the benefit of parasitical philosophers, thereby aligning all with the interests of a political and economic elite. Strauss is neither a liberal nor a democrat. He sees politics as an "indoctrination of the masses, the imposition of form onto the stupid, aimless, gullible masses."[105] At the end of the day, Strauss's esoteric thinking aims at the crass instrumentalization of the political community and the separation of lofty philosophy from the "dirty, yet necessary" realm of politics.[106]

Criticism of Strauss's esotericism is usually characterized by a polemic tone overriding any objective engagement with Strauss's ideas. This most likely derives from the nature of esoteric philosophy, which forces analysts to either enter the circle of the select few and succumb to Strauss's enchantments or stand against him from the outside and exercise critical judgment without direct contact with the object in question.

In examining Strauss's esoteric philosophy, a methodological question emerges as to whether the demands of a historically oriented examination of political philosophy can be reconciled with the imperative to analyze an author's ideas without recourse to their historical context. Indeed, we must also inquire into the criteria for judging esoteric-exoteric texts. Unfortunately, Strauss leaves this question unanswered. It would also be necessary to clarify how the dangers of misapprehension when reading between the lines can be either avoided or defused.

While esotericism constitutes an essential element of Strauss's philosophizing, it cannot be construed as a "misunderstanding of literalness."[107] Critics have to admit that Strauss — at least according to his professed self-image — argues for the esoteric-exoteric way of writing out of a pro-society attitude. The economic treatment of truth, which Strauss ascribes to the great philosophers of history and apparently to himself, is based on the conviction that there are certain truths that pose a threat to society and must therefore remain hidden in order not to threaten the social order. The esoteric Strauss constructs his own self-understanding out of a perceived responsibility for the existing social order. His understanding of these dangerous truths appears to be framed against a post-Enlightenment age in which true knowledge is revealed in emancipatory terms that reflect certain Christian principles. Strauss's esotericism is in many ways an important moment in his critique of Enlightenment, which began with *Philosophie und Gesetz*. His affirmation of the esoteric could therefore be formulated in such a way that a reason that had succeeded in disempowering religion would not need to hide the negation of religious ideas slyly between the lines. Strauss's esoteric method must be rigorously analyzed within this context. However, such an analysis would have to overcome an enormous difficulty. A reconstruction of Strauss's train of thought would have to be intimately familiar with his esotericism. And such esotericism can be unpredictably contagious!

Each of the approaches to interpreting Strauss sketched above could potentially be justified. Nevertheless, all of them share two forms of structural weakness. Each analyzes Straussian philosophy one-dimensionally by placing one facet of his oeuvre in the center. They also undervalue his relationship with medieval Islamic philosophy.[108] The importance of Averroes and Averroism for Strauss's early critique of religion unfolded in the study of Spinoza is neglected. The enormous impact made by al-Fārābī on Strauss has been subsumed under Strauss's relationship to the thought of Maimonides. And the radical change that Avicenna's statement about the treatment of prophecy and religious law in Plato's *Laws* caused in Strauss is finally attributed to chance, without any consideration of the foundations of the Avicennian view and its consequences for Strauss's response to the crisis of modernity.

The exaggerated reverence toward Strauss is reflected, on the one hand, in the remark of Allan Bloom (mentioned previously) whereby the prospect of judgment by future generations is made out to be the leitmotif of engagement with Strauss's work. On the other hand, the undeserved venom against Strauss is characterized by his portrayal as a "sphinx without a secret." In contrast to these approaches, my analysis of Strauss will be characterized by a sober seriousness in which Strauss will be taken at his word without conjecture as to any unarticulated esoteric views. The task of this work is to explicate Strauss's relationship to the Islamic philosophers named here. I will attempt to derive two main lines of analysis: on the one hand, the scope and position of the interpretation of Islamic philosophy in Strauss's oeuvre as a whole and, on the other hand, the thematic impact of his treatment of Islamic philosophers on his critique of modernity. Thus, the following investigation aims at filling a substantial gap in the existing interpretations of Strauss's work. It will serve as a substantive corrective for the existing lines of interpretation that I have sketched above. I will focus on the early and middle periods of Strauss's academic engagement, in which Strauss's treatment of medieval Islamic philosophy was at its peak. In order to reveal the deficits in the existing literature and achieve a greater appreciation for Strauss's philosophy more broadly, I will pursue a detailed depiction of Strauss's treatment of al-Fārābī, Avicenna, and Averroes. Al-Fārābī's impact on Strauss's philosophizing will be given a prominent place in this analysis and serve as a unifying thread.

Indeed, as mentioned previously, al-Fārābī was most influential for the development of Strauss's Platonic form of political thought. Strauss viewed the history of philosophy as defined by decline and the potential for rejuvenation. Al-Fārābī is characterized by him as a force for the renewal of philosophy following its destruction at the hands of revealed religion. He mediates between Plato and Aristotle and thereby creates a unified form of philosophy. Al-Fārābī is the founding father and guiding light of the epoch in medieval Islamic and Jewish philosophy that consumed Strauss. Strauss viewed himself in turn as the originator of a new form of thought that would be termed "the fourth wave of modernity." This mode of thinking would be characterized by a restoration of the form and rigor of philosophical questioning demonstrated by Plato and Aristotle.[109] His project of restoration would resemble al-Fārābī's in his attempt to nullify the serious differences between Plato and Aristotle, thereby deriving a unified portrayal of classical political philosophy that could then be applied to modern discourses in political thought.[110] Thus, the question emerges whether Strauss, who viewed himself as ensconced in the crisis of modern philosophy, did not project this self-perception onto al-Fārābī. Was it necessarily al-Fārābī who was responsible for Strauss's desire to augur a philosophical breakthrough, a breakthrough that would subsequently have recourse to a historical recovery of Platonic modes of philosophy and esoteric writing?[111]

A lack of critical studies and understanding exists regarding the relationship of Leo Strauss to the Islamic philosophy of the Middle Ages. Interpreters and critics of Strauss will, therefore, only be treated in the following six chapters and epilogue inasmuch as they touch on this particular theme. The first chapter will deal with Strauss's early critique of religion as reflected in his treatment of Spinoza and subsequently Averroes. It will demonstrate the influence of the medieval philosopher Averroes on Strauss's interpretation of Spinoza's critique of religion. The second chapter will begin with the dilemma in which Strauss found himself following his study of Spinoza and from which he emerged thanks to the help of his engagement with the philosophy of Avicenna. I will discuss Strauss's complete change in philosophical orientation resulting from his treatment of Avicenna. In the third chapter, the fruits of Strauss's investigations into Avicenna's thought will be revealed. The influence of al-Fārābī on Strauss, and on his Platonism in particular, will be observed in Strauss's engagement with Carl Schmitt's *Begriff des Politischen*, in his new understanding of religion in *Philosophie und Gesetz*, and in five further studies in which he dealt with al-Fārābī's political philosophy and interpretation of Plato. In the fourth chapter, we will observe Strauss's reaction to the crisis of modernity through the portrayal of a medieval Judeo-Islamic conception of religion heavily infused with

Platonism. At the center of this picture stands the prophet, whom Strauss, with an eye to al-Fārābī's ideas, combines with the figure of the philosopher-king in order to address the problem of revelation in philosophical fashion. In the fifth chapter, I will examine the relationship between reason, religion, and politics, three elements that are uniquely juxtaposed in Strauss's work. The equivalence Strauss draws between nomos and sharia and the philosophical treatment of revelation (along with the political meaning of religion that emerges therefrom) are discussed. The chapter ends with Averroes's religiously oriented justification of philosophy and Strauss's interpretation of its hermeneutic imperative. In the last chapter, I will analyze the primary position of political philosophy in Strauss's work against the backdrop of his interpretation of al-Fārābī. I will also explore the relationship between Strauss's understanding of the political and the Arabic concept of *siyāsa* (politics). The art of esoteric-exoteric writing, so significant for Strauss's work, will be discussed with reference to al-Fārābī's influence. In the epilogue, Strauss's philosophic project as a whole along with his interpretation of al-Fārābī will be critically assessed. The conclusion of my investigation will pose the question of whether Strauss's treatment of medieval Islamic thought actually succeeded in helping him philosophically treat the self-perceived crisis of modernity.

CHAPTER ONE

On the Genesis of Leo Strauss's Thought

SPINOZA AND AVERROES

Introduction

When Strauss's political thought is traced back to its roots, it becomes clear that this work is inseparable from his intense study of medieval Islamic philosophy. Leo Strauss was born to a conservative Jewish family in Kirchhain, near Marburg, on September 20, 1899. After graduating from high school in 1917, he served in the German army. It was only after World War I that he entered university, studying philosophy, mathematics, and natural sciences in Marburg, Frankfurt, Berlin, and Hamburg. Under the supervision of Ernst Cassirer, he wrote his doctoral thesis, "The Problem of Knowledge in the Philosophical Doctrine of Friedrich Heinrich Jacobi," and received his doctoral degree in 1921.[1]

Strauss's first publications after his doctorate were limited to short newspaper articles and reviews in which he mainly discussed specifically Jewish religious and political questions, such as Zionism.[2] However, Strauss dealt with the famed neo-Kantian Hermann Cohen's interpretation of Spinoza in two articles. Here, Strauss casts a far more favorable light on Spinoza and his Jewish context than the more critical Cohen.[3] These two papers laid the foundations of what would become Strauss's first major publication, *Die Religionskritik Spinozas als Grundlage seiner Bibelwissenschaft*, which he composed between 1925 and 1928.[4] This book, which was first published in 1930, is an exhaustive interpretation of Spinoza's *Tractatus Theologico-Politicus*. Taking Spinoza as a starting point, Strauss illustrates the genealogy of the modern critique of religion, going back as far as Epicurus. He attempts to expand the analysis of the old conflict between Enlightenment and religious orthodoxy into a more comprehensive and radical interpretation.

This book marks the beginning of an undertaking that would occupy Strauss throughout his entire life. While reflecting on *Die Religionskritik Spinozas als Grundlage seiner Bibelwissenschaft* in 1964, Strauss could rightly state that the theological-political problem had remained at the core of his intellectual preoccupations throughout his career.[5]

It seems that this book and the two aforementioned articles constitute Strauss's attempt to rehabilitate Spinoza's position in the sphere of Jewish scholarship. The motivation for this endeavor was Hermann Cohen's previously authoritative critique of Spinoza that went so far as to accuse Spinoza of heresy. It is this latter attack by Cohen that Strauss tries to refute.[6] Strauss's defense assumes that Spinoza's biblical studies are "first and foremost a product of intellectual history." They are preceded by the critique of revelation, which is actually a prerequisite for the critique of scripture. Strauss therefore attempts to situate Spinoza's critique of religion in its philosophical-historical context. This positioning, in turn, allows him to use historical argumentation to identify Spinoza's true concern along with the actual target of his critique.[7]

The following sections highlight the importance of Averroes for the genesis of Strauss's thought. Strauss realized that Averroes's ideas were crucial to Spinoza's *Tractatus Theologico-Politicus*.[8] Subsequently, Averroistic philosophy belonged to a great extent to the intellectual nourishment of the young Leo Strauss. I will try to show this above all by strictly following the Straussian view of Spinoza's relationship to Averroes. However, the primary aim of this chapter is not to relate Spinoza to Averroes or to investigate their relationship. Instead, it uses Strauss's perception of this relationship to reconstruct the position of Averroes's philosophy in Strauss's early work.[9]

A Historical Account of the Critique of Religion: Spinoza between Epicurus and Averroes

Leo Strauss discusses the place of Spinoza's critique of religion within the Epicurean tradition. This tradition claims that religions have their roots in a lack of knowledge and understanding of natural phenomena, a fact that causes anxiety in people. It is the fear of the inexplicable and the dire that disposes the human being to believe in the hidden power of God. This constitutes the fundamental bipolarity between science, on the one hand, and religion, on the other. While the latter stems from fear of death, the former would liberate humans from the pressures of religion that had emerged mainly a result of anxiety.[10] It was probably Strauss's familiarity with the Jewish tradition that made him associate the critique of religion with Epicureanism. As early as the second century CE, in the *Tractate Sanhedrin* of the Mishnah, the Epicureans are listed as among those who would not take part in the world to come. Gradually, Epicureanism became synonymous with a radical critique of religion that, among similar critiques, would deny the divine roots and basic principles of the Torah as well as the interpretations of religious scholars.[11] Strauss had evidently understood from Maimonides's *Commentary on the Mishnah* that the Epicureans among the Jews repudiated prophecies, especially those of Moses. Moreover, they dismissed the idea that humans could possess superior knowledge of God or that God had knowledge of particular human deeds.[12] In his *Guide of the Perplexed*, Maimonides eventually equates Epicureanism with atheism.[13]

In hindsight, Strauss explains that the antagonism between Spinoza and Judaism ultimately presented itself to him as a moral antagonism. Therefore, he deems it useful to further equate atheism and Epicureanism: "For the understanding of that moral antagonism, the Jewish designation of the unbeliever as Epicurean seemed to be helpful, especially since from every point of view Epicureanism may be said to be the classic form of the critique of religion."[14] From Strauss's perspective, Spinoza was an atheist. Following the widespread practice in Jewish philosophy of religion of equating atheism with Epicureanism, Strauss calls Spinoza an Epicurean, in order to put Spinoza's critique of religion into sharper focus from a Jewish perspective.

Nonetheless, equating Spinoza's critique of religion with Epicureanism fails to adequately capture this critique because, as Strauss continues, "Epicureanism is hedonism." But Epicureanism was foreign to the nature of Spinoza's thought. Hence Spinoza must have been much more than an Epicurean: "Unlike Epicurus, who fought against religion applying theory but not for the sake of theory, now it was also and in particular the representatives of pure theory (to the extent that their theories taught a different doctrine than did religion), who found themselves obliged to wage a more or less concealed war against religion. For it was no longer possible, or not yet possible, simply to disregard religion or to live as if religion did not exist."[15] This new critique of religion, which Strauss alludes to in the quotation above, was motivated by the concerns of theoretical philosophy. It came into being only after living and philosophizing without reference to religion had become impossible since religion started to be equated with revealed religion, namely a form of religion that claimed to have exclusive access to knowledge and truth. This constituted an entirely novel situation. In addition, those scholars who were hitherto indifferent to religion were now obliged to come to terms with it in every conceivable context. It was medieval Islamic philosophy that opened this new chapter in the history of philosophy.

This explains why Strauss traces Spinoza's critique of religion back to Averroes. In a bold move, he extends Spinoza's critique of religion — hitherto considered to have targeted only Judaism — to all revealed religions. He thereby reevaluates Spinoza's critique from a new angle. According to Strauss, it is from Averroes's oeuvre that the critique of religion as revealed religion originates.[16] The strong influence of Averroes on the philosophy of subsequent epochs, in both the East and West, was not restricted to his groundbreaking commentaries on Aristotle but also included his conception of religion. This conception of religion in turn paved the way for a politically infused notion of religion that possessed the capacity to shape societies. As it became obvious to Strauss, Spinoza's *Tractatus Theologico-Politicus* was influenced more by Averroes than by Epicurus.[17]

According to Strauss, the views of Epicurus and Averroes differ in their understanding of happiness and the right way of life for the individual. He emphasizes that the original views of Averroes are not identical with those of "the radical Christian-Averroistic tradition" of the Occident.[18] To Epicurus, it is the satisfaction of desires that leads to eudaimonia, which all people are capable of achieving. Averroes, on the other hand, follows in the steps of Aristotle and restricts happiness to theoretical reasoning and therefore to a small group of sages. From the latter point of view, the populace, or "nonphilosophers," who cannot reach happiness through theoretical reasoning, need other arrangements and provisions that promote happiness in order to secure the foundations of social life. These arrangements, to be sure, must go beyond political regimes that merely organize practical deeds but are not sufficient to maintain the order of the polity.[19]

Political rules alone are not sufficient for creating and maintaining an all-embracing order among affective human beings. For Strauss, following the Averroistic tradition, it is exactly this inability that makes religion necessary. The corpus of religion, Strauss continues, consists of those measures that are necessary to establish and maintain social order: "Religion is a regulator of order in social life. It bears on the life of the populace. It is not a necessary and spontaneous product of the life of the many, but a code of law prescribed for the many by higher intelligences (prophets). Religion is not by nature, but by institution." Later on, Strauss calls religion "a postulate of reason."[20]

At this point, Strauss finds Epicurus's critique of religion to exist in stark contrast with the Averroistic critique of religion. Epicurus rejects religion as a mere product of human anxiety in response to the inexplicable phenomena of nature. In the Averroistic tradition, on the contrary, religion has its roots in the leadership and deeds of a few individuals (prophets) who stand out among the many and who combine reason and imagination in order to speak to the populace as leaders. The prophets demand from the crowd, otherwise incapable of genuine virtue, to behave virtuously by replacing the sensual happiness they seek with a promised eternal one. They promise the reward to the obedient and the punishment of God to the disobedient. Such a functioning religion is "an excellent means also for princes to restrain their peoples and to exact obedience. This conception of religion, which found crude expression in the catch-phrase of the three impostors, is originally supported by the interest in theory as the perfection of man. It is this very connection which is still an element in Spinoza's thinking."[21] Strauss highlights three differences between the Averroistic and the Epicurean conceptions of religion that are crucial to Spinoza's critique of religion:

1. In the Averroistic tradition, religion is not a natural and spontaneous product of human existence, as Epicurus saw it. It is, rather, a "code of law prescribed for the many by higher intelligences," which regulates the social order among affective people given the inability of politics to do so.
2. Religion uses sanctions and promises happiness to those who obey commandments that are instrumental for the functioning of society. Thus, religious fear acquires a sociopolitical function. Therefore, religion should not be rejected, as Epicurus suggests, but instead channeled and instrumentalized.
3. The previous concept relies on the Aristotelian assumption that the individual reaches perfection only in theory. Aristotle equates the latter with true happiness, which can only be achieved by a few wise people.

This study will ultimately reveal that these three factors have remained decisive for the development and formation of Strauss's political thought. It is in Spinoza's critique of religion that Strauss claims to have found the true Averroes, whose thought had been superseded by the legend of Averroes in "Christian Europe." For this Averroes, it was theory, not pleasure, that would bring about human perfection, while priests and princes used religion with fraudulent intent. In the same vein, Strauss refers to another momentous occasion in the history of philosophy which was equally influential in the formation of Spinoza's critique of religion, a development which also had clear Averroistic features. He observes that Machiavelli transferred mundane ambitions such as honor and fame into the center of political power, while at the same time rejecting, like Giordano Bruno, the quietist Christian ideal. "This transvaluation gives new life to the Averroistic conception of prophecy as a product of the imagination." However, Strauss also points to the fact that Machiavelli's critique of religion is limited to Christianity and does not aim at a rejection of religion in and of itself. Furthermore, he asserts that Machiavelli's evaluation of religion's role in relation to politics was only of lasting influence to the extent to which it remained Averroistic: "For the free-thinkers of the following age, this kind of critique is effective only through those elements which it shares with the Averroistic type of thinking. This combination permeates the 'politicians' of the seventeenth century."[22]

Averroes and the State Theory of Spinoza

Closely linked to Spinoza's critique of religion is his state theory, which Strauss gives equal treatment in *Spinoza's Critique of Religion*. The most important aspects of this state theory can be summarized as follows:

The rather traditional notion of "beatitude," which Spinoza retains, elevates science qua philosophy to the primary means for the attainment of happiness, thereby rendering happiness into a rarefied state that only philosophers can achieve. This engenders a need for a source of political power capable of guiding the masses of ordinary people, crowds that cannot be tamed unless they are afraid. In this regard, religion earns appreciation as a useful and even indispensable tool. Apart from the radical distinction between the wise and the unwise, there is a further categorization of the unwise into the superstitious and the pious. Here, "theory" and "religion" even stand together against "superstition," and it is as a result of this alliance that religion turns out to be a necessity for the state.[23]

The preceding explanations of the political functions of religion within the state bear similarity to passages from Averroes's *Tahāfut at-tahāfut*.[24] In the course of his explanation as to why the philosophers do not reject the notion of bodily resurrection, Averroes — as translated by Simon Van Den Bergh — states,

> [The] philosophers believe that religious laws are necessary political arts, the principle of which are taken from natural reason and inspiration, especially in what is common to all religions, although religions differ here more or less. [. . .] the religions are, according to the philosophers, obligatory, since they lead towards wisdom in a way universal to all human beings, for philosophy only leads a certain number of intelligent people to the knowledge of happiness [. . .] whereas

religions seek the instruction of the masses generally.[25]

Indeed, this statement by Averroes actually contains important elements that can be found again in Spinoza's critique of religion. These elements are also authoritative for Strauss's later conception of religion. Religious laws are considered political artifices whose principles stem from both natural reason and revelation and that can therefore hardly be differentiated. Additionally, religion is assigned a political role based on the assumption that philosophy can give direction to only a limited number of intelligent people, whereas the populace needs the guidance of religion.

While explaining the political function of religion in the state, Strauss also takes up Spinoza's critique of theocracy. From Spinoza's point of view, theocracy readily accepts the enslavement of men for security's sake, subjugating their minds and restraining them with superstition. If superstition is considered inherent in human nature, theocracy can persist eternally and may even appear to be the regime most consistent with imaginative and affective life. Strauss identifies the foundations for such a critique in Spinoza's theory of natural law, which he subsequently discusses in order to explain problems in the critique of theocracy and to highlight the proper role of religion for the state.[26]

To Strauss, Spinoza's theory of natural law holds that all existing entities have equal rights. Since the populace is more numerous, this equality means that the majority will be more powerful in state affairs than the wise. Natural law, hence, is on the side of the majority, which seems justified in Spinoza's philosophy inasmuch as his doctrine of natural law "is primarily metaphysical or cosmological" and thereby discounts the human.[27]

Such a notion of power, of course, entails that the power, and accordingly the rights, of the state or society always override the power and the rights of the individual. However, this power structure appears to be the raison d'être of the state, which is fundamentally intertwined with the fact that affective life requires the guidance of reason. Given that affection dominates the populace, the raison d'être of the state mainly consists of governing or, as the case may be, of both governing and being governed. Governments can only persist as long as the affections of the populace are contained. From this viewpoint, the reason behind the state seems to be identical with the harmonizing of diverging forces within the state. However, apart from this equalization of reason and harmony, Strauss also points to another element in Spinoza's doctrine of natural law: the people's natural desire for freedom. The freedom that humans aim at, though, can be defined as the freedom to lead an affective life. As a result, the natural state is declared both a state of perfect freedom and a state of perfect equality. This difficulty is only resolved by interpreting the coincidence of freedom and equality not as the origin but as the telos of the state. As long as people show stronger tendencies toward hatred and conflict than toward peace, there is the indispensable need for a power that could endow human society with a powerful, intimate bond. It is at this point that religion is embedded into the theory of state, for "reason exercises only little influence on the majority of men. Not reason, but religion, teaches the multitude to love one's neighbor."[28]

Strauss says that Spinoza's state theory, as discussed above, is deeply rooted in the tradition of Averroes, who had already shown an inclination to assign religion the role of ensuring the existence of the state. Spinoza carries this tendency to its extreme conclusion.[29]

This judgment is based on the insight that Spinoza, like the Muslim philosophers, recognizes a perfect state that people without wisdom are incapable of achieving. Therefore, like the Muslim philosophers, he postulates special norms to which the majority must adhere. As a consequence of this fundamental intellectual and political difference between those possessing philosophical wisdom and the general populace, it is necessary to turn to religion as an efficient means for establishing the state and the social order. With religion adopting a political role, political doctrine receives a stabilizing theological underpinning. It is the inconceivable origin of the commandments and the prohibitions revealed by religion that provide individuals with the motivation to observe them. This is how Strauss can state that "the part played by philosophy in the life of the wise, and by superstition in the life of the vulgar, has its correlate in religion for the life of the nation. Since Spinoza asserts that an unbridgeable gulf separates the multitude from the wise, he is obliged to attribute to religion, as distinct from superstition, a function of significance."[30] Like Spinoza, Strauss differentiates between institutionalized religion and mere superstition. The former can induce "the multitude, trapped as it is in the life of the passions and the imagination, [. . .] to adopt behavior not indeed guided by reason but to some extent conformable to reason, socially useful, supporting not merely any state — for superstition would suffice for this — but a free state." With this conclusion, Strauss asserts that Spinoza is in line with the tradition of Islamic philosophy. He acknowledges that both Spinoza and the medieval Muslim philosophers reserved perfection for philosophers and emphasized the importance of religion as a normative authority for the multitude. Religion, as the work of prophets, "stands midway between philosophy and superstition" and is recognized as a political principle only.[31]

Averroes and Spinoza's Critiques of the Bible

In his analysis of Spinoza's theory of the state, Leo Strauss emphasizes the conformity of reason with scripture, a principle that even Spinoza acknowledged. Such agreement is rooted in "man's natural inclination to view things teleologically," which are interpreted "in such a way that they can lead to belief in a law-giving and judging God."[32] This parity involves the generation of both religious and political obedience among individuals. Spinoza thereby adopts the same pattern as used by Averroes in order to demonstrate the correlation between theoretical reasoning and religious scripture. Averroes holds that it is the function of philosophy to draw human thought to the Creator through the contemplation of Creation, and that therefore its purpose must be equated with the purpose of the law.[33] It is generally known that Averroes intended to justify the teleological identity of philosophy and religious law based on the content of religious scripture. However, Spinoza assumes that this teleological identity of philosophy and scripture presupposes a political meaning of religion, thereby agreeing, as Strauss sees it, with Averroes. This is why Strauss's interpretation of Spinoza can be considered a reference to the teleological link of philosophy and religion in Averroes's thought.

Strauss's identification of the foundation of Spinoza's biblical critique reveals the extent to which Spinoza's view of scripture corresponds to the Averroistic position on this same issue. The core notion is very concisely summarized by Strauss as follows: "Scripture teaches nothing about those points on which it expresses itself in contradictory fashion; however, where scripture teaches nothing, reason can teach everything for which it is able to assume responsibility."[34] Strauss does not here disclose the source of this hermeneutical principle, which ascribes to reason the capacity for teaching and self-accountability and, moreover, is meant to grant a freer hand with the text to the interpreter of the scripture, a scripture that is considered holy. However, for anyone familiar with Averroes, the Averroistic origin of this notion, so fundamental for Spinoza's critique of religion, cannot remain hidden. The clear demarcation between the scopes of scripture and of reason is structurally in line with the traditional argument made by Averroes that the Qur'ān does not contain everything worth knowing and therewith does not prevent the believers from applying reason in order to draw conclusions. On the contrary, it encourages the believer to engage in reasoning.[35] On this point — namely, that reason is fully qualified to fill the gaps in scripture's teaching — Spinoza is in full agreement with Averroes; however, he has a different philosophical motive. While it fell to the latter to justify philosophy before religion's jury, the former's intention was to deprive religion of the right to set binding standards for scholarly inquiry. Under the influence of scientific progress and the work of Descartes, the apologetical tendency of Averroes undergoes further noteworthy development up until Spinoza's polemic.

The critique voiced by the Jewish philosophical orthodoxy that Spinoza thus remains dependent on the authority of scripture and must then forbid himself to speculate[36] does not strike at the Averroistic core of the argument. Averroes did not intend to abolish the authority of the Qur'ān. On the contrary: he wanted its authority to prevail for the sake of philosophy.

Spinoza between Maimonides and Averroes

In the course of his work on the most important elements of Spinoza's critique of religion, Strauss investigates Spinoza's relationship with the medieval Jewish philosopher Maimonides (1135 or 1138 to 1204). Although not a Muslim (like the Christian Yaḥyā Ibn ʿAdī [893/4 to 974] before him), Maimonides is considered one of the most brilliant philosophers of the age of Arabic-Islamic philosophy.[37] The reference to Maimonides is clearly discernable in Spinoza's *Tractatus theologico-politicus*. Aware of this relationship, Strauss extensively discusses the links between the two philosophers. Strauss contends that they both acted in the religious context of Judaism and rendered the Bible, and the Torah in particular, an object of criticism.[38]

Despite his recognition of the Maimonidean influence on the development of Spinoza's rationalism, Strauss deems the influence of Averroes more important. In contrast to Maimonides, both Spinoza and Averroes follow Aristotle in holding the view that the world is not created but eternal, although they do so as a result of different scientific preconditions.[39] However, Strauss does not fail to notice that Spinoza's radical attitude toward revelation breaks away from both Averroes's and Maimonides's positions. Spinoza's denial of the creation of the world, and hence of the reality of revelation, goes against the pivotal theological precondition of the identity of God's reason and will in the act of creation. Strauss asks if this theological precondition is the "first cause," thereby resulting in the rejection of both teachings. His answer, which he gave in the form of a handwritten side note in his author's copy of *Spinoza's Critique of Religion*, reads as follows: "No. For also Ibn Rushd recognizes the sharīʿa and the allegorical interpretation, and teaches the eternity of the world."[40] In this marginal note on page 139 of the first edition, Strauss alludes to the option of philosophy rejecting the doctrine of the creation of the world without at the same time rejecting the possibility of revelation. Strauss obviously opposes Spinoza's uncritical rejection of the possibility of revelation solely on the basis of the rejection of the createdness of the world. He brings to his side Averroes, who does not accept the doctrine of a creator God, which is crucial for all monotheistic religions, but who recognizes religion as sharia — in other words, as religious law. A discussion of how Averroes uniquely declared the world to be both eternal and dependent on God is beyond the scope of this book.

In this context, Strauss uncovers another point on which Spinoza, through Averroes's philosophy, turns against Maimonides. To Strauss, Spinoza's attempt to "prove that philosophy and theology are irreconcilable by assuming that philosophy is a matter for the wise minority, and that socially intended religion is a matter for the unwise majority, [. . .] belongs to the context of the critique of Maimonides." Maimonides assumed the existence of two different categories regarding articles of faith. These are, on the one hand, the fundamental truths, which must be believed by all. On the other hand, there are the articles of faith that should be followed for the sake of maintaining social order. This distinction illustrates Maimonides's attempt to bridge the gap between those who know and those who do not possess philosophical knowledge on the common ground of religion. In the same vein, Spinoza differentiates between "the fundamental" and "merely pious dogmas" but recognizes the "comprehensive unity of lex divina," which "conveys fundamental truth as well as merely pious dogmas" only for the sake of the state: "For it is only the wise elite who, by their insight into the fundamental truths, are directly induced to conduct themselves in a manner favorable to social life. The majority, the unwise, need quite other methods of education. They must be brought to believe in God's mercy and punitive justice."[41] Eventually, Strauss realizes that, in stark contrast to Maimonides, Spinoza does not grant the multitude access to the fundamental truths. These truths are based on knowledge that can only be obtained from proofs. Furthermore, Spinoza discards the possibility of the philosophers conveying these truths to the multitudes. By highlighting Maimonides's acknowledgment of one single truth for all people, their wisdom notwithstanding, Strauss intimates his suspicion that Spinoza adheres to the doctrine attributed to Averroes, namely the existence of a double truth dependent on the immutable heterogeneity of humans' capacities to perceive "the" truth.[42]

In a detailed note, Strauss discusses Leon Roth's conclusions on the relationship between Spinoza, Descartes, and Maimonides.[43] Strauss, whose book aims at justifying Spinoza's critique of religion vis-à-vis Judaism, notes,

> Roth overestimates the importance in intellectual history of Spinoza's relationship to Maimonides, which is doubtless important in Spinoza's philosophical development. Roth does not sufficiently take into account that the theories regarding which Spinoza stands with Maimonides against Descartes

> (and against the kalām) are for the most important part not peculiar to Maimonides, but are the common property of "the philosophers."[44] Spinoza's agreement with Averroes is certainly of greater objective importance than his agreement with Maimonides. Our interpretation is to be understood within this limitation, and this is justified, since we are considering Spinoza's relationship to Maimonides not in regard to Maimonides' importance in general in the history of philosophy, but as an element in Spinoza's critique of religion.[45]

Strauss does not dwell on those points on which Spinoza stands with Averroes against Maimonides. Indeed, a detailed analysis of the relationship between Spinoza and Averroes is beyond the scope of this book.[46] Nonetheless, this remark illustrates that Strauss was well aware of the influence of Averroes and Averroism on Spinoza's thought. Strauss probably had good reasons to mention this only in a footnote. Nonetheless, this mere footnote contains important elements of Strauss's perception of Maimonides. While the Jewish elements in the thought of this medieval precursor of the Enlightenment must not be neglected, Maimonides's oeuvre originates from and develops primarily within the context of Arabic-Islamic philosophy. This is what Strauss had realized from the beginning of his philosophical career and what he makes unmistakably clear in his *Philosophy and Law* as well as in his subsequent studies on the conception of religion in the Islamic and Jewish Middle Ages. After all, essential elements of his early works go back to the philosophy of Averroes, and it is against this background that Strauss's early work has to be understood.

Summary

Leo Strauss, through Spinoza, understood that the doctrines of revealed religions appear to be false prejudices that people believe out of habit. This habit stems from the "basic human prejudice," which "is the assumption that all things, and even God Himself, act as men do, according to purposes." This prejudice presupposes two conditions: the ignorance of true causality and the tendency of men to consider natural things as a means of self-preservation. In this attitude one can find the origin of belief in a Creator and in providence. Should daily experiences arouse doubts regarding the existence of divine providence, people seek consolation in the assumption that divine acts transcend human comprehension. This is how the ignorance of true causality effectively affirms God through human imagination. Furthermore, Spinoza states that inadequate imagination only causes affection and that, in turn, the imaginative-affective life is a fertile breeding ground for revealed religion.[47]

As is well known, it is on this imaginative-affective rationale for religion that Spinoza builds his own critique of religion, which downgrades revealed religion to an excellent means of subduing the populace in order to maintain social order. According to this view, religion is inherited from the prophets and necessary due to human nature. Reason therefore demands it. Strauss concludes that Spinoza, influenced by Averroes, can only admit a certain coalescence between reason and scripture: Both "agree that God's eternal word is graven on the hearts of men." One could even say that the preaching of the prophets appeals to "the word of God which is written in the hearts of men" and is not addressed "to believing and learned men but, essentially, to the multitude."[48]

At this point, Strauss detects a contradiction in Spinoza's doctrine: "Spinoza's conception of religion cannot be reconciled with his principles so long as it is assumed that the passive (passionate-imaginative) life is the basic stratum of human life, in such a manner that in only a few men does reason rise above this stratum and against it. However, what is acted upon must be, in itself, act. Being acted upon is only the counter-effect of an original agent upon effects produced from without." Implicitly, Spinoza seems to recognize natural religion: Assuming that there is a divine spark engraved in every human heart, people strive for love and justice even though they often live in darkness. This divine spark is often buried under the influences of the external world. In this eternal — albeit obscured — word of God, Spinoza still is able to evoke a popular image of God and, as a consequence, the possibility of a pious life.[49]

To what extent is there a need for institutionalized religion if natural religion is already recognized? If the prophets "had very vulgar opinions about God" suitable only for the multitudes, how can it be explained that philosophers took such an interest in religion? Indeed, Strauss already observed this fact when studying Spinoza in the light of Maimonides and Averroes. Moreover, Spinoza does not specify the political role religion should play.[50]

CHAPTER TWO

Discovery and Change

Introduction

The preceding chapter made clear the Averroistic traits of Spinoza's theological-political thought, traits that did not escape Strauss's notice. Both Averroes's and Spinoza's critiques of religion eventually yielded a positive role for religion to play in establishing an independent, constructive disposition toward the state. Within the scope of this book, the question of whether Averroes could imagine a polity independent of any religious authority must remain unanswered.

Unlike Epicurus and the inhabitants of his pleasure garden, Averroes appears to constitute a "more sophisticated believer" and is by no means an atheist. Like al-Fārābī, he holds that religion is a practical vehicle employed for conveying theoretical truths to the multitudes, thereby functioning as a necessary condition for the maintenance of social peace in the state.[1] Spinoza adopts the same line of argument when he assigns religion a strong political function that guides the populace, thereby stabilizing both the social order and the ruling authority.

While working on *Spinoza's Critique of Religion*, Leo Strauss must have also noticed Averroes's tendency to understand religion (Islam, in this particular case) as sharia — that is, as religious law. In all likelihood, Strauss also realized that Averroes was specifically concerned with the relationship between philosophy and religious law when investigating the relationship between philosophy and religion in general.[2] Later on, in *Philosophy and Law*, Strauss begins to consistently designate religion as "law," a usage recalling Averroes's conception of religion. Nonetheless, Strauss was not content with these appropriations from Spinoza and Averroes regarding the theological-political problem. The problem of revelation remained a thorn in his side.

The Discovery

Strauss examined and followed Spinoza's argumentation in his *Tractatus theologico-politicus* "with a view to the question of whether Spinoza had in fact refuted orthodoxy." But he found that the attacks of Enlightenment on religion had left the theoretical claims of religious orthodoxy almost untouched.[3] It seems that Strauss was not satisfied with the answers rationalism offered in response to the challenges of revealed religion. This dissatisfaction in turn nourished Strauss's suspicion that modern rationalism had actually caused the self-destruction of reason.[4] Strauss was aware of the new possibilities that Nietzsche had developed in his critique of the underlying principles of the European tradition and that Heidegger's destruction of that very philosophical tradition had further revealed. This awareness undoubtedly contributed to his turn to premodern rationalism. Nevertheless, there is likely also a more direct explanation for his turn to medieval Jewish and Islamic philosophy.

On November 30, 1933, Strauss wrote in a letter to Dr. Cyrus Adler that his work on Spinoza had compelled him to read the Jewish philosophers of the Middle Ages, in particular Maimonides. He was also inspired by Hobbes's political science. This was reason enough to push Hobbes and the prophetology of the Jewish and Islamic philosophers of the Middle Ages to the forefront of his future research. It was the search for the philosophical sources underpinning Gersonides's *Milchamot ha-shem*, which Strauss was initially commissioned by the Academy for the Science of Judaism to analyze, that prompted Strauss to go beyond Maimonides and to read several manuscripts of Islamic philosophers, some of them in Arabic. At this point, he realized that the relationship between Jewish and Islamic medieval prophetology, on the one hand, and Platon's *Politikos* and *Nomoi*, on the other, had not been sufficiently analyzed and evaluated.[5]

We learn from this letter that after studying Spinoza, Strauss turned to the prophetology of the Jewish and Islamic philosophers. Both al-Fārābī and Avicenna were interested in analyzing the relationship between religion and politics primarily in terms of prophecy. The fact that in Islam the figure of Muhammad as both prophet and statesman may have compelled this kind of prophecy. Likewise, Moses was the religious and political leader of his people. The Muslim medieval prophetologies could therefore become role models for the Jewish prophetology to be developed later. It was due to his studies of Maimonides's prophetology and the philosophical sources of Gersonides that Strauss read Islamic philosophers other than Averroes.[6] Both "Cohen und Maimuni" and "Maimunis Lehre von der Prophetie und ihre Quellen," two papers Strauss probably wrote in 1931,[7] reveal that Strauss was mainly interested in Avicenna's Arabic writings.[8] One passage in Avicenna's *Fī aqsām al-ʿulūm al-ʿaqliyya* (*Treatise on the Divisions of Rational Sciences*) attracted his special attention.[9] What does this passage, which has become important for Strauss, say? Strauss notes that Avicenna, after enumerating the objects of politics, continues as follows:

> Of this, what has to do with kingship is contained in the book [sic] of Plato and of Aristotle on the state, and what has to do with prophecy and the religious law is contained in both of their books on the laws . . . this part of practical philosophy (viz. politics) has as its subject matter the existence of prophecy and the dependence of the human race, for its existence, stability, and propagation, on the religious law. Politics deals both with all religious laws as a whole and with the character of the individual religious laws specific to nations and epochs; it deals with the difference between divine prophecy and all invalid pretensions.[10]

This passage caused a profound alteration of Strauss's philosophical orientation. This alteration, which is only briefly alluded to here, was twofold: First, the medieval conception of revelation became a subject matter of political philosophy and was interpreted from a Platonic viewpoint. Second, Strauss aligned his own philosophizing, which centered on the theological-political problem, with Plato's political philosophy.[11]

However, a discussion of the philosophical consequences of this discovery is predicated on an analysis of the discovery itself. Given the importance of this text, it merits more attention. First and foremost, we must ascertain whether Strauss's understanding of Avicenna's statement was correct or only partially so.

To begin with, I shall address Avicenna's treatise, which begins with a definition of philosophy as a speculative occupation (*ṣināʿat an-naẓar*). From this speculation, one gains insight into the nature of all beings. Furthermore, one acquires knowledge that is ultimately translated into acts that render his soul sublime, perfect, and relatable to the existing intelligible world. As far as human power allows it, philosophy can teach humans to prepare for the highest form of bliss in the afterworld. Avicenna goes on to explain that which he considers the two divisions of philosophy: theoretical and abstract philosophy, on the one hand, and practical philosophy, on the other. The former aims at providing certainty about the state of those beings that have not come into existence through human action, offering theoretical perspectives to this end. The purpose of the latter is to produce healthy insights into the effects of human acts and to extract from them what is good. Eventually, practical philosophy produces opinions for the sake of action. Whereas truth is the purpose of the theoretical division, the practical division aims at the good.[12]

Avicenna continues by dividing theoretical philosophy into three parts: Physics, mathematics, and metaphysics.[13] Practical philosophy can also be divided into three parts, for it refers to the conduct of life (*tadbīr*), which is situational: It can refer either to the solitary individual or to a human being in company, whether such company consists of the household or the society. Unlike the divisions of theoretical philosophy, Avicenna does not name the divisions of practical philosophy but rather describes their areas of application.[14] However, regarding the divisions of theoretical philosophy, he goes even further into detail and enumerates the subsequent divisions of physics, mathematics, and metaphysics as well as other areas of inquiry arising from these respectively.[15] Finally, he discusses the different divisions of the science of logic.[16] Avicenna ascribes most of the divisions to a classical work of philosophy by Aristotle. Only two Platonic writings are mentioned: the *Politeia* and the *Nomoi*.

Avicenna divides practical philosophy into three groups, according to the different spheres of human life: The first division deals with individual ethics and instructs the individual regarding the appropriate moral opinions and actions that can lead to bliss in this life and in the life hereafter. Avicenna ascribes these teachings to Aristotle's *Ethics*. The second division is concerned with domestic life and gives advice on how men should administer their household (including spouses, children, and slaves) in order to transform it into a place of happiness; the book for this topic is *Arunos*.[17] The third division concerns society (*ijtimāʿ madanī*). It deals with different kinds of administration and leadership (*as-siyāsāt wa-r-riʾāsāt*), positive and negative forms of human society, and how and why they persist, decline, or alter in form. At this point, the passage provoking Strauss's philosophical turn appears.[18]

When one compares the Arabic text, published in 1880 or 1881 in Constantinople, with the passage translated by Strauss, several deviations can be noticed. Whereas the Arabic text mentions the two books on the laws without specifying their author or authors (*kitābān fī n-nawāmīs*), Strauss clearly ascribes the two books to Plato and Aristotle. In this case, Strauss obviously follows the Gotha manuscript, which he used by his own account for "the establishment of the text."[19] Yet Strauss deviates from both Arabic texts in another case: neither Arabic version states that politics deals with all aspects of religious law as well as with the difference between divine and fraudulent prophecy. It seems that Strauss put these words into Avicenna's mouth.

As mentioned above, the version from Constantinople alludes to two anonymous books about the laws. The manuscript of the library in Gotha that Strauss used to "establish" or reconstruct the text clearly assigns the books to the philosophers Plato and Aristotle (*kitābāhumā l-mawḍūʿ fī n-nawāmīs*).[20] Hence, the manuscript seemingly provides more information than the edition of 1880/1881, which may have been the reason why Strauss decided to rely on the former. Only the use of the manuscript allowed Strauss to link Avicenna's statement on the discussion of prophecy and religious law to Plato's *Laws*.

However, this sentence in the manuscript raises a problem that Strauss, curiously enough, disregards. Not only Plato but also Aristotle is mentioned as the author of a book on laws, even though no such book has come down to us. Neither does the list of pseudo-Aristotelian books contain a title on law.[21] Arabic thinkers were aware of at least parts of Plato's book about the laws from Galen's *Synopsis*. Al-Fārābī wrote the *Epitome of the Laws*, although it remains disputed whether he was aware of Plato's dialogue itself (or maybe even an Arabic version of it) or had to rely on Galen's *Synopsis*. So far, it seems highly unlikely that al-Fārābī was familiar with the text in its entirety.[22] The statement about the two books on the laws, one by Plato and one by Aristotle, can therefore be considered incorrect. The Constantinople version seems to be the more accurate one, as Aristotle must be rejected as a possible author.

Nonetheless, this version does mention two books on the laws. Moreover, it differentiates between two different conceptions of the notion of *nāmūs* (nomos): one of them philosophical and the other popular. According to this classification, the philosophers understand *nāmūs* to mean revelation, namely a religiously infused way of life that constitutes a constant ideal. To put it differently, Avicenna's description of the "philosophical" category of *nāmūs* corresponds to the meaning of revealed religious law and the idea of the ideal human being that the latter contains. Avicenna underpins this conception of *nāmūs* by referring to the common use of the word in Arabic: the angel who descended to bring revelation was also called *nāmūs*. It seems that the philosophical notion of *nāmūs*, which Avicenna introduces, has to be regarded as a synonym for revelation inasmuch as it includes, apart from the messenger, the content (the ideal conduct of life) and mystery of revelation.[23] In addition to the philosophical use of *nāmūs*, Avicenna points to a popular usage that signifies cunning and deceit.[24]

A Pseudo-Platonic *Book of Laws*

The aforementioned quotation of Avicenna's text conveys two meanings of *nāmūs* (pl. *nawāmīs*). One is used by the philosophers and pertains to prophecy and religious laws. The other one is rejected by the philosophers as it constitutes cunning or fraud. Regarding the former meaning, Avicenna explicitly refers to the two *nawāmīs*-books.[25] As for cunning or fraud, Avicenna does not mention any reference book. Is it therefore possible that there are writings that contain the latter two meanings, which the Arabs could have mistaken for Plato's *Nomoi* (*Nawāmīs Aflāṭūn*) in the Middle Ages?

There were indeed three Arabic books entitled *Nawāmīs Aflāṭūn*. First, there was a pseudo-Platonic book on magical deeds and the feats of charlatans such as walking on water or on air, appearing in the guise of animals, magical rainmaking, or the conjuring of flashes or pillars of fire. Apart from these, this *Nawāmīs Aflāṭūn* deals with the burning of people from a distance, talking to the dead, the fission of the sun and the moon, and the creation of snakes and dragons from sticks and ropes.[26] In short, these topics perfectly correspond to the conception of *nāmūs* rejected by Avicenna. Apart from al-Fārābī's summary of Plato's *Nomoi* (or Galen's *Synopsis* thereof), there is a third pseudoepigraphic book entitled *Nawāmīs Aflāṭūn*. It comprises three treatises and does in fact contain long passages on religious laws and prophecy.[27] The following sections will investigate these passages on prophecy and religious law. This is a necessary step toward an understanding of the true meaning of Avicenna's statement on the two *nawāmīs*-books on prophecy and religious law and, accordingly, toward an evaluation of Strauss's interpretation of this statement and its philosophical consequences.

Religious Law in the Pseudo-Platonic *Book of Laws*

In this pseudo-Platonic book, we find both the Arabic word *sharīʿa* and the Arabized, originally Greek word *nāmūs*. Both designate religious law. Once, they even appear combined as *nāmūs ash-sharīʿa*.[28] So, which conceptions of religious law are actually conveyed in this book?

Before the anonymous author of this book sets out to discuss religious law and its purpose, he emphasizes its necessity. Since religious law steers human intentions clear of evil and toward good deeds, both of which are of consequence in the afterlife, its necessity is made doubly manifest. On the one hand, it allows for the establishment of justice essential for human society while meeting the exigencies intertwined with the human need for social life. On the other hand, the author indicates that compliance with religious law is awarded by eternal life.

The text also holds that religious laws came into being because of God's intention to provide humanity with the necessary guidance to meet their spiritual and material requirements. Still, from the very beginning, the text gives the proviso that religious law is fundamentally not concerned with particular matters but is rather oriented toward the whole. As far as material needs are concerned, religious law gives instructions and thereby frames the conditions for a just human society where those needs can be met. Inasmuch as religious law ensures the fairness of human behavior, it ensures the persistence of the political order.

It is obvious that the relationship between religion and politics is of relevance to the author. Initially, both seem to share common ground inasmuch as they share the concern of upholding the social order. Nevertheless, a clear distinction separating religious law from politics accentuates the contours of religious law. Contrary to those who confound the two, the text states that their purviews are different and only tangential to one another. Religious law would supersede the rights inherently granted by politics. Political rights only target the external aspects of the social order, while religious law restrains human passions by dictating religious praxis. The latter results in just social dealings together with the maintenance of society. Moreover, religious law is concerned for the human soul and compels it to perpetuate its ties to the cosmic order. Religious law ultimately transcends political rights. It is evocative of the return of the souls to heaven and thus tries to keep human beings from descending into a life dominated by lust and wrath. Political life, in turn, benefits from the exigencies of religious law, although the latter is not confined to this role. Rather, it aims directly at the essence of human nature. It is out of internal conviction that human beings comply with such religious laws. In this conceptual framework, religious law exhibits mainly spiritual traits.

Another point of contact between religious law and politics is the attempt to use political rules to ensure continued compliance with religious precepts. The text does not directly mention the political motives behind this but suggests the following interpretation: Constant observance of religious commandments creates in people a tendency to obey higher authorities. People learn to submit to the will of others. According to this logic, the tendency to submit to the political order grows with the tendency to obey religious law. This is confirmed by a Pythagorean quotation that holds that people find it less difficult to resist their king than to resist religious law, for the latter is more deeply rooted in the human character than political rule. This is why political rulers often use religion as a shield. Therefore, a stabilizing religious power also stabilizes political power, which explains the political interest in compliance with religious law. From this perspective, religion and politics must necessarily interact.

However, it is widely believed that religious law has an authority that political power cannot violate. The text gives the example of two prophets who criticize the practices of the political regime in an uninhibited way. The fact that religious law is fundamentally independent from politics is also illustrated by the final story relayed by the text, in which the guardian of the laws escapes the death sentence pronounced by the king, doing so by means of magical abilities that the political ruler is powerless to impede. This story suggests that while the political rulers may preside over religious acts, they do not wield power over the content or the guardians of religious law. On the contrary: in the opinion of the author, politics acts like a servant to the master, which is the religious law. This opinion most likely stems from the author's conviction that, because of its divine character, religious law stands above politics.

In accordance with the Islamic type of revelation, the author of the pseudo-Platonic treatise states that religious laws are sent down (*tanzīl*), thus making the revelation of the Qur'ān the model of the origin of religious laws par excellence. But it is remarkable how the text explains the plurality of religious laws. This plurality is held to result from the differences existing between human societies. Religious laws differ from each other according to the degree of comprehension possessed by the respective society to whom the laws have been delivered. Additionally, such laws have come into being in different epochs with great variation because human ignorance and obstinacy made the renewed promulgation of these laws necessary. Herewith, the text conveys the author's belief that God truly wants human beings to understand his will. This is why he sends down different religious laws that are individually tailored to the culturally determined capacities of the respective human societies. Furthermore, God takes into account that human beings also have animalistic features that sometimes prevent them from understanding religious law and acting accordingly. In this context, the text gives the example of the donkey that only drinks upon repeated whistling. Hence, God must repeatedly send religious law to humanity.[29]

Prophecy in the Pseudo-Platonic *Book of Laws*

It is in the context of drawing a comparison with philosophy that the text mentions prophecy for the first time. In this passage, the prophet is portrayed as a unique figure of his era who has a capability to explain circumstances that the philosopher lacks. The text describes an encounter between a prophet and a philosopher, which betrays a hierarchy: the philosopher has to rely on the prophet's knowledge and is well-advised to follow the latter's instructions. Prophetic insight takes priority over philosophical insight because the former comes directly from above and is only received by the prophet. Philosophical insight, on the other hand, is the result of (human) intellectual effort. However, prophetic knowledge has a transcendental and supernatural source and is therefore all-embracing.

Prophets gain their insight from revelation (*waḥī*), although the text hints at a process of revelation without the personal participation of the prophet. The prophet receives the fully formed revelation passively while in a dormant state and passes it on without any alteration. At this point, the text compares prophecy to divinatory practices such as astrology and soothsaying, which may appear similar to prophecy. However, unlike these practices, prophecy does not require human intervention and conveys accomplished insights to a recipient who does not need to be technically trained. A further difference between divination and prophecy consists of the moral attitudes of those who receive and disclose particular insights. The prophet stands out in merit of his conduct marked by asceticism, mental purity, and abstention from the material and profane.

Contrasted with divination on the one hand and with philosophy on the other, the notion of prophecy becomes clearer. Prophecy consists of the aptitude on the part of a person who is unique in their era and often vested with magical powers to receive revealed knowledge directly from God without any effort of their own. The prophet imparts this religious knowledge in unaltered form to the people. During the process of revelation, the prophet is entirely passive. Their role is restricted to that of a mouthpiece of God or to that of a medium between God and his addressees. The content imparted by God passes through them, and this is why they need to be of high moral purity to adequately perform this intermediation. The moral and spiritual characteristics the prophet is endowed with contrast sharply with the intellectual and theoretical capabilities of the philosopher. Due to their moral power and revealed knowledge, the prophet can criticize and reprehend the philosopher from a higher position. By the same token, the prophet can criticize the political regime and gain the upper hand when disputes with the latter arise. The fact that it is God's word that they proclaim lends them authority. However, it is also important, for the sake of their virtue, to remain distant from the realm of politics, intervening only if necessary. Thus, the prophet's role with regard to politics is that of an ethical corrective.

Comments

It is noteworthy that the pseudo-Platonic *Book of Nawāmīs* under scrutiny here bears a resemblance to concepts and terminologies in well-known writings of the Sufi tradition.[30] The pseudo-Platonic treatises show a certain tendency toward abstinence from the profane, the discipline of the soul, and the quest for the proximity to God. As is common in Sufi literature, our text appeals to the self-emancipation from passions, while death is the liberation of the soul held prisoner by the body.[31] In elaborating this point, the following observations can be made:

> The text uses terms specific to Sufi literature such as the following: *irtiyāḍ an-nafs* (the self-discipline of the soul, p. 197),[32] *al-maʿād* (the return to heaven, pp. 200, 211), *baṭin* (the interior or hidden, p. 200), *az-zahāda* (abstinence, pp. 200ff., 223)[33], *al-faqr* (the poverty, p. 201),[34] *aʿājīb, muʿjizāt* (the miracles, pp. 202, 209), *yaghshāh* (to assail him suddenly, p. 202),[35] *al-qawma ʿalā sh-sharīʿa* (the persistence in religious law, pp. 221, 223)[36], *safar* (journey, p. 222),[37] and *ṭarīq al-ikhlāṣ* (the path of truthfulness, p. 224).[38]

> The conception of prophecy in the treatises is evocative of an early Sufi tradition that distinguished three often-combined ways of receiving and, accordingly, three types of recipients of divine messages. The first way can be described as "the sending by God" (*risāla*), the second prophecy (*nubūwa*), and the third inspiration (*ḥadīth*). The messenger of God (*ar-rasūl*) "proclaims something from God and is sent to a particular people in order to convey lore as well as God's message." He is the bearer of a law that he has received from God to call upon the people to comply with it. The prophet (*an-nabī*), on the other hand, "prophesies, but has not been sent to anybody. Only if he is asked or solicited to do so does he speak about it to the people. In so doing, he summons people to God, admonishes them and explains to them the paths within the law of the messenger of God (*rasūl*). [. . .] The prophet, who himself is not sent, acts on the law of the respective messenger. He encourages the people to adhere to the law the messenger has conveyed."[39]

The demonstrated similarities of the pseudo-Platonic *nawāmīs* with early Sufi writings make the perception of the former as "Platonic" even more probable,[40] which in turn helps to explain important elements of this spurious text. The conception of prophecy especially benefits from this. Prophecy seems to be the gift of being capable to receive the revelation and to pass it on without alterations. God vested chosen people in different eras with this gift. Prophecy does not necessarily entail law giving. Only few among the prophets are designated messengers of God and in charge of law giving.[41] The theological,[42] mystical, and philosophical[43] tradition of early and medieval Islam acknowledges the appearance of numerous prophets in the history of humanity. These prophets express God's will and presence in their words and miracles, thus admonishing the people to adopt righteous attitudes and a virtuous conduct of life. The notion of prophecy is therefore historical and open. It is not restricted to the prophets of the Bible and allows for an inclusion of antique rulers and sages among the prophets.[44]

Although the reception of a sudden and miraculous revelation remains a fundamental feature of prophecy, the characteristics of prophecy in this text go beyond this reception of revelation. According to a saying attributed to Muhammad, prophecy also includes other qualities such as thrift, right conduct, and good behavior.[45] It seems that, according to this conception, prophecy shares characteristics commonly attributed to important historical figures, such as vision and acumen. Furthermore, the recognition of numerous pre-Islamic prophets is compatible with the Islamic idea of Muhammad as the seal of the prophets. Implicitly, this underpins the doctrine of Muhammad's exceptional position.

Avicenna and the Pseudo-Platonic *Book of Laws*

Discussing prophecy, Avicenna concludes that prophets and messengers of God use symbolic language and a vocabulary full of insinuations. As a proof, Avicenna quotes a statement of Plato's to be found in this *nawāmīs*-book. According to this statement, those who are unable to understand the meaning of the messengers' (*ar-rusul*) symbols will not reach the divine kingdom (*al-malakūt al-ilāhī*).[46] It is obvious that such a statement cannot be found in Plato's *Nomoi*. Thus Avicenna's quotation suggests that his knowledge of Plato is based upon a corrupted transmission. Hence, the conclusion that this false transmission may in fact be the pseudo-Platonic *nawāmīs*-book under scrutiny here can potentially be inferred.[47]

What justifies the assumption that Avicenna had knowledge of this book? And is it possible at all to find commonalities between Avicenna's writings and the *nawāmīs*-book? In the above-quoted passage from the treatise *On the Divisions of the Rational Sciences*, Avicenna mentions two different conceptions of *nawāmīs*: whereas the multitude understands the *nāmūs* to connote cunning or fraud, *nāmūs* as the philosophers understand it means the right conduct of life (*sunna*); the constant, established ideal (*al-mithāl al-qāʾim ath-thābit*); and the descent of revelation (*waḥī*). There are indeed parallels with this categorization in the falsified *nawāmīs*-book. The latter equally describes the laws as revealed and stresses on several occasions that they are an ideal to be followed. Additionally, Avicenna holds that the last division of practical philosophy that the text discusses meets the human need for laws. The author of the *nawāmīs*-book also holds that human beings need to live in society and that laws are necessary to uphold this society. Avicenna also recognizes the diversity of the laws, which differ depending on the people and the era they live in. This idea is also clearly expressed in the pseudo-Platonic book. Finally, Avicenna assigns to this division of practical philosophy the knowledge of the existence of prophecy and the ability to distinguish between divine prophecy and invalid claims to prophetical insights. Avicenna's description of prophecy also shows a remarkable similarity with the notion of prophecy as understood by the author of the pseudo-Platonic book. Both writers attribute prophecy's existence solely to divine revelation while also clearly separating prophecy from divination.

However, to address the relationship between prophecy and religious law in both Avicenna's and the pseudo-Platonic *Book of Nawāmīs*, it is necessary to provide an account of the most important features of Avicenna's prophetology. At this point, I am only concerned with this one relationship. The subsequent discussion of Avicenna's prophetolgy does not claim to be comprehensive.

A fundamental source of Avicenna's prophetology[48] is the Aristotelian doctrine of the soul and its cognitive power, a discussion that goes back to the third part of *De Anima*. The doctrine, as Avicenna knew it, had been further developed by commentators, most importantly by Alexander of Aphrodisias. According to this Aristotelian doctrine, all intellectual cognition results from the action of the separate active intellect on the human intellect.[49] This Aristotelian framework had already been enriched by Stoic, Neoplatonic, and Hellenistic elements. It was in this "extended" form that Aristotle's doctrine of the soul was passed on to and received by the Islamic philosophers.[50] Avicenna's reception of this doctrine must be viewed against the background of its previous definitions by al-Kindī and, in particular, by al-Fārābī. Avicenna agrees with al-Fārābī when he describes the prophet as a human being of exceptional intellectual capabilities who does not require any external instructions, yet receives his comprehensive knowledge through revelation. It seems that the intellect of the prophet, as al-Fārābī saw it, had to undergo all stages of development common to the philosophers in order to finally receive revelation. Hence, as it pertains to this issue, al-Fārābī did not depart too markedly from Aristotle's position. Avicenna, on the other hand, adapted al-Fārābī's prophetology in such a way that revelation could also not occur "at the end of a noetic development but as something sudden, happening with a coup."[51] In his opinion, the intellect of the prophet is pure and, therefore, able to directly connect with the active intellect.

There is another element of Avicenna's conception of prophecy worth pointing out: Avicenna acknowledges that the celestial bodies affect the human soul and, accordingly, the human cognitive faculty. To him, the celestial bodies enable humans to foresee future events. Yet he makes sure to differentiate between prophets and astrologists while also casting doubt on the validity of astrological foretelling.[52] Furthermore, he distinguishes prophetic revelation (*waḥī*) from similar forms of inspiration (*ilhām*).[53] This distinction between different kinds of anticipatory knowledge is meant to differentiate between the personages of prophet and mystic. According to Avicenna, the mystics may possess prophetic faculties as well.[54] He seems thus to recognize several forms of prophecy.[55]

Another element Avicenna added to al-Fārābī's conception of prophecy pertains to miracles and theurgy. It seems that, in explaining miracles, Avicenna resorted to the Stoic and Neoplatonic conceptions of the cosmos. According to the latter, there is a link between the human soul and the cosmos that allows only humans to perform miracles. This link owes its existence to the divine nature of the human soul. It is only due to this divine nature that the soul is capable of dominating the body. In establishing this link, prayer plays a crucial role, though Avicenna admits that black magic is also an option.[56]

To Avicenna, a religious law proclaimed by a prophet is necessary in order to contain excessive self-interest and thereby establish justice in society. In *an-Najāt*, he advances the opinion that the human will is exposed to different celestial and earthly influences that go beyond the sphere of any individual's control. This is why religious rites such as prayer and almsgiving are required to acquit humans of sin and wrongdoing. These rites also help anchor religious laws within souls, thereby furthering their felicity in the afterlife. However, the final aim of religious law is spiritual. While religious rites are certainly supposed to protect human existence, Avicenna's prophetology leaves no doubt that these rites were introduced to purify human souls from carnal desire and bring them to God.[57]

Conclusion

It was the purpose of this chapter to demonstrate that Avicenna's discussion of prophecy and religious law is actually based on the pseudo-Platonic *nawāmīs*-book and not, as one would believe, on Plato's *Nomoi*. There is now striking evidence of the commonalities between Avicenna's conception of prophecy and the respective statements in these pseudo-Platonic treatises. This assumption is underpinned by the absence of similar parallels in al-Fārābī's summary of Plato's *Laws*. In particular, the idea that humans need to live in society and thereby necessarily require laws is an idea that cannot be found in al-Fārābī's synopsis of the *Laws*. The same holds true for the aforementioned recognition of multiple celestial and earthly influences upon the human will and the consequential purpose of revelation. Finally, the remarkable similarities that characterize prophetic figures and the distinction of prophecy from divination are absent in al-Fārābī's summary.

But what does all of this mean for our examination of Leo Strauss? As mentioned above, Avicenna's statement on prophecy and religious law in Plato's *Laws* was crucial for Strauss's philosophical development. Due to this statement, Strauss changed his perception of medieval Jewish and Islamic philosophy. He henceforth claimed that the latter conceived religious law as the equivalent of the ancient Greek nomos and, consequently, as a political phenomenon. To Strauss, the consequences of this conception were not limited to the history of philosophy. More importantly, Strauss himself adopted it and tried to interpret religion politically in the light of a political philosophy that adhered to Plato's model.[58]

The impact of Avicenna's statement on Strauss is well-known to Strauss specialists, who interpret his works from this viewpoint. Against the background of Avicenna's statement, it becomes clear that Strauss tried to settle the dispute between philosophy and revealed religion in the same manner as he tried to explain Plato's dispute with the poets.[59] My conclusion that Avicenna must have referred to a pseudo-Platonic book when pointing to the discussion of prophecy and religious law in two *nawāmīs*-books considerably weakens Strauss's basic assumptions.[60]

The fact that Avicenna's statement is related to a non-Platonic *Book of Laws* must lead to a nuanced reconceptualization of Strauss's efforts regarding the interpretation of this text. The "Platonic" thought Avicenna derived from this book is not identical with Plato's own philosophy. This leads to the unanswered and unavoidable question of whether Avicenna would have referred to Plato regarding prophecy and religious law had he known the true content of Plato's *Nomoi*.

At this point it is helpful to provide a sketch of how Plato was imagined in the Arab Middle Ages. Plato was considered not only a philosopher but also an alchemist and astrologer who wrote about magic.[61] Plato the philosopher and his teacher, Socrates, were credited with strong ascetic characteristics and often appeared in the form of religious preachers.[62] It is repeatedly indicated that the confusing image of Plato in the Middle Ages reflects both the life and the transmitted texts and teachings of the philosopher.[63] Muslim philosophers viewed Plato through the eyes of Plotinus and Neoplatonists such as Proclus and the Syrians Iamblichus and Ammonius, together with their students Olympiodorus and John Philoponus.[64] Al-ʿĀmirī, a philosopher from the tenth century, reported that Plato, alongside Empedocles, Pythagoras, Socrates, and Aristotle, belonged to the pillars of wisdom and received his wisdom from the prophets.[65] This statement clearly indicates that there was no fundamental disjunction between the wisdom of prophecy and the wisdom of philosophy in the consciousness of al-Fārābī's contemporaries. Indeed, they considered the wisdom of the philosophers as derived from the wisdom of the prophets. This assumption has certainly been decisive for the understanding of Platonic philosophy among the Islamic philosophers of the Middle Ages. In an Islamic cultural realm infused by philosophy, the image of Plato was adapted to new religious circumstances. The beneficiaries of the Greco-Arabic translation movements apparently did not possess any complete Platonic dialogues but rather longer or shorter fragments mostly derived from Arabic translations of Greek commentaries that had first been translated into Syriac.[66] The corrupted nature of the transmission of Platonic texts into Arabic led to the emergence of a unique image of Plato among Arabic-speaking philosophers that must be considered. We must evaluate Avicenna's reference to Plato and the concepts he builds upon in a more nuanced fashion.

This now leads us to a difficult question regarding the encounter between Arabic philosophy and the philosophical legacy of antiquity that took place in the religious and cultural realm of Islam. This question deserves its own study. However, it must be emphasized here that there are numerous indications that the reception of ancient philosophy in Islamic culture was not conceived in terms of hellenizing Islam. Instead, these Muslim thinkers attempted to construct their own framework from the building blocks of these newly received sciences and understandings. If strong elements of the "old world" remained in transmission, they were attributed to the nature of the topics in question and were not to be negatively judged. Nevertheless, appropriated elements were modified such that they would fit into new cultural and religious parameters. In this sense, the great philosophers of antiquity were held to be prophetic figures, with Plato in particular described as "divine." Indeed, Islamic philosophers were not passive in the face of this transmitted knowledge. They exercised a great degree of autonomy, which becomes apparent in the treatment of a Platonic work by two important philosophers. Plato's *Politea* served as a model for al-Fārābī's *Ideal State*, a book that was later commented upon by Averroes. However, al-Fārābī did not copy the Platonic *State* but rather changed certain elements in the structure of the work and the figure of the ruler such that this book would be considered the product of a Muslim who was influenced by Plato, a Muslim who was cognizant of the exigencies emerging from both his religious membership and philosophical training. How successful he was in this endeavor is another story. Averroes, for his part, undertook formal changes to the structure of the Platonic book so that the reader of his summary would not recognize anymore that Plato composed the text in the form of a dialogue. Furthermore, Averroes posited a content-based relationship between Platonic ideas and the political situation of his age. This provides good reasons to think that his commentary was primarily intended to offer a political critique of his present situation.[67]

Strauss's hermeneutics is based on a return to the history of philosophy. He mandates that we understand the philosophers of history in the way in which they understood themselves.[68] My conclusions regarding the significance of Avicenna's hint, which became effective for Strauss, show that Leo Strauss did not understand Avicenna correctly. He did not address the question of which of the two books of *nawāmīs* Avicenna was referring to when he spoke about prophecy and religious law. Instead, he made a hasty and singular connection with Plato's *Nomoi*.[69] It is difficult to prove that Avicenna even had access to an Arabic edition of the Platonic text; modern scholarship has serious doubts about this prospect.[70] One could say that Strauss was correct in his assertion that Avicenna had Plato in mind. Yet this claim lacks any justification. Any Plato that Avicenna may have encountered was different than the one posited by Strauss. This falsely attributed text contains ideas that do not match Strauss's interpretation of Plato's views. *The Book of Nawāmīs* does not doubt the divine origin of the religious law or the truth of revelation but rather attributes divine origin to the event of revelation. It points out that the ultimate goal of religious law is to lead people to eternal life, thereby transcending temporal events. It distinguishes religious law from politics and declares that religious law transcends its interface with the people who encounter it, for it refers to the wisdom revealed to the prophets, a wisdom beyond the reach of philosophy. Finally, it is clear that Avicenna does not reduce prophecy to the political interpretation of the laws, as Strauss imagined Spinoza to do in his theory of prophecy. Instead, he endows prophecy with elements that go far beyond this dimension.

Leo Strauss claimed that true Platonists — such as al-Fārābī — did not interest themselves in historical (accidental) truth because they were solely interested in (essential) philosophical truth. This pushes them to engage in the practice of philosophical rhetoric.[71] In this case, one could say that Strauss behaves similarly while constructing the bridge between Avicenna and Plato, a bridge that did not actually exist. He engaged in what he thought was an authentically Platonic art of philosophizing. One thing is certain: Strauss's philosophical enterprise, based on the Avicenna theorem already mentioned several times, must lack the philosophical-historical and thematic foundation it claims if Avicenna's strong commitment to Plato's political philosophy is to be questioned.

CHAPTER THREE

The Fruits of Change

Introduction

Avicenna's supposed recourse to Plato's *Laws*, discussed in the preceding chapter, caused a profound shift in Leo Strauss's thought. One aspect of this shift is reflected in Strauss's conviction that religion, which Strauss went on to perceive as law, could be explained philosophically by Plato's political philosophy. While contemporary research has tended toward an Aristotelian interpretation of medieval Islamic philosophy, Strauss highlighted its essentially Platonic and political character. At the same time, he saw a possibility to perpetuate and situate the dispute between Enlightenment and religious thought within the framework of Platonic political philosophy.

The first of Strauss's publications to reflect this change is his paper "Anmerkungen zu Carl Schmitts Begriff des Politischen," which was published in 1932.[1] An English translation of the paper was included in the American edition of *Spinoza's Critique of Religion*.[2] It is within the preface to this edition that Strauss admits that his "change of orientation [. . .] found its first expression, not entirely by accident, in the article published at the end of this volume."[3] Strauss does not explain how and to what extent his essay on Schmitt's treatise is the first expression of his reorientation. Therefore, the following account will investigate whether there is a connection between Strauss's reception of Avicenna and his increased interest in Islamic philosophy, on the one hand, and his critique of Carl Schmitt, on the other. If such a connection is proved to exist, we must explore its precise contours. It is therefore necessary to shed more light, in particular, on the implications of Avicenna's statement for Strauss's discussion of Schmitt's concept of the political. A detailed assessment of Strauss's critique of Schmitt, as well as a discussion of the mutual relationship between the two philosophers in general, must be left aside in this context.[4]

In addition, this chapter will discuss the studies produced by Strauss after his philosophical turn that manifest this new way of thinking. These are the book *Philosophie und Gesetz* (1935) and the papers "Quelques remarques sur la science politique de Maïmonide et de Fārābī" (1936), "Eine vermißte Schrift Fārābīs" (1936), and "Der Ort der Vorsehungslehre nach der Ansicht Maimunis" (1937). These writings are valuable for our analysis since Strauss extensively draws on Islamic philosophers, and al-Fārābī in particular, in order to develop his political thought in the most robust fashion possible. Indeed, the first two works contain the substrate of his entire mature philosophical program. Over the following decades, Strauss would merely extend these fundamental insights to specific topics or adapt them to the American context. Additionally, I will examine two important studies by Strauss dedicated to al-Fārābī's interpretation of Plato's philosophy. Both "Fārābī's *Plato*" (1945) and "How Fārābī read Plato's *Laws*" (1957) reveal the unique medial position al-Fārābī occupies between Plato and Leo Strauss.

Leo Strauss, Avicenna, and Carl Schmitt's *Concept of the Political*

Already at the beginning of his "Notes on Carl Schmitt's *Concept of the Political*," Strauss states that Schmitt's treatise is "in the service of the question of the 'order of human things' [. . .], i.e., of the state" and, because "the state has become so questionable in the present," wants to achieve its understanding through the "'elementary exposition' of what the reason of the state is, and that is: the political." According to Schmitt, the concept of the state presupposes the concept of the political, which is now to be asserted against liberalism. Liberalism was "characterized by the negation of the political," which was meant to establish "rational social relations" but failed to do so. However, liberalism "killed not the political but only the understanding of the political," and this is why Schmitt intends "to remove the smokescreen over reality that liberalism produces" and to reverse the negation of the political.[5]

Strauss argues that liberalism turns culture into a genus "within which the nature of the political and thus of the state is to be determined." Therefore, Schmitt first tries to negate the equation of the political with other "cultural provinces" by emphasizing the specificity of the political. In the case of the political, this peculiarity consists of "the distinction between friend and enemy." The division of humanity into friendly and hostile groups gives rise to political tensions in the event of an "emergency." It seems that the possibility of war not only constitutes the political but makes it more immanent due to "the real possibility of physical killing." Therefore, it is no longer possible to consider the political "equivalent and analogous" to other domains of culture.[6]

In Schmitt's argument, the special status of the political is based on the real possibility of war, which Hobbes had already declared to be the *status naturalis* of the human species. But there is a difference between Hobbes and Schmitt, which Strauss does not fail to notice. While Hobbes saw it as the natural political state of individuals, Schmitt located the *status belli* between exclusive groups. For Strauss, Schmitt's reference to Hobbes, whom he considered the "founder of liberalism," was motivated by the intention to "strike at the root of liberalism."[7] However, it is noteworthy that Hobbes's conception of the political is self-negating inasmuch as it contradicts the founding of liberalism. Schmitt's thesis of the "dangerousness of man" is the final precondition for the position of the political. The dangerousness of man and the mere possibility of political polarities are supposed to justify the inescapability of the political.[8]

Strauss continues, "Accordingly, dangerousness means *need of dominion*. And the ultimate quarrel occurs not between bellicosity and pacifism (or nationalism and internationalism) but between '*authoritarian* and *anarchistic*' theories."[9] Schmitt's affirmation of the political aims at awakening the "seriousness of human life" and is ultimately nothing other than the affirmation of the moral.[10] For Schmitt's position eventually requires abandoning the security of the status quo while at the same time "expecting to regain the order of human things from a 'from the power of a knowledge of integrity.'"[11]

Furthermore, Strauss notes that Schmitt's polemic against morality is directed against a particular kind of morality, which he calls "humanitarian." However, Schmitt remains a prisoner of the very morality he attacks, essentially making a moral judgment himself. While he tries to keep his judgment unnoticed, his writings nevertheless betray an aporia that stems from the fact that Schmitt's position on the political presupposes a judgment — that is, a private statement. The same position characterizes the nature of the political in such a binding way that it withdraws it from any private convenience.[12]

Strauss goes on to observe that the primacy of the political over the moral lying at the heart of Schmitt's argument inevitably leads to an indifference toward what the belligerents fight for in the "dire emergency." The affirmation of the political appears thus as liberalism in reverse. This is why Schmitt fails to supplant liberalism. According to Strauss, Schmitt's last word is not the affirmation of the political in and of itself but the affirmation of "the order of human affairs." He remains mired in the polemics against liberalism and is therefore distracted from his original purpose. This is not a failure resulting from sheer coincidence but rather a necessary consequence "of the principle 'that all concepts of the spiritual sphere [. . .] are to be understood only in terms of concrete political existence' and that 'all political concepts, ideas, and words' have 'a polemical meaning.'" As long as Schmitt's critique of liberalism remains within the horizon of liberalism and as long as his illiberal tendencies are constrained by the systematics of liberal thought yet to be overcome, the critique "against liberalism can [. . .] be completed only if one succeeds in reaching a horizon beyond liberalism." Such a critique of liberalism needed to be radical and had to occur within the same conceptual horizons that had oriented Hobbes's foundational formulation of liberalism.[13]

At this point, Strauss's thought reaches a breakthrough. *Spinoza's Critique of Religion*, as Strauss admits in hindsight, "was based on the premise, sanctioned by powerful prejudice, that a return to pre-modern philosophy is impossible."[14] To Strauss, this return became not only a possibility but a necessity for his attempt to retrieve the intellectual horizons required for replacing systematic liberalistic thought through a new form of systematic thinking — the step that Schmitt had failed to take. It was only after reading Avicenna that Strauss concluded that this form of return was necessary. The required intellectual horizons for such a philosophical programmatic needed to go beyond Hobbes (and even beyond Machiavelli) and back to the Islamic and Jewish philosophy of the Middle Ages. The latter provided Strauss with the instruments both for the critique of modernity and for the way back to antiquity.[15]

But how exactly did Avicenna's statement influence Strauss's critique of Schmitt and the resulting notion of the political?

A crucial aspect of this critique argues that a concept of the political based primarily on opposition and manifested in war as a result of a "dire emergency" lacks the fundamental nature it claims to possess. Like the aesthetic or the moral, the political becomes nothing more than a product of culture. Soon after, in *Philosophy and Law*, Strauss would oppose this view by stating that both politics and religion were "the facts that transcend 'culture,' or, to speak more precisely, the original facts." Strauss identifies the "fact of the political" as one "crux of the philosophy of culture," whereas the other crux is the "fact of religion."[16] Culture primarily presupposes "human nature; and because man is by his nature an animal sociale, the very human nature upon which culture is based is the natural social relations of men. The way in which man, prior to any form of culture, behaves toward other men" is considered the natural state of human affairs.[17] The political constitutes the natural human state because human beings cannot but live in society. The political, therefore, holds a radical position that goes beyond the mere binary of friend and enemy. To Strauss, this opposition did not sufficiently explain the fundamentality of the political. Given the aforementioned human need for rule, the order of human things requires a fundamentally stabilizing factor that concretizes the foundation of a society. For this reason, Strauss adds the religious to the political. Henceforth, both appear as original facts of human existence.

Only shortly before coming to these insights did Strauss take notice of Avicenna's dictum glossing religion as religious law, a dictum that anchored the philosophical work that Strauss would later call Plato's "most political work." At the same time, Strauss would observe that this was Plato's only text beginning with the word "God."[18] Plato is known to be the only philosopher with whom Strauss's political thought remained closely connected. This "most political work" of the history of philosophy begins with the word "God," which is probably the reason why Strauss singled it out. Avicenna's sentence provided Strauss with a transcendental-pragmatic meaning of the political resulting from its reference to revealed law. Linking politics and religion, he could now turn the political into the most radical basis of human existence. While Schmitt's concept of the political remained mired in liberalism, Avicenna's statement enabled Strauss to transcend this barrier twice: First, Strauss's historical starting point precedes the inception of modernity, and, second, its content has divine origins. Strauss took the main features for his concept of the political from Avicenna. In due consideration of the human need for domination, he regards the natural state of human affairs as a necessary ordering of human things. According to Strauss, it is God who, caring for this order, sends prophets capable of transmitting the laws necessary for the maintenance of human existence.[19] Whereas Schmitt supposedly failed to develop the concept of the political into an essential principle for all spheres of human culture, Strauss underpins the political through a pragmatic and therefore de-theologized divine foundation. With Avicenna's help, he was able to turn the political into an unquestioned basis for human existence.

Strauss comes to believe that a radical critique of the concept of culture is only possible if this critique is of a theological-political nature. However, this critique "must take exactly the opposite direction from the theologico-political treatises of the seventeenth century, especially those of Hobbes and Spinoza." Whereas the latter aimed at a separation of politics and religion for the sake of the liberty to philosophize, Strauss, taking his cue from Avicenna, viewed religion and politics as radically united in religious law. The rational justification for this radical unification of religion and politics lies at the foundation of philosophy.[20]

Philosophy and Law

When the shuttering of the Berlin Academy of Jewish Studies appeared imminent, Strauss successfully applied for a scholarship at the Rockefeller Foundation, enabling him to go to Paris (1932) and London (1933). In Paris, Strauss met the outstanding Arabist Louis Massignon, who made "the strongest impression" on him, as Strauss confided in a letter to Schmitt.[21] The fruit of his work in Paris and previously in Berlin was *Philosophy and Law*, which in 1935 could still be published in Germany. The rather lengthy introduction to this book also represents an attempt to "somewhat repair" the formal errors from which his previous book *Spinoza's Critique of Religion* suffered.[22] Three chapters followed. The first one deals with Julius Guttmann's account of Judaism in the light of the *querelle des anciens et des modernes*.[23] In the other two chapters, Strauss presents a general outline of his new interpretation of Islamic and Jewish philosophy in the Middle Ages. He goes back to this philosophical age in order to revive, on the one hand, the justification of philosophy in a religious forum and, on the other hand, the philosophical foundation for prophecy that had been laid at that time.[24]

Philosophy and Law stands out among Strauss's writings because, more than any other of his works, it relates to his biography and the political circumstances of Germany in the 1930s.[25] But its philosophical content seems to be of even greater importance for the extraordinary nature of this book. The title, to begin with, consists of two contradictory terms and betrays the contradictory nature of the content to be discussed. Drawing on the studies at his disposal, he reignites the conflict between rationalism and religious orthodoxy. The reason for reopening this old problem is his opinion that rationalist Enlightenment had failed to overcome faith. Strauss revives this old dispute between skeptical rationalism and obedient religiosity, or between reason and revelation, but gives it a new name: *Philosophy and Law*.

Strauss blames the modern tendency to assume extreme positions for the failure of the Enlightenment to win the battle against traditional religiosity. This tendency turned extreme thought into the measure of understanding the natural and ordinary. Strauss made the same critique of Carl Schmitt. Following in Nietzsche's footsteps, he now turns against this modern extremist tendency. His philosophy is supposed to continue and to radicalize the "critique of the principles of the tradition," both "Greek and Biblical, which in turn can take place only through history of philosophy." Such an undertaking presupposes an original understanding of those principles. To this end, the critic is not only entitled but bound to historicize philosophy. This historicization begins with the seventh book of Plato's *Politeia*, which contains Plato's allegory of the cave. As is well known, this allegory likens the nonphilosophers to the inhabitants of a cave who can only perceive shadows of natural things. This cave, where all people save for the philosophers remain, appears to be a "natural" cave where philosophizing can fail due to "natural" reasons. To Strauss, modern humans can no longer be compared to the "natural" ignoramuses in Plato's cave. Modern human beings are in a second cave, much deeper than that of the happy ignoramuses with whom Socrates had to deal with. The natural cave can only be regained by an ascent from that second, unnatural cave. The latter cave has its origins in the accumulation of tradition and the polemics of Enlightenment against tradition that precluded human thought from grasping the original purpose of philosophizing. Regaining this first, natural cave is, according to Strauss, the purpose of the historicization of philosophy. This process is supposed to permeate the dark and opaque layers of the history of philosophy in order to recover its foundations. From this process, the philosopher expects to glean true insights into the original relationship between philosophy and religion, which he would be able to draw upon to criticize both modernity and religious orthodoxy.[26]

It is in his daring introduction to *Philosophy and Law* that Strauss attacks traditional religiosity most vehemently. For the first time, he avows the "atheism of intellectual probity," which he makes sure to differentiate from the "atheism at which the past shuddered."[27] Strauss fails to indicate which of these two kinds of atheism he is indeed distancing himself from. However, I presume that Strauss wanted to distance himself from the kind of Epicurean atheism discussed in *Spinoza's Critique of Religion*.[28] Thus, his critique of religious orthodoxy distances itself from Epicurean atheism while at the same time adopting a position on the denial of God that is capable of confronting both orthodox religiosity and modern rationalism. This critique of rationalism forms the basis for a new critique of religion and is justified by the assumption that the Enlightenment failed to solve the problem of religion.

Strauss was only capable of criticizing modern rationality because he resorted to the arguments of earlier rationalists who handled the problem of revelation more effectively. The latter were the medieval rationalists who did not altogether reject revelation but rather affirmed it. Their position became the measure of Strauss's critique of modern rationalism. Hermann Cohen had already considered Maimonides to represent "'classic rationalism' in Judaism."[29] Strauss adopts this view of Maimonides and intends to illustrate his own critical model with the help of a revelation-bound rationalism resembling Maimonides. This step is of paramount importance for Strauss, as it allows him to enter the realm of Islamic philosophy. "In view of the authoritative influence these [the Islamic] philosophers exerted precisely during the flowering of medieval Jewish philosophy and particularly on the 'philosophy of religion' of the Jewish Middle Ages," Strauss had to go back to Islamic philosophy in order to properly understand Maimonides's thought. The mode in which "Islamic Aristotelians from al-Fārābī to Averroes" dealt with religion becomes formative for Strauss's critique. Ultimately, Strauss takes the criteria required for his twofold critique of modern rationalism and religious orthodoxy from the medieval Islamic philosophers.[30]

Philosophy and Law not only reveals a new and groundbreaking understanding of Islamic and Jewish medieval philosophy in light of Platonic philosophy, it also contains the mature Straussian philosophical program essentially concerned with the problematic relationship of reason and revelation. This new approach is based upon a negative foundation resulting from an insight Strauss attained while writing *Spinoza's Critique of Religion*. He intuited that the attack of modern rationalism on religious orthodoxy remained defective and was, consequently, doomed to failure. The reading of Avicenna provides a positive impulse, prompting Strauss to address his critique not only toward conservative religiosity but also to the rationality of Enlightenment. Methodologically, this new orientation is constituted through a return to the history of philosophy, namely to the Middle Ages. This process comprises two formal steps. First, he applies a hermeneutical principle that aims at understanding past philosophers as they understood themselves. Second, his return to the Middle Ages comes along with the discovery of exoteric-esoteric literature, which hides true opinions in the face of potentially fatal situations. Strauss seems to have regarded this literature as a necessary complement to a certain kind of open hermeneutics with universal aspirations. Later on, this discovery would become one of the defining characteristics of his philosophic programmatic. In any case, the pivotal element of this new constellation is the revaluation of the status of religion between the conflicting priorities of philosophy and law. The main conclusion that Strauss drew from Avicenna's statement was the conviction that the Muslim philosophers as well as Maimonides were, at their philosophical cores, Platonists. When they transformed revelation, prophecy, and providence into components of politics, they built on Plato's *Laws*. When they regarded the foundation of the perfect city as the raison d'être of revelation, they were referring to Plato's *Politeia*. Strauss can start from the premise that Platonic philosophy as carved out by the Muslim philosophers provides insight into how "the unbelieving, philosophical foundation of the belief in the revelation" can be grasped.[31]

Strauss's critique of modernity was sparked by his attempt to find an effective mode of criticizing religious tradition. He begins his critical undertaking with a discussion of Julius Guttmann's approach to "the problem of the methodological value of religion." Strauss approaches the conception of revelation propagated by the medieval Jewish and Islamic philosophers from the viewpoint of a modern understanding of philosophy of consciousness. He advances the opinion that the Jewish and Muslim medieval philosophers at least formally recognized the authority of the materialized revelation as a self-evident presupposition of their philosophy. However, the philosophy of consciousness deprives religion of its character as revealed religion. It turns religion into a merely interior matter connected with subjectivity, thereby never really overcoming it. Inasmuch as Muslim and Jewish philosophers strove to establish a philosophical foundation for the possibility of revelation, they only confirmed what had been certain prior to the philosophical establishment of such a foundation.

To put it differently, this tradition established the *posse* of revelation from the angle of its *esse* insofar as revelation had been a priori imposed on human thought. This imposition obliges human thought to recognize revelation as a higher authority. Medieval philosophy does not primarily conceive of this higher authority as a dogma but rather as a comprehensive entity or revealed law that claims to be perfect and to be able to guide humanity toward the true purpose of life. As such, it has remained of central importance for those philosophers.[32]

Strauss intended to demonstrate that the philosophical recognition of the law constituted a higher authority. He approached this goal from two directions. The first was through the Muslim philosophers — most notably Averroes — and their legal foundation of philosophy as an authority for the interpretation of religious scriptures. The second deals with what Strauss called the philosophical foundation of law. The latter path consists of the treatment of religious law, prophecy, and divine providence as political subjects, a mindset mostly attributed by Strauss to al-Fārābī and Avicenna.

For Strauss, al-Fārābī viewed Plato as his philosophic role model. And given that Maimonides was Strauss's bridge to the Islamic philosophers, Maimonides serves as a convenient starting point for our virtual journey back to al-Fārābī and his work.[33] Indeed, Hermann Cohen had called Maimonides a Platonist.[34] In principle, Strauss is of the same opinion, but he extends Cohen's judgment by considering the Islamic philosophers. By taking this step, Strauss is distancing himself from Cohen (whom he held in high esteem), a process that had already begun with the publication of *Spinoza's Critique of Religion*. His discovery of Maimonides's dependence on his Islamic predecessors and on al-Fārābī in particular "forces" him to take this drastic step.[35] The truth is obviously of greater importance than his esteem for Cohen.

Maimonides is a particularly suitable instructor for Strauss's studies of al-Fārābī. The philosopher from Cordoba had clearly instructed his student and translator, Samuel Ibn Tibbon, "not to concern himself" with books of logic "except those composed by the wise Abū Naṣr al-Fārābī; for what he has composed in general, and in particular his book *The Principles of the Beings* — all of this is of the purest flour." Furthermore, Maimonides adds that despite their merits, Avicenna's writings were not comparable to those of al-Fārābī.[36] It seems that Strauss followed Maimonides's instructions. Between 1935 and 1957, he dedicated four studies to al-Fārābī. Another paper on Maimonides's doctrine of providence, published in 1937, makes clear reference to al-Fārābī and therefore deserves equal attention in this context.

Leo Strauss's Five Studies on al-Fārābī

In the papers to be discussed in this section, Leo Strauss persistently develops his interpretation of medieval Islamic and Jewish philosophy against a Platonic horizon, first presented in *Philosophy and Law*. In the course of these studies, his earlier thoughts become richer and gain depth and clarity.[37] The importance of al-Fārābī as a founding father of the Platonic tradition of political philosophy is unflinchingly reemphasized and voiced with conviction. Strauss would stick to this interpretation throughout his entire life.

"Quelques remarques sur la science politique de Maïmonide et de Fārābī"

This more detailed study was published shortly after *Philosophy and Law*.[38] Here, Strauss expounds on the insights of the earlier book and confirms its main theses. Like a sequel, the paper begins where the previous book had ended: the Islamic and Jewish medieval philosophers had developed political science as the primary framework through which they explained the phenomenon of religion. This framework constitutes itself around the central figure of the prophet and the comprehensive law imparted by him. According to this view, divine law is a consistent law that regulates the religious, civil, and moral affairs of humanity, and, as Strauss claims to have taken from Avicenna, Plato provides with his *Laws* the explanatory template.[39]

What is Strauss's intention behind this study? To begin with, it contains various proofs for al-Fārābī's overwhelming impact on Maimonides's philosophy and his interpretation of the Torah.[40] Moreover, Strauss definitively anoints al-Fārābī as the philosopher responsible for reestablishing philosophy after its destruction by the domination of religious dogma. He is portrayed as the founder of a rationalist philosophy accepting and incorporating revelation, which Strauss calls "politique platonisante."[41] From this viewpoint, al-Fārābī's "platonizing politics" is a "philosophical politics." It assumes that, after revelation, the foundation of the Platonic ideal state has been fulfilled. Hence, there is no need to strive for the creation of such an ideal state anymore. Rather, philosophical politics is supposed to make the phenomenon of revelation philosophically acceptable by explaining prophecy from a political perspective. Understanding al-Fārābī is an indispensable precondition for understanding a medieval rationalism capable of underpinning Strauss's simultaneous critique of modernity and religious orthodoxy. This explains Strauss's effort to uncover the reasons behind al-Fārābī's attempt to revive a particularly Platonic philosophy by means of Aristotelian rationalist physics in the Islamic context. These reasons remained determinant for the entire history of medieval philosophy.[42]

Strauss takes Maimonides's allusions toward al-Fārābī's book *as-Siyāsa al-madaniyya* as a starting point for his study of al-Fārābī's political philosophy. The explicitly political title points to content dealing with both metaphysics and politics, following in the footsteps of Plato's *Politeia* and *Nomoi*. This commonality already testifies to the strong bonds between al-Fārābī and Plato and the connection between theology and politics in his thought. Strauss assumed that the religious and political situation of al-Fārābī's time was crucial for his alignment with Plato's philosophical position. Strauss calls Plato's philosophical position, which al-Fārābī appropriates in order to create a metaphysical framework, "truly critical." By "truly critical" he means that this philosophical position, a position taken in an era marked by both rationalist Enlightenment and messianic expectations, managed to reject both cruel naturalism and religious extremism. Whereas the former aims at subordinating human passions to the power of reason, the latter obviously envisages moral enslavement. However, al-Fārābī found in Plato's philosophy the golden mean that nonetheless does not constitute a synthesis of the two extremes. Rather, this "golden mean" subordinates the two extremes to the power of political thought and uproots them through radical questioning. In this context, metaphysics, traditionally thought of as the "first philosophy," becomes a formative body of thought for the ideal society, as the title of al-Fārābī's *Ideal State* reveals.[43] Strauss alludes to this title when he emphasizes that politics provides a real framework for the development of metaphysical ideas and thereby plays a primary role for the elucidation of metaphysics. He goes on to explain that, although he started from the prerequisite position of a Platonizing politics, al-Fārābī nonetheless had to draw on Aristotle's *Physics* for his critical undertaking. As Strauss saw it, al-Fārābī needed Aristotle to overcome forms of hybrid speculation that threatened the revival of Platonic political thought. Hence, Aristotle's science prepared the ground for al-Fārābī's examination of the world of the "sens commun" (common sense) along Socratic and Platonic lines.[44]

Compared to *Philosophy and Law*, this paper describes the doctrine of prophecy in a more concise and significant manner. In this exposition, Strauss discards any lingering doubts when he states that the foundations of a theory of religious law — that is, religion itself — are to be found only in prophetology. Indeed, prophetology is considered an essential political fact by the three great Muslim philosophers: al-Fārābī, Avicenna, and Averroes. For Strauss, this position is demonstrated by the fact that these philosophers counted the virtue of courage among the crucial character traits of prophets, thereby vesting the prophet with essential qualities for political leadership. This political function of the prophet is mentioned alongside two other equally important prophetic functions, namely philosophy and divination. But when it comes to teleology and the final goal of prophecy, leadership is accorded greater importance. For al-Fārābī, the main task of the *ra'īs al-awwal* ("chef premier" or "first chief") is the foundation and ruling of the ideal city. Assuming that this prophet is at the same time an imam, philosopher, and legislator, the foundation of the perfect city appears as the "raison d'être" of revelation.[45]

In no other study does Strauss put a stronger emphasis on the role of the political in the dispute between philosophy and revealed religion. He even abandons the view, previously adumbrated in *Philosophy and Law*, that the philosopher's dependency on revelation stemmed from the insufficiency of human reason.[46] From this point onward, the prophet and philosopher are understood to be operating on the same level of cognitive facility. When Maimonides and the Islamic philosophers proceed to accord the prophet a loftier position compared to that of the philosopher, Strauss interprets this difference as a result of the political function of the prophet. He ceaselessly tries to find proofs for his thesis that the philosophy of Maimonides and of his Muslim teachers contains a political science. To clearly illustrate the political character of Islamic philosophy, he quotes numerous passages from six of al-Fārābī's works, as well as other treatises such as the *Rasā'il Ikhwān aṣ-Ṣafā'* (*Epistles of the Brethren of Purity*) and Averroes's commentary on the *Politeia*. At the same time, these quotations demonstrate the extent to which Strauss was familiar with Islamic philosophy. Furthermore, he evaluates some of al-Fārābī's writings with a focus on their political content.[47] Strauss shortens several of al-Fārābī's statements in order to exclude his ethical views on life after death from his argumentation.[48] Ethics becomes thus a part and parcel of politics, and it is politics that is responsible for providing the framework for virtuous acts.[49]

"Quelques remarques sur la science politique de Maïmonide et de Fārābī," like *Philosophy and Law*, clearly demonstrates the overwhelming influence of Maimonides on Strauss's thought. By the same token, al-Fārābī's powerful influence on both Strauss and Maimonides becomes clear.[50] To Strauss, al-Fārābī even seems to have answered hitherto unsolved questions on purely Jewish matters such as the theological-political status of the people of Israel in the world.[51]

"Eine vermißte Schrift Fārābīs"

Strauss composed this paper[52] in reaction to a statement by Israel Efros. The latter claimed that the second part of Falaquera's *Reshīth Ḥokma*[53] (*The Origin of Wisdom*, written around 1240) was nothing more than a literal translation of al-Fārābī's "eminent" writing *Iḥṣā ʾ al- ʿulūm* (published in English under the title *On the Introduction to Knowledge*).[54] To Strauss, this statement called for a correction and further explanation. Consequently, he undertook a masterful philological analysis of parts of Falaquera's book, with the intention of proving that the latter relied on writings by both al-Fārābī and Avicenna.

The detailed comparison of the texts demonstrates that large sections of the second part of Falaquera's book had indeed been taken from al-Fārābī's *Iḥṣā ʾ al- ʿulūm*. However, the remaining sections were a "(more or less) verbal translation of the corresponding passages in Ibn Sīnā's *Encyclopedia* (*Iqsām al- ʿulūm*) or were taken from al-Fārābī's text on the philosophy of Plato and Aristotle."[55]

Eventually, an examination of these texts demonstrated that even the fourth chapter on the development of the sciences, which seems to represent the most important original contribution by Falaquera, can undoubtedly be traced back to al-Fārābī's ideas in *Iḥṣā ʾ al- ʿulūm* or *Kitāb taḥṣīl as-sa ʿāda*. Strauss also finds that a speech contained in this same chapter is evocative of al-Fārābī. This speech deals with the development of the sciences in the nation or nations and thus alludes to a political function of science.[56]

Apart from these commonalities, Strauss also observed one essential difference between Falaquera's book and his Fārābian model. Whereas the former contains quotations from the Bible and can therefore be considered a "truly Jewish book," al-Fārābī abstained from quoting from the Qur'ān or from any other Islamic sources. His book is philosophical and cannot be called "Islamic" to the same extent as Falaquera's book is Jewish. This points to different intentions behind the two books. While Falaquera admits his intention to demonstrate the congruence between doctrines of philosophy and of law, al-Fārābī pursues "philosophical and not religious goals." Accordingly, the latter does not attempt to harmonize the relationship between philosophy and religion but rather subordinates religion to political science quite early in his attempt to classify the sciences. In his classification of the sciences, he already defines "the religious sciences (*fiqh* and *kalām*) [. . .] as branches of political science" and thus assigns religion a position subordinate to philosophy. While referencing his own discussion of Averroes's book *Faṣl al-maqāl* (*Decisive Treatise*) in *Philosophy and Law*, Strauss notices that Falaquera distances himself from al-Fārābī even though his intentions with this analysis are fully in line with Averroes's position.[57]

However, Strauss placed greater importance on the sources in the third part of Falaquera's book. Already, Moritz Steinschneider had speculated that this part had been taken from a book on the philosophy of Plato and Aristotle penned by al-Fārābī, which was thought to have disappeared.[58] According to Strauss, this book by al-Fārābī consisted of three parts: (1) *Kitāb taḥṣīl as-saʿāda* (*Attainment of Happiness*), which the Hyderabad edition had made accessible for the first time; (2) an account of Plato's philosophy; and (3) an account of Aristotle's philosophy.[59] Over the course of his comparison of the text, Strauss concludes that the third part of Falaquera's book is actually a translation of al-Fārābī's missing work. Two accounts bear witness to the fact that al-Fārābī wrote such a book: there is an account by the Muslim scholar al-Qifṭī and a reference by Averroes that Strauss adduces in this paper.[60] Eventually, the last sentence of the edited *Kitāb taḥṣīl as-saʿāda* mentions the "philosophy of Plato, its divisions and the ranking of these divisions from the first to the last." This, at least, is what Strauss, in the introduction to his section on Plato's philosophy, claims to have understood.[61]

Strauss concludes from his arduous philological study that reconstructing al-Fārābī's missing book grants access to one of his most important writings while simultaneously allowing for a new interpretation of his doctrine.[62] In this paper, he argues for the first time that al-Fārābī was ahead of his time because he revived Plato's and Aristotle's philosophy, recognized it as the philosophy par excellence, and adopted its style for his own philosophizing. Strauss suggests that al-Fārābī's project was to harmonize the opinions of the two sages, Plato and Aristotle, thus challenging the traditional view that the two were opponents. If it is true that philosophy is exclusively Platonic-Aristotelian, this philosophy is consequently of ambiguous character. As a matter of fact, Strauss does not go into detail regarding the character and quality of such an ambiguous philosophy. From Strauss's allusion to al-Qifṭī's reference to al-Fārābī's missing book, as well as a marginal note on a quotation from Averroes, we get a better picture of the ambiguous conception of philosophy suggested by Strauss here.

From al-Qifṭī's summary of the content of al-Fārābī's missing book, Strauss understands that the part dedicated to Plato deals with all aspects of Plato's philosophy and is more elaborate than the treatise on Aristotle's philosophy, which neglects the *Metaphysics*. Al-Qifṭī explains that this odd neglect of the *Metaphysics* was due to a corruption of the manuscripts. Strauss, on the contrary, argues that al-Fārābī omitted the Aristotelian treatise on metaphysics on purpose but does not give any reasons for this opinion. However, a possible explanation can be obtained from connecting this opinion with Maimonides's reference to al-Fārābī's book *On the Principles of the Soul*, which Strauss quotes on several occasions. One can hardly avoid the impression that the Platonic-Aristotelian conception of philosophy that Strauss attributes to al-Fārābī only considers Platonic ideas on metaphysics. According to such ideas, the cosmic hierarchy is part of political philosophy because it presupposes the hierarchy of the city. To Strauss, Aristotle's *Metaphysics* are abandoned for the sake of Plato's and al-Fārābī's conception of metaphysics, which occurs in a political framework.[63]

Next to Averroes's reference to al-Fārābī's work on the two philosophers, Strauss made the following marginal note: "(sc. Die exoterische und die esoterische Philsophie!)."[64] When Strauss designates philosophy as both Platonic and Aristotelian, he is referring to two different styles of philosophizing, one esoteric, the other exoteric. In this paper on al-Fārābī's missing book, which is marked by arduous and dry philology, this thought fails to be clearly expressed. However, it is implied in Strauss's attempt to reconstruct al-Fārābī's missing book and to reinterpret al-Fārābī's philosophy in the light of the aforementioned ambiguity.[65]

"Der Ort der Vorsehungslehre nach der Ansicht Maimunis"

Already at the end of his "Remarks on the Political Science of Maimonides and Fārābī," Strauss argues that Maimonides's *Guide of the Perplexed* contains dogmatic politics in which the theological and the political are connected. On the one hand, the inapprehensible theological notions of the Old Testament, such as the attributes of God, are expressed as political patterns of behavior. On the other hand, theological convictions are deployed to facilitate the establishment of the political order. It is Maimonides's doctrine of providence that explores the scope of this dogmatic politics. In this regard, Strauss assumes that Maimonides draws on the doctrine of providence developed in Plato's *Laws*, of which the Jewish medieval philosopher was likely aware by way of the accounts of Alexander of Aphrodisias and Galen.[66] "The Place of the Doctrine of Providence according to

Maimonides" (1937) ties in with this earlier remark and tries to locate the doctrine of providence in Maimonides's philosophical system.[67]

At the beginning of the paper, Strauss points to the two different kinds of providence discerned by Maimonides: (1) the "general providence," which is the sensible and skillful guidance of the world in its entirety, and (2) the "particular providence," which can be understood as the system of divine reward and punishment for human action. Maimonides dealt with the former within the framework of theoretical philosophy, while he argued that the disposition of the *Guide* excluded the question of particular providence (as well as the closely connected question of divine omniscience) from theoretical philosophy, thereby assigning it to the realm of politics.[68]

Strauss admits the oddity of Maimonides's division of providence into a general and a particular variety, with the latter being assigned to politics. Historians of philosophy may find it unusual because occidental philosophy considers this subject matter to be part of natural theology, and thus of theoretical philosophy. Furthermore, such a view could not be found in the metaphysical compendiums of Avicenna or Averroes.[69] However, Maimonides is in line with the *kalām* tradition even though he holds the view that the doctrine of providence pertains to politics. In Strauss's view, this can be traced back to an actual philosophical tradition. Maimonides's position, therefore, consists of two layers, one exoteric and the other esoteric. The aforementioned pattern stemming from the *kalām* tradition thereby fashions an exoteric foreground that requires and at the same time hides an esoteric backdrop consisting of philosophical and political convictions.[70]

Strauss contends that the politicization of the doctrine of providence in Islamic philosophy is a consequence of assigning the doctrines of prophecy and law to the realm of politics. At the same time, this politicization is a necessary result of the philosophical discussion of the topic, which required a structural transformation of the doctrine of providence itself.[71] In the first instance, Maimonides philosophically illustrates this necessary transformation by differentiating between his own doctrine of providence and a version of that doctrine provided by religious law. While the law teaches that the good and bad things that befall individuals are rewards or punishments for their actions, Maimonides argues "in a concealed manner"[72] that providence depends on the intellect. This, according to Strauss, asserts a differentiation that is relevant from a practical perspective: "The exoteric teaching asserts that moral virtue and external happiness are *coordinated* with one another [*Zugeordnetheit*]; the esoteric teaching, on the other hand, asserts the *identity* of true happiness with knowledge of God." From this esoteric angle, the philosophical doctrine of providence is not concerned with moral acts, which pertain merely to external happiness. Rather, it identifies true happiness with the knowledge of God, the latter being the result of philosophical inquiry. This judgment equates the esoteric doctrine of providence with the theory of true happiness. In this regard, Maimonides follows al-Fārābī, who had already discussed the latter notion within the framework of political science.[73]

Ultimately, Strauss comes to the conclusion that Maimonides elucidates a doctrine of providence in a context devoted to the explanation of the commandment of reversal, that is, a context that was supposed to be edifying. For Strauss, this was just another proof that such a doctrine was necessarily connected to politics, "for edification is nothing other than didactic politics, and for Maimonides there is no politics that is not primarily didactic that would be primarily 'Realpolitik.'"[74] By regarding religious edification as a didactic politics of the realpolitik variety, Strauss binds religion completely to politics. This is why he perceives the *Guide of the Perplexed* as a political book, whereas Maimonides by his own account presents the text as nothing other than the "science of the Law." In addition, the structure of this book corresponds to the structure of the Law, consisting of a theoretical and a practical part in accordance with al-Fārābī's fundamental "division of 'religion' into opinions and actions."[75]

By assigning the doctrine of providence to the realm of politics, religion is disempowered. It is downgraded to a means of politics for the preservation of political order. Religion is deprived of its promise of true happiness, which is thereby turned into an asset of philosophy.[76] And it is al-Fārābī whom Strauss views as the originator of this way of thinking.

"Farabi's *Plato*"

Strauss's paper "Farabi's *Plato*" (1945) is dedicated to al-Fārābī's treatise on Plato's philosophy, which had been edited shortly before Strauss viewed it.[77] Both at the beginning and at the end of this text, Strauss justifies his interest in this treatise by highlighting al-Fārābī's importance for Maimonides. Furthermore, he admits that the treatise has functioned as a replacement for those other writings of al-Fārābī that he cannot easily access.[78] However, Strauss informs the reader over the course of this paper of the true reason for his interest in this treatise: al-Fārābī's account of Plato's philosophy possesses an intrinsic value. This account is the core of a three-part work on the *Intentions of Plato's and Aristotle's Philosophy*, hence occupying the center of classical philosophy: "What Fārābī regarded as the purpose of the two philosophers, and hence what he regarded as the sound purpose simply, appears with all the clarity which one can reasonably desire, from his summary of Plato's philosophy, and from no other source. This purpose is likely to prove the latent purpose of all *falāsifa* proper."[79] Al-Fārābī's treatise on Plato's philosophy contains, as Strauss saw it, an account of the results of his more mature Plato research.[80] In this article, al-Fārābī presented genuinely Platonic views. To Strauss, he appears to be a real Platonist concerned with philosophical truth rather than the historical circumstances of a text. Furthermore, Strauss regards this treatise as an appropriate means for the investigation not only of al-Fārābī's thought but also of the ideas of successive philosophers. For this text is less exoteric than his other writings and offers more esoteric truth.[81] Strauss also argues that al-Fārābī's role cannot be restricted to that of "a mere epitomist of a lost Greek text" because men like Avicenna and Maimonides held him in such a high esteem. The fact that Strauss draws on the historical importance of al-Fārābī's entire philosophy in order to highlight the significance of this very treatise on Platonic philosophy may stem from his subjective classification of this treatise as "esoteric" philosophy. Therefore, Strauss's reference to Maimonides's and Avicenna's admiration for al-Fārābī may not suffice to illustrate the importance of this treatise among al-Fārābī's complete works. One must engage in a thorough discussion of the treatise's content.[82]

Strauss contends that al-Fārābī's treatise on Plato has two layers of interpretation. The first layer consists of the content he presents to his readers. The second one represents al-Fārābī's own view on which ideas he considers genuinely Platonic. He is determined to bring those ideas to the close attention his philosophical readers. Furthermore, this form of double-layered interpretation serves as a disguise for the writer, allowing him to hide behind the immunity of the commentator and to express views he could not have expressed on his own behalf. Thus, Strauss introduced a second ambiguity into his interpretation of the treatise: al-Fārābī's own ideas are hidden behind the comments. The treatise, therefore, was not only a source of Plato's authentic ideas but also, to the same degree, of al-Fārābī's convictions. From this double-layered interpretation, it seems that Strauss viewed al-Fārābī's treatise as a prime example of an exoteric-esoteric "art of writing."[83]

Additionally, Strauss's account reveals an ambiguity. The subject matter of his interpretation is itself an interpretation. Strauss draws a picture of al-Fārābī's image of Plato. It is al-Fārābī's *Plato* who is contrasted with Strauss's view of al-Fārābī. To Strauss, the two pictures are identical, and it is such reflection that can facilitate an understanding of Plato's authentic philosophy. The writings of this great medieval Platonist introduced by Strauss into modernity can yield most profound insights.[84]

What is this Platonism that Strauss describes as the basis of al-Fārābī's work and that he apparently adopts himself? Applying Strauss's method of double-layered interpretation, an answer can be obtained. This method of philosophical writing corresponds to the Platonic mode of philosophizing and combines the styles of Socrates and Thrasymachus. Whereas the former can only be understood by philosophers, the latter can be used to present philosophy to society.[85] To Strauss, another featured trait of al-Fārābī's Platonism becomes manifest in his innovative approach to the interpreted text. He directs his attention to the consistent thoughts, i.e., those that remain valid despite changing historical circumstances.[86] In this way, the quotation from Lessing that Strauss placed at the beginning of his essay can be explained.[87] The thought remains the same although it might take a different value in a different concrete context. The value of a thought depends both on its conceptual value and its social effects. However, contrary to its fluctuating value, the thought proper does not change. These are ideas that true Platonists — and Strauss would like to count al-Fārābī and himself among them — had in mind.[88] Platonists have used the method introduced above to express views that, being perceived as dangerous, can be addressed only by means of careful writing. They mainly concern the purpose of philosophy, the goal of human life, and the existence of God.

The central part of the paper is devoted to the relationship between philosophy and politics. Years prior, Strauss had claimed that al-Fārābī represented the idea of "Platonizing politics." Al-Fārābī had modified authentic Platonism by considering revealed religion to constitute the realization of Plato's ideal state.[89] In his account of Plato's philosophy, al-Fārābī gave the equal impression that the nature of philosophy is political. However, the most important purpose of this paper seems to be the positing of a clear separation of philosophy from politics with al-Fārābī's assistance. Hence, Strauss asserts that philosophy essentially is a theoretical occupation that goes beyond the realm of morals and politics and addresses politics only if pressured for justification.[90] By the same token, philosophy transcends morals, which are counted among the inferior practical arts, providing humanity only with "the happiness of this world." According to al-Fārābī, not even moral perfection can be identified with true happiness. True happiness, like theoretical philosophy, is the ultimate goal of all human actions.[91]

If al-Fārābī uses the form of a commentary to conceal but nonetheless convey his own views, Strauss can explain why important passages of al-Fārābī's interpretation differ significantly from the Platonic original. This is reason enough for Strauss to assign to this treatise on Plato's philosophy a special position among al-Fārābī's complete works. He goes so far as to draft an interpretive "canon," which he describes as follows: "Apart from purely philologic and other preliminary considerations, one is not entitled to interpret the *Plato*, or any part or passage of it, by having recourse to Fārābī's other writings. One is not entitled to interpret the *Plato* in the light of doctrines, expounded by Fārābī elsewhere, which are not mentioned in the *Plato*."[92] The paper is a piece of philological brilliance. Strauss ascribes to al-Fārābī a technique of writing that hints at the hidden views and intentions of the author by thoroughly and systematically using certain words and inaccurate repetitions. In turn, Strauss claims to be able to discover these hints.[93] He focuses his attention on detecting linguistic details, which he then uses to draw and underpin conclusions. However, he attaches excessive significance to some of these details. Strauss reads a great deal into the Arabic text. In the following discussion, I will highlight those passages based on philological interpretation and note some of the discrepancies with the Arabic text.

> Strauss alleges that al-Fārābī used the Arabic word *tafaḥḥaṣa* instead of *faḥaṣa* to underline the importance of the philosopher at the beginning of his passage on Phaedrus. However, both *tafaḥḥaṣa* and *faḥaṣa* mean "to examine," and the difference in meaning between the two related verbs is too small to conclude that the passage is rated higher. Moreover, the verb *faḥaṣa* is used eight times in this passage.[94]
>
> Strauss concludes from §18 of the treatise that al-Fārābī does not consider philosophy and the royal art to be identical — not even when governing the ideal city.[95] Yet the Arabic text clearly contradicts such an interpretation: the philosopher and the king are identical, as are the royal art and philosophy in the ideal city. What al-Fārābī describes is obviously Plato's teaching on the philosopher-king.[96]
>
> Strauss overrates al-Fārābī's use of the two verbs *sharaʿa* (to begin) and *iʿtaqada* (to be of an opinion, to believe). Contrary to Strauss' view, neither verb has a religious connotation in the text.[97] Likewise, Strauss exaggerates the significance of the personal pronoun *huwa* (he), which, in the two passages quoted by Strauss, merely marks the difference between Plato's views and those that are most widespread.[98]
>
> Strauss relies on Falaquera's translation when he differentiates between, on the one hand, true happiness that only philosophy can grant and, on the other hand, the happiness of this world that can result from a morally perfect way of life. However, nothing justifies such a differentiation in al-Fārābī's text. The notion *hādhihi as-saʿāda* (this happiness) refers to the true happiness that can be achieved through a virtuous conduct of life. Al-Fārābī clearly distinguishes this kind of happiness from illusory happiness.[99]
>
> Strauss contends that al-Fārābī uses the attribute *ilāhī* to designate something humanly sublime. Examination of the respective

> passages in al-Fārābī's text where *ilāhī* appears seven times[100] reveals that, contrary to Strauss' view, *ilāhī* designates something that transcends humanity. *Ilāhī* describes something praiseworthy (*maḥmūd*), contrasted with the unpraiseworthy (*madhmūm*) and human.[101] Furthermore, the text adjures persons to direct all their yearning toward divine things. Otherwise, their mental attitudes are to be considered animalistic, and they will live like animals.[102] The passage in al-Fārābī's text that Strauss regards as a repetition of a previous passage is not concerned with human desire and its subject matter but rather with the concrete conduct of life. The latter can either be called human or animalistic. Contrary to Strauss' interpretation, this later dichotomy of "human-animalistic," which the passage mentions, does not therefore replace the earlier dichotomy of "divine-human."[103]

"How Fārābī Read Plato's *Laws*"

This paper, a treatment of al-Fārābī's *Talkhīṣ Nawāmīs Aflāṭūn* (*Summary of Plato's Laws*),[104] was first published in Damascus in 1957 and reprinted two years later without any significant changes in the edited volume *What Is Political Philosophy?*, which deals with the most important topics of Strauss's work and had already been called "a microcosmos" of his entire oeuvre. The paper in question appears in the middle of *What Is Political Philosophy?*; its central position in this volume may indicate the central position of al-Fārābī in Strauss's philosophical world, a world which, in its entirety, can be understood as a reconstruction of the history of political philosophy that Plato had shaped. This paper also testifies to Strauss's enthusiastic admiration for al-Fārābī's free treatment of Platonic thought.[105]

"How Fārābī Read Plato's *Laws*" is the result of decades of analysis of al-Fārābī's treatise, parts of which Strauss and Paul Kraus had translated from Arabic into German in Berlin in 1931 to 1932.[106] Like "Farabi's *Plato*," this study is characterized by remarkable philological efforts. At first glance, the text seems to be a "pedantic, pedestrian and wooden writing which abounds in trivial or insipid remarks."[107] Strauss claims that this wooden language is necessary for the detection of al-Fārābī's opinions about Plato's philosophical method, the meaning of the law, and the existence of God. Again, Strauss explains al-Fārābī's contradicting statements by pointing to his alleged art of exoteric-esoteric writing.[108]

To begin with, Strauss discusses al-Fārābī's preface to the nine tracts of the treatise. This preface is divided into three parts: The first part consists of a general statement, and the second part consists of a story. The third section applies the insights from the previous two parts to a reading of Plato's *Laws*. In the first part, al-Fārābī is concerned with those sages who rely on the human tendency to make generalized judgments so that they can offer differing opinions and remain unmolested. This procedure is illustrated by a story about a persecuted ascetic who feigns drunkenness. Such feigned drunkenness allows him to reveal his true identity without being believed. According to al-Fārābī, Plato pursues a similar strategy. Plato was known to impart his views using an "allusive, ambiguous, misleading and obscure" language. This language permitted him to occasionally utter clear and explicit views that went unnoticed. The picture Strauss draws of Plato is that of a man who pretends to never clearly and unmistakably utter his thoughts on topics of primary importance. And it is exactly this pretension which makes it possible for him to nonetheless accomplish this feat without being taken seriously. Regarding al-Fārābī, Strauss correspondingly argues that the medieval philosopher meant to allude to Plato's thoughts but without the intention of explaining them.[109] Strauss writes, "Just as Plato before him, Fārābī does not permit himself the seeming generosity of trying to help all men toward knowledge but employs a kind of secretiveness which is mitigated or enhanced by unexpected and unbelievable frankness."[110] To Strauss, al-Fārābī pursues the very same strategy of hiding true opinions as Plato had done before him. His *Summary* has two layers, for he intends to help those who wish to understand the *Laws* while at the same time making short statements for those who are incapable of arduous research. This "secretiveness" entails the imperative to not only deal with his explicit statements but also with what he omits saying. The unsaid must also be compared with other writings.[111]

Strauss's interpretation relies on the hermeneutical principle to not only consider what al-Fārābī has mentioned but also what he has left unsaid. Strauss analyzes al-Fārābī's treatise on Plato's philosophy and finds that, contrary to this earlier treatise, his *Summary* does not mention philosophy or numerous philosophical terms. To Strauss, this omission corresponds to the deficiency of notions such as God/gods, the afterlife, or the sharia in Plato's philosophy, whereas al-Fārābī's *Summary* abounds with these notions. Therefore, Strauss concludes that the relationship between these two treatises reflects the relationship between philosophy and divine law "as between two entirely different worlds." Additionally, Strauss explains al-Fārābī's pronouncement that his *Summary* would mostly be concerned with the "roots of the laws." The fact that derivations of the root *k-l-m* appear twenty-six times in this text, while this very same root is utterly absent in Plato's philosophy, is significant for Strauss, who concludes that the *Summary* showcased Plato's *kalām*, while Plato's *Philosophy* indeed presented his philosophy.[112]

Although seemingly cursory, this last remark on the *kalām* in the *Summary* is of utmost importance. According to al-Fārābī's classification of the sciences, *kalām* is the part of Islamic theology that deals with both the roots and the defense of religion.[113] At the beginning of his analysis, Strauss asserts that al-Fārābī's *Summary* does not take into account the tenth book of the *Laws*, "i.e., Plato's theological statement par excellence."[114] This is how Strauss insinuates his belief that al-Fārābī denies Plato's theology any theological implications. This is also how one might explain another of Strauss's remarks, namely his speculation regarding how al-Fārābī would interpret the tenth book of the *Laws* if he were in a position to do so. From a Straussian perspective, al-Fārābī would read the tenth, theological book of the *Laws* only with respect to its explication of punishment in the afterlife. Previously, Strauss had already declared that the doctrine of providence, which includes sanctions on the individual, was a political topic. Furthermore, Plato's theology is perceived by Strauss as a political theology without intrinsic theological worth. Al-Fārābī expressed this understanding in his *Summary*, which Strauss calls "personal" because of the frequent occurrence of the personal pronoun.[115]

Strauss explains that the treatise may give the impression that al-Fārābī had tried to give an account of the content of the *Laws* without having properly understood them. The opposite is in fact the case: al-Fārābī assumed that the reader of his *Summary* was already familiar with the *Laws*. His intention was not to give an account of the obvious content of the *Laws*, but to cautiously unveil the views that Plato himself kept secret. Furthermore, his style was less monotonous than it appeared to be. From his wording, one could not only discern Plato's thoughts but also al-Fārābī's own verdict on these thoughts. To Strauss, the main purpose of al-Fārābī's *Summary* was to shed light on the differing nature and weight of Plato's statements, which a dull reader would consider to be of the same weight and nature. Such an approach not only explained the divergence between Plato's statements in the *Laws* and al-Fārābī's statements in the *Summary*, it justified the necessity of this divergence.[116]

Strauss further explains the great discrepancy between Plato's original and al-Fārābī's *Summary* by pointing to al-Fārābī's awareness of the difference between Plato's laws and Islamic law. However, Strauss does not insinuate that al-Fārābī modified Plato's doctrine with the intention of bringing it into accordance with the demands of his religion, as one might expect of him. On the contrary, this assumption suggests that al-Fārābī was critical of religion and therefore applied some of Plato's views on past laws of antiquity to the sharia.[117] Strauss goes on to state that other opaque statements by al-Fārābī, particularly those that concern the problems of any law supposed to be universal, have their roots in al-Fārābī's critical stance on religion.[118] Al-Fārābī's language was often opaque and difficult to understand because he had to keep his opinions secret.[119]

Like "Farabi's *Plato*," "How Fārābī Read Plato's *Laws*" expresses doubts regarding al-Fārābī's belief in God. Strauss underpins these doubts by highlighting that, whenever al-Fārābī mentions God, he does so in the context of a quotation from Plato, not by means of his own words: "Fārābī himself speaks exclusively of gods." He goes on to remark that, in a passage of the *Laws*, al-Fārābī went so far as to replace "God" with "gods"[120] and to disregard God in central parts of his treatise. The ground for this omission was prepared by this special use of language. As Strauss saw it, al-Fārābī neglected to refer to a passage in Plato's *Laws* that mentions God's omnipotence. Later in the text, he replaces "God" with "gods" and entirely ignores a reference by Plato to the gods. At the beginning of the fifth and central chapter of the treatise, al-Fārābī goes on to omit Plato's hint at God and discuss the significance and nobility of the soul instead. He declared the soul to be the most noble among things that deserved to be venerated. Furthermore, Strauss analyzes those passages in al-Fārābī's *Plato's Philosophy* and his *Summary* that deal with "divine things" and where the attribute "divine," according to Strauss, stands for the excellent quality of the nature, achievements, and goals of human beings. When Strauss goes on to argue that the soul constitutes not only a trait but something possessing its own dignity, he seems to imply that al-Fārābī considers the soul and what relates to it to be referents of the divine. Al-Fārābī's tacit negation of God, as Strauss saw it, peaked in the omission of the tenth book of the *Laws*.[121]

As in "Farabi's *Plato*," Strauss's interpretation of al-Fārābī's understanding of Plato is based on philological observations. Such an interpretation implies al-Fārābī's knowledge of Plato's unabridged and complete writings. However, such an implication becomes untenable when the corrupt transmissions of Greek texts into Arabic are considered. It seems that Strauss's argument rests on a thin philosophical foundation. This is particularly evident in his reasoning regarding the central issue of atheism, which Strauss attributes to al-Fārābī and which he sees as the root of al-Fārābī's exoteric-esoteric writings. In the end, one cannot help but feel that Strauss's interpretation of al-Fārābī lacks a solid foundation.[122]

CHAPTER FOUR

Crisis and Prophecy

Introduction

The departure point and overall trajectory of Leo Strauss's thought must be understood in light of what he perceived to be a deplorable crisis of modern philosophy.[1] His complex critique of the negative manifestations of modernity constitutes his most influential legacy.[2] Neo-Kantians and disciples of Dilthey had previously diagnosed this crisis of philosophy and interpreted it as a general crisis of European civilization. The defeat in World War I and the unstable social and political circumstances, particularly in Germany, intensified the sense of crisis. The title of Spengler's book *Der Untergang des Abendlandes* (*The Decline of the West*) is instructive with regard to this mood.[3] Strauss similarly extends the notion of a crisis of philosophy to a general crisis of the modern Western world.[4] To him, this crisis was reflected chiefly in the individual's loss of orientation, itself the result of calling into question humanity's most highly cherished aspirations, such as progress, peace, and freedom.[5] The crisis resulted both from theoretical challenges to philosophy in the form of Nietzsche's and Heidegger's attacks and from more concrete challenges posed by technological progress. However, the causes of this crisis go deeper, and concern the foundations of modernity itself.

Strauss's diagnosis highlighted several aspects of this crisis of modernity. What stands out is his critique of the complacency of post-Enlightenment culture, with its belief in technological superiority, trust in the power of reason to organize political life, and the exclusion of religion from the public sphere. Parallel to and as a result of this critique of modernity, Strauss developed a critique of religion that harkens back to Plato and concentrates on the Islamic-Jewish conception of the prophet in the Middle Ages. This critique of religion, he claims, can unveil the deep-rooted causes of the crisis.

This chapter will be dedicated to Strauss's theory of the crisis of modernity, the crisis's underlying causes, and the paths Strauss proposes to take out of this crisis. It has often been noticed by scholars that Strauss's critique of modernity makes use of a rhetorical style that resembles the rhetoric of the biblical prophets.[6] However, the context of Strauss's examination of the medieval prophetological theories of Maimonides, Avicenna, and al-Fārābī has gone unnoticed. Shedding light on this context is a further goal of this chapter.

The Crisis of Modernity

For Leo Strauss, modernity consists of a project unfolding in three stages, or "waves." The first wave began with Machiavelli and was carried on by Hobbes. This wave was marked by a break with tradition and the claim to a human right of self-determination. It introduced a new understanding of nature, claiming to manipulate nature and thereby adapt it to human needs. The lowest of these human needs, namely individual security, became the highest goal of politics.

The second wave of modernity turned out to be more radical than the first. It was initiated by Rousseau, who, on behalf of virtue, protested against the ideas of his predecessors and attempted to transcend the state of nature. To him, the general will of humanity was the trigger of human development, which takes the form of a historical process. The third and most radical wave of modernity crested in Nietzsche's thought. Like Rousseau, Nietzsche rejects the natural state and places unprecedented philosophical emphasis on the unfolding of historical developments. However, he fails to recognize any other impetus for development than the will to power.[7]

According to Strauss, modernity suffers from a crisis rooted in the idea of progress and its effect on Western culture. While technological progress and the development of science have unfolded rapidly, no analogous growth of human wisdom or kindness can be observed. Technological progress did not bring affluence to all people, and the catastrophes, the wars, and the barbarism that have haunted humanity in the twentieth century have left little hope for any form of moral progress. The West has had to witness the destruction of its vision of a future where the entirety of humanity benefits from progress. The current state of humanity is marked by purposelessness and uncertainty. This situation necessarily results in doubts regarding any kind of possible progress. As progress became the defining characteristic of Western modernity in the course of the nineteenth century, the age-old distinction between good and bad or right and wrong was replaced by the distinction between progressive and reactionary through the philosophical, political, and religious discovery of history. The shattering effect of such a belief in progress has thus led to the crisis of modernity itself.[8]

Strauss highlights three characteristics of modern thought. The first consists of an anthropocentrism that has replaced the theocentrism of the medieval era and the cosmocentrism of classical thought. The second is that the anthropocentric character of modern thought has been accompanied by a radical shift in moral orientation that has liberated the passions. Consequently, even virtue becomes understood as a passion that is to be gradually replaced by freedom. The third feature consists of the human dependence on history.[9] In addition, the aforementioned moral uncertainty evokes strong doubts regarding the project of modernity, which, according to Strauss, had essentially been initiated by philosophers in order "to satisfy in the most perfect manner the most powerful natural needs of men."[10] The individual and the fulfilment of their needs have been thrust into the center of modern thought, a position that had hitherto been occupied by the question of God.

According to Strauss, modern Western civilization has two roots: the Bible and Greek philosophy. Yet both have suffered damage from the effects of modern rationalism. On the one hand, such rationalism has aimed at separating biblical morals from biblical theology, thereby depreciating the value of the Bible. Rapid scientific and technological progress, on the other hand, has rendered philosophy into an apparently ineffectual discipline. Therefore, rational morality, the main legacy of Greek philosophy, was necessarily eliminated.[11]

Strauss conceives of the crisis of modernity as a crisis of a fundamentally theological nature. He defines the crisis in terms of an "all-important question which is coeval with philosophy although the philosophers do not frequently pronounce it — the question quid sit deus."[12] The question of God has been largely superseded by the question of how the life of the individual should be shaped. It is this latter question that has given rise to the insolvable conflict between the two roots of modernity. From Aristotle onward, philosophy has regarded theoretical contemplation as the highest form of human action that does not require divine guidance. The Bible, on the contrary, has portrayed obedience to God's laws, piety, and the human need for God's mercy as the most important features of a good way of life. This conflict was "the core, the nerve of Western intellectual history, [. . .] the secret of the vitality of Western civilization."[13] Life in Western civilization, he argues, takes place as a fundamental tension "between two codes," whereby none of the participants can be both philosopher and theologian. Thus, Strauss categorically rejects any possibility of circumventing this conflict or resolving it through synthesis.[14]

This irreconcilability of philosophical and religious forms of conduct forms the basis of modernity while, at the same time, animating it by means of the resulting tension. To Strauss, this conflict has characterized both the West and the entirety of the Mediterranean realm. While the conflict has had mainly theoretical roots, it has been waged in the form of a secular praxis that could only bind itself to one of the competing moral alternatives. In this context, the argument of philosophy against religion has revealed that the former was not so confident in itself anymore. Using the example of Spinoza, Strauss indicates that the philosophical refutation of revelation has failed. However, religion has also not entirely succeeded in defending itself against the attacks of philosophy. Both antagonists and their respective camps continue to be hostile to each other. In the face of this situation, Strauss asserts that the decision to embrace philosophy at the expense of religion has relied on a certain kind of belief. Even the quest for self-evident insight has not relied on evident assumptions. Philosophy has remained mired in its critique of revelation, which the self-destruction of reason and the related crisis of modernity have demonstrated.[15]

Albeit in another context and with different terminology, Strauss had already presented this line of argumentation equating the crisis of philosophy with the general crisis of modernity. In his daring introduction to *Philosophy and Law*, Strauss reopened the conflict between modern rationality and Bible-believing religiosity in the Jewish context of the Weimar Republic.[16] In this context, what was presented as the particularly "Jewish problem" of assimilation turns into a more universal and fundamental question reflecting an antagonism between human philosophy and divine revelation that cannot be resolved by political or rational means. This conflict between philosophy and revelation, as Strauss himself apparently experienced and deliberated upon it, mirrored the irreversible human dualism of religious law and the autonomy of reason. The question preoccupying Strauss in the Jewish context appears to him as "the manifest symbol of the human problem as a social or political problem."[17]

Ever since *Philosophy and Law*, Strauss had regarded the current state of philosophy as marked by two alternating imperatives, namely enlightenment and orthodoxy. Consequently, Strauss believed that the only remaining solution was a variety of atheism characterized "by its diligence and by its morality" inasmuch as it was "a descendant of the tradition founded in the Bible."[18] The point of reference for this atheistic attitude presented by Strauss and the biblical tradition is the fact that such atheism seemingly did not altogether reject the position of the Bible but rather planned to maintain it. While Strauss rejects any true synthesis of the two opposing positions, those of Jerusalem or Athens,[19] the atheism he proclaims nonetheless puts forth a claim for maintaining biblical elements. At the same time, this kind of atheism, "free of both the polemical bitterness of the Enlightenment and the equivocal reverence of romanticism," is vested with the capacity to attain to the "original understanding of the human roots of the belief in God" in order to "radically overcome orthodoxy."[20] The next subsection will shed some light on how Strauss conceptualized this special form of atheism.

Progress by Return

The philosophical position that Strauss never ceased to hold deplores the crisis of modern philosophy and aims at tracing back its causes to their roots. Therefore, a historical approach must have appeared necessary to Strauss. His intentions in this regard were twofold. On the one hand, philosophy could be revived through retrieving forgotten, seemingly antiqued philosophical thinking. One the other hand, a radical understanding of philosophy's foundations could restrain the worst impulses of unbridled religious orthodoxy. The fact that Strauss resorts to a historical approach does not stem from nostalgia or an interest in history for history's sake but is rather "a consequence of modernity's unease with itself." Indeed, Strauss wishes to have a fundamental discussion regarding a contemporary problem.[21] Strauss's view that the crisis of modernity is not only the end but also a "focal point" of philosophizing can be justified from such a perspective.[22]

Strauss believed that it was impossible to solve the crisis of modernity with modern means. Rather, this undertaking required a vantage point outside of modernity's horizons, which could apprehend modernity in its entirety, thereby offering an appreciation of the full magnitude of modern rationalism's self-destruction. Through this philosophical inversion, Strauss can transcend modernity. Such an inversion aimed at abandoning any prejudices that would incline a philosopher to think that a return to premodern rationalism was no longer feasible. In fact, such a position of supersession had already been rendered possible by Husserl and Heidegger.[23] However, Strauss's philosophical change of direction only took place after reading Avicenna's musings about the philosophical treatment of religion in Plato's *Laws*. In this case, a work of classical philosophy is regarded as capable of discussing prophecy and religious law, thereby informing Strauss's position that the rationalism of antiquity permeating medieval thought had not lost its ability to explain revealed religion. From Strauss's perspective, the return to classical philosophy is inevitable and even implied in the notion of modernity, for "modernity was understood from the beginning in contradistinction to antiquity."[24] Contrasting modernity and antiquity will facilitate better understanding of the problems of modernity.

The connection Avicenna drew between the medieval Islamic conception of religion and Platonic philosophy, and the appropriation of this line of thought by other Muslim and Jewish philosophers, provided Strauss with a model toward which he could orient his constructive critique of modernity.[25] Whereas philosophy was officially recognized and placed under the strict control of the church in the medieval Christian world, Strauss argues that it is precisely the precarious situation of philosophy in the Islamic-Jewish world, a position that confined it to private study, that — odd as it may seem — granted it more liberty. But what exactly did Strauss discover in medieval Jewish and Muslim philosophy that allowed him to turn to its representatives for answers to the crisis of modernity?[26]

In *Philosophy and Law*, Strauss admits that the discouraging state of modern philosophy, especially regarding the phenomenon of religion, made him "go to school to the medieval philosophers."[27] By considering the importance ascribed to revelation, the situation of philosophy could change radically. Muslim philosophers, ever since al-Fārābī, were ceaselessly confronted with the authority of revelation, and their philosophy could not but take its reality into account.[28] Compared to modern rationalism, this form of rationalism developed by grappling with the theological tradition, therefore enhancing its ability to cope with the phenomenon of revealed religion.[29] According to Strauss, it is precisely Platonic philosophy that constituted the basis upon which these philosophers stood when dealing with revelation. Yet he also recognizes that references to a "factor of revelation" indicated the emergence of a new, non-Platonic precondition of medieval philosophizing that could not but reshape the Platonic framework. Against the background of this insight, Strauss developed his plan to lead contemporary philosophy out of crisis using the guideposts that the Muslim philosophers of the Middle Ages had provided. The return to the Middle Ages is not just a sojourn on the path back to antiquity. Rather, medieval philosophy is essential for establishing a discussion between revealed religion and philosophy. Al-Fārābī, Avicenna, Averroes, and Maimonides, philosophers intensely preoccupied with the relationship between religion and philosophy, are the most important references for Strauss's critique of modernity in a Platonic context aimed at a revaluation of religion.[30]

According to Strauss, Muslim and Jewish medieval philosophers considered revelation not only as a miraculous act of God but also most essentially "as the law given by God through a prophet." This, in turn, makes revelation a "subject matter of philosophy" within the framework of prophetology.[31] As Strauss saw it, the teachings of those philosophers regarding prophecy required a philosophical examination of religious law with respect to its nature, development, and purpose. The preconditions for a modern philosophical treatment of religion seemed to him to lie with the medieval Islamic and Jewish doctrines of prophecy. It was therefore his intention to thoroughly examine those doctrines, thereby revealing the foundations of the medieval conception of religion. The resulting insights, in turn, are rendered applicable to the current discussion of the crisis of modernity. Strauss's remarks further make clear the extent of al-Fārābī's influence on his philosophizing, which is actually committed to Plato's political philosophy.

Medieval Doctrines of Prophecy

It is again Avicenna's statement on the treatment of prophecy in Plato's *Laws* that forms the background against which Leo Strauss interpreted the Muslim and Jewish teachings of prophecy and eventually developed his new understanding of religion.[32] The Islamic-Jewish conception of prophecy remained of continued interest to Strauss, as it explains the extraordinary phenomenon of prophecy and, consequently, the origins of revealed religion conceived as "emerging from human nature." It does so by attaching certain prerequisites to prophecy that concern the person of the prophet. These conditions are the perfection of the intellect, morals, and imaginative faculty. If an individual is vested with perfection in all three areas, such a total state of perfection will allow him to receive revelation and impart it to the people. While the perfect intellect enables the prophet to directly receive the revelation of fundamental truths, a fact that also renders him a philosopher, the perfect imaginative power gives him the ability to depict theoretical truths in order to make them understandable for his fellow human beings. The prophet possesses perfect knowledge, whereby the prophetical process of cognition was thought along the lines of the Aristotelian epistemology predominant at that time.[33] According to this theory of cognition, the active intellect, *intellectus agens*, whose agency is defined by God, renews and feeds the effectiveness of both perfect capabilities of the prophet, whereby he is able to gain an understanding of heaven. The insights he derives from these processes can be taught to the people, including the philosophers.

The Straussian account of the medieval doctrines of prophecy starts with the study of Maimonides's conception of prophecy. The link to modernity is provided by Hermann Cohen's insight that "Maimonides was in deeper harmony with Plato than with Aristotle."[34] Strauss adopts this assertion of Cohen and consequently views Maimonides as a Jewish philosopher who understands Judaism in a Platonic framework. He nonetheless differs from the neo-Kantian Cohen in maintaining not a transcendental-ethical interest but rather a political-philosophical one.[35] He argues that prophetology is "a central part of the doctrine of the *Guide of the Perplexed*" and that "Maimonides, in his prophetology, follows a centuries-old philosophical tradition whose premises he no longer even mentions." However, this philosophical tradition contains a fully developed conception of prophecy that Maimonides explicitly refers to.[36] Strauss finds that the Maimonidean conception of prophecy contains a fundamental difficulty that puts its validity into question. Because his concept of prophecy relies on the actualization of both the intellect and imaginative faculties, it postulates the coterminous action of two diametrically opposed features that essentially differ from and ultimately hinder one another. Maimonides fails to provide Strauss with an answer to this essential problem, thereby compelling him to search for answers in the works of Maimonides's philosophical progenitors, namely the writings of al-Fārābī and Avicenna.[37]

According to Strauss, al-Fārābī broaches the issue of prophecy in two passages of *On the Perfect State*. "In each of these passages he treats a different kind of prophecy, although without expressly saying so."[38] The first passage can be found in two consecutive chapters on the origins of dreams and revelation. The kind of prophecy presented here solely stems from the imaginative power and mainly consists of gaining knowledge about the future.[39] The second passage is contained in the chapter on the head of the perfect state. Strauss argues that what al-Fārābī presents here is a secondary typology of prophecy that not only relies on the perfected imaginative faculty but also results from the actualization of the intellect. Satisfying both conditions allows for the reception of divine revelations through the impact of the active intellect on the intellect and, thereafter, on the imaginative power of the apt individual. This emanation of insights "flowing" to the intellect turns the individual into a philosopher. The perfection of the imaginative faculty equally enables the individual to successfully convey to the people what their intellect has received. Such a prophet combines philosophy and prophecy in their person and "stands at the absolute highest rank of humanity."[40]

Strauss compares al-Fārābī's prophetology to that of Maimonides, thereby concluding that the latter rejects al-Fārābī's first typology of prophecy. In this fashion, he makes the highest rank of humanity coincide with the perfect imaginative faculty. Furthermore, he highlights the fact that "al-Fārābī denies the possibility of supra-philosophical knowledge of the upper world through prophecy" and, consequently, diminishes the prophet by reducing the influence of the active intellect on their intellect to "nothing other and nothing higher than a philosopher." Strauss underpins his judgment by highlighting an objection made by Ibn Ṭufayl, who argued that, according to al-Fārābī, prophecy is chiefly the result of imaginative power and hence exists on a lower level than philosophy. At this point, Strauss discerns an important difference between al-Fārābī and

Maimonides in that the latter ascribes to the prophet the unlimited supremacy of knowledge.[41]

It was Strauss's intention to maintain the versatile relationship between Maimonides and the Islamic philosophers in an unrestricted fashion. He therefore argues that Maimonides's doctrine of the direct knowledge of the prophet can be found in Avicenna's works. Avicenna, as Strauss saw it, appropriated al-Fārābī's doctrine of prophecy but deemed the "capacity for direct knowledge, not based on syllogisms and proofs [. . .] as the highest capacity distinguishing the prophets."[42] Strauss's account of Avicenna's conception of prophecy concentrates on the following features. The prophet is the most excellent among men because, in addition to his possession of an intellectual and moral perfection, which other excellent individuals might also attain, he distinguishes himself by three further psychological capacities: the perfection of the imaginative capacity, the capability to perform miracles, and the possession of direct knowledge. He receives revelations, hears God's word, and views His angels "in visible form." Furthermore, a hierarchy exists among the features of prophecy. The imaginative faculty ranks the lowest, followed by the performance of miracles. Prophecy, "consisting in the absolute highest perfection of the theoretical intellect," ranks highest. This hierarchy of the prophetical capacities is arranged in such a way that the prophet "does have at his disposal also the capabilities of the prophets of both other ranks."[43]

Strauss's examination reveals the dependence of Maimonides's prophetology on al-Fārābī and Avicenna. Nevertheless, he also discerns differences between the two conceptions of prophecy explained above. One of the differences between Maimonides and al-Fārābī, the one regarding direct prophetic knowledge, has already been mentioned. The comparison of Avicenna's prophetology with that of Maimonides demonstrates that the latter deviates from the former only with regard to those "miraculous powers" that Maimonides, contrary to Avicenna, does not mention. Maimonides's position on this matter relies on the philosophical principle of the plurality of causes. He nonetheless acknowledges the divine power as the final cause of all events, agreeing on this matter with the Islamic *kalām*.[44]

This is how Strauss solves the riddle of the disputed imaginative faculty. The latter has a practical purpose and, in this sense, can be integrated into a conception of prophecy. By virtue of the influence of the active intellect on the prophet's intellect, the prophet "becomes a philosopher, a theoretical man; and, if both his intellect and his imaginative faculty are influenced by the active intellect, he becomes a prophet." Furthermore, the activation of the intellect by the active intellect turns the prophet into a teacher of men. By virtue of this influence on his imaginative faculty he is also "able to fulfill his practical task," thereby becoming a political guide. The capacities ascribed to the prophet, namely the capacity to function as a politician, a lawgiver, a veridical dreamer, a predictor of the future, and a magician, can all be traced back to the impact of the active intellect on his imaginative power.[45]

The Purpose of Prophecy

Through these studies, Strauss recognizes the dependence of the philosopher on the prophet. Two factors underpin this position. The first centers upon the insufficiency of philosophical insight compared to knowledge gained from revelation, a medieval notion that Strauss elucidates in *Philosophy and Law*.[46] Accordingly, the prophet does not only make use of perfect theoretical knowledge, like the philosopher, but also of the perfect practical skills he has accomplished through the perfection of the imaginative faculty. Under the influence of al-Fārābī, Strauss subsequently abandons the idea of the insufficiency of philosophical knowledge while nonetheless retaining the second factor for the superiority of revelation over philosophy, namely the prophet's creation of the perfect society.[47] Strauss concludes that the medieval philosophers conceived of prophecy as a union of philosophy, on the one hand, and politics, divination, and magic, on the other. This compels Strauss to inquire after the final purpose of prophecy.[48]

Based on the Aristotelian dictum of man as *zoon politikon*, who more than other creatures has need of communal life,[49] Islamic philosophy quite early on proclaimed the individual's dependence on society. Associated with this conception is the view that religious law provides the necessary regulation of society. With religious law existing as a precondition of society, it turns out that perfect legislation can only ensue from the art of prophecy. Avicenna specifies the idea of the necessity of law and the excellence of the law given by a prophet while explaining the emergence of the laws in terms of a work of divine providence. Laws give any organism or creature the required strength to survive and, consequently, also provide for the existence of prophetic lawgivers.[50]

Therefore, Strauss can conclude that the Islamic philosophical tradition considers the establishment of a perfect society to be the core purpose of prophecy and revelation. On an elementary level, it meets the characteristic human need for communal living, which distinguishes human beings from other creatures. Yet it also causes complications due to individual differences among human beings.[51] This purpose, nonetheless, fulfils more than just elementary needs. The perfection of the human being in the proper sense is the perfection of his soul. Bodily perfection, in this sense, only serves the perfection of the soul. The law that targets the soul's perfection is called the "divine law" and is proclaimed by a prophet.[52] Strauss concludes that "the prophet must be philosopher/statesman/seer/(miracle-worker) all at once so that he may be the founder of the community directed to the specific perfection of man, the perfect community."[53] According to Strauss, these extraordinary prophetical faculties answered the call for the establishment of a perfect society, thus lending these faculties significance and importance. They enable the prophet to outperform the philosopher, who is obviously not capable of establishing this perfect society. Rather, the philosopher seems to be "dependent on a law given by a prophet." He must obey the prophet since, as a human being, the philosopher is reliant on social life.[54]

When he asserts that humanity needs prophecy, Strauss is mainly referring to the position held by Avicenna. Avicenna instituted a difference between these two kinds of laws, dividing them into "the part of politics dealing with *kingship* and the part dealing with *prophecy and religious law*." Strauss draws upon two further passages from Avicenna's treatises in order to demonstrate that he distinguished prophecy "from all that is merely political." Strauss adduces from the first of these passages that Avicenna defined the "utility of *politics*" in terms of providing humanity with knowledge about "how the communal relation among human individuals must be fashioned in order for them to mutually help one another towards the well-being of *bodies* and the maintenance of the human race."[55]

The second passage Strauss refers to in order to demonstrate Avicenna's position that religious law ranked higher than the "mere political" concerns the prophetical mission (*ar-risāla*). In Strauss's relatively loose translation, this passage reads as follows: "The (prophetic) mission is the inspiration whose end is "the welfare of *both* worlds, that of (eternal) subsistence and that of passing-away, through science *and* political government. The messenger (the prophet) is he who proclaims what he has learned . . . through inspiration, so that, through his views, *the welfare of the sensible world may be achieved through political government, and [the welfare] of the intelligible world through science*."[56] From these remarks, Strauss concludes that prophecy consists of political action, which nonetheless differs from "mere political guidance." Prophecy not only aims at a more perfected state of the sensible world but also aims at "the perfection of the intellect, the specific perfection of man." The prophet is distinguished from the statesperson in that the former's guidance aims at the comprehensive material and spiritual well-being of man. The statesperson in the Platonic model may also be a philosopher. They may also be concerned with the spiritual welfare of their fellow human beings. But the prophet is superior to the philosopher because revelation gives him "direct knowledge of the upper world," which in turn makes him "capable of that government of men which is proper to him, namely, politics and science united in one." Therefore, according to Avicenna, the superior position of the prophet derives solely from revelation, which the philosopher, despite their access to the best knowledge, does not possess. Only knowledge that comes from God enables the prophet — and only the prophet — to address the welfare of humankind in both realms, the realm that can be grasped with the senses and the realm that can only be grasped with the intellect.[57]

Strauss deems the actions of the prophet to be political. Defining the purpose of prophecy as the establishment of the ideal society, he takes the first step toward the systematic interpretation of medieval Islamic philosophy as a form of Platonic philosophy. In Strauss's writings, the medieval concept of prophecy takes on markedly Platonic features.[58] These features are reflected in the primacy of philosophy and politics for the emergence and continued existence of prophecy. At the same time, Strauss ascertains that the philosophers he had analyzed distinguished the prophet (and the attendant "founder of religion" figure) by their success in achieving what Plato failed to accomplish, namely the creation of an ideal state.[59]

Strauss's interpretation not only distinguishes the prophet from the Platonic philosopher-king; it also highlights the prophet's access to revealed knowledge and ability to found the ideal community, elements that emanate from such access. At the same time, it posits prophetic actions as political actions emerging from the combination of political abilities and philosophical knowledge. It stands to reason that this depiction represents contradictory elements in Strauss's interpretation. How, after all, can Strauss connect the Platonic idea of the union of philosophy and politics with such elements as revelation and prophecy, elements that go well beyond Plato?

An Islamic Platonic Philosophy of Religion

Strauss argues that the prophet fulfills what Plato had ultimately demanded, namely the creation of the ideal state. Therefore, he considers al-Fārābī to be the "author of this view of prophecy." Al-Fārābī's concern with Platonic politics is "attested most manifestly by the fact that he composed an 'epitome' or 'summa' of Plato's *Laws*." Furthermore, al-Fārābī differentiates between two variations of prophecy. The superior form, or prophecy in its proper sense, "differs from vulgar divination of all sorts in its political mission." This mission consists of the founding of a state that aims at the perfection of man and that is usually referred to as an excellent or perfect state. The sovereign of this state can only be a prophet who has "by nature the qualities which, according to Plato's requirement, the philosopher-kings must have by nature."[60]

These accounts contain two key identifications: First, religion is equated with the Platonic ideal state. Second, the prophet corresponds to the Platonic philosopher-king. This is also reflected in the characterization of the foundation of religion as a political act of the prophet. In order to set revealed religion and Plato's ideal state on an equal footing, Strauss relies on Avicenna. However, Strauss only equate the prophet and philosopher-king by placing the *ra'īs al-awwal*, the head of al-Fārābī's ideal city, between the two figures. The positing of the philosopher-king, prophet, and the *ra'īs al-awwal* as coeval figures enables Strauss to develop his own Platonic conception of revealed religion, a conception he first expressed in his interpretation of the medieval Islamic philosophy of religion. This notion, again, is based on the connection between prophecy and religious law with Plato's *Laws*, which Strauss claims to have found in Avicenna's writings. In the following sections, I will explain in more detail what Strauss understood by what he termed the Platonism of the Islamic philosophers. I will then show how and to what extent he succeeded in making the teaching of the Islamic medieval philosophers compatible with Plato's ideal state. Finally, I will explore Strauss's equation of the prophet and the philosopher-king.

Critical Islamic Platonism

According to Strauss, the Muslim medieval philosophers along with Maimonides are all Platonists. However, he simultaneously admits that this claim will raise many objections. Indeed, these philosophers have mainly been considered Peripatetics and their teachings Aristotelian and thus Neoplatonist rather than strictly Platonist.[61]

Nonetheless, he is convinced of medieval Islamic and Jewish Platonism, particularly with respect to these philosophers' practical or, in Straussian language, political philosophy.[62] To him, the medieval philosophers showed an "essential dependence" on Plato that could not be sufficiently examined without "evidence of exact source analysis." It was therefore necessary to understand the possibility of "the *emergence*" of their teaching from Platonic philosophy.[63] Yet what exactly makes these philosophers Platonic in Strauss's view?

Strauss highlights three main points to underpin his claim. First, these philosophers fully recognize the primacy of the law given by the prophet, and "they derive from the law their *authorization* to philosophize as a legal *duty* to philosophize." It is this latter point that Strauss considers to be Platonic: they fulfill "what Plato called for, that philosophy stand under a higher court, under the state, under the law." Plato, contrary to Aristotle, did not allow the philosophers to limit their philosophizing to "the contemplation of the truth" but rather obliged them "to care for and watch over others."[64]

To Strauss, the philosophers' obliging themselves by recourse to religious law bears a similarity to Plato's reference to his daimon. However, revelation adds to this transcendental justification of philosophizing an intensity unfamiliar to Plato's oeuvre: it is not a daimon anymore who admonishes Socrates to philosophize, giving him cryptic signs, "but rather the one God obliges the men suited to it, by a clear, unequivocal, simple command of His revealed law, to philosophize." This, at least, was what even the most radical thinkers of the Middle Ages, including Averroes himself, pleaded "in their exoterical writings" in order to justify their philosophical work. The second Platonic feature of those philosophers, as Strauss saw it, was the fact that they had to defend their philosophizing before religion, although they advocated, like Aristotle, for the primacy of theory.[65]

The third argument Strauss offers to justify his view of the Muslim philosophers as Platonists concerns their reception of the revelation: "The Platonism of these philosophers is given together with their *situation*, with their de facto standing under the law." From this position "under the law," they perform their philosophical work. Yet they do not have the same intention as Plato. For them, revealed law is the actualization of Plato's ideal state. They do not need "to seek the law, the state, to inquire into it: the binding and absolutely perfect regimen of human life is given to them by a prophet." All that those philosophers try to do is "to understand the given law" and this they can do "only by Plato." Strauss believed that on their way to achieving their Platonic goal, they were required to inquire after beings, the soul and its parts, and science in an Aristotelian manner.[66]

However, Strauss also discerns a certain degree of autonomy in the attitude of the Muslim philosophers toward Plato. Plato's demand for the conjoining of philosophy and political power in the perfect state, as well as his notion of the philosopher-king, merely forms a framework within which those philosophers promoted a concept of prophecy that respects revelation. Revelation is assumed by the Muslim philosophers as a matter of fact. Since those philosophers understand revelation as an immovable and binding starting point, a groundwork that they continuously take into consideration and that legitimizes their philosophical activities, they ultimately end up starting from a non-Platonic point of origin. They advance revelation as a precondition, thereby altering the Platonic framework they had adopted. They read Plato's politics with the intention of understanding revelation in its light. Thereby, they extend the Platonic framework, adding new elements such as knowledge about the future or the miracles of the prophet. However, the framework does not unravel as a result. For them, "it remains the spiritual bond that unites philosophy and politics." The consequences of taking revelation as fact implicitly contained, as Strauss saw it, "a critique of Plato." Subject to this critique are the nature of the ideal state and its founder. The Muslim philosophers recognize the prophet as the founder of the ideal society, but, contrary to Plato, they rule out the potential founding of the ideal society by a philosopher. This is how they, and al-Fārābī in particular, modify what can be deemed authentic Platonism. Their "ruler-philosopher must be more than a philosopher." He must be of superhuman dimensions. Hence, as insufficient as Plato's draft concept may have been, it nonetheless has the merit of predicting revelation, thereby providing those philosophers with a framework to philosophically explain revelation.[67]

Strauss considers the medieval Platonic philosophers to be Platonists, based on observations from the history of philosophy and derived from the Arabic translations of Plato's *Politeia* and his *Nomoi*, which al-Fārābī and Averroes commented upon. Yet recent scholarship has suggested that al-Fārābī only commented on Galen's synopsis of the *Nomoi*. Therefore, Strauss's assumptions need to be put into a new perspective. Averroes admits that he commented on Plato's *Politeia* because he did not have access to Aristotle's *Politics*. It must be borne in mind that, at that time, Plotinus's *Enneads* were thought to be the "Theology of Aristotle." As a result, Plato's and Aristotle's teachings did not seem to essentially differ from one another. This explains why Averroes did not hesitate to draw upon Aristotelian postulations in his commentary on the *Politeia*, which he had linked in any event to his commentary on the *Nicomachean Ethics*.[68]

It seems that Strauss discerns a dialectical relationship between the Islamic philosophers and Plato. While Plato enables the Muslim philosophers to understand the factuality of revelation, that very same revelation induces them to expand the original Platonic framework.[69] This expansion originates in the provision granting the necessity of law's revelatory event. At this point, a gap emerges between the understanding of revelation in medieval Islamic philosophy and the Straussian interpretation. The medieval philosophers view revelation as a miraculous event that only God can perform. They discuss the requirements for revelation, which must be present in the person of the prophet, thereby explaining the origins of revelation as a process of emanation of the active intellect on reason and the imagination of the prophet. However, intellectual effort reaches its limits at this point, for the secrets of revelation have their origin in God and cannot be explained by the intellect.[70]

In this regard, the prophet and philosopher-king constitute distinct figures, thus enabling the Islamic philosophers to go beyond the horizons of Plato's thought. However, Strauss's interpretation of their prophetologies suggests that he assigns revelation a mere functional significance in the political-philosophical framework. Ultimately, this amounts to the subordination of revelation to the political action of an ideal state's founding, whereby Strauss remains firmly on the ground of Platonic political philosophy. It seems as though Strauss deviates here from the original standpoint of those Islamic philosophers who were the primary objects of his studies. As mentioned above, the next section will shed more light on Strauss's Platonization of the Islamic philosophers, using Strauss's equation of revelation and the ideal state as a primary example.

Revealed Religion as Ideal State

For Strauss, prophecy is political inasmuch as it serves the purpose of establishing the perfect society. In this sense, he attributes to Muslim philosophers an interpretation of revelation as the realization of Plato's concept of the ideal state. The society founded by a prophet and the Platonic ideal state coincide in Strauss's interpretation. Strauss justifies this conjunction with the brief remark that the "classic model of the ideal state is the Platonic state."[71]

Strauss must admit that a different idea pertaining to the purpose of prophecy was at work in Maimonides's thought. However, he argues that his own definition of the purpose of prophecy is only "within the meaning" of Maimonides's vision.[72] That said, a huge gap exists between the purpose of prophecy according to Maimonides and the views held by his Muslim predecessors. They regarded prophecy as an endowment given to society aimed at the perfection of humanity. Strauss thereby projects a political interpretation of this teaching. However, the notion of a perfect society created by a prophet cannot tacitly be equalized with Plato's notion of the ideal state. And Strauss clearly admits to this gap in his argumentation.[73]

When Strauss attempts to equate revealed religion with the Platonic ideal state, he does so by referring to several passages in Avicenna's writings: The first reference regards Avicenna's statement that Plato's *Laws* was the classic work for the discussion of prophecy and religious law. The second passage claims that the perfect society, created by a prophet, had to be called "the excellent city" or the "city of good way of life."[74] Strauss concludes, therefore, that Avicenna must have been referring here to Plato's ideal state, particularly as Avicenna did not have access to Aristotle's *Politics*.[75] Additionally, Avicenna's passage about the legislator's division of the city's population into leaders, craftspeople, and guardians provides Strauss with an indication that Avicenna considered the prophet as the founder of Plato's state, with Islam serving as the realization of Plato's ideal state.[76]

According to Strauss's conception, the perfect society of revealed religion corresponds to Plato's ideal state. Plato's concept of the ideal state described in the *Laws* serves as a paradigm for understanding revealed religion, and Islam and Judaism in particular, from a philosophical perspective. This assumption leads Strauss to two further coequal pairings. As mentioned previously, prophet and philosopher-king are equated, although the philosopher-king's faculties have been extended to also include divinatory practices. Additionally, religious law is equated here with the Greek nomos. Strauss's most important judgment, namely that the Islamic philosophers regarded revealed religion as the realization of Platonic political philosophy, is based upon this fact.[77]

Averroes is the author of the only known commentary on Plato's *Politeia* in Arabic. It is mainly as a result of Strauss's reference to it that this commentary has attracted the attention of modern scholarship. When one investigates whether Averroes's commentary is compatible with Strauss's interpretation, one finds that Averroes did not consider Plato's project to be foretelling the political order established by revealed religion. Rather, Averroes viewed it as an ethical-social project aiming at the foundation of a just state, but not as the foundation of a religious order.

For Averroes, as for Plato before him, the existence of the ideal state depends on the condition that "the king is simultaneously a philosopher." However, he inserts the four preconditions enumerated by Aristotle in his *Book of Demonstration* into the Platonic argument while describing this very philosopher. He argues that the head of the ideal state needs to master both theoretical and practical sciences and must possess all ethical and intellectual capacities since he functions simultaneously as a philosopher, king, and lawgiver. Drawing on al-Fārābī, he concludes that the philosopher, the king, and the lawgiver are synonymous and combines them with the Arabic word *imām*, "due to the fact that in Arabic, the *imām* is the one whose actions are emulated as role models."[78] Averroes turns the founder of the ideal state, whose actions are exemplary, into the imam in the absolute sense, that is, the human being to be followed unconditionally. He adds, "As to whether it should be made a condition that he be a prophet, this requires more detailed investigation, and we shall investigate it in the first part of this science, God willing.[79] [If this were the case], it would be best; however, it is not necessary."[80] This passage demonstrates that Averroes clearly differentiated between the founder of the ideal state and the prophet.[81] For Averroes, the Platonic text upon which he is commenting does not contain a Platonic conception of Islam but rather the model of a just and perfect state, which, to be sure, can be realized under Islam if the necessary conditions are met.[82] In several passages of his text, Averroes critically comments on the social and political circumstances of Andalusia, which is another indication of Averroes's purely political perception of Plato's ideal state.[83]

In summary, it seems that Averroes did not equate Plato's ideal state with revealed religion. Additionally, Avicenna's statement at the end of his compendium of metaphysics *ash-Shifāʾ* (*The Healing*), which Strauss drew upon to support his thesis, seems to be driven by Avicenna's active role in politics. Plato's ideal state may have appeared to him as a way out of political chaos in the Persia of his time. Furthermore, Avicenna's treatment of Platonic ideas, which were in any case mixed with non-Platonic elements, may have been under the influence of his affiliation with the Shia and his inclination toward Sufism. It is therefore extremely difficult to prove that he regarded Islam as the realization of the Platonic state.

Prophet and Philosopher-King

Equating the prophet and the philosopher-king seems to be of even greater importance when evaluating the idea of revelation as the realization of the Platonic ideal state. Strauss assumes this correspondence when he declares the foundation of the perfect society, that is, Plato's ideal state, to be the raison d'être of revelation.[84] In this sense, he notes that in the prophetology of the Muslim philosophers and of Maimonides, "the union of philosophy and politics is presupposed as a condition of the perfect state, whose founder alone can be a prophet." Furthermore, he states that Plato's concept of the philosopher-king marked out the framework, "the filling of which, carried out with regard to the factual revelation, results in the prophetic concept" of these philosophers. Strauss concludes, therefore, that the prophetology of those philosophers depends upon the relationship between the notion of the prophet and the Platonic notion of the philosopher-king.[85] Accordingly, he points out that, even in the Hellenistic age, it was taught that "in primeval times ruler, philosopher, and seer coincided." Strauss goes on to attribute the distinctive feature of prophecy, namely the thaumaturgy of the prophet, to "neo-Pythagorean views" and the doctrine of the direct knowledge of the prophet to Philo's notion of the pneuma.[86]

At the beginning of his paper "Quelques remarques sur la science politique de Maïmonide et de Fārābī," Strauss asserts that the Muslim philosophers of the Middle Ages defined the prophet as someone combining the essential features of the philosopher, the lawgiver, and the king in his person.[87] Al-Fārābī's notion of the *ra ʾīs al-awwal*, the head of the virtuous city, is obviously Strauss's source for the unification of prophet, philosopher, lawgiver, and king. Several of Strauss's remarks suggest that he built his own concept of the prophet according to this paradigm. He highlights, for example, that al-Fārābī vests the head of the virtuous city not only with the features of the Platonic philosopher-king but also with those of the prophet and his prophecy. Both are the products of revelation. Therefore, in the eyes of al-Fārābī, this *ra ʾīs* ranks highest among human beings. Such prophecy properly considered differs from all other kinds of prophecy on account of "its political mission." Furthermore, Strauss points out that al-Fārābī describes the head of the virtuous city as a particularly brave and audacious individual whose "faculté du courage" is germane to the prophet and serves as the representation of his political function.[88]

Strauss regards the clarification of the relationship between the prophet and the philosopher-king as a precondition for the proper understanding of prophetology and the related identification between the ideal society founded by the prophet and Plato's ideal state. Yet Strauss fails to achieve clarity in this regard. He may have assumed that al-Fārābī had already completed the fusion of the two notions in his depiction of the *ra ʾīs al-awwal*. Hence, al-Fārābī's *ra ʾīs al-awwal* is the decisive element in Strauss's attempt to equate the prophet and philosopher-king, thus serving as an illustration of the relationship between the two notions.[89] Strauss concludes the following: "The philosopher-politician-soothsayer triad is immediately reminiscent of Fārābī's policy that the 'first ruler' of the perfect city must be a philosopher and soothsayer ('prophet')."[90] To Strauss, al-Fārābī's head of the virtuous city corresponds to the philosophical notion of the prophet who combines the features of the Platonic philosopher-king and the prophet-lawgiver. This notion forms the very basis of Strauss's Platonic interpretation of the prophetology of the Islamic philosophers and of Maimonides, as well as for his equating revealed religion with Plato's ideal state. Strauss merges Avicenna's theory of the agency of the prophet with al-Fārābī's concept of the *ra ʾīs al-awwal* of the virtuous city to produce a medieval Islamic notion of the prophet that seems to be compatible with Plato's philosopher-king.[91] In *Philosophy and Law*, the head of the virtuous city is vested with the features of the Platonic philosopher-king and declared a prophet, since his prophecy serves the political goal of both the foundation and the rule of the city.[92] In "Quelques remarques sur la science politique de Maïmonide et de Fārābī," Strauss further sharpens the union between prophet and philosopher-king by pointing to the concept of the head of the virtuous city. He writes, "In medieval politics, the prophet occupies the same place as the philosopher-kings in Platonic politics: by fulfilling the essential conditions for philosopher-kings enumerated by Plato, he founds the perfect city, i.e., the Platonic ideal city."[93] According to Strauss, al-Fārābī taught that the "first chief" of the perfect city had to be a prophet and an imam. Furthermore, the notions "first chief," "imam," and "lawgiver" are rendered synonymous, and, therefore, "the 'first chief' is, as such, the founder of a religion. [. . .] He is Plato's philosopher-king."[94] Among the Jewish prophets, only Moses resembled the "first chief," being vested with characteristics such as courage and a rhetorical talent, features stemming from the Islamic prophets rather than the Platonic philosopher-king.[95]

Al-Fārābī's head of the virtuous city is the actual prophet because he is at once a philosopher and a political ruler. In this conception, philosophy and politics correspond with one another and, thus united, represent the characteristics of prophecy itself. The fact that Strauss renders political rule into a characteristic of prophecy entails that philosophy and politics become pillars of prophecy. At the same time, the faculty necessary for receiving the revelation, which is usually the characteristic par excellence of the prophet, is relegated to a secondary position. The emphasis on the importance of both philosophy and politics for prophecy comes along with an emphasis on the realms of autonomous human thought and action at the expense of the importance of revelation. From such a perspective, the theoretical contents of faith take their meaning from their political function.[96]

At this point, one cannot but notice a contradiction in Strauss's interpretation of the conceptions of Islamic and Jewish prophecy. There, it is revelation that is the decisive element of the medieval philosophical conception of prophecy. Revelation gives the prophet priority over the philosopher and allows him to gain insights the philosopher cannot reach. It is revelation that enables the prophet, unlike the philosopher, to serve as founder of the perfect society. Nonetheless, in Strauss's interpretation, revelation must cede its eminent position to philosophy and politics. It seems that Strauss's understanding of prophecy, based on Avicenna's and Maimonides's prophetology, deviates from its role models with respect to this very central dimension even though Strauss continues to claim its correspondence with his sources.

Excursus: al-Fārābī's notion of *ar-ra'īs al-awwal*

The description of the *ra'īs al-awwal* is one of the topics al-Fārābī dwells on in his *Perfect State*. Al-Fārābī describes the *ra'īs al-awwal* as a perfect man, in possession of all the faculties that Plato ascribes to his philosopher-king in the sixth book of the *Politeia*. He is necessarily perfect with respect to his body, his reason, his imagination, and his memory. Furthermore, his intelligence and his verbal skills are accomplished. He prefers teaching, knowledge, and the truth while abhorring lies. He must be of a dispassionate nature when food, beverages, sexual intercourse, and all other worldly pleasures are concerned. Instead, he needs to be of a noble and eminent mind, unconcerned with property ownership, and fair-minded. Resolute, brave and fearless, he allows for justice to prevail.[97]

However, the head of the virtuous city outperforms the philosopher-king by virtue of both his perfect intellect and his perfect imagination. These capacities allow him to be in contact with the active intellect. Thereby, he becomes an accomplished philosopher and prophet who recognizes current problems and predicts future practical issues. He holds the highest rank in the hierarchy of the virtuous city, which exists through his person and is managed by him. This city resembles the perfect and healthy body, or even the well-ordered cosmos. Its parts have different natural arrangements, and some of them outperform others. They form a well-ordered hierarchy, and their relationship among each other is marked by cooperation. Nevertheless, the inferior parts follow the higher ones and emulate them. The *raʾīs* is similar to the First Cause. The relationship of the parts of the virtuous city to the *raʾīs* is similar to the relationship of all beings to the First Cause: they owe their existence to it and follow it according to power and rank, imitating it and being guided by it. The coincidence of all the required features existing in one person is rare, and therefore so is the existence of such a *raʾīs*. Al-Fārābī nevertheless does not rule out the simultaneous existence of several chiefs (*ruʾasāʾ*). However, these chiefs will be of the same soul and of the same mind. Their unity will not be damaged. In case the *raʾīs al-awwal* is absent, the virtuous city can be ruled by a second chief (*raʾīs*). This latter *raʾīs* needs to possess wisdom and philosophical ability as well as the capacity to learn the laws and rules of his predecessors. Furthermore, he needs to be able to identify missing principles and to renew rules and orders according to the requirements of current circumstances. Just like the first chief, he needs to be eloquent. Finally, he must be physically fit and experienced in the conduct of war.[98]

If these features cannot be found simultaneously in one individual but only divided among two individuals, these two individuals shall rule the city together.[99] If the complete features can only be found in a group of people, this group shall rule the city. In the event that wisdom disappears from the city, it will remain without a ruler and perish before long.

In his treatise *as-Siyāsa al-madaniyya*, al-Fārābī explains that the *raʾīs al-awwal* does not need instructions or advice from anybody else, as he possesses scientific insight and understands all matters. He is therefore able to guide all other people toward beatitude. He disposes of the acquired intellect that comes into being through contact with the active intellect. Such a man is indeed someone whom the ancients had called "King." He deserves to be called someone who receives revelation, for a man can only receive revelation if no further medium is required to connect him and the active intellect. Those men who follow the guidance of the *raʾīs* are the virtuous, chosen, and felicitous. If they form a nation, this nation is virtuous. Gathering together at their places of residence, they form a virtuous city. However, if they live scattered in different places whose inhabitants are ruled by other chiefs, these virtuous people will remain alien to their environment. They live dispersed either because they do not yet have a city or because they needed to leave their former city due to hostile attacks, epidemics, or droughts.[100]

Al-Fārābī equates the meaning of the concept of *raʾīs al-awwal* with the meaning of "philosopher," "lawgiver," and "imam."[101] Yet it seems that he avoids religious terminology. This could be explained as an attempt to differentiate his philosophical position from the theological position of the *mutakallimūn*. He carefully chooses neutral wordings that are close to the normal semantic range of the Arabic. The word *imām*, which in Islam normally connotes the leading figure of a group gathered for prayer, is employed by al-Fārābī in a very literal sense. In the English translation by Mahdī, the Arabic word "Imam" means "the one whose example is followed and who is well-received: that is, either his perfection is well-received or his purpose is well-received."[102] With this definition, al-Fārābī obviously wants to illustrate that "imām" does not have any religious meaning in the respective context. Rather, the word "imām" is used for those individuals who are perceived as excellent and whom the people follow as a role model. In this sense, the *raʾīs al-awwal* can be called an *imām*.[103] However, he adopts an entirely religious tenor in another passage. He explains that the leaders (*ruʾasāʾ*) are the just imams and the real kings, who, when absent, are replaced by the religious jurists (*fuqahāʾ*).[104]

Due to a lack of biographical knowledge about al-Fārābī and his work, it is impossible to decide which religious, philosophical, or political figure he had in mind when describing the *raʾīs al-awwal*. The philosophical influence is striking and appears to be an amalgam of neo-Platonic, neo-Pythagorean, and Stoic elements.[105] Additionally, an Islamic resonance can be discerned.[106] For this reason, some researchers view al-Fārābī's combination of philosophy and prophecy as his contribution to the defense against the attacks of skeptics who denied prophecy.[107] The ability of the head of the virtuous city to receive revelation does not necessarily turn him into a counterpart of the prophet Muhammad. Recent studies have shown strong parallels between al-Fārābī's *raʾīs* and the concept if the *imām* in Shiite Islam.[108] Furthermore, the *raʾīs* bears similarities to the traditional image of the caliph.[109] All these elements of influence call for a more sophisticated description of the *ra'īs al-awwal*. An unqualified identification with the prophet and founder of Islam, as contended by Strauss, is an undue simplification.

It seems that al-Fārābī did not consider it important to allude to historical figures of philosophy and Islam. Rather, his focus is on creating a concept of ideal leadership through the *ra'īs al-awwal*. This concept refers to leadership in any kind of organized society without being limited to political leadership.[110] However, al-Fārābī establishes a personified model of perfect leadership here. It is possible that he chose this personification of leadership for the sake of a critical comparison with a specific political leader. Nonetheless, the *ra'īs al-awwal* represents the art of excellent leadership of any sort, an art that is the fruit of the harmony of philosophical and religious values. The practice of these arts results in a perfect society, with "perfect," in this context, implying that this society aims at realizing its immanent telos. The historical circumstances in which al-Fārābī lived probably gave him more than one cause to design such an ideal type of consistent leadership. As is well known, the decline of the Abbasid Empire was followed by a power vacuum that eventually resulted in a turbulent period of internal and external struggles for political power.[111]

In al-Fārābī's concept of the *ra'īs al-awwal*, the coeval nature of philosophy and revelation forms the basis of perfect leadership. This perfect leader unites the faculties of the philosopher with the faculties of the prophet.[112] Prophet and philosopher are united with the *ra'īs al-awwal* in order to create perfect leadership. There is also a pedagogical aspect to this perfect leadership. It is among the tasks of the leader to spread theological and philosophical truths among the inhabitants of the virtuous city and to guide the people toward happiness by combining ethical and cognitive elements.[113] Clearly, al-Fārābī deems this union of philosophy and revelation unproblematic because both philosophical knowledge and revelation originate from the same source.[114] This common source is the active intellect, which, according to al-Fārābī, mediates between God and human and guides the latter toward absolute beatitude.[115] Within the notion of the *ra'īs al-awwal*, all components are of equal importance, for perfection leaves no room for gradual differences or nuances. Al-Fārābī admits that there has hardly ever been a man capable of uniting all the features of the *ra'īs al-awwal* in his personhood. Therefore, he conceives of a second constellation that makes for a "less perfect" leadership. In case no single person fulfills all the demands of a perfect leader, he even considers the possibility of a group of leaders. Evidently, his main concern is not a certain person but a certain constellation of characteristics required for virtuous guidance and the establishment of a virtuous order that allows human beings to live happily.

Undoubtedly, al-Fārābī is an idealist. But he is also a realist. Taking reality into account, he admits that the simultaneous occurrence of all the characteristics required for perfect leadership of the virtuous city is a rare event. In fact, it is difficult to find a group of people who possess all of these qualities together and thus qualify for leadership. Among these qualities, prophecy is the rarest and most uncommon. Therefore, leadership without prophecy must also be possible.[116] Leaving idealism aside, al-Fārābī — being, after all, a philosopher — abandons all necessary features of leadership but one: wisdom. Wisdom is the most important characteristic that a person can acquire through their own personal effort. When all virtues disappear from the city, wisdom must remain lest the city perish. Considering human reality, wisdom is the best guarantee for a just society. Wise leadership, in turn, is a matter of political philosophy, whereby "political" is conceived by Strauss in a broader, classical sense.[117]

Speaking of wise leadership brings us back to the realm of political philosophy, a realm primarily concerned with problems of the social order. Mahdī contends that al-Fārābī saw the problem of philosophy as closely interlinked with political philosophy. Therefore, political philosophy plays a significant role in his writings.[118] Strauss treads in al-Fārābī's footsteps when he turns the crisis of modern philosophy into a subject matter of political philosophy. His intention thereby is to employ the rehabilitated mode of political philosophy as an answer to the crisis of modernity by making prophecy and, consequently, the question of God into an issue of political philosophy.[119]

Summary

The main insights from this chapter can be summarized as follows:

> Strauss declares the theory of prophecy to be a central element of Maimonides's philosophy. Strauss is driven by a political interest to interpret it. However, Maimonides's conception of prophecy shows certain weaknesses and contradictions that Strauss can only solve by resorting to the prophetologies of Avicenna and al-Fārābī. The teachings of the two Islamic philosophers are of utmost importance not only for the understanding of Maimonidean prophetology but also for Strauss's political interest in revelation.
> Strauss follows in the footsteps of the medieval philosophers when he recognizes the priority of the prophet over the philosopher. This prioritization results from the prophet's access to direct knowledge from revelation and the related foundation of

> an ideal society that meets the material and spiritual needs of humanity. However, Strauss clearly deviates from the medieval philosophers when he attributes human spiritual needs to reason alone and when he interprets the activities of the prophet and founder of religion as merely political.
>
> According to Strauss's view of prophecy, revealed knowledge serves a political purpose. The role of revelation, therefore, seems to be limited to the implementation of this political aim of prophecy. Consequently, revelation can only be explained by its political purpose. Strauss thereby undeniably reduces the importance of revelation for prophecy.[120]
>
> The fact that Strauss describes the prophet as teacher, leader, philosopher, and wonderworker together in one person suggests that prophecy also contains combined elements of philosophy, politics, and revelation. Yet Strauss reevaluates these elements. Revelation is pushed aside and, contrary to the medieval theories, is not regarded as a characteristic of prophecy any longer. This becomes clear when Strauss argues that the particular leadership skills of the prophet rely upon the union of politics and science. Therefore, it is not revelation but politics and philosophy that are the most important ingredients of the extraordinary leadership faculty possessed by the prophet. Furthermore, Strauss singles out politics as the sole context in which prophecy can be properly understood.[121]

Strauss's recourse to the medieval Islamic and Jewish philosophers and their theories of prophecy represents his reaction to the crisis of modernity, which he attributes to a popular loss of orientation in the face of the disappearance of religious values. To be sure, the reasons that prompted Strauss to resort to those doctrines of prophecy, which appear old-fashioned today, were not of a religious nature. He clearly admitted to his "honest atheism." His motivation is of a political nature, and the "honesty" of his atheism is in my view quite limited. Strauss's atheism exploits theological doctrines he does not actually believe in, employing elements selected from these doctrines for his political thought. Avicenna's statement on the treatment of prophecy in Plato's *Laws* is used by Strauss in order to fuse philosophical horizons from different eras, thereby allowing for a Platonic conception of religion. The prophet is at the core of this undertaking. He is the human being whom God endowed with the authority to found a society that meets people's material and spiritual needs, promising them the good both on earth and in heaven. The question of heaven seems to be of secondary importance to Strauss. According to his conception, prophecy is a political mission, and he interprets it against a political background.

The prophet, if we believe Strauss, is the philosopher-king who returns to establish the long-desired ideal community of justice and excellent leadership.

In this fashion, he surpasses his predecessor in one dimension, namely access to revelation. On behalf of the Jewish and Muslim philosophers of the Middle Ages, Strauss turns religion of revelation into the realization of the Platonic ideal state. By the same token, it seems that Strauss considers their religion to represent one version of the Platonic law. However, neither Avicenna's nor Maimonides's prophetologies sufficed to justify these parallels. It is only in al-Fārābī's writings on the *Nomoi* that Strauss believes he has found such a conception of religion. Nevertheless, of even greater importance to Strauss is al-Fārābī's notion of the head of the virtuous city. It serves Strauss as a vehicle for identifying the prophet with the philosopher-king. This, in turn, seems to allow Strauss to equate revealed religion with Plato's ideal state along political lines.

Al-Fārābī's notion of the *raʾīs al-awwal* is unique. Although it may combine elements related to the philosopher-king with the faculty of the prophet to receive the revelation, it cannot be equated with either one of these two dimensions alone. Strauss's conception of the prophet coincides with al-Fārābī's idea of the *raʾīs al-awwal*. Yet it is guided by his interest in politics. He neglects the event of revelation although this very event is crucial for the head of the virtuous city to emerge. This fact does not qualify as the precondition for equating religion and the ideal state as assumed by Strauss. Al-Fārābī's *raʾīs al-awwal* cannot justify Strauss's conflations. Contrary to Strauss's intentions, the *raʾīs al-awwal* implies and presupposes the belief in the existence of revelation. This belief is based on contents conveyed by revelation that philosophy fails to explain because they cannot be reduced to politically relevant laws.

Therefore, it seems that Strauss's attempt to equate revealed religion with Plato's ideal state falls prey to a vicious circle. The characteristics this prophet needed to demonstrate were already among the preconditions for the ideal state to begin with. Nonetheless, Strauss's preoccupation with prophecy and his original intention to offer a radical interpretation of religion did prove fruitful. Strauss managed to salvage at least one idea, namely the idea that political philosophy could help solve the problem of religion in the modern age through a conception of religious law.

CHAPTER FIVE

Reason, Religion, and Social Order

Introduction

Leo Strauss conceived the Islamic and Jewish religion of revelation "primarily as law." Avicenna's statement about the treatment of the sharia in a classical book of *Laws* gave him the impression that the attempt of the Muslim and Jewish philosophers to understand revealed religion must have been guided "by the original, ancient idea of law as a unified, total regimen of human life."[1] Therefore, their justification of revealed law was entirely disconnected from the revelation they actually believed in. Strauss perceives the sharia as rationally explained through the nomos, with both notions claiming divine origins. The notion of "divine law" thereby becomes "a common ground" for both religion and philosophy.[2]

The preceding accounts of Strauss's thought contain several elements of programmatic relevance that shall be further explained in this chapter. First, I will investigate the relationship between nomos and sharia as conceived by Strauss while drawing on al-Fārābī's interpretation of the *Laws*. Second, Strauss's critique of religion, which he developed against the background of his interpretation of al-Fārābī's conception of religion, will be discussed. Then, I will examine the consequences of equating religion and law for both the self-conception of philosophy and philosophical attitudes toward religious texts. The conclusion will offer a critical review of Strauss's interpretation of the medieval philosophy of religion that undergirds his own conception of religion.

Nomos and Sharia

To Strauss, Avicenna's statement was proof that the Muslim medieval philosophers viewed the sharia in the context of Plato's nomos. In *Philosophy and Law*, Strauss argues that Plato "transforms the 'divine laws' of Greek prehistory into truly divine laws" by interpreting them in such a way that makes their divine nature philosophically recognizable. Plato's interpretation anticipated the philosophical interpretation of revealed law in medieval Islamic thought. "In his [Plato's] approximation to the revelation without the guidance of the revelation we grasp at its origin the unbelieving, philosophic foundation of the belief in the revelation." Strauss considers the idea of divine law to constitute "the required highest perspective acknowledged in common by both Plato and the medieval philosophers."[3] The idea of divine law was the most important common denominator between Plato and the medieval Muslim philosophers, for whom the notion of divine law was of central importance. According to Strauss, the Muslim philosophers had understood revealed law from the perspective of Plato's *Laws*, thus rendering them true Platonists.[4] But how does Strauss interpret their conception of nomos?

Al-Fārābī's Conception of the *Laws*

Strauss mainly relies on al-Fārābī's summary of the *Nomoi* (*Talkhīṣ Nawāmīs Aflāṭūn*) to illustrate how the notion of nomos was interpreted by the Muslim philosophers of the Middle Ages. In all likelihood, this short treatise attracted Strauss's attention for more than three decades because it contains al-Fārābī's understanding of the nomoi, which ultimately becomes normative for the field of Islamic philosophy.[5] In "How Fārābī Read Plato's *Laws*," Strauss presents not only the mature fruits of his long-standing work on al-Fārābī's interpretation of the *Laws* but also his own attitude toward Plato's political work par excellence.[6] This is how he describes the methodical foundation of al-Fārābī's interpretation of the *Laws*, which corresponds to his own interpretation: "The *Laws* is not a book of whose content one can merely take cognizance without undergoing a change, or which one can merely use for inspiring himself with noble feelings. The *Laws* contains a teaching which claims to be true, i.e., valid for all times. Every serious reader of the *Laws* has to face this claim."[7] This statement reveals both Strauss's starting point and path for the interpretation of al-Fārābī's understanding of Plato. To him, the *Laws* was not an ordinary book that would merely inspire sublime feelings in the reader. Instead, it contained a doctrine claiming unconditional truth and validity. This brings us to the core of Strauss's insight: Plato's *Laws* clearly resembles the religious laws of Judaism and Islam. It can even compete with religious law.[8] Furthermore, he argues that any Muslim in the Middle Ages faced this dilemma and had to take one of the following three paths: (1) He could reject the Platonic claim by countering that Plato lacked the guidance provided by revelation. (2) He could apply Plato's standards to specific Islamic institutions, thereby judging and criticizing them, or even rejecting Islam altogether. (3) He could argue that only Islam contained those values postulated by Plato and try to find a purely rational justification for the content and origins of Islam on a Platonic basis.[9]

Strauss gives the impression that al-Fārābī opted for the second path, although he fails to clearly state this fact.[10] For instance, Strauss, highlights that al-Fārābī knew that Greek and Islamic laws differed in their approach to music and singing, yet he considered Greek laws pertaining to those issues to be more appropriate. As for other aspects of law, al-Fārābī recognized that Greek law and Islamic law often coincided in many respects. In fact, both laws indicated that virtue did not consist solely in observing the law. Moreover, both sets of laws were similar in that they had come into being naturally and would necessarily pass away. Strauss's judgment on the coinciding views of al-Fārābī and Plato reads as follows: "Fārābī agreed with Plato certainly to the extent that he, too, presented what he regarded as the truth by means of ambiguous, allusive, misleading, and obscure speech."[11] Strauss argued that al-Fārābī found implications for revealed law in Plato's *Laws*. Indeed, al-Fārābī's adaptation of the book implicitly contained his own views about revealed law. Strauss reconstructs a line of argument from the first chapter of al-Fārābī's treatise that is supposed to demonstrate how al-Fārābī interpreted the idea of revealed law from Plato's perspective. This line of argument consists of the following elements: Abiding by the laws seems to be connected to their alleged divine origins, yet the philosopher stresses the necessity of rational justification, thereby putting the existence of God into question. The laws that are enforced can be those of the victors and are not necessarily better than those they have replaced as a result of war. Just as there exists a difference between true and false lawgivers, there is also a difference between human and divine virtues, whereby the former are the preconditions for the latter. However, the boundaries between the two kinds of virtues are blurred. In the end, it does not become clear how the law renders human virtues into divine virtues. It even seems as though the laws were not necessary for the achievement of virtue. They exist solely to fashion the emergence of religious life. The gods are above the laws. The degenerate, those who by nature have a bad character, must abide by the laws. Logic allows for the genuine knowledge of the laws, which, in their essence, represent rational morality. This morality consists of a rational mediation between the intellectual and the animalistic power of the soul in the case of conflict. The link between human virtue and the practice of logic paves the way for the conclusion that reasonable human beings do not require the guidance of the lawgiver. However, the actual virtue and praiseworthiness of a human being who does not know anything but the laws and acts accordingly remains an open question.[12]

Strauss's interpretation of al-Fārābī's view of the *Laws* amounts to the conclusion that al-Fārābī considered not only the revealed law but also the nomos to have a divine character. The Straussian reading of al-Fārābī's notion of the "divine" means nothing more than the "excellently human," thereby identifying the laudable passions and characteristics of a human being. To demonstrate this view, Strauss adduces the example of the "divine laws," which are designated as "divine" because they are excellent despite being the result of "the work of a human legislator."[13] The attribute of "divine" applies to both the sharia and the nomos because defining the laws as "divine" facilitates their implementation and recognition. The philosopher stands above both, thereby allowing his position to resemble the position of the gods. He has the capacity to distinguish between true and false laws and to recognize the virtues inasmuch as they represent rational morality and not religious life per se.

According to Strauss, al-Fārābī also recognized the problematic character of the law, and it is this very fact that is responsible for al-Fārābī's contradicting statements regarding the validity of the *Laws*: While al-Fārābī had stated previously that only the degenerate had to abide by those laws, he applies them to all inhabitants of the virtuous city in *The Philosophy of Plato*. In this treatise, al-Fārābī attributes the sciences and arts to Socrates and argues that both were a part of the *Nomoi*, although he should have known that Socrates is absent from this dialogue. To Strauss, this contradiction can only be resolved by al-Fārābī's distinction between the Socratic and the Thrasymachian methods of philosophizing and the subsequent conclusion that Plato had actually provided a correction to the Socratic method. The philosophers following in Plato's footsteps had actually known that they did not need the laws in order to live a good life. However, they hid this insight from the multitudes, knowing that the masses, the only group of people that were truly politically significant, needed those laws. Such a judgment originates from Platonic political philosophy, which, because of the fates of Socrates and Thrasymachus, had to learn how to behave toward society. To Strauss, al-Fārābī highlighted the *Laws* in his interpretation of Plato because he understood their essential importance for Plato's political philosophy. Yet his own statements did not always reflect the content of the Platonic dialogues.[14]

Law of Reason versus Law of God

Based on his interpretation of al-Fārābī's understanding of the *Laws*, Strauss describes the nomos as a category of universally valid commandments that transcend time and space, thereby disregarding individuality.[15] In order to demonstrate the necessity of the nomos, Strauss refers to al-Fārābī, who defined the law as "a substitute for the government of a perfect ruler who governs without written laws and who changes his ordinances in accordance with the changing of times as he sees fit."[16]

Strauss defines the origins of nomos as follows: "The primeval notion of 'custom' or 'way' is split up into the notions of 'nature,' on the one hand, and 'convention,' on the other. The distinction between nature and convention, between physis and nomos, is therefore coeval with the discovery of nature and hence with philosophy."[17] The nomos, therefore, originates from the philosophical division between nature and convention. From the beginning, nomos contrasts with nature, with the discovery of nature serving as the beginning of philosophy. Nomos relies on convention and tradition. Philosophy, on the other hand, is the quest for the origins of all beings and thus stands as a necessary challenge to the notion of nomos.[18]

In his study of Judah Halevi's *Kuzari*, Strauss points to the fact that the Muslim and Jewish medieval philosophers termed Plato's nomoi as "Plato's rational laws" and that the philosopher who takes part in the dialogue is actually the first figure to use the term "law of reason."[19] The "laws of reason" were the "laws of the philosopher," their role model being Plato's *Laws*. The nomos, therefore, is a notion emanating from philosophy. Nevertheless, Strauss distinguishes between both the law of reason proper and the *lex naturalis*. He also differentiates between the law of reason and other rational laws such as the elementary rules of social behavior necessary for the continuation of human society, irrespective of the character of its individual members. Strauss presents the nomos as "a complete code [. . .] identical with 'the religion of the philosophers.'" Rational laws contain a rational morality that is by no means compulsory. Such rational laws were not invented in order to meet the provisional needs of a specific human being or a group of human beings. They have been created by the philosophers in order to meet the immutable needs of the human beings, so that they are rational in an emphatic sense. To him, philosophical laws rooted in reason are "codes fixing the political or other conditions most favorable to the highest perfection of man," and therefore they contain both a political theology and the philosophical but nonpolitical codes of behavior of the philosopher in seclusion.[20]

These philosophical codes can be described in terms of the conduct of life of the philosopher, regardless of whether they are part of the best possible society or lead a solitary life of contemplation. While the life of solitude is indeed a life that should be preferred to "any other religion," the philosopher should not isolate themselves from political life.[21] Nonetheless, the philosophical laws of reason are not appropriate as "governmental laws."[22] It is the revealed law that the philosopher in *Kuzari* characterizes as "political" (*siyāsī*), and it is based upon rhetorical prowess rather than the power of reason.[23] The laws of reason attributed to the philosopher, if we are to believe Strauss, are the sum of the codes of conduct that enable them to live a life in contemplation. They are addressed to all philosophers, irrespective of their different historical contexts. Hence, they are of a general nature. Their individual application under certain circumstances is left to the cautious decision of the individual philosopher, thus turning them into the framework "of all private codes of all individual philosophers." They form a kind of *regimen solitarii*, with their purpose to enable the philosopher to reconcile themselves with God, that is, to achieve a state of purity for the soul.[24]

In a relevant passage of *What Is Political Philosophy?*, Strauss describes the relationship between nomos and religious law as follows:

> Whereas the *nomos* entails a religion that is in the service of government, the divinely revealed law which is a subject of the same branch of political philosophy as the *nomos* puts government in the service of religion, of the true religion, of the truth. The divinely revealed law is therefore necessarily free from the relativity of the nomos, i.e., it is universal as regards place and perpetual as regards time. It is then a much loftier social order than the *nomos*. Hence it is exposed to dangers which did not threaten the pagan nomoi. For instance, the public discussion of "the account of creation," i.e., of physics, did not harm the pagans in the way in which it might harm the adherents of revealed laws. The divinely revealed laws also create dangers which did not exist among the Greeks: they open up a new source of disagreement among men.[25]

According to Strauss, both the nomos and the revealed religion are subjects of political philosophy, since both are ultimately concerned with the political guidance of human beings. However, they follow different processes. The nomos puts religion in the service of the government; religion, on the other hand, puts the government in the service of the truth. Truth becomes the "true religion" and thus the subject matter of philosophy.[26] Philosophy may not claim to be in possession of the truth but rather turns the achievement of truth into the perpetual subject matter of all its activities. Religion instrumentalizes government for the purposes of philosophy. Religious law lacks the relativity that characterizes the nomos in that it claims universality and eternity. Religion contains essential doctrines and therefore may, unlike the nomos, be attacked from a scientific perspective. Since each religious law claims to be universal, Strauss regards religious laws as the source of human conflicts. The nomos, on the other hand, is the generally recognized law that the philosophers have defined. Since nomos is neither dogmatic nor compulsory, it does not cause discord.

Commonalities and Differences between Nomos and Sharia

Strauss's interpretation of the relationship between nomos and sharia encounters both historical-philosophical and systematic difficulties, as this section will show. There is no simple answer to the question of how the Muslim philosophers viewed the relationship between nomos and sharia. The corrupted transmission of both the ancient Greek texts in the Arabic Middle Ages and the Arabic philosophical texts of the Middle Ages in the present is an obstacle. The authenticity of the text that al-Fārābī took for Plato's *Laws* is actually heavily debated among scholars.[27] H. A. Wolfson had already counted the term *nomos* among the "amphibolous terms" in Islamic philosophy and in al-Fārābī's works in particular. The example adduced by Wolfson points to an Aristotelian use of the word *nomoi*, namely as civil laws.[28]

It is impossible to establish a direct link between Plato's *Laws* and al-Fārābī's *Talkhīṣ Nawāmīs Aflāṭūn*, given how many Neoplatonist influences, Syriac intermediaries, and unknown Greek summaries have blurred the tradition's reception.[29] Upon closer look, al-Fārābī's treatise reveals that he apparently was not referring to a book that he deemed comparable to the revealed book of the sharia.[30] Regarding the statement in Plato's *Laws* that Zeus was the origin of the laws (*nawāmīs*), al-Fārābī adds that the Greeks considered Zeus to be the father of all human beings.[31] It becomes clear that al-Fārābī is establishing a fundamental difference between the respective origins of the laws:

The nomoi do not stem from God but rather from Zeus. While the Greeks considered Zeus the father of all human beings, he nonetheless could not be compared to the omnipotent creator God of monotheism. The numerous Greek gods are divided into two groups: the heavenly and the earthly. The nomos contains regulations regarding the sacrifices and ritual acts the respective gods are entitled to.[32] Unlike the sharia, the nomoi are used in their plural form.[33] Later on, al-Fārābī would argue that not every lawgiver is a true lawgiver because the true lawgiver needs to be created by God. God must have vested him with the requisite capacities just like the master of any form of art.[34]

To be sure, the Islamic philosophers saw a link between the rationality of the nomos and the rationality of the sharia. Both deal with the human being as a *zoon politikon* and try to enable them to reach a state of bliss, indeed the highest state of life on this Earth. Indeed, both share human life as a common concern. Practical subsections of philosophy, ethics, economics, and politics regulate the life of the individual. Such a regulation constitutes both an end in itself and a functional role in the context of familial affairs and political society. Revealed religion addresses its commandments and prohibitions directly to the believers to encourage them to live a life of perfection. Both nomos and sharia presuppose honesty and correct opinions because only these traits can result in ethical behavior.[35] This apparatus overlaps with those ritual practices regulated by the nomos as a subcategory of social affairs.[36] The performance of ritual acts, at least when performed in public by several people, is a matter of politics. For the sake of social peace, these acts needed to be regulated by political law. Indeed, the intersections of nomos and sharia mainly pertain to questions of social order. They give the impression (not only in the works of medieval Islamic thinkers) of running parallel to or overlapping with each other in certain areas of social existence. These striking similarities, especially where social duties are concerned, may have compelled those philosophers to develop a philosophical interest in the political meaning of the sharia. Of course, they pursued this interest under the influence of Plato and Aristotle.

At this point, the similarities end and the differences begin to appear. Al-Fārābī views the nomoi as numerous and dependent on the circumstances of specific peoples in history. Each people has its own nomos that comes into being under favorable circumstances, ultimately perishing together with the respective society, either due to natural catastrophe or defeat in war.[37] The nomos, therefore, is a phenomenon marked by specific geopolitical or ethnic circumstances that regulate the ethical, cultural, and political life of a people. Its existence is tied to the existence of a particular people.[38] The sharia, by contrast, addresses all peoples irrespective of their ethnic or cultural allegiances. It is not the work of a human being but rather the result of divine interaction with human existence. Contrary to the nomos, it is independent of any ruling political power. However, once the sharia exists, it interacts with politics. When political power declines, the sharia can survive through its core mission. Moreover, the sharia can detach itself from the political regime in place when it is practiced under a regime professing a different faith or no faith at all. Politics is but one function of the sharia.[39]

Furthermore, nomos and sharia differ regarding the final ends of regulating the *zoon politikon*. The nomos aims at the well-being of the citizen by providing for justice in society. The establishment and maintenance of the social order is reached through statutory provisions, with the transgression of those provisions punished by the law.[40] The sharia, on the other hand, contains commandments and prohibitions that promise the believer a twofold form of happiness, namely well-being in this world along with eternal bliss. The attitude of the human being toward the sharia has consequences for the afterlife. Both the origin and the purpose of the sharia possess a transcendental dimension.

The nomos, as al-Fārābī viewed it, stems from reason and regulates all matters of social actions and political life, both for the individual and political society. Therefore, it is also concerned with ritual acts. Since social acts based in truth imply good dispositions, the nomos also demands this rectitude from every individual. Hence, when the nomos interferes with the spiritual sphere of human existence, it does so in order to create the ideal conditions for political action, thereby limiting itself to this purpose. The interest of the nomos in gods and their relationship with humanity, therefore, only serves practical ends. The nomos is not concerned with any purely spiritual relationship with God. This relationship may have an impact on the behavior of the individual in society, but it is not conditioned by it.[41]

The sharia constitutes something entirely different. According to the sharia, the relationship between man and God is the ultimate principle undergirding good deeds. It is the belief in God and prophecy that forms the basis of ritual acts. Faith may have an inner dimension, but it is unthinkable without the ritual acts prescribed by religious law, because humans are social creatures. It is in social acts that faith materializes. The purely spiritual dimension of the sharia is a feature that the nomos lacks. Whereas both agree about social practice, the belief in revelation is clearly a constitutive feature only of the sharia.

Al-Fārābī did not doubt revelation. As a philosopher, he tried to explain revelation by philosophical means, presenting it as a natural process. It is here that he makes use of Plato's characterization of the philosopher-king and of Aristotle's method of cognition. Al-Fārābī did not aim at diminishing the importance of the sharia. If this had been his goal, he would not have striven for the harmonization of religion and philosophy. The impression that his philosophical writings seem to deviate from theology can be attributed to his method of philosophizing. This method came into being only as a result of the Islamic reception of Greek philosophy in an Arabic-speaking context, and this reception was partly shaped by the attempt to distinguish philosophy from theology (*kalām*).[42]

A closer look at al-Fārābī's treatise reveals that he did not think of his work on Plato's *Laws* as a theoretical foundation of his philosophical approach to revealed law. On the contrary, he considered Plato's nomoi and the sharia as belonging to different realms. Neither al-Fārābī nor his successors equated monotheism with polytheism. While he ascribes philosophy priority over religion, he does so because philosophy is, in his view, the perfect theoretical and practical wisdom that can only be achieved by a few elite individuals. Religion, on the other hand, addresses the multitude and must be delineated from philosophy. Al-Fārābī did not consider Plato's *Laws* to be a religious book but rather an ethical one. Hence, we cannot but conclude that Leo Strauss misunderstood al-Fārābī.[43]

The Muslim philosophers were able to absorb new ideas originating beyond their own religious horizons. Their intellectual stance was an open one, but they always adhered to the unity of truth. They adopted ideas from ancient ethical texts on the life of the individual and their behavior in the sphere of both family and society. The philosophers did not fail to consider the historical circumstances of those writings. Indeed, the non-Islamic origins of these thoughts did not compromise their ethical validity since they were concerned with general human problems. As the Muslim medieval philosophers saw it, the ethical postulates of these Platonic dialogues did not differ from those of the sharia but rather confirmed them. To be sure, the stipulations of the sharia had a higher degree of assertiveness, but their validity was strengthened by virtue of their agreement with those philosophical teachings that predated revelation. As a result of this agreement, a certain degree of identification with the origins of those laws also took place. Plato, for example, received the attribute "divine" (*Aflāṭūn al-ilāhī*); the ancient philosophers and sages were called "apostles" or "divinely inspired."[44] A precondition for this identification was the assumption that only one first cause exists for everything. This view can be held by both religion and philosophy and was considered a precondition for the assimilation of both divine and human wisdom. From the perspective of a believer, God is both wise and the source of wisdom. He is also the creator of human reason. The benefits of reason, therefore, are a product of what God has created. Only the belief in God's unity enables the Islamic philosophers to recognize one consistent form of reason for all human wisdom.

"Critique of Religion"

Having investigated Spinoza's critique of religion, Strauss concluded that modern rationalism was not capable of solving the problem of revelation. As Strauss saw it, the Jewish and Muslim philosophers of the Middle Ages differed from modern philosophers in that they did not consider revelation primarily in terms of conveying articles of faith. Rather, they regarded revelation as a form of law targeting social order (sharia) and regulating not only adherents' actions but their thoughts and opinions as well. Thus, religion is posited in terms of a primordial facticity that completely transcends culture.[45] It seems as though Strauss shares this view, yet he transcends it when he identifies nomos and sharia with each other. His critique of religion is accompanied by two simultaneous steps: The first consists in questioning the importance of faith for such a conception of religion. The second foregrounds the connection of religion and politics. Avicenna's literal connection of revealed law with the nomos directs Strauss to build his own critique of religion. However, he develops the critique further by basing it upon al-Fārābī's conception of religion.

Strauss's View on al-Fārābī and Religion

According to Strauss, al-Fārābī is the first philosopher who formulated a critique of religion with a political interpretation of revealed religious law. Both the Muslim successors of al-Fārābī and Maimonides had considered religious law to constitute a substitute for classical political philosophy.[46] Referring to al-Fārābī's political teaching, Maimonides sees the Torah as being "foremost a political fact, a political order, a law; it is the ideal law, the perfect *nomos*, of which all other laws are more or less imitations."[47]

The necessity of the law stems from the human need for social life and the attempt to defend against the obstacles hampering the possibility of such a life. Thus, religious law achieves a primarily political function for Strauss. In his opinion, it was the task of the lawgiver to harmonize the different dispositions and affections among the people by providing one single consistent law. Such a law had to appear divine and could only be promulgated by a prophet who combines the features of the philosopher and the statesperson.[48]

The priority of the divine law over the human law, as Strauss viewed it, resulted from the fact that religious law contained conceptions of God and the angels tailored to the cognitive capacities of the multitudes. The prophets can use metaphors and exoteric speech in order to convey to the people truths whose esoteric meaning only philosophers can grasp. The principles are conveyed by the medium of analogous physical and sense-based illustrations. Strauss continues that

> the external meaning of the prophets' speeches is sometimes more than a means to indicate the esoteric truths; there are cases in which the exterior meaning has a value in itself: it may be that the prophet pronounces some speeches which communicate by their esoteric sense a speculative truth, while their

> exoteric sense indicates "a wisdom useful for many things, and among others for the improvement [amelioration] of the state of human societies." There is then among corporeal things, worthy of being employed for the representation of the principles, a class which particularly lends itself to this use, namely, political matters.[49]

The statements of the prophet not only exist as a means through which exoteric truths can be conveyed but are also conducive to beneficial social behavior. Al-Fārābī argued that political matters were specifically suitable for allowing the people understand esoteric truths.[50] Strauss adds to this that those comparisons cannot be taken literally. While they contain an esoteric truth, their exoteric content is also of great value to political life: "The divine law attaches so great a value to the representations, useful for political life, of divine matter that it invites men to believe not only in the most important speculative truths, but also in certain things which are 'necessary for the good order of political conditions.'"[51] Inasmuch as religious law is of political importance, it becomes a subject matter of politics. Strauss declares politics the "crown and seal of metaphysics."[52] By the same token, Strauss ascribes to the Muslim philosophers as well as to Maimonides a "dogmatic policy" that uses religious teachings for political ends. The doctrine of providence is particularly amenable for this purpose.[53] Strauss argues that "a city governed by laws and not by philosophers cannot be perfect unless the belief exists that God rewards or punishes men according to their actions."[54] The meaning of the doctrine of providence for politics relates to the belief that God takes care of people's affairs and that he sanctions their views and actions. This belief causes men to be politically obedient and to abide by the laws.[55]

The philosophical interest in religion corresponds to the importance of religion for the political order. In "Farabi's *Plato*," a study that reflects Strauss's own interpretation of how al-Fārābī understood Plato's philosophy, Strauss illustrates al-Fārābī's attitude toward religion. He does so within the framework of his analysis regarding the relationship between philosophy and religion. He imputes to al-Fārābī the desire to hide behind the role of the commentator in order to deny important religious doctrines. In Strauss's opinion, al-Fārābī annulled the difference between the happiness of this life and the highest forms of happiness in the life hereafter, admitting only to the happiness that philosophy can yield. Any comments pointing to opposite views were labeled hallucinations and untrue accounts by old women. Therefore, Strauss concludes that al-Fārābī tacitly rejects Plato's doctrine of the immortality of the soul, even going so far as to avoid the notion of the "soul" in his summary of both the *Phaidon* and the *Politeia*.[56]

According to Strauss, al-Fārābī, in his treatise *The Enumeration of Sciences*, places the religious sciences of *fiqh* and *kalām* within the realm of political science. Strauss treats this linkage as an esoteric hint and concludes that philosophers first looked at revealed religion as a political fact. Al-Fārābī wanted to pave the way for a potentially potent revealed theology that differed from metaphysics. Nevertheless, in the course of his interpretation of Plato, al-Fārābī clearly stated that speculation on religion, religious inquiry into beings, and religious syllogism "do not supply the science of the beings, of which man's highest perfection consists, whereas philosophy does supply it." To Strauss, al-Fārābī even went so far as to put religious knowledge in general and religious speculation in particular on the lowest rung of cognitive practices. Al-Fārābī considered religious knowledge to be dependent on a certain human community just like a language.[57] Al-Fārābī articulated thereby carefully a rejection of religion's claim to be universal and capable of providing bliss. Furthermore, he ascribed to Plato a critique which Plato could never have possibly uttered, namely the critique of the value of Islamic *fiqh*.[58]

According to Strauss, the way in which al-Fārābī dealt with the religious doctrines of his own society perfectly illustrates the philosopher's attitude toward religion. Al-Fārābī had stripped religion of its promise of human happiness and replaced it with politics. For Strauss, the rejection of religious dogma by philosophers reflects an irreconcilable conflict between philosophy and society, a conflict that poses a danger to both sides. Al-Fārābī avoids this conflict by stipulating that any future philosopher must at least provisionally agree with the views of the religious community they grew up in.[59] It is out of "philanthropy" that the philosopher does not destroy the widely accepted religious views of their own society, as these views are politically useful.[60]

Religion and Social Order

In *Philosophy and Law*, Strauss argues that there is a necessary "connection between politics and theology" that he had "discovered by coincidence." This connection demonstrated that "metaphysical problems were not to be left aside" but rather examined in light of the ancient, Platonic notion of the divine law.[61] The discovery of the idea of the divine law enabled Strauss to develop a nomistic conception of religion. According to this conception, religion functions mainly as a factor of social order and can thus be made acceptable for the modern discourse of political philosophy. At the same time, the value and place of belief within the framework of religion changes: "We do not deny, as need hardly be mentioned, that the problem of 'faith and knowledge' is the central problem of medieval rationalism. Our quarrel with Guttmann is only about the meaning of 'faith' here, and it seems to us more precise to say 'law and philosophy' rather than 'faith and knowledge.' For the 'believed truths,' which are identical with philosophical truths for the rationalists, are, qua 'truths of faith,' part of a comprehensive whole, viz. the law."[62] The questions of faith, which Strauss counts among the core problems of metaphysics, gain new meaning in this newly developed conception of religion that is so closely connected with politics. In this conception, faith refers to theoretical objects that constitute only a part of the revealed law. For revealed law mainly consists of rules and regulations aimed at ordering the ethical and social life of the individual.[63]

If revealed religion is regarded as a law, faith cannot exist as a decisive criterion for law's evaluation any more, given that theoretical views rooted in faith are only a part of this law. The value of faith can be elucidated only by the socially and politically relevant functions of revealed religion. With this interpretive move, Strauss intends to solve a crucial dimension of the crisis of modernity: Enlightenment philosophy's limitation of religion to an individual's conscience had contributed to the crisis of modernity. However, Strauss demonstrates the necessity of religion for society by engaging with the medieval Islamic philosophers. He even assumes that religion is rooted in the political nature of the individual. Through the radical politicization of these notions, Strauss believes that he can "rescue" religion. Unlike Marx or Nietzsche, Strauss does not reject religion but turns it into a necessary condition for social harmony even if revelation is not considered true. For Strauss, the appropriate philosophical perception of revelation is its political interpretation. Revelation as law becomes tangible when it is rendered both religious and political.[64]

Strauss held that a philosophy based on faith no longer constituted philosophy because philosophy is ultimately meant to continuously pose questions and search for satisfying answers.[65] Yet society requires stability. It must cope with existing circumstances if it does not wish to risk its very existence. In this regard, religion provides important stabilizing elements that are recognized by philosophy. Religion obliges philosophy to accept it as an important foundation of the continuity of society. According to Strauss, the philosopher does not have the capacity to instantiate divine law even though, as philosopher, they recognize its rational principles. What the philosopher lacks is the ability to individually intuit the various designations that prove constitutive for law. Therefore, they remain dependent on religious law. For the philosopher is a political being themselves.[66] As a result, an unavoidable dilemma arises, with philosophy continually fluctuating between the rejection of belief and the acceptance of religion. In the solution proposed by Strauss, belief is replaced by law, thereby granting religion a role in the philosopher's scheme for maintaining social order. Strauss's path towards this solution was provided by Avicenna's hint regarding the *Nomoi*. For Strauss, socially useful religious law represents a healthy relationship between the archnemeses religion and philosophy, one that does not argue for their synthesis. "Humanly speaking," the nomos is the common ground upon which philosophy and religion can meet. Where the specific prescriptions of human society are concerned, Strauss did not see any differences between the contents of Plato's laws and religious law.[67]

What is the origin of the necessity of religion for the social order? Strauss writes, "Man cannot live without light, guidance, knowledge; only through knowledge of the good can he find the good that he needs. The fundamental question, therefore, is whether men can acquire that knowledge of the good without which they cannot guide their lives individually or collectively by the unaided efforts of their natural powers, or whether they are dependent for that knowledge on Divine Revelation. No alternative is more fundamental than this: human guidance or divine guidance."[68] Strauss conceives of man as maturing into adulthood shaped by opinions and convictions based chiefly on conceptions of God, nature, morals, and humanity, and hence by religious ideas.[69] The fact that Strauss admits to human and divine leadership as alternatives indicates that there are human beings who have the capacity to guide others and themselves: the philosophers. The philosophers do not require any divine direction and are therefore independent of religion. However, other people are in need of guidance and they can be divided into two groups: those who are guided by religion and those who are guided by philosophy. The radical difference between these two classes of individuals lies in the difference between autonomy and paternalism. The philosophers are the only individuals who are truly autonomous, and this is why they are capable of guiding other people. Indeed, philosophers constitute a real challenge for religion, which Strauss believes relies on tradition and is considered by the masses as "ancestral."[70] Whereas most people are dependent on religion, the philosopher alone is autonomous. Human existence is ruled by two authorities that are diametrically opposed.[71]

While Strauss takes the autonomy of philosophy for granted, his analysis of human law had revealed to him that it was not free of contradictions. Human law understands itself as essentially good and necessary for the well-being of any political being. At the same time, it seems to correspond to the general opinion of the majority of the citizens and, therefore, cannot be altogether good and noble. At times, human law can even appear to be foolish and unfair. This leaves doubts whether "the makers of laws are as a rule wiser than 'you and I'; why, then, should 'you and I' submit to their decision?" It seems that the degree of human wisdom inherent in law giving could be subject to doubt: it can be called into question and nullified by the same power that had created it.[72] The political can circumvent this dilemma by declaring the laws "sacred" and thereby lending them a higher degree of dignity. They can then transcend the bounds of political life.[73]

By the same token, Strauss held that the establishment of justice constituted the ultimate aim of religion. The final part of Plato's *Laws* was dedicated to the central topic of the *Republic*.[74] It was only through divine law that justice was possible.[75] Premodern atheists had already recognized the necessity of religion for society: "no premodern atheist doubted that social life required belief in, and worship of, God or gods."[76] If religion is important to philosophers, it is not because of truth but because of its utility for social life inasmuch as religion precludes civil strife which may result from human greed.[77] Nonetheless, Strauss deems the diversity of the laws designated as "divine" to be problematic. Some of the doctrines underpinning those different laws are irreconcilable, with one law capable of judging something as bad while another one deems it good. Consequently, the question of the right law becomes an essential question of philosophy.[78] Strauss writes,

> In order to arrive at a clear distinction between the natural and the conventional, we have to go back to the period in the life of the individual, or of the race which antedates convention. We have to go back to the origins. With a view to the connection between right and civil society, the question of the origin of right transforms itself into the question of the origin of civil society or society in general. This question leads to the question of the origin of the human race.[79]

Searching for an answer to the question of the nature of religion, philosophy finds itself faced with an original question related to the establishment of human society. On this fundamental level, all religions seem to be equal and their differences secondary. Religion essentially seems to be the original condition for the establishment and the continuity of humanity. With this view, Strauss clearly treads in the footsteps of al-Fārābī, Avicenna, and Averroes. They all tied the necessity of religion to the essential human need for social life.[80]

What Strauss creates is a nomistic notion of religion that conceives of all religions as "codes." All those codes have their origin in the human instinct for survival.[81] Such a conception of religion clearly displays political features and Strauss deems this essential link between religion and politics as the "theological-political problem" par excellence. First, this notion points to an irreconcilable conflict between reason and revelation that Strauss observed in Spinoza's works. This conflict plays out not only in the realm of religion but also in the realm of politics. Strauss agrees with Spinoza when he argues that revelation as a purely religious experience cannot be appropriately understood because religion plays an important political role in the state. Nonetheless, it seems that the Muslim philosophers of the Middle Ages strengthened Strauss's perception of the "theological-political problem" while at the same time enriching it with the dimension of religious law. To be sure, this does not mean that Strauss declared the conflict between reason and revelation resolved. He continued to consider this conflict in terms of the psychic drama of Western man, thereby lying at the core of the crisis of modernity. Strauss argued that this psychic drama stemmed from the radical and insolvable opposition between Jerusalem and Athens.[82]

Regarding Strauss's idea of the divine but politically useful law, Strauss transcends the level of mere description to constructively solve the crisis.[83] Spinoza rejects religion by claiming that religion constitutes an instrument by which those in possession of political power can rule the passion-driven multitude.[84] Strauss agrees with Spinoza's description of the problem but not with his solution. Based on his interpretation of the Muslim philosophers, and al-Fārābī in particular, he concluded that society needs religion and that revelation must not be denied because it contains necessary and politically useful, although untrue, doctrines.[85] Contrary to Spinoza, Strauss does not mind religious belief. Instead, he views it as an important foundation of the political order inasmuch as men are not easily guided by reason. It is precisely because religion is political (*siyāsī*) that it is important.[86]

Strauss's idea of the "divine" introduces a new philosophical perspective on the role of religion in society or the state.[87] He was aware that the question of whether revelation is real or not does not belong to the realm of reason. Thus, Strauss refrains from asking this question. Obviously, he is convinced that the issue of revelation must be treated not ontologically but rather socially and existentially. Therefore, he takes an assumed reality of revelation as a starting point and asks to what extent it can be important, that is, useful for human existence.[88] At least since Aristotle, it is philosophically clear that human existence can be considered secure in a politically organized society. Therefore, the question of the meaning of revelation becomes a question of political philosophy. Strauss makes the question of God's existence its central theme, which he calls the theological-political problem.[89]

Strauss highlights three different alternatives of how the philosopher can face the religion of their society. First, the philosopher can be indifferent to any cult or affiliation with a religious, ethnic, or political group. Second, they can create their own religion in order to better regulate their own behavior at home or in society. Third, the philosopher can adopt the rational laws of the philosophers as a religion and thus aim at the purity of the soul. In any case, Strauss is convinced that the "religious indifference of the philosopher knows no limits."[90] Stanley Rosen reports a quite similar quotation attributed to Strauss: "Philosophers are paid not to believe!"[91] It is the task of the philosophers to investigate the eternal order and the eternal cause of all beings. Inspired by the eros of the search for truth, they dare to render God into a question. To them, divinity depends on veneration, which, in turn, depends on a degree of knowledge.[92] To Strauss, the rule of law becomes necessary only in the absence of a philosopher-king. Where philosophy rules, there is no need for laws. However, the rule of philosophers, "the best regime," is only possible under ideal circumstances and therefore must remain utopian. The laws, among them the religious law, are all, to some extent, incomplete regimes. They also work under much less fortunate circumstances and are therefore legitimate, or even necessary, because religion seems irrefutable under the normal circumstances of human existence.[93]

For Strauss, Socrates constitutes the archetype of the philosopher. He abides by the law and does not deprive it of its validity in society because he is aware of that the destruction of the political order and society would result from the destruction of the law.[94] For "divine approval and divine assistance seem to be indispensable for salutary political action."[95] Whenever laws are called into question, he withdraws from the discussion because he is banned from any political activity. This, in turn, also allows him to avoid engaging in dialogue while also holding back his own opinions. To him, the question of divine law is subordinate to the ethos of philosophical inquiry. Even the lawgiver is Athens's enemy.[96]

The Religious Justification of Philosophy

Strauss held that the understanding of the religion of revelation as law obliged the Muslim and Jewish rationalists of the Middle Ages, who believed in revelation, to defend philosophy before the bar of religion. This concern seems to have been of such essential importance that they felt compelled to operate as jurists and philosophers simultaneously.[97] The conception of religion as a perfect form of law revealed by God and sufficient for guiding human life must necessarily have put the legitimacy of philosophy into question. Any act of philosophizing would be required to take this preconceived and prephilosophical notion of revelation as a starting point. Philosophy was subordinate to the power of revelation, while revelation's justification was deduced from the necessity of finding a religious interest in philosophy.[98]

Religion's Need for Philosophy

For Strauss, it is Averroes who showcases the paradigmatic religious justification of philosophy in the Middle Ages. Unlike other medieval Islamic and Jewish philosophers, he dedicated a separate treatise to this topic, thus presenting it in a coherent way.[99] However, it seems that systematic philosophy, the framework in which Averroes treated this subject, was not sufficient for demonstrating the necessity of philosophy. Jewish philosophers later examined by Strauss, such as Maimonides and Gersonides, followed in the footsteps of Averroes.[100] In this section, I will demonstrate how Strauss reconstructed Averroes's justification of philosophy in religious law and to what extent this reading of Averroes influenced Strauss's subsequent thought.

To begin with, Strauss describes Averroes's treatise as "speculating according to the law" (*gesetzliche Spekulation*)[101] and states that it seeks to clarify the link between philosophy and religious law. Strauss goes on to explain that it is this very same religious law that Averroes uses as a source for the different qualifications required for engaging in philosophy. He asks whether this understanding of the law allows, prohibits, or demands philosophizing. This categorization applies to any human act. For Strauss, it indicates that Averroes does not give philosophy priority over any other human action but rather subordinates it to the law. Philosophy, as Averroes understood it, constitutes "the consideration of the beings in their relation to their maker." Therefore, the Qur'ān would not only allow philosophy but demand it. Consequently, it would also be a duty to study Aristotelian logic, which encompasses physics and metaphysics. Logic serves as an instrument for the contemplation of all existing things philosophically and for deriving reasonable conclusions regarding their creator. Like any other instrument, the sciences should be employed purely with an eye to their utility, without taking offense at their pagan pedigree.[102]

By turning philosophy into a tool for the contemplation of creation, Averroes guides humankind to its creator and to the highest level of bliss. Averroes can equate the purpose of philosophy with the purpose of the law, thereby elevating philosophizing above all other human actions. It is not only the teleological identity of philosophy and religious law that is justified from the viewpoint of authoritative law, thereby precluding conflict between the two. Inasmuch as it is declared to be a Qur'ānic duty, philosophy is justified.[103]

In order to justify philosophizing, Averroes relies on the commandment of the religious law that a Qur'ānic saying must be interpreted in cases where it conflicts with philosophical insight. For the Qur'ān contains hidden meanings that only "people capable of demonstration" (*ahl al-burhān*) can recognize. Other people do not possess access to those meanings because they lack either natural ability, habits of mind, or capability to instruct themselves. God shows understanding for this class of people and conveys to them those hidden meanings in the form of pictures and parables, thereby compelling them to believe. These parables also enable nonphilosophers to believe in God on the basis of rhetorical and dialectic demonstrations: "This is the reason why religious law is divided into an outer (*ẓāhir*) and an inner (*bāṭin*) dimension. The outer dimension consists of those parables that were made for the expression of those meanings. The inner dimension contains those meanings that are only revealed to the people of the demonstration."[104] It is due to this division of the scripture into outer and inner dimensions that the Qur'ān requires interpretation. Furthermore, it stipulates that only philosophers who have direct access to the truth through demonstrative science conduct this form of interpretation. Indeed, this very form of interpretation must remain "prohibited" to those who can only recognize the truth by means of rhetorical and dialectic arguments. The violation of this commandment constitutes a lack of faith at best, or heresy at worst. Strauss sums up the commandments as mentioned by Averroes as follows: "Thus, those suited to philosophizing are commanded: (1) to philosophize; (2) in case of a conflict between philosophy and the literal sense of the law, to interpret the law; and (3) to keep the interpretation secret from all the unqualified."[105]

Strauss asks the question of whether "philosophy as authorized by the law is *free*" to teach "everything that it establishes for itself" "without concern for the law."[106] For Averroes, the freedom of philosophy seems to prove itself above all in the interpretation of Qur'ānic passages seemingly contradictory to philosophical doctrine. Therefore, Strauss modifies the essential question of the freedom of philosophy with respect to the law and turns it into a hermeneutical question. He asks whether, according to Averroes, religious law allows the philosophers to interpret scripture without any restrictions. Averroes appears to provide five conditions for the interpretation of scripture. These five conditions, or rather Strauss's reconstruction of those conditions, will now be discussed in terms of their broader implications:

> The first interpretive restriction is of a linguistic nature. It stipulates that an interpretation may not go against the usage of the Arabic language. It must be in harmony with the rules of interpretation in Arabic.[107] Strauss concludes that this condition does not restrict the freedom of philosophizing. Any statement about the law that seems to contradict reason and that cannot be interpreted by the standard rules of interpretation should be considered "rhetorical" and therefore only valid for the multitudes. However, Strauss goes beyond Averroes's statements to claim that the "interpretation of the law as a whole makes

the 'interpretation' of the single passages superfluous in certain circumstances."[108]

Second, one must complement any interpretation of a Qur'ānic passage with a second passage whose meaning confirms the interpretation of the first passage.[109] Again, Strauss does not consider this a real restriction because there is hardly a philosophical doctrine that cannot be confirmed or at least underpinned by a passage of scripture.

The third restriction concerns those passages "which, according to the true consensus of the Muslims, are to be understood literally." Averroes had already highlighted the weakness of this restriction: A true consensus on speculative questions is impossible because the inner meaning of texts had not been made public at the time of Islam's emergence. Therefore, these passages in question could not be subject to interpretative consensus. Divergent conceptions of the relayed remarks must be ensured.[110]

The fourth restriction concerns the interpretation of doctrines "which are known by all three modes of persuasion — by demonstrative, dialectical, and rhetorical argumentation."[111] Strauss correctly notes that this is "not even formally a restriction of the right of interpretation," since a passage should and can only be interpreted if it contradicts the result of the demonstration.

Interpretation should not be allowed when it is aimed at denying "the existence of things" that "belong to the principles of law." Only the "quality of these things" pertaining to their transmission through revelation should be made available for interpretation.[112] Strauss also weakens this limitation. Philosophers do not have any reason to engage in the interpretation of statements pertaining to the principles of the law because, according to Averroes, these principles "are also and necessarily accessible to philosophic cognition."[113]

What conclusion does Strauss draw from these conditions for textual interpretation? He remarks that these conditions laid out by Averroes lose their force upon more in-depth examination. Nevertheless, three points can be ascertained that highlight the complexity of the task.

On the one hand, philosophers are free to interpret the wording of the law according to their convictions. However, they cannot cross certain boundaries and spread sinful ideas leading to the denial of God, the prophets, or eternal punishment.

Philosophy does not have the right to set for itself the ultimate standards by which to judge whether an interpretation is in error. The decision about it follows certain qualifications that come from the sacred text itself.

It follows that Averroes ultimately grants primacy not to

> philosophy but to religion, for philosophy presumably does not have the power to accept or reject the principles of faith by means of rational deliberation.

Therefore, Strauss concludes that philosophy, according to Averroes, stands in an ambivalent and not altogether stable situation vis-à-vis law. Averroes recognizes "*those truths prescribed by law*," which do not have the character of "supernatural truths" but whose "recognition or denial [. . .] certainly has the character and consequences of the recognition or denial of a dogma."[114] Strauss sees a deficiency in Averroes's teaching because philosophical freedom is made intimately bound to the law: "Philosophy can thank the law for its authority and freedom; *its freedom is based on its bonds*. Philosophy is not sovereign. The beginning of philosophy is not the absolute beginning, for the law retains primacy. The literal meaning of the law can only be divulged when its opposite is proved; it is not the case that a standpoint outside the law is taken from the outset, from which one can advance along the path of reasonable consideration to submission to the law."[115] Strauss further notes that Averroes bows to the primacy of religious law over philosophy. He was "not the Voltaire of the twelfth century."[116] Against the background of an analysis of Maimonides's and Gersonides's justifications of philosophy from the Torah, Strauss demonstrates once again the radical aspects of Averroes's law-based justification of philosophical activity. He emphasizes the significant agreement between Maimonides and Averroes concerning the agreement of philosophy and law conceived in terms of their respective ultimate purposes. He also insists on their common imperative that individuals in possession of knowledge interpret the figurative passages of a sacred text.[117] From the vantage point of Maimonides, Strauss engages with Averroes in order to emphasize that Maimonides viewed an acknowledgment of the insufficiency of human understanding as a necessary precondition for answering questions regarding creation or the eternity of the world. Averroes, he contends, assumed a more radically rationalistic position in maintaining that this question was "dialectical" and "dogmatically irrelevant," given that he "fundamentally recognized the sufficiency of human understanding."[118] Strauss maintained that Averroes was a more radical rationalist than Maimonides in that he viewed those sections within the text corresponding to the overwhelming theoretical power of revelation vis-à-vis rationality as sections of text that simply "require interpretation."[119]

The question of religious justification for the interpretation of certain sections within sacred texts is of great interest to Averroes given the more fundamental question of the freedom of philosophy in a society dominated by religion. It is not the act of interpretation in and of itself but rather the act of philosophizing as a whole that is the object of Averroes's justificatory efforts. Inasmuch as revelatory religion remains a central theme for Averroes and his compatriots, the interpreter of religious texts is posited ultimately as a representative of philosophy. Indeed, this perspective would justify the study of logic. The conception of how ultimately to justify philosophy from the scared text and to demonstrate that the revealed book does not prohibit philosophy is more important than the question of potential addressees of this mode of interpretation. It is necessary to empower reason to bring harmony to seemingly contradictory statements in the text. Reason presents itself as an appropriate basis for religious justification of philosophy, as God is not "unreasonable" for believers.

The Benefit of Hermeneutics

Strauss, through his excellent analysis of Averroes's justification of philosophy before the religious law, proves that the medieval philosophers unequivocally recognized the bounded nature of their philosophizing with revelation. Nevertheless, it can be observed that Averroes's conception of philosophy is not unconditionally subordinate to religion. Dogmas can be explained through demonstration and difficult sections in sacred texts can be clarified. Statements within scared texts must be compatible with the postulates of reason. If not, their inherent reasonability needs to be drawn out by the interpreter. In this way, reason seems to have the upper hand over revelation. However, revelation strikes a balance by claiming to legitimize the intervention of reason in its works. The action of reason is justified by the fact that it does not lead away from God but contributes to the glorification of the Creator through the knowledge of Creation and that reason, created by God, does nothing more through its interpretive activity than to bring to light the rational meaning of the revealed scriptures. This meaning is initially revealed only to the eye of the knower, who makes it visible to other members of the religious community.[120]

In contradistinction to modern philosophy, medieval philosophy not only wished to recognize the authority of revelation as a self-explanatory precondition for philosophy; instead, it also sought a philosophic justification for this recognition.[121] Whether Averroes recognized the primacy of law outside this framework must remain an open question. The Averroistic representation of the interpretative relationship with the Qur'ān points toward a suspenseful and often tense relationship between philosophy and religion in the medieval period. Averroes's limitations on allegorical interpretations of Qur'ānic passages could potentially be posited as impotent or merely ostensible in nature, thereby allowing philosophers a free hand in the interpretation of the sacred text. Nevertheless,

Averroes recognizes the integral differences between philosophy and religion. Philosophy can be brought to bear on religion, yet it cannot take a fully skeptical position. In turn, Averroes does not emerge as a fully liberated philosopher, for he must operate from within the bounds provided by religion. One cannot speak of absolute freedom, as the freedom of philosophy derives from its being bound to the law. This contradicts the intentions of a philosopher who wishes to enjoy the right to philosophize without limitations. Later, Strauss would seek to dissolve this tension through his division of philosophical writing into the esoteric and the exoteric, linking the trepidations of certain philosophers regarding certain statements to their sense of caution.

Averroes provided philosophers with the right to interpret statements within sacred text that often seemed to contradict philosophically held convictions. Yet he predicated this effort on a recognition of both philosophy and religion as separate entities containing different parameters. The freedom granted to philosophy to explore truth lies within the bounds of the religious law. This defines the outer realm of truth, or, as Strauss would put it, the exoteric side of truth. However, the inner realm, the esoteric, remains an area of absolute freedom for those philosophers possessing deep knowledge. They may then employ the appropriate and necessary tools for recognizing the true core of revealed statements. Philosophies remain in their theory-bound fortress, which allows them to conduct free inquiry. Since they do not require any other pleasure, they may find the highest degree of happiness there. The boundaries provided by religion offer walls of protection, behind which they can freely philosophize without worrying about the meddling of ignorant people. These conditions, which may appear like handcuffs, are meant to protect philosophers and philosophy. At this point, the question arises as to whether the same Averroistic thought also decisively determines the philosophizing of Leo Strauss. For he understands philosophy as an interpretive instance that penetrates to the true meanings of every kind of text, and he exercises philosophical power in the interpretation of writings. He seems to have given the answer with his choice of interpretation as the vehicle of philosophizing.

Conclusion

The question whether Strauss was an atheist is highly debated. Rosen, among others, is convinced of this.[122] However, Colmo objects that Strauss is convinced of the importance of the existence of God and his relationship to man with regard to the question of the right way of life and therefore does not reject religion.[123] Orr posits the question in a Straussian manner. She asks whether Strauss was a "cautious nihilist" or more of a "reluctant believer."[124] She concludes her analysis with the claim that the most important teaching in Strauss's works pertained to the impossibility of any modern synthesis of philosophy and religion, as both are "powers to be reckoned with," which presents itself as a nonpious enterprise that can produce "pious intentions and pious results."[125] Shadia Drury claims that Strauss was conducting a secret revolt against God through his mode of philosophizing, citing Jacob Klein's statement that Strauss was an Orthodox Jew who later radically changed his religious orientation, "tying the question of god or gods to this political reasoning, without letting his own life be dependent on any divinity or on any religious rites."[126]

Strauss admitted his own atheism while grounding it paradoxically in the Bible.[127] He negates God but confirms the Bible. His denial of God did not mean the negation of religion. On the one hand, he rejects the understanding of religion as a private matter of the individual. At the same time, he rejects an understanding of religion that differentiates religion from society and leads to the formation of exclusive and exclusionary identities. He criticized religion that focuses too intently on external religious praxis or maintains too much pride in its own irrationality.[128] At the same time, he affirmed religion as a political reality that emerges out of the constant need for order and justice. Religion is also a permanent reaction to the inherently difficult situation of humankind. He arrived at this understanding because his philosophizing was centered on political affairs. In this context, he understood that a politically organized society needed the holy. From a position that recognized religion as a force of order, Strauss could reject forms of tyranny that used (or eventually would replace) religion.[129]

Strauss's philosophy developed on the path leading to Zeus's cave. For Strauss, the path is more important than the goal. The path is the nomos, the sharia, the direction and way of life. However, for the determination of the way, it is significant that its beginning is set in a hidden, divine realm. Yet one cannot know whether such a hidden divine realm really exists. The question of God's existence is irrelevant for Strauss because it cannot be answered one way or another by reason. From the failure of Enlightenment to rid itself of the question of God, Strauss learned not to even deal with the topic, which is at the core of faith. He believed philosophy existed in a state of continuous, radical questioning and therefore could not coexist with self-satisfied faith.

According to Strauss, the ascertainment of God's existence is not a human matter. "Deus est quem dei deum esse declarant." Nevertheless, divinity could be ascertained in terms of its utility for politics.[130] The divine would therefore be associated with everything that contributed to a good, socially viable way of life. Therefore, social faith in revelation is more important than whether revelation is true.[131] The existence of revelation cannot be a concern of reason. However, the effects of revelation are indispensable for the attainment of social peace. In this sense, Strauss is an Averroist.[132] In religion, he finds an instrument to overcome relativity and stabilize the political order.

Strauss could render religion politically applicable by conceiving it in terms of law. Therefore, he returns to the Muslim and Jewish philosophers of the Middle Ages who oriented their treatment of religion toward Plato's *Laws*. In their name, and relying mainly on al-Fārābī's authority, Strauss dissolves the difference between Plato's rational laws and the law of revelation. In doing so, he attempts to show that the medieval, politically oriented conception of religion is an extended version, in terms of the fact of revelation, of the philosophy contained in Plato's *Laws*. Strauss's designation of these philosophers as Platonists appears to stand or fall on his identification of sharia with nomos, and the prophet with the philosopher-king. From the perspective of the history of philosophy, as has been already mentioned, this position is difficult to maintain. Strauss himself does not bring any content-based justification for this claim. Instead, he refers to various moments in medieval thought in order to confirm his opinions without engaging in proper argumentation. The only argument that could potentially buttress his position is the explicit negation of revelation. Strauss would never go down that path due to reasons connected with his conception of political philosophy. His dilemma regarding religion centers on whether the interpretation of religion as law renders the rejection of revelation into a politically destructive interpretation imperiling the social order.

Strauss's interpretation of the philosophical conception of religion in the Middle Ages appears incoherent regarding at least one point. On the one hand, he emphasizes that Muslim and Jewish philosophers of every generation differentiate themselves from the philosophers of both antiquity and modernity because of their serious belief in revelation. On the other hand, he claims that these philosophers equated the Greek nomos with the sharia, thereby locating the philosophical foundation for their understanding of the sharia within the nomos. Yet accepting this postulate would mean nothing less than the denial of revelation's reality for these philosophers. Since Strauss himself was committed to a diametrically opposite stance, we may accuse him of either self-contradiction or the instrumentalization of medieval philosophy for his own atheism.

The concept of divine law enabled Strauss to push the two competitors, philosophy and religion, onto the same playing field. Their irreconcilable coexistence in the reality of human life was transformed into a notion of political compatibility. With the concept of divine law, political philosophy could unite revealed precepts with the decisive capacities of reason in securing a moral way of life. Strauss's atheism appears to be socially cognizant in that it relegates the question of God to a question of political philosophy, thereby positing the religion of revelation as an ordering principle of society. Löwith's reproach that Strauss himself kept alive "the tradition of philosophizing" under the religious law — that is, "of revelation" — seems to be correct.[133] However, if one takes into account that Strauss essentially understands religious law as a political instrument, his philosophizing in the garb of political interest appears to be emancipated from the pressure of religion, even bending it under the power of the political. For Strauss, the power of God in human, that is, social existence is the power of a metaphor.

The core of Leo Strauss's political-theological problem is contained in the question of how God's law could be rendered useful for political purposes. Nonetheless, he needed to fight on two fronts in this regard: against a liberalism that would eagerly jettison religion from the public sphere to the private sphere, and against forms of religious orthodoxy that would not tolerate Strauss's instrumentalized, metaphorical conception of religion. Against both, he forges the weapon of a political philosophy that rests on a theological foundation, albeit a suppressed one, for the dialectic of atheism and revelation remains open in his work.

CHAPTER SIX

Leo Strauss, al-Fārābī, and the Primacy of Political Philosophy

Introduction

Leo Strauss traces the crisis of modernity back to the crisis of political philosophy, which, in his view, has been mired in a process of decline and decay. This is evident because its methods, function, utility, and even its very "possibility" have been called into question. Its original academic domain has been spliced up into newly created sciences.[1] Strauss blames the lack of interest in political philosophy on the rise of positivism and historicism, viewing his own engagement with political philosophy in terms of confronting these new academic developments.[2] His response to this self-diagnosed crisis is focused on rehabilitating a classical, Platonic-Aristotelian philosophy and applying it to modern philosophical discourse. It must be said that he is not interested in history, per se, but rather a better understanding of modern political and philosophical problems.[3]

The point of departure for Strauss's mode of political philosophizing is the assumption that philosophy and society do not stand in a harmonious relationship with one another (as the modern social sciences would have one believe). Rather, society is inclined to tyrannize philosophy. Both stand in an antagonistic relationship with one another. Indeed, this type of relationship emerges from the diametrically opposite compositions of these two entities. While philosophy is rooted in radical, skeptical questioning, society is characterized by custom and tradition. Despite its precarious position in society, philosophy remains dependent upon it. From this basic proposition, Strauss develops the notion of the necessity of political philosophy from a paradoxical state of affairs, in which philosophy is inscribed in, engages with, and challenges society "philosophically."

Therefore, the core attribute of "the political" attains a special meaning. It is both an object and, ultimately, a mode of philosophizing. Political philosophy thereby attains new elements that elevate it above other philosophical disciplines.[4]

In al-Fārābī, Strauss discovered the chief protagonist and founder of a new epoch in philosophy. He renewed philosophy after a period of crisis through a newly propagated reception of classical philosophy that allowed his philosophical teachings to flow within new political boundaries. Through examining al-Fārābī's oeuvre, Strauss wished to delineate the difference and relationship between theoretical and political philosophy. With his interpretation of Platonic philosophy, Strauss wished to markedly illustrate the exoteric representation of philosophy. With al-Fārābī, and especially his interpretation of Platonic philosophy, Strauss placed himself against the telos of the philosophical tradition and elevated political philosophy to philosophia prima. This mode of philosophy points to a notion of "the political" contained within the Arabic tradition of *siyāsa* (politics).

In the following, I will illustrate Strauss's reception of al-Fārābī's philosophy. Thereafter, I will proceed to depict how Strauss's concept of political philosophy emerges. The Arabic concept of *siyāsa* will then be analyzed. Building upon this explication, I will explore the problem of "truth" and its concealment. I will conclude with a final critical assessment of Strauss's enterprise.

Al-Fārābī's Political Philosophy According to Strauss

In his restoration and consolidation of the classical philosophical tradition in light of the crisis of modern philosophy, Strauss takes his cue from al-Fārābī. Indeed, al-Fārābī is the one responsible for reviving philosophy in the Arabic-speaking world following centuries of obsolescence. According to Strauss, al-Fārābī was cognizant of the fact that political philosophy lay at the core of Plato's and Aristotle's philosophical efforts. From this observation, he was able to extract the identity of their esoteric teachings.[5] He depicts the totality of philosophy within a political framework. This allows the philosophers to both circumnavigate the authority of religious law and interact with it in a productive way.[6] The departure point for his conception of political philosophy is the social nature of human beings, conceiving human need in terms of the dependence on law giving. This conception allows humankind to achieve peace, moral perfection, and an understanding of the highest truth. Religious law and its chief disseminator, the prophet, lie at the center of his political philosophy. This approach emerged in a dominant form in the work of al-Fārābī's successors.[7] Al-Fārābī and those in his wake did not orient their thinking toward

Aristotle's *Politics* but rather primarily toward Plato's *Laws*. There they found religion to be the framework within which religious law could be reformulated in a philosophic fashion. According to Strauss, they apparently did not conceive of revelation in a traditional manner. Instead, they connected revelation with the demands emerging from a concept of reason.[8] Al-Fārābī may also have had two other motivations for conceiving his political philosophy in a Platonic manner, namely, to defend the sharia against skeptics and heretics, and to provide a philosophical vocabulary for the Shiite longing for the return of the Hidden Imam (whereby his philosophical attitude reflects something akin to Plato on his way to Syracuse).[9] According to Strauss, al-Fārābī does not fully reject religion altogether but rather is interested in its existence for rational reasons.[10] The following investigation attempts to analyze Strauss's interpretation of al-Fārābī's political philosophy through such central themes as the relationship between politics and happiness, and between philosophy and society.

Al-Fārābī's Science of the Political and the Problem of Felicity

In his study of al-Fārābī's and Maimonides's political science, Strauss depicts al-Fārābī's description of the *ʿilm al-madanī* in his book *Iḥṣāʾ al-ʿulūm* (*Enumeration of the Sciences*).[11] Strauss's very brief summary makes it clear that political science's primary objects of inquiry are autonomous action and ways of life. This inquiry focuses on both the ends to which these constructs aspire and the sources of their derivation. Indeed, this differentiation between goals and modes reveals that human beings do indeed have a specific end goal, which is true happiness. Such a distinction also suggests that the praiseworthy goods and virtues are those that lead to happiness, and that their existence in humanity depends on perfected models of action and ways of life that are oriented on a hierarchical level to the life of states and nations. In fact, they exist at a level independent of these political constructs. In this way, Strauss goes beyond what al-Fārābī claimed. Al-Fārābī does not locate the notion of true felicity within the confines of the political or even in "this life" but rather relegates it to the afterlife. This point is obscured by Strauss. He places happiness at the center of political science, which determines how it is constituted and how it can be achieved individually. In his view, al-Fārābī clearly builds the doctrine of happiness into political science when he treats it in the *Ideal State* only after the doctrine of the first ruler and the "excellent city." Strauss sees this as an indication that happiness in al-Fārābī's conception is the result of the ideal political order.[12]

Though felicity, according to Strauss, is the subject of political philosophy, its attainment does not come from political praxis but rather through theoretical reflection. According to this interpretation of al-Fārābī, political philosophy is empowered to deal with matters of divinity. The composition of al-Fārābī's most consequential political works indicates that profoundly metaphysical questions are placed under the rubric of the political. According to al-Fārābī, philosophy and politics are both equally necessary for the attainment of happiness. In the essay "Farabi's *Plato*," Strauss distinguishes between two layers of al-Fārābī's argument that are on display in his interpretation of Platonic philosophy. The reader's first impression would indicate that al-Fārābī appears to understand Plato's philosophy as having a primarily political meaning connected to the attainment of felicity and the articulation of philosophy's relationship to that very happiness.[13] However, al-Fārābī's treatise on Plato's philosophy conveys two different meanings of philosophy, a narrow, theoretical one and a comprehensive one underlying al-Fārābī's expression "Plato's philosophy." The two meanings can be reconciled by including felicity in the argument. The theory-wielding philosopher must justify the very practice of philosophy in response to the question, Why does the practice of philosophy exist in the first place? This question is deeply connected with the "natural aim" of humankind, namely, the pursuit of felicity. Due to human beings' essentially political nature, this question can only be answered within a political framework. It posits the general question of how one should live one's life. Again, the pursuit of felicity functions in al-Fārābī's concept of philosophy as a transitional moment between a narrow, theoretically hued practice and a broader, politically charged endeavor. Strauss firmly believes that "philosophy proper on the one hand and the reflection on the human or political meaning of philosophy, or what is called moral and political philosophy, on the other, do not belong to the same level."[14] Al-Fārābī's explicit identification of philosophy with statecraft goes against Strauss's insistence on ranking theoretical philosophy above political philosophy. Al-Fārābī echoes Plato when he posits the *homo philosophus* and the *homo rex* as the same entities.[15] Nevertheless, Strauss believes that al-Fārābī's concepts of philosophy and statecraft exist parallel to one another. He believes that al-Fārābī's positing of them as identical is an act of "extravagant philanthropic observation" that functions as a "provisional solution," and he offers three reasons why the reader should not understand al-Fārābī literally on this issue.[16]

> If the pursuit of happiness was exclusively attributed to speculative philosophy, this would mean that most people do not possess the chance of actually becoming happy. A charitable perspective toward the distribution of happiness necessitates

> the engagement with statecraft in order to permit the pursuit of happiness for nonphilosophers.[17]
> The identification of philosophy with statecraft functions as a "pedagogical device" intended to guide the reader to the correct understanding that only theoretical philosophy is capable of enabling the pursuit of happiness.[18]
> Linking philosophy and politics in light of the pursuit of happiness is necessary, according to Strauss, because the philosopher necessarily lives in a political society. By virtue of shrewd, politically attuned writing, the philosopher navigates the "understandably difficult relationship" between himself and his "vulgar" fellow citizens.[19]

Strauss decisively ascribes to al-Fārābī the consequential and problematic position that the pursuit of happiness exists only "in consideration *scientarium speculativarum*" and deduces two consequences: al-Fārābī's denial of the immortality of the soul and the monopolistic placing of the pursuit of happiness into the hands of the philosophers. Both positions reflect a blatant abandonment of the teachings of religion. This pushes al-Fārābī to express his personal denial of the immortality of the soul by simply leaving the topic out of his exposition of Plato's philosophy, thus avoiding taking a stand on the issue.[20]

According to Strauss, al-Fārābī ties the pursuit of happiness and human perfection inseparably to philosophy. Their realization can occur only in the virtuous city, at whose core lies the philosophers. He posits this virtuous city as "the other city" of the philosophers, a city that stands between this world and the afterlife. It exists as a "virtuous city" only "in speech." Yet Strauss's al-Fārābī does not leave the matter at that. He points to law giving as the vehicle for the realization of the virtuous city. Strauss assumes that al-Fārābī posits the figure of the lawgiver as the prophet who founds a religion. This is supported by the fact that in al-Fārābī's conception the function of the prophet is not aimed at the highest human perfection and that the diversity of virtuous cities is recognized.[21]

Philosophy and Society

According to Strauss, al-Fārābī's political philosophy expresses the deep dichotomy between the philosopher and broader society. In his summary of Plato's *Republic*, al-Fārābī demonstrates that the philosopher who strives toward perfection faces two alternatives. Either they are killed or they must dispense with philosophy. Wishing to reconcile the pursuit of perfection through philosophy with the realities of social life, the philosopher seeks to create an alternative society in which they are not threatened with the death penalty and in which everything necessary for the pursuit of happiness is readily available.[22] In the context of the establishment of religion, the pursuit of an ideal city becomes a symbol of the pursuit of ideal conditions for a philosophical life in which justice reigns unhindered.[23] In Strauss's vision, al-Fārābī goes beyond Plato by emphasizing life in a political community as the central element of what it means to be human. He declares that those human beings who live outside a politically organized society should be treated like animals, with those deemed useful to be employed and those deemed dangerous to be killed.[24]

The gap separating philosophers from the rest of society presents a clear and present danger to them. Al-Fārābī, as the first interpreter of Plato to truly understand the consequences of combining Socrates's radical behavior and Thrasymachus's clever assimilatory political machinations, was able to avoid the conflict with the masses that plagued Socrates. While Socrates's abrasive mode of philosophizing was only appropriate for the political elite, Thrasymachus's style was more appropriate for the youth and layperson. In this fashion, Plato replaces the "revolutionary" search for the other city with a more "conservative" praxis acceptable across a broader cross-section of society. However, such praxis must still replace broadly accepted opinion with an approximation of truth.[25] In Strauss's eyes, the combination of Socrates's and Thrasymachus's approaches in "Plato's own politics" constitutes a correction of the Socratic method first observed by al-Fārābī. The purpose of this philosophical politics is to teach truth to the elite, who for him constitute the potential philosophers. This is achieved by systematically deconstructing commonly held opinions while simultaneously only bringing the masses an approximation of truth or a depiction of it that appeals to the imagination.[26]

Strauss believes that al-Fārābī denied direct political rule to the philosophers. Al-Fārābī's Plato comes to the conclusion that philosophers, in contradistinction to lawgivers, cannot expect to be worshiped as "divine."[27] He therefore replaces the public rule of Socrates's philosopher-king with the covert monarchal rule of philosophers who disseminate their teachings exoterically without blatantly contradicting popular opinion, thereby undermining such popular opinion's sway. The kingdom of the covert philosopher comprises the potential philosophers, who alone can recognize truth.[28] His exoteric philosophy is, according to Strauss, none other than political philosophy.

The Priority of Political Philosophy

According to Strauss, al-Fārābī distinguishes between pure philosophy and political philosophy. Philosophy is at its core theoretical and is imparted by reflecting on the proper pursuit of happiness. However, political philosophy is practically oriented and applies to the outer form of philosophizing. Such an outer form offers philosophers access to truth, while the masses of humanity must satisfy themselves with images of truth upon exposure to it. The belief that truth and the pursuit of happiness lie solely within the province of the philosopher provokes the hatred of the masses and presents a challenge to the promise of revealed religion to provide eternal felicity to those who adhere to religious obligations. The destruction of the expectation of felicitous reward for adhering to religious law is destructive both for society and for philosophy. If nonphilosophers were to discover that philosophers deem them foolish and incapable of understanding truth, they would attempt to exact revenge on the philosophers out of a sense of resentful hopelessness. They will have nothing to lose if the philosophers completely remove this hope. This situation would risk the disintegration of any social order that professes to ensure its citizens' pursuit of happiness. Philosophy would indeed become scandalous in such circumstances. Thus, political philosophy means the coping mechanisms deployed by philosophy to deal with this naturally occurring phenomenon. It is this very praxis that is its justification. Since it situates itself at the front lines of philosophy, political philosophy finds itself in a position of necessity and priority among the philosophical disciplines.

The primacy of political philosophy in al-Fārābī's oeuvre is, therefore, exoterically contingent and defines itself primarily in its relationship to the field of ethics.[29] It is not ethics but political philosophy that is capable of distinguishing between true and false felicities and the proper modes for pursuing true happiness. Beyond political philosophy, Strauss does not see moral virtue and its practice as the goal of life. This renders such moral virtues understandable only in reference to politics. Morality, or what Strauss calls "common sense morality," belongs therefore in the realm of commonly accepted opinion, the "*endoxa*" that comprise societal demands and not the demands of theoretical understanding.[30] Strauss's conception of the primacy of political philosophy is also rooted in the fact that it is not concerned with the life of a singular individual but with the well-being of the political community as a whole. It is therefore concerned with a more consequential and substantive process, an object of inquiry that goes beyond the happiness that ethical practice confers on the individual. If happiness follows from good ethical action, political science examines the conditions that make happiness possible in the political community. It thus has a more fundamental approach and a broader subject matter.[31]

Politics is likely to appear dominant in this conception when, in the interest of social order, it even claims control over society's metaphysical views insofar as they affect the organization of public life.[32] According to Strauss's interpretation of al-Fārābī, true metaphysics is apparently nothing other than a "collection of the opinions of the inhabitants of the ideal city."[33] Moreover, Muslim philosophers expressed their conviction of the paramount importance of political science by attributing to it the treatment of prophecy. According to Strauss, al-Fārābī intertwines the political with the divine when he entrusts the sharia with the task of presenting esoteric truths in an exoteric manner. These truths are known to philosophers only through demonstration. However, in this conception, divine principles and deeds are represented by equivalent expressions taken specifically from the realm of the political and used for the purpose of establishing political stability. The intertwining of theology and politics is further expressed by Strauss when he defines the content of faith as the views of the prophet in the context of a political community.[34] At the end of the day, Strauss ascribes to al-Fārābī subordinating religious sciences to politics, thereby making religion the subject of politics.[35]

The Relationship between Theory and Practice

The relationship between theory and practice lies at the crux of Strauss's interpretation of al-Fārābī's *Plato*. By rendering speculative philosophy as the sole and sufficient condition for the attainment of felicity, every practical dimension of human ambition is considered incapable of helping a person achieve felicity. Not only does politics appear to be incapable of this task, but religion and morality are also powerless in this regard given the fact that all these disciplines require rational justification.[36] Strauss ignores the fact that al-Fārābī, in his explication of the connection between religion and politics, does indeed make the king, the imam, and the philosopher equivalent in their ability to combine theory and praxis at the highest levels.[37] However, religion as well as politics is subordinate to philosophy in Strauss's own interpretation of al-Fārābī, an interpretation that strictly divides theory and practice.

Christopher Colmo has demonstrated that while the philosophical life is to be considered the best way of life in Strauss's interpretation of "Farabi's *Plato*," such a realization should be classified as "practical." Colmo therefore classifies Strauss's interpretation as incoherent. According to Colmo, this insight provided by Strauss and al-Fārābī is to be considered a matter of political philosophy. His main argument against Strauss focuses on the fact that the recognition of the theoretical life as the best way of life can only be based on a theoretical position. Otherwise, it cannot be considered a philosophical insight in the strict sense.[38]

Strauss rightly observed that al-Fārābī's initial insight posits the achievement of felicity as a product of a specific scientific discipline and way of life. The necessary discipline is therefore the theoretical science of the essence of beings.

Nevertheless, Strauss believes that the necessary way of life for the achievement of the highest felicity is not one of virtue. Virtue can only protect "the felicity of this world," and it must be distinguished from true felicity.[39] There is a broad agreement between the behavior of moral individuals and the behavior of philosophers. This agreement allows one to use the word "virtue" to describe both cases. However, the philosopher and the moral individual interpret the same virtuous behavior differently. The difference between the true, virtuous way of life and all other ways of life is not based on a difference of ends or the quality of the will in question but on a difference in understanding.[40]

According to Strauss, the moral way of life possessed by the philosophers does not differ in an external sense from that of nonphilosophers. Differing understandings of the same behavior is a matter of insight. While the nonphilosopher behaves morally out of obligation and honor, the philosopher utilizes the moral way of life in order to ensure a higher, theoretically oriented way of life necessary for the attainment of felicity. In contrast to Colmo's interpretation, Strauss appears to believe that insisting on the prioritization of the theoretical life is indeed a theoretical insight. However, his mode of argument should be located within a rhetorical dialectic employed regarding praxis. In light of the absolute claims put forth by politics, theoretical concepts must have a double meaning. When speech functions as a mode of political praxis in and of itself, every insistence of theoretical expression must be expressed in an oftentimes contradictory fashion due to its own claim of possessing truth.[41]

The Result: Exoteric-Esoteric Philosophy

According to Strauss, al-Fārābī holds, in the context of his interpretation of Plato, views that do not correspond with the teachings of Islam. In this framework, al-Fārābī is seen as denying not only the afterlife but the very existence of God and the divine. He sees philosophy as having a monopoly over a felicity anchored purely in this life. In his interpretation of al-Fārābī, Strauss describes the philosophers' position in society in the following fashion: The philosophers, who rule in the other city existing in speech, present themselves as gods among men. They are deemed intellectually superior to other people and therefore hated and persecuted. They have no direct political power, but they play a certain political role. They heed people's need for divine law and allow it to be the second-best form of rule. Yet they realize that their positions endanger both the stability of society and their own personal security. Consequently, they conceal their true convictions and reveal them only in the context of interpreting the works of others. Only potential philosophers have the capacity to access the hidden truth latent in these texts through rigorous training. For them there is only one truth, namely that religion and morality are noble lies because they are socially useful. The dangerousness of this truth forces the philosophers to communicate it to the suitable ones by means of twofold writing, which becomes the characteristic of political philosophy.[42]

For Strauss's al-Fārābī, philosophy is the path toward the science of being in contradistinction to a science of human behavior. It must be understood as a path toward scientific understanding rather than science itself, as a mode of researching rather than as a result of such research. Understood in this fashion, philosophy can be considered as science "in action," identical to σκέψις (skepticism) in the original meaning of the word. It is considered the real search for truth and buttressed by the conviction that it alone can ascribe meaning to life. This increases the intensity of the philosophers' conviction that philosophy expresses doubt about the individual's natural tendency to immobilize themselves by beliefs that are seemingly satisfactory but ultimately unclear and unproven. Al-Fārābī understands philosophy to be a skeptical enterprise concerned with providing a radical and skeptical critique of accepted opinion. It develops its own convictions based on critical thinking. These convictions are to be differentiated from those found in the usual textbooks and monographs. In the manner of determining the identity of the philosopher par excellence, Strauss says with regard to al-Fārābī, "But what made him a philosopher, according to his own view of philosophy, were not those convictions, but the spirit in which they were acquired, in which they were maintained and in which they were intimated rather than preached from the house-tops."[43] This point is crucial in understanding how Strauss himself views philosophy and philosophers.

It was not the convictions that al-Fārābī held about important questions but the attitude of mind, the manner and inner attitude in which he acquired, maintained, and proclaimed them, that made him a philosopher. For Strauss, it is the conscious way of philosophizing that makes the philosopher. He does not describe it but defines it *ex negativo* when he calls it the opposite of preaching from the housetops. The way of philosophizing and proclaiming philosophical views that he emphasizes is the way isolated from external influences, carried out in a small circle that carefully handles the proclamation of philosophical views by means of exoteric-esoteric writing.

Through his interpretation of al-Fārābī's philosophy, Strauss attempts to define the object and goal of philosophy. He explains that, according to al-Fārābī, philosophy consists of the theoretical science of the essence of all beings as well as the examination of the things. This science is called "science of beings," whereby "beings" and "things" must be distinguished from one another. Indeed, all instantiations of being are things, while not all things are beings. To understand things means to understand their existing essence. Philosophy thereby becomes the "science of the essence of all things." Al-Fārābī considers natural beings to be "beings *par excellence*." When he refers to "divine beings," he means "simply the most outstanding group of natural beings in the sense of beings 'which are bodies or in bodies,' i.e., the heavens."[44] Strauss interprets the attribute "divine" as the excellence of things and credits al-Fārābī with using it in the "divine-human" or "divine-bestial" dichotomy, replacing "divine" with "human" when repeating the passage in question. Strauss avoids making a judgment regarding al-Fārābī's conception of *substantiae separatae*. He is satisfied with the observation that this point is not central to al-Fārābī's philosophy.[45] However, al-Fārābī does not really have anything in common with a "non-philosophical faithful" and can readily be classified as a "philosophical materialist." By virtue of his interpretation of al-Fārābī, Strauss appears to be harnessing the philosophical materialization of the divine and rendering it into the object of esoteric philosophy, which he depicts as "essentially and purely theoretical."[46]

Strauss's Political Philosophy as Philosophia Prima

For Leo Strauss, philosophy is simply what it has always been in a classical sense: the search for wisdom, universal knowledge, knowledge of the whole. Insofar as the whole implies the nature of all things in their totality, it cannot be apprehended spontaneously. The central task of philosophy is to replace the "opinions regarding the whole with true knowledge."[47] It does not claim to possess the truth but rather envisions itself as a continuous process aimed at achieving knowledge. It often appears comparable to a thankless, Sisyphean task, especially compared to the results achieved. Of course, philosophy is always accompanied, supported, and preserved by eros.[48]

As demonstrated by Strauss's interpretation of al-Fārābī, Strauss distinguishes between theoretical philosophy in its strictest sense and political philosophy, though he considers the latter to transcend disciplinary confinement. The following will elucidate the characteristics of Strauss's conception of political philosophy.

The Object of Political Philosophy

The term *political philosophy* invests philosophy with the attribute of the political. As demonstrated throughout his critique of Carl Schmitt, Strauss understands that the political constitutes the fundamental significance of natural human life. Thus, philosophy is regarded as the deep and comprehensive way of dealing with political matters; the attribute "political" here indicates the subject and function of philosophy, as well. Accordingly, political philosophy treats the nature of political affairs in a manner appropriate to political life. Its object is for Strauss the ultimate goal of political action, and its subject is the great question of humanity, namely, how freedom and rulership properly relate to each other. However, this must not be confused with a politicization of philosophy.[49]

In Strauss's view, political praxis aims at maintaining the good already present in society while changing the bad. All political praxis derives by its very nature from an epistemological understanding of the good, that is, the good life or the good society, whose attainment constitutes the ultimate purpose of political praxis. Philosophy, as rendered into a discipline, is closely related to human life. It is therefore apparent why political philosophy cannot accept a division between "facts" and "values."[50]

Strauss conceives of political philosophy as the attempt to understand the nature of political objects, an attempt that orients itself toward political knowledge in its original, prescientific form. This kind of understanding is dependent not only on particular political situations but on political life and human life in a broader sense. Indeed, a coherent philosophical approach toward politics concerns itself with these important prerequisites to understanding the political circumstances of a particular time and place.[51] The prevailing, historically accumulated opinions about the foundations of politics are replaced by knowing them. This results in the intertwining of the philosophical and the historical with one another, for which reason philosophy becomes the adversary of historicism.[52]

Strauss's primary goal is to render political philosophy operative by separating it on all sides from neighboring disciplines. He distinguishes it from political thought, an enterprise unconcerned with the task of distinguishing opinion from knowledge. He also distinguishes political philosophy from political theory, an enterprise concerned with reflection on current events. He distinguishes it from political theology, an enterprise consistently oriented toward divine revelation and hence accessible to human understanding apart from philosophical guidance.[53] Insofar as it enables a genuine knowledge of political things, it presents itself as the philosophical discipline that does not neglect the study of natural things but subordinates it to the study of questions of human life.[54] Finally, the political philosophy presented by Strauss claims to recover the scientific character of philosophy, allegedly lost by the historical separation of philosophy and science.[55]

The Problem of Ideal Governance and the Solution of Law Giving

Leo Strauss understands his version of political philosophy as a modern resuscitation of the classical political philosophy founded by Socrates and brought into coherent form by the harmonization of Plato's and Aristotle's political philosophy through their direct orientation toward political life.[56] According to Strauss, the main theme of classical political philosophy relates to the search for the best political system. This naturally provokes the question of what should be considered the best form of governance, the best governing class, and the best laws. All these components are fused together by political regimes tasked with producing a specific way of life for their respective states and societies. The regime is a comprehensive whole consisting of the totality of politics and society, the form of government, and the general ethical attitude. It is thus called the "spirit" that generates the laws and customs of a society and promotes human perfection.[57]

The naturally occurring differences between human beings produce a situation whereby something that is good for one person is bad for the other. This mandates that political decisions be flexible and permeated by wisdom. At the core of Plato's *Republic*, which is chiefly concerned with the question of the best form of rulership, lies the rule of philosophers. It should be considered the best form of governance since, as opposed to other forms governance, it is based on acute intelligence and cognizance of changing circumstances and personages. The rule of wisdom allows for the good within humans to be individually identified and a more flexible form of governance responsive to variable emerging conditions. Strauss explains that "the best regime is that for which one would wish or pray."[58] Therefore, the best regime constitutes an object of hope, replacing the ideal community envisioned by religion. When the attainment of the best regime is impossible, classical political philosophy becomes concerned with the practical attainment of the best possible regime. The rule of acute intelligence should, in these circumstances, be replaced with wise laws. Strauss considers this to be the second-best form of governance given that it reflects reality by combining wisdom with the power to punish.[59] A wise lawgiver establishes a code of law that embodies wisdom and is freely accepted by the citizenry. The laws would be administered by people close to the philosophers and completed according to the circumstances. In Strauss's view, these people are the "gentlemen" who come from rich families. Aristocratic rule under the law is presented as a "mixed regime" that replaces the absolute best rule of the philosophers, which is wise and flexible.[60] In this sense, Strauss writes that "the legislative skill is, therefore, the most 'architectonic' political skill that is known to political life."[61]

The lawgiver, considered by Strauss in the ideal sense to be a prophet, must be responsive to both the needs of his community and universal political questions that concern law giving universally. Law giving must be oriented toward the cosmic order of nature.[62] Given the fact that the political philosopher is primarily concerned with the search for the best system of political order, they become the teacher of the lawgiver and thereby find the solution for the most fundamental political question concerning which class should rule and become communal lawgivers.[63]

Based on his interpretation of the meaning of law giving for political philosophy, Strauss explains that the character of classic political philosophy is most pointedly operable in the best possible mode of political order represented by the Athenian in Plato's *Laws*.[64] The old Athenians who came to Crete to study the best laws realized that these laws are considered optimal because of their long history and divine origin. The divine origin of these laws, as presented in the beginning of the book, must remain unquestioned even though they are justified by poetic panegyrics. Therefore, the question is aimed at the inner value of the laws and introduced by a discussion concerning the consumption of wine, a practice forbidden in Crete. In the course of the conversation, wine drinking is presented as a way of educating people to learn courage and bravery, but also moderation. Just as apparent is the fact that the Athenian plans to institute new laws and institutions that he considers to be good. According to Strauss, the same is true of political philosophy. It is characterized from the outset by replacing the old, fixed opinions and habits of an established society with new practices based on knowledge. Therefore, it avoids immediately denying or at least questioning the sacred character of the ruling laws. Instead, after the necessary preparation, it questions the concrete content of the laws by ascending from the sacred to the natural. Political philosophy, like drinking wine, requires courage, fortitude, and moderation.[65]

The Importance of Education for Political Philosophy

Strauss observes that the Athenian together with his interlocutors undergo a process of adaptation. It is at this juncture that we can raise the important question regarding the role of education. In *Persecution and the Art of Writing*, Strauss writes that "Education [. . .] is the only answer to the always pressing question, to the political question par excellence, of how to reconcile order which is not oppression with freedom which is not license."[66] Education, in this conception, provides an answer to the ultimate political question of how to reconcile an order that is free from oppression and a freedom that is not contradictory to order. This reconciliation is an important guarantee for the establishment of social stability. For Strauss, freedom as a goal is ambiguous, since it can be the freedom to do good or to do evil. In this sense, education aims to establish virtue through the formation of character and modes of adaptation. It is aimed at the children of the wealthy, since they do not have to work and therefore have the time and energy to devote to philosophy.[67] "Socrates was the political educator *par excellence*."[68]

The Essence of Political Philosophy

The following aspects of Strauss's political philosophy have thus far been presented: It is the constant attempt to replace opinions that are politically relevant with real knowledge in order to achieve the best form of political order in which rulership and freedom can be reconciled. An important tool of political philosophy is education. Education is the social process that most concerns philosophy, as it protects true knowledge from political realities. Indeed, this occurs in a "political," careful fashion. Strauss identifies a further characteristic of political philosophy whereby the attribute "political" is applied to the mode of analysis. Political philosophy primarily points to "the political, or popular, treatment of philosophy, or the political introduction to philosophy — the attempt to lead the qualified citizens, or rather their qualified sons, from the political to the philosophic life."[69] It is here that we encounter the essence of the Straussian concept of political philosophy. Philosophy and the philosophical life are to be distinguished from political philosophy and the political life. In order to further clarify Strauss's concept of political philosophy, we must contrast the early and later designations of political philosophy. In its earlier meaning, political philosophy is presented as part of the philosophical endeavor. It is a radically comprehensive and knowledge-seeking mode of being aimed toward "an ontology of political phenomena."[70] Its goal is the best regime, one in which freedom and governance are reconciled in order to render their establishment possible in the first place. With the second definition, Strauss presents political philosophy as the way in which the whole of philosophy is presented to society. Thereby, philosophy operates "dialectically" or in an "ad hominem" fashion proceeding from commonly accepted opinions in order to replace them with true knowledge. Of course, this form of political philosophy is addressed to discrete individuals, who should be made capable of transcending the political in favor of active philosophizing.[71] Political philosophy thus becomes a political means of introducing philosophy, or even the framework in which philosophy in its entirety is introduced into society.[72] The first designation is external and general, while the second seems to be something quite specific to Strauss. The first is necessary for society, while the second is only considered necessary for philosophers to spread their teachings in society and to recruit students. Political philosophy is thus seen as exoteric philosophy, the inner core of which is only apparent to the philosophers themselves. According to Strauss, philosophers believe that the essence of the best political order lies in the elimination of the tension between rulership and freedom. Furthermore, they strive to elevate philosophy as the absolute best way of life through the education of aristocrats.[73]

Such a concept of political philosophy, despite its seeming simplicity, is actually connected to a complex conception of philosophy that unifies four distinct moments in classical philosophy: the philosophical interest in cosmology, the characterization of philosophy as a way of life leading to felicity, the skeptical character of philosophy that contains elements of both danger and endangerment, and the necessarily existing political dimension.[74]

> Since philosophy is characterized by the striving toward universal knowledge, cosmology is its most important component.[75] Socrates, in his investigations of human affairs, distinguishes himself from his predecessors by virtue of the fact that he replaces an understanding of the whole with an understanding of its parts. As the whole is nothing but the totality of its parts, knowledge of the whole is predicated on an understanding of those parts, which must first be identified as partial rather than as those complete entities in and of themselves.[76] This same principle applies to the understanding of humanity and its affairs. Socrates views humanity as a part of the cosmos and therefore part of the secret nature of the whole. The philosopher is therefore not dependent on any one specific conception of cosmology but rather the "humanizing search for the eternal order of things." This view of the cosmos renders it the source of human inspiration and intuition.[77] According to Strauss, the hierarchical ordering of the cosmos is particularly important since it serves as a prototype for the order of the polis and as a model for its laws.[78]
> Philosophy implies not merely a collection of teachings but rather a way of life in which theoretical knowledge and praxis are closely related. Indeed, philosophy consists of a substantial ethical moment. The question "How should I live?" proves itself to be the most exigent question for the philosopher. The answer to this question does not lie in the acknowledgment of the ethical norms already dominant in society but rather in the light of self-knowledge. The search for the philosophical way of life leads to a more fundamental question, namely, "Why philosophy?," a question that thematizes the necessity of philosophy for society. The justification of philosophy is therefore part and parcel of the philosophical way of life that reaches its apotheosis with the theoretical apprehension of all beings.[79]

> Philosophy is characterized by subjecting everything that exists to radical questioning in an effort to replace opinions with true knowledge. However, traditional opinions regarding religion, morals, and politics are significant for the composition and survival of society. Therefore, philosophical questioning of these fundamentals should be considered a threat to the security of society. This position will ultimately lead to the discontentment of most citizens, who see the philosopher as a parasitical creature, one that enjoys theoretical contemplation at society's cost and in conspicuous self-isolation.[80]
> This fundamental antagonism between philosophy and society leads philosophers to act in a careful fashion. Since philosophical skepticism contradicts the natural human tendency to desire ready-made solutions to problems, leading in turn to the endangerment of society's sense of security, the public pronouncements of the philosophers must be made charitably. Their ethical responsibility toward society necessitates that they not endanger its security. They also must act to protect themselves against political, religious, and social persecution. They must therefore philosophize in a "political" way. According to this view, to pursue political philosophy means two things: on the one hand, to deal radically and comprehensively with questions that are important for political life and, on the other hand, to philosophize politically — that is, to philosophize cautiously and in a way that is compatible with the political order, thus avoiding the mutual endangerment of philosophy and society.

The Primacy of Political Philosophy

Strauss's depiction of the relationship between philosophy and society appears quite complex. In addition to the aforementioned antagonism, he highlights a further aspect of this problematic relationship, namely the independence of philosophy on the political community. "Philosophy has its home in the cities," writes Strauss.[81] On the one hand, the philosopher is a human being who depends on the community in order to fulfill their material needs. On the other hand, the political order creates the necessary conditions so that they may do their philosophical work in peace and disseminate their teachings.[82] Despite this, the philosopher leads a natural, happy life on the margins of society in order to provide a service to their fellow citizens.[83] Philosophy therefore does not have the ability to implement anything. In the time of Socrates, it needed to be integrated into a larger apparatus influenced heavily by rhetorically effective poetry in order to be protected and completed.[84]

Strauss's philosopher, therefore, does not pursue a political role, for

> [he] is led to realize that the ultimate aim of political life cannot be reached by political life, but only by a life devoted to contemplation, to philosophy. This finding is of crucial importance to political philosophy, since it determines the limits set to political life, to all political action, to political planning. Moreover, it implies that the highest subject of political philosophy is the philosophic life. Philosophy — not as a teaching or a body of knowledge, but as a way of life — offers as it were, the solution to the problem that keeps political life in motion. Ultimately, political philosophy transforms itself into a discipline that is no longer concerned with political things in the ordinary sense of the term.[85]

According to this interpretation, the philosopher deems political life in and of itself to be insufficient. It is, rather, a means to enable the practice of philosophy, which should be considered the ultimate end. This implies that the highest object of political philosophy is the philosophical life. Political philosophy thus transforms into a discipline that can only be characterized as metapolitical inasmuch as it does not concern itself with political affairs in a normal sense. Socrates's fundamental question about the best way to live is thus reduced to a choice between a philosophical and a political life.[86] In light of philosophy, politics can be seen as derived from an apolitical form of theory.[87] For Strauss, philosophy's essential reclusiveness from political life is illustrated by Socrates's absence from Plato's *Laws*. Indeed, this indicates that the political is ranked below the philosophical.[88] This first constitutes a way of life anchored in the cave, while the latter constitutes the best life, one lived in the light of the sun.[89] Thus, the philosopher is able to place human beings in a position between the gods and the animals. To be useful for and compatible with the needs of the political community, the demands of philosophy must be lessened so as to not constitute "dynamite for civil society."[90]

From the foregoing discussion, we can determine that political philosophy possesses a dual function. It ensures the continual constitution of both society and philosophy. It is the outer layer of philosophy that protects the core when philosophy is introduced to society. It also helps philosophically talented young people move from everyday political questions to philosophical inquiry in their respective polities.[91] It is not simply a subdiscipline of philosophy but rather, in a much more profound sense, the art of how to philosophize in society. Therefore, it presents itself as the broad framework of philosophy in its entirety — or, in Strauss's words, the surface — which contains the totality of philosophy.[92] As Strauss writes in *The City and Man*: "In its original form, political philosophy broadly understood is the core of philosophy, or rather 'the first philosophy.'"[93] Against the philosophical tradition, Strauss considers not metaphysics but political philosophy, in its newly resuscitated form, to be the philosophia prima. His justifications for this new designation can be summarized in the following fashion. Political philosophy emerges primarily out of the political life of the community in which one lives and is concerned with matters pertinent to that particular community. It lays a path that moves from prephilosophical activity to philosophical inquiry concerning not only matters imminently pertinent to that community but also matters applicable to all political communities.[94] Due to the fact that its area of concern relates to human questions and implies the existence of further philosophical subdisciplines, it assumes a methodological priority.

Six structural features can be gleaned from Strauss's definition of political philosophy:[95]

> Political philosophy views communal life as necessary for the continued survival of human existence. Since political philosophy has always been chiefly concerned with the conditions necessary for political order and community, its object of inquiry proves to be fundamental. However, inquiry into relations among human beings requires that further topics of essential inquiry, such as the nature of humanity, law, freedom, and justice, assume priority.[96]
> Political philosophy goes beyond its originally narrow framework and in doing so transcends itself. For an appropriate explication of the social nature of humanity, it is necessary to pose broad questions that apply to human and nonhuman matters. In this fashion, political philosophy escapes its narrow field and touches upon matters of physics, metaphysics, and psychology. In order to comprehend the nature of the human being, a being rooted in both a cosmic and social landscape as part of a whole, it is necessary to explore the nature of such a totality in its broadest sense.[97]
> Political philosophy can be considered the best introduction to philosophy. Its treatment of questions related to political life leads to a grappling with diverse questions of a macrocosmic nature. This becomes especially apparent in the depiction of Socrates's trial, in which the explication of questions related to human nature leads to further philosophical questions that nevertheless do not forget their very human origin. In this fashion, a conversation regarding what is good for people in a specific condition leads to a discussion regarding the idea of the good as an ontological principle. Similarly, human objects point to objects related to nature in its entirety, while grappling with the microcosmos proves to be essential for comprehending the whole.[98]

> Political philosophy is a serious endeavor. It takes the essential problem of human existence seriously, namely that the world cannot be rid of evil. It proceeds to deal with the problems resulting from this state of affairs such as the establishment of justice within society.[99] The seriousness of philosophy is justified by the fact that an examination of political affairs is necessary to understand nature as a whole.[100]
> Political philosophy defuses the revolutionary character of philosophy by giving political consideration to the tendency of philosophers to replace traditional unexamined opinions with the true views they discover. The resulting politically attuned rejection of established opinions implies a replacement with something new without causing public resistance, which arises among the public in response to the misinterpretation of traditions of venerable origin. Enlightenment, carried out in a political way, causes the unobtrusive exposure of social foundations, especially those tied to religion. Given the fact that this all relates to tradition, a conflict with philosophy naturally emerges in that philosophy requires the radical freedom to think. Political philosophy sees religion as an institution necessary for maintaining social peace. In its function as law, religion is especially adept at serving this function, given the fact that it demands obedience from citizens. For this reason, it becomes an important partner to politics. Political philosophy requires that the natural antagonism between philosophy and religion be transformed into a form of compatibility between philosophy and law. The enmity between philosophy and religion is thereby overcome, with religion rendered useful for the maintenance of social order, something always seen as essential by philosophy.[101]
> These considerations invariably lead to a new evaluation of political philosophy. It becomes the philosophical practice par excellence. This is done by giving a new weight to the political, which enables it to present itself as the factor that integrates philosophy into society. The political becomes the social manners of philosophy, even the methodology necessary for the philosopher to develop ideas in view of their social effect. Political philosophy is the framework in which theoretical philosophy presents itself as well as the function with which philosophy attains its social justification, thereby protecting its core.[102]

Strauss demonstrates that philosophers rule society through persuasion achieved through subtle and noble deception.[103] He is fully convinced that every society necessarily requires a fundamental untruth comprising two elements: the replacement of universal human brotherhood with the limited brotherhood of citizens in their own homeland and the tracing back of the existing social hierarchy to its divine origin. Consequently, the task of philosophy is to replace untruth with truth, which presupposes the ability to address the mass of people in such a way that they can be convinced. Strauss remarks that al-Fārābī is the sole philosopher in the history of philosophy who recognized this fact in Plato's *Republic* and who brought out the necessity of combining the Socratic method for dealing with elites with the method of Thrasymachus for dealing with the masses. The Platonic philosophy that emerges from this combination gives itself the ability to philosophize and to deal with society. It is the political philosophy that Strauss brings into being in modernity on the basis of al-Fārābī.[104]

Strauss's Concept of the Political

Leo Strauss radicalizes the political in that he separates it from its strict modern usage and uses it in relation with the natural state of affairs for humanity. This is based on the conception of the human being as a political, or rather social, being. Strauss became convinced of the importance of this move through his exposure to Arabic Peripatetic philosophy. This sets up a conception of the political that should be seen as diametrically opposed to the friend-enemy schematic of Carl Schmitt. Strauss's concept of the political should be seen as an existentially significant designation of the relations between human beings as well as the art of statecraft. Both are necessary for the continued existence of man as well as the securing of life. Both elements within the political build a concept of political philosophy in which philosophy is capable of interacting with society and where both society and philosophy remain secure. The political exists as a complementary element to philosophy that enables it to be effective in society and thereby capable of withstanding external political forces while successfully communicating its ideas to young people.

This form of political philosophy is inserted by Strauss into the context of modernity with the intention of defining the political anew, thereby facilitating a rapprochement with society. The political is meant to overcome a certain discrepancy between philosophy and society. A specific concept of politics is obviously deployed here that differs from the common concept of politics and does not basically mean "that which is proper to the polis" or, more precisely, the action aimed at shaping public life in the ancient polis or in the modern state.[105] Rather, it denotes the art of treatment, which implies the inequality of the treating and the treated.[106] Anyone with knowledge of Arabic will notice that Strauss's conception of the political is related to the Arabic concept of *siyāsa*, particularly in his view that the Socratic student of politics (probably referring here to himself) has much to learn from the way horses and dogs are trained. Indeed, the affinity with the Arabic concept of *siyāsa* is unmistakable.[107] Strauss can only have come to this conception through his engagement with Islamic philosophy, and particularly with al-Fārābī. I will now examine this concept more closely.

Excursus: The Arabic Concept of *Siyāsa*

The Arabic word *siyāsa* is derived from the verb root *sāsa* (*sa-wa-sa*) and originally meant the management and training of animals, especially horses. The *sā'is* is the one charged with the care and dressage of horses. This person also knows how to ride them.[108]

From these origins, the word *siyāsa* has come to be associated with the leadership and governance of people and of human societies as well as the administration of human affairs. The one tasked with the *siyāsa* of human beings is the one that rules the community by putting their wisdom and capacities at its disposal, thereby augmenting its well-being and improving the relationships therein. *Siyāsa* thereby assumes the meaning of "taking care of human beings and leading them to something better." The concept not only indicates a relationship to others, whether they be humans or animals, but also applies to inner processes concerning the ways in which individuals deal with themselves. Therefore, it can also indicate self-control over the body and the passions through reason and spirit.[109]

The term brings forth a mode of rule that bases itself upon the natural inequality between the ruled and ruler.[110] Reason is posited as a central instrument of governance that leads to general betterment. Regarding animals, it implies irrational creatures that must be saved from the wild by the direction of a person possessing reason. In the case of human beings, it concerns the rule of one or more superior persons who are capable of leading and administrating the affairs of those ruled. In the case of the rule over one's own self, a higher rationality rules over a deeper irrationality. As these examples demonstrate, *siyāsa* aims to develop a class of people capable of benefiting from such rule. In this fashion, the one to whom *siyāsa* is entrusted is tasked with providing physical, moral, spiritual, and intellectual advantages to his fellow people. This activity can be considered in terms of a "policy or system of organization where people are managed or tended in such a manner as to enhance their lives and put them in a right or proper state."[111]

This term, in the sense of rule, administration, or government, appears in the Qur'ān and the Ḥadīth. In these sources, multiple forms of *siyāsa* appear with varying principles and goals at work. Medieval Arabic readers considered the Socratic dialogues as discussions about *siyāsa*. Numerous tractates and books regarding ethics and moral living belong to the vast *siyāsa* literature in Arabic. This treasure trove contains any number of ethical recommendations aimed at both leaders and other groups within society. *Siyāsa* comprises the mastery of the self, the administration of the household (treatment of spouses and servants along with the education of children), and the proper manner of dealing with subordinates.[112] *Siyāsa* therefore assumes a close relationship to the sum of behavioral regulations (*adab*).[113]

In the essay cited previously, Fauzī Najjār offers numerous examples regarding the usage of the term *siyāsa* by Muslim jurists (*fuqahā'*) and philosophers. The jurists treat the topic as part of religious jurisprudence (*fiqh*) and derive its normative principles from the sharia. In this sense, al-Ghazālī considers the highest form of *siyāsa* to consist of legal or prophetic teachings (*siyāsa shar'iyya* or *siyāsa nabawiyya*) that guarantee stability and prosperity in this world and secure salvation in the world to come. Within these teachings, both the eternal and the temporal, as well as the spiritual and the material, become intertwined so that this reality becomes a model of ideal governance worthy of imitation by Muslim rulers. Al-Ghazālī elevates *siyāsa* to the noblest and most necessary of the four principal activities (*ṣināʿāt*) necessary for human existence.[114] According to al-Māwardī, the *siyāsa shar'iyya* ensures that the government is functioning according to divine law and that the administration of every day matters within the state (*siyāsat ad-dunyā*) functions within its framework.[115]

Najjār makes it clear that *fiqh* theorists understand *as-siyāsa ash-shar'iyya* as a perfect form of leadership, whose standards are taken from sharia and which has ethical, religious, and, in a narrow sense, political elements and goals. By virtue of the connection between religion and politics in Islam, spiritual and narrowly defined political moments become enmeshed with one another. However, the spiritual is of primary importance because it possesses elements whose chief aim is eternity. This life is indeed aimed at preparation for the one to come. In this framework, all human activity assumes religious relevance.[116]

Bernard Lewis provides examples of the nonreligious literary usage of the word *siyāsa* in order to demonstrate that it means "a skill or craft" in classical Arabic and therefore is better translated as "management" (although not in terms of the commercial or administrative) or "statecraft" (especially in the political sense). It can also be observed that the word appears in book titles from the ninth century onward, in which it assumes the meaning of "the art of good treatment and leadership."[117]

In philosophical works, the concept of *siyāsa* assumes specific characteristics due to Greek influence. In contradistinction to the jurists, the philosophers are concerned that human reason should assume a certain autonomy in relation to the divine. They therefore support their arguments rationally in order to demonstrate the necessity of social life for mankind. Their deliberations are thus able to assume a universal character grappling not only with principles of Islamic government and behavior but with principles in a general sense that are grounded in reason. According to their teachings, the prerequisites for the art of leadership include natural and rational elements in addition to theological ones.[118]

Al-Fārābī defines *siyāsa* as the way of management, which in the absolute sense is not a genus for different kinds of *siyāsāt* (plural) but a common name for many things that are different in themselves and by nature.[119] *Siyāsa*, therefore, means the activity of leading and is designated according to the intellectual and ethical attitude of the leader. In this fashion, a *siyāsa fāḍila* (virtuous form of leadership) is contrasted with a *siyāsa jahiliyya* (ignorant form of leadership). While the first form is both simple and unique, representing good leadership in an absolute sense, the latter is constituted by different forms of ignorant governments that are joined together. Only the first form of rule leads to felicity in this world and the next, thereby elevating it to kingly practice.[120] The rulers (*aṣḥāb as-siyāsāt*) render the ruled into stand-up individuals trained to routinely behave well.[121] *Siyāsa* also assumes a pedagogic function. Al-Fārābī divides philosophy into theoretical and practical parts. The theoretical (*al-falsafa an-naẓariyyā*) comprises three parts: mathematics, physics, and metaphysics. Practical philosophy (*al-falsafa al-ʿamaliyya* or *al-falsafa al-madaniyya*) comprises ethics and politics (*al-falsafa as-siyāsiyya*).[122]

In a less widely known tractate attributed to al-Fārābī, *Risāla fī s-siyāsa*, he refers to regulations of behavior (*qawānīn siyāsiyya*) useful for dealing with superiors, peers, and subordinates, on the one hand, and with oneself, on the other, in order to achieve felicity. Therefore, *siyāsa* comes to connote a comprehensive and ethical mode of behavior or way of life necessary for social interaction and whose details vary according to the level and status of those affected.[123]

Avicenna similarly uses the term *siyāsa* to mean the art of leadership, whose different areas of applicability are mentioned in the third part of his practical philosophy.[124] *Siyāsa*, along with knowledge (*ʿilm*), belongs also to the essence of a prophet's message, by means of which he brings salvation to the sensible world.[125] In his commentary on the *Politeia*, Averroes utilizes the word *siyāsa* to apparently mean order, leadership, and governance, and, like Plato, he distinguishes between their virtuous and nonvirtuous forms.[126]

Thus, it appears that Islamic philosophers viewed *siyāsa* as the capability and art of leading and governing humans and human affairs with the goal of understanding order and felicity. The concept does not seem to imply an ideology or a system of doctrines that has its analogy in religion but rather a procedural activity of leadership that can be characterized in various ways and that, at its best, can be applied by philosophers in a reasonable and flexible way. Like theologians and jurists, philosophers are convinced of the necessity of social life for human beings and therefore develop a concept of leadership whose ultimate goal is the preservation of the community. But they look at leadership from a different point of view, one that allows them to delve into the works of the great philosophers — especially Plato and Aristotle — and to identify the guideposts for effective governance that they see as acting in complete harmony with the texts provided by revelation.[127] *As-siyāsa al-madaniyya*, in their eyes, characterizes the art of governance that utilizes human reason rather than seeking constant confirmation from Qur'ānic sources like *as-siyāsa ash-shar'iyya*. Even the political goals of both forms of scholarship regarding leadership appear to be different. Leadership that bases itself solely on the Qur'ān demands the establishment of a divine order. In the strictly political sense, this means the establishment of theocratic divine rule. For the philosophers, such scholarship intends to describe a virtuous political order that is not only desired by God but also ensures the attainment of felicity, whose highpoint is achieved through philosophical reflection that ultimately sets its sights on God, the ultimate origin of all beings. The philosophers would like to have reason guide the way to this goal in a fairly autonomous fashion, a process ensured by the concept of *siyāsa* in its original sense. Whether its gaze is set on horses or humans, *siyāsa* must be based on reason. According to the philosophers, religion would also affirm this idea unconditionally.

Philosophical Politics and the Concealment of Truth

Strauss's mode of philosophy assumes the fact that an indissoluble conflict exists between philosophy and society. This assumption leads Strauss to the belief that the relative greatness of a philosopher should be measured by the disharmony between that figure and the broader social landscape. In *Persecution and the Art of Writing*, Strauss presents a "sociology of philosophy" that depicts the antagonism between philosophy and society as well as the attendant multifarious dangers that face philosophers. In this fashion, philosophers, regardless of time or place, come to constitute an elite class. What unites them is stronger than any relationship between philosophers and nonphilosophers, even when they live in the same time and place.[128]

It seems that the idea of a consistent dichotomy between philosophy and society, and the resulting need for esoteric writing, came to Strauss through his encounter with medieval Islamic philosophers.[129] According to Strauss, philosophy held a problematic status in medieval society, owing primarily to the fact that its teachings differed significantly from dominant religious dogma.[130] This dichotomy is most readily observable in the writings of al-Fārābī. Strauss attempts to delineate how "real philosophers" behaved in light of this problem.[131] Through the immunity offered to the mere commentator or historian, al-Fārābī is able to express an opinion regarding controversial questions, something he could not dare to put forward under his own name.[132]

The Analogy of the Rider and the Horse

Strauss explains that al-Fārābī's summary of the Platonic *Laws* is a twofold book. He compares this type of text with men that sit on horses. He writes, "One can articulate the two-foldness of works of this kind by comparing them to men on horseback: to seeming wholes which consist of a discerning and slow ruler and a fast and less discerning subject, and which are well fitted for unexpected attack as well as for flight."[133] In this portrait of the rider, we can discern two figures:

> The rider has a mind and is able to think. This provides him with the ability to lead the horse. Even though he is slower than the horse, he is in a superior position due to the strength of his mind. He is the master in this constellation. Because he has reason, he possesses total control over decision-making in critical circumstances, namely when to fight and when to flee. His role in a fight is more important than that of the horse.
>
> The horse only possesses instinct and therefore can only behave instinctively. It is stronger and faster than man but is nevertheless controlled and dominated by him. It must remain obedient, as it will be punished otherwise. Its function is not to fight but rather to carry the true fighter. In the case of flight, its role becomes greater than the rider's.

This image also implies that there are two types of readers, namely those who read slowly and carefully no matter how hard the text, fight with it, and therefore understand its true content, and those who read the text quickly and fleetingly. They flee from difficult texts and therefore only apprehend their outer layer of content.

The deployment of this image to characterize the twofold exoteric-esoteric art of writing recalls the Arabic concept of *siyāsa* that anchors Strauss's conception of the political. It points toward Strauss's conviction that a close relationship exists between political philosophy and the esoteric-exoteric art of writing.

Political philosophy and twofold writing appear to belong with one another and contribute to the regulation of the philosopher's relationship with society.

Ascetic and Philosopher

Al-Fārābī's impact on Strauss's teaching of exoteric-esoteric philosophy should be considered stronger than has previously been recognized. According to Muhsin Mahdi, Strauss dealt with al-Fārābī's *Summary of the Nomoi* in 1931 to 1932.[134] It is primarily the initial description of Platonic philosophy and the history of the ascetic capable of using deception to save himself from death that probably alerted Strauss to this twofold art of writing. One thing is clear: the word *exoteric* first appears after this date.[135] Thirty years later, Strauss dealt afresh with al-Fārābī's remarks and story.[136]

At the beginning of his *Summary of the Nomoi*, al-Fārābī presents the general observation that the human differs from other creatures in their ability to identify and acquire those things that are useful. Experience plays a large role here, in that observation of parts of objects leads to an understanding of generally applicable judgments. While the wise ones (the "men of judgment," in the words of Strauss) can pass judgment on true experiences in a differentiated fashion, the rest of humanity is naturally inclined to make sweeping judgments from partial observations. When someone repeats the truth once, twice, or many times, the mass of people are likely to assume that they are being honest. Since wise individuals understand this human proclivity, they often repeat things over and over again and are thus judged accordingly. If they act differently in an isolated circumstance, it generally goes unnoticed.[137]

Al-Fārābī illustrates his general point with the following story. An ascetic known for his goodness, respectability, piety, and reclusiveness wanted to flee the city because of his fear of a tyrannical ruler. Because the tyrant ordered the city gates to be manned in case of just such a circumstance, the ascetic was forced to disguise himself during the escape. He dressed like a vagabond, took a cymbal in his hand, and posed as drunk. Upon nightfall, he approached the city gates. The guard asked him to identify himself, and he answered, "I'm that pious ascetic." The guard took him to be joking and let him go. In this fashion, the ascetic was able to save himself without lying.[138]

In his commentary, Strauss establishes the fact that the hero of the story is someone with a strong moral and religious character. His actions are motivated by the wish to save himself. He does what is useful for himself. In an isolated incident, he is forced to depart from his usual mode of behavior, but he is nevertheless regarded as honest. The public will not attack his outstanding character even when he behaves irregularly in this one instant given the fact that the uninhibited expression of opinion is part and parcel of the ascetic's essential character. The ascetic lied not with his statement but with his deed. However, his truthful expression is a part of his deed that can nonetheless be considered justifiable in light of persecution. From this story, Strauss concludes that one can speak a dangerous truth when one finds oneself in the proper circumstance.[139]

This story told by al-Fārābī in his introductory remarks helps explain Strauss's teachings regarding exoteric-esoteric writing. This art of philosophical writing is necessary because it contains a dangerous truth that must remain hidden so that the philosopher does not risk persecution or death. Deeply rooted public opinion will not be reinterpreted when presented with philosophical truth. Rather, the opposite will occur. This provides the philosophers with security and enables them to express such truth in the appropriate setting.[140] They do not lie "in speech" but rather "in deed" through their act of writing. Their texts are conceived as masks and camouflage true philosophical positions so as to prevent their being accessible to the broader public and thereby endangering the safety of the philosophers.

Through al-Fārābī's description of Plato's art of writing, Strauss concludes that Plato should be considered to possess good judgment. Plato was concerned about not only what was useful for himself but also the existence of science "in the cities and amongst the nations."[141] He thereby assumed the reputation that he was not always clear about what he thought about the "most important matters" in every circumstance. This allowed him to express his positions without being taken seriously each time. Strauss differentiates Plato from the ascetic by virtue of the fact that Plato did not always say explicitly and precisely what he thought. Nevertheless, both were sometimes forced to pronounce truths that could lead to either their own endangerment or the endangerment of others. Because they both possess the power of judgment, they behaved similarly in similar circumstances. They express the dangerous truth through their written formulations in a hidden way that outwardly communicates something very different to most people.[142] Strauss's comparison between Plato and the ascetic concludes with the judgment that while the ascetic acted out of self-love, Plato was motivated by the desire to save science from attack. This should be understood as a critical allusion to religion, represented by the ascetic. Strauss posits philosophy, as represented by Plato, as exalted above religion.

The Anonymous Truth

Strauss addresses the question of whether al-Fārābī was or was not attracted to subjects and ideas that should have repulsed him as a man of faith. He also addresses the question of whether al-Fārābī became confused through this proclivity, so much so that he could view philosophy and religion as two thoroughly separate entities like a Latin Averroist. Strauss concludes that al-Fārābī was "a man of a different stamp." In contradistinction to the Latin Averroists, who directly professed extremely heretical views, al-Fārābī possessed milder views that he expressed with an extreme ambiguity, with one particular view standing out: the Platonic understanding of life after death.[143] Strauss posits al-Fārābī as a true Platonist who used the interpretation of Plato's works as a vehicle for ambiguously expressing ideas that might be considered shocking for society. Strauss writes, "Platonists are not concerned with historical, (accidental) truth, since they are exclusively interested in the philosophic (essential) truth. Only because public speech demands a mixture of seriousness and playfulness, can a true Platonist present the serious teaching, the philosophic teaching, in a historical, and hence playful garb."[144] For Strauss, the Platonist is a philosopher unconcerned with the historical context of particular text. Instead, he is concerned with the truth. Such truth remains unchanged regardless of historical circumstances.[145] The deployment of a historically oriented interpretation functions as a camouflage for serious philosophic teachings. By virtue of his exoteric-esoteric mode of writing, al-Fārābī achieves an ahistorical purpose. In that he communicates "the most valuable insights" not in systematic works but in the guise of a historical account, al-Fārābī hints at his view of "originality" and "individuality" in philosophy: What becomes visible as the "original" or "personal contribution" of a philosopher is infinitely less significant than his private and truly original and individual understanding of the necessarily anonymous truth.[146]

Strauss considers al-Fārābī's treatment of Platonic philosophy as paradigmatic for the Platonic mode of dealing with texts. He expresses his commitment to such philosophical writing with an enthusiastic awe at how al-Fārābī was able to obliquely express Platonic views.[147] However, this mode of philosophizing belongs to the essence of political philosophy. It should not be considered as a conglomerate of lies. Political philosophy requires operating with "noble lies" in order to neutralize the dangers inherent in the interaction between philosophy and society and to allow the philosopher to function as a "secret king" of a group of young men, thereby having an impact on society.[148]

According to Strauss, al-Fārābī combines the figures of the philosopher and the king in his interpretation of Plato. He excludes the lawgiver from this constellation, thereby rendering philosophy the highest theoretical art and kingship the highest practical art. Strauss strips revealed religion of the ability to provide a path to felicity. Al-Fārābī posits a fundamental and secular alliance between the philosophers and the philosophy-friendly kings and inaugurates a tradition continued by Marsilius of Padua and Machiavelli. The power of the philosophers, practiced in this way, replaces, from a philosophical point of view, the other life, but it is "truly earthly" and is exercised not "in action" but "in speech."[149]

The Justification of Twofold Writing

Thus, Strauss's philosopher is somebody whose views differ from the followers of the three monotheistic religions. Philosophers comprise a "sect" in the context of the religious community to which they belong. While they do not share all views inherent in their respective religions, they also do not wish to dispose of many of these views. The philosophers recognize the role of such views in enabling social order. More than anything, the belief in the afterlife possesses a social function since it motivates people to behave ethically.[150] The philosopher's profession of atheism cannot run amok. He needs to demonstrate a certain piety that bases itself upon the practice of political philosophy.[151]

Philosophers know, Strauss says, that religion operates with noble lies and pious deceptions and that the determination of what is moral depends on the difference in knowledge. They are also convinced that only philosophy grants true happiness, which can only be attained in this life. However, they hide their true views not only out of fear of maltreatment by the masses but out of a sense of responsibility emerging from the unavoidable conclusion that religion is an inescapable factor in ensuring the social order. They must therefore carefully express their "shocking" convictions and differentiate between exoteric and esoteric teachings.[152] The use of this twofold mode of writing not only protects philosophers from persecution but also ameliorates the threat philosophers pose to society. Because opinion constitutes the fundamental element of society, philosophy becomes the attempt to dissolve this element in which society has its being. The imperative therefore arises for philosophy to become the reserve of a small minority of society and nonetheless be respected by society despite the philosophical understanding they possess. Respect for their opinions does not mean accepting these opinions as true. For this reason, the philosophers adopt a mode of writing that allows them to only partially reveal that which they believe to constitute truth without destroying those opinions necessary for society to continue to function. In this fashion, esoteric teachings are distinguished from socially useful teachings. While esoteric teachings are only accessible to careful and well-trained readers engaged in intensive study over many years, exoteric teachings are aimed at reaching a wider readership.[153]

The exoteric-esoteric form of writing becomes unavoidable for philosophy in Strauss's view since philosophy and its political surroundings are in an indissoluble form of conflict. The fundamental gap between philosophers and nonphilosophers will not disappear with any amount of broad educational advancement.[154] Against the modern perspective that understands philosophy to be capable of aiding the progress of society, Strauss posits an intractable problem of communication between philosophy and society. Philosophy, in his opinion, "is essentially private and trans-political."[155] It can only enjoy esoteric freedom and will henceforth be ejected from society if it becomes incapable of communicating its own utility.[156] The twofold method of communication is an integral part of ancient philosophy. Its chief protagonists deemed it necessary because of the nature of philosophy and its relationship to the world.[157] According to this formulation, philosophy is dangerous for society yet is nevertheless dependent on the political environment in which philosophers have to operate. Their daimon, or the commandment of the religious law, forces them to descend again into the cave of human reality, because they feel the urge to spread the teachings that they hold to be true, after all. They are moved not only by the self-preservation instinct of philosophy but also by a prudent urge to enlighten.[158]

According to Strauss, the crisis of modernity is caused by the generalized Enlightenment. Opinions are pronounced without consideration for their impact on society. The philosophical attack on religion that reaches its apotheosis when God is declared dead engenders a loss of orientation in modern humanity. Strauss, conversely, is convinced that society needs religion.[159] He engages with medieval Muslim and Jewish philosophers because they were convinced of religion's social importance. Opinions that do not conform to religion are dissimulated in a politically canny art of twofold writing. Commentary on works by past philosophers has the benefit of serving as a mouthpiece for the careful philosopher. The best practitioner of this art, according to Strauss, is al-Fārābī. His commentaries on Plato are paradigmatic for a philosophical representation containing a double meaning. Strauss undertakes this act of interpretation in order to speak what, with respect to "the loftiest topics," is unspeakable, in a politically canny manner relevant to the philosophical discourse of modernity.[160] He makes it clear that "[T]he exoteric teaching was needed for protecting philosophy. It was the armor in which philosophy had to appear. It was needed for political reasons. It was the form in which philosophy became visible to the political community. It was the political aspect of philosophy. It was 'political' philosophy."[161] The exoteric type of philosophizing is identical to political philosophy according to Strauss. It is the garb in which philosophy presents itself to society.[162] The radical antagonism between philosophy and society produces a state of mutual endangerment that compels the philosopher to formulate his opinions in an exoteric fashion out of fear of mistreatment and a sense of social responsibility. The philosopher must develop two forms of philosophy, an outer and an inner form. Such forms are necessary to prevent the endangerment of social cohesion and to protect the esoteric core of their teachings through the exoteric shell of political philosophy. The distinction between an inner and an outer philosophy emphasizes the distinction between truth and utility. Political philosophy, conceived in this way, demands reflection on the tension between the search for an often-dangerous truth and the demands of society. The political function of philosophy is secured by the establishment of a secret form of rule. Strauss believes that philosophers must philosophize in a political way if they are to enable a society lacking reason to philosophize in any meaningful sense. His political philosophy aims to establish the proper channels of communication between philosophy and society by educating potential philosophers and advising rulers.[163]

Strauss's theses regarding the necessity of twofold communication are important not merely in connection with the interpretation of past thinkers. He seems to have abided by them himself. He reuses his essay "Farabi's *Plato*" in his introduction to *Persecution and the Art of Writing*. However, the recapitulated version contains a striking difference from the original. The classification of philosophy as a purely theoretical activity solely necessary for the achievement of felicity, an opinion reflected in the original essay, falls away completely in the new version. Here we see that al-Fārābī identifies the philosopher with the king. This statement, made at the beginning of the essay, is relativized a few lines later as Strauss designates philosophy as the highest theoretical art and the art of kingship as the highest practical art. He also emphasizes that the fundamental difference between theory and practice remains relevant to al-Fārābī. Strauss does not attempt to reconcile these contradictory explications but rather explains that al-Fārābī was concerned with adding an extension to philosophy that could promote felicity. This extension was to be found not in religion but in politics. Al-Fārābī replaces religion with politics as the handmaid of philosophy in the search for felicity.[164]

If we see Strauss as concealing the truly Platonic view of philosophy's monopoly on happiness, the same is true of the position Strauss attributes to al-Fārābī. The exoteric (and some might say rather condescending) justification for this position is that nonphilosophers should not be made aware of the necessary inaccessibility of happiness to them and their ilk.[165] Can it be assumed that Strauss, for similar reasons, decided to suppress these views in a publication available to a wide audience? It need not be the case, but it may well be. The studies that contain the above passage deal with persecution and its effect on the way philosophers write. According to Strauss, persecution is coterminous with philosophy and can take many forms.[166] In his view, nothing has changed in this regard, even in the modern age. In the age of religious indifference, religiously based moral values still retain their significance for most of society by providing orientation. The sole possession of happiness by theoretical philosophy is an esoteric idea that corresponds to the relegation of morality and virtue to a matter relevant only to the masses, thereby marginalizing religion. Strauss seems to follow al-Fārābī on this point by concealing the privileged position of philosophers. Platonic politics, which is added to philosophy in this process of philosophizing, is nothing else than political philosophy, which is suitable for the exoteric presentation of philosophical ideas.

Summary

Strauss distinguishes between philosophy as an unrestricted theoretical search for the constant truth of objects and political philosophy, which, with Alexander Kojève, he describes as "philosophic politics." He describes its exigency in the following manner:

> In what then does philosophic politics consist? In satisfying the city that the philosophers are not atheists, that they do not desecrate everything sacred to the city, that they reverence what the city reverences, that they are not subversives, in short, that they are not irresponsible adventurers but good citizens and even the best of citizens. This is the defense of philosophy which was required always and everywhere, whatever the regime might have been. [. . .] This defense of philosophy before the tribunal of the city was achieved by Plato with a resounding success. [. . .] What Plato did in the Greek city and for it was done in and for Rome by Cicero [. . .] and for the Islamic world by Fārābī and in and for Judaism by Maimonides.[167]

Political philosophy, according to Strauss, arises from the discrepancy between philosophy and society and is posited as the necessary rhetoric of the social justification of philosophy. This is done primarily through the defense of philosophers in a public tribunal where they, like Socrates, are accused of atheism. Political philosophy seems to have the task of disproving the philosophers' denial of God in the court of public opinion, thereby convincing their fellow citizens that they are good citizens and do not intend to destroy society by undermining all that is considered sacred. Such a political philosophy is philosophy's most effective advocate.

Strauss ascribes a Platonic character to political philosophy, a Platonism whose character is largely applicable to al-Fārābī's oeuvre as well. Strauss identifies al-Fārābī's Platonism through three observations that can be considered central to political philosophy. First, Strauss views al-Fārābī's mode of commentary as truly Platonic because of the innovative way in which it treats Platonic texts. Such a modus operandi focuses on what is universally and timelessly applicable rather than the literal meaning of the text.[168] Second, in the structure of al-Fārābī's political writings, he sees philosophy presented in a political framework, which allows him to declare political philosophy exoteric, preserving the theoretical core in itself. Finally, Strauss sees al-Fārābī's interest in Plato's *Laws* as a model for the philosophical treatment of religion, which political philosophy no longer attacks but must preserve for the stabilization of the social order.[169]

According to Strauss, philosophy's treatment of the idea of the best social order paradoxically implies the exalted position of theory over practice. However, theoretical knowledge cannot be fully separated from the political realm. In a much more significant fashion, theoretical understanding can be derived from a prescientific understanding of human beings' political nature and elaborated in the context of political arrangements.[170] Moral and political phenomena are illuminated in this regard by an exalted and classically conceived mode of theoretical observation.[171] As Aristotle probably recognized, the philosopher finds himself in the tension between the benefits of theoretical reflection and the natural impulse of social life that encourages a person to lead an autarchic life. Plato's philosopher-king and Aristotle's identification of good people with good citizens in the best regime are posited as an answer to the diametrically opposed demands of philosophy and politics.

Leo Strauss designates political philosophy as the political treatment of philosophical themes aimed at bringing people from political to theoretical activity. Philosophy becomes the end goal of politics. Political philosophy is the exoteric side of the inner-philosophical preoccupation with truth. It posits itself as the bridge between philosophy and society and is, in this regard, the politics of philosophy within society. Strauss's political philosophizing requires a dialectical interaction between the philosopher and the surrounding world. The duality of thought and praxis is eliminated so that philosophical ideas conceived in light of their political consequence can be expressed and the philosophical enterprise made possible.

Through these investigations into the history of philosophy, we can see that Strauss's conception of political philosophy is based on an important hermeneutical principle: One must understand the philosophers of the past in the way that they understood themselves. The connection between political philosophy and this type of hermeneutic indicates a belief that the fundamental questions of humanity possess a permanent character. According to this conception, contemporary philosophic problems do not differ from those of the past, thereby justifying the philosopher's attempt to retrieve old philosophical traditions and to insert them into contemporary philosophical discourse. The assumption of this type of fixed structure for human existence and its central problems prepares the ground for the utilization of past thought while deterministically fashioning future history. The repeatability of past questions and ideas also necessitates the determination of a future incapable of renewal. Leo Strauss appears to extend Nietzsche's idea of the eternal return of the same onto the political. One can observe deterministic traits in his conception of political philosophy.[172] The capability to justify rebellion that some have attributed to him does not seem to be sufficient.[173]

Through his analysis of al-Fārābī, Strauss identified the widely held medieval position that Plato and Aristotle were hiding their true opinions and only communicating them through signposts and insinuations.[174] He also interpreted Maimonides in this way given that he taught his student solely through insinuations (*talwīḥāt*) and signposts (*ishārāt*) in order to assess his capacity to understand the secrets of the prophetic books before offering that knowledge to him.[175] However, Strauss linked the question of mediation and withholding of knowledge, which was emphasized in late antiquity and transferred to the medieval Islamic world, exclusively with his thesis of the philosophers' fear of persecution. Nevertheless, at least in the case of al-Fārābī and Avicenna, there is no connection between the expression of philosophical views and the threat to philosophers. One should not, therefore, make generalizations about Islamic philosophy based on Strauss's assessment.[176] Al-Fārābī identifies three reasons for Aristotle's opaque mode of expression: (1) testing whether the student possesses the necessary intellectual capacities to be instructed, (2) the withholding of philosophy only for the worthy, and (3) the intellectual exercise of the student through the toils of research.[177] The use of a symbolic style in philosophical works appears to have a primarily pedagogical function. It allows for a proper disciplinary interaction with philosophy to be maintained and for students to develop intellectually. The truth is hidden primarily for positive, "non-defensive, philosophic reasons."[178] Fear of persecution is certainly a reason for this - but apparently not a decisive one for the Muslim philosophers of the Middle

Ages mentioned by Strauss.[179] Finally, al-Fārābī's story of the ascetic could have a religious Shiite background, which can certainly be linked to the description of the Platonic method, taking into account the prevailing image of the ascetic Plato at that time.[180]

The esoteric understanding of philosophical works neglects the meaning of historical contingency for thought. When a philosopher sees more commonality with other philosophers regardless of historical differences and political circumstances than with his own fellow men, what kind of relationship could possibly form between himself and the political life of his time and age? It is difficult to reconcile the praise of the invention of statements in the interpretation of historical works with a serious attitude toward reality.[181] The commitment to the esoteric, of course, grants philosophy immunity from worldly politics. However, the differentiation of the two isolates philosophy from social concerns and relegates it to an ivory tower existence concerned primarily with itself.[182] In this schematic, politics is also deprived of immanent meaning. Both are posited as antagonists. Fred Dallmayr senses a certain metaphysical reception at play in the establishment of this dichotomy. The antinomy between philosophy and politics lies within a tradition of previous antinomies such as episteme and *doxa*, reason and faith, essence and phenomenon. Furthermore, he critically remarks that Strauss's distinguishing between esoteric and exoteric in philosophy possesses distinct post-Kantian or neo-Kantian characteristics and is easily identifiable with the differentiation between the noumenal and the phenomenal. Strauss's thought can therefore be considered more modern than Strauss's own self-identification as an antimodernist would have it.[183]

For Strauss, political philosophy is primarily concerned with the question of the best order. This central theme seems to fade into the background when political philosophy is seen as transcending itself. Why do philosophers need to consider the question of the best order when they can enjoy the pleasures of theoretical reflection? When they pursue this question, do they not instead provoke the suspicion of their opponents that they are acting only in their own interest? The transcendent nature of political philosophy identified by Strauss could imply the negation of philosophical interest in the realization of the best philosophical society. Any change in established political relations could threaten philosophy if the discipline is seen as a purely elite endeavor. Even the political responsibility that Strauss ascribes to philosophy does not seem to imply that philosophy is required to meet the needs of the many or of the community as a whole. Instead, philosophers possess a kind of political common sense that allows them to assess their position in society. With this recognition, they should learn to justify themselves in the context of the political community. The justification of philosophy before the tribunal of the political community and in its language seems to consist in the need for philosophers to descend into the realm of popular opinion and convince the political community of the necessity and healing power of philosophy. In this scheme, the suspicion that political philosophy (so conceived) is concerned with influencing society only out of self-interest seems quite justified.[184]

Strauss's variant of political philosophy presents itself as an answer to the question of the best social order. However, his stance on this question is passive, since he rejects political action for philosophers.[185] The gap that Strauss posits between philosophy and society proves to be a theoretical barrier to the philosophical goal of social and cultural betterment. It indicates a philosophical self-contradiction and can lead to a division of truth. A society convinced that its condition can only improve through philosophical impulses needs to confront that position with a healthy degree of skepticism. In contrast to Strauss's interpretation, theory and practice are complementary in al-Fārābī's philosophy. In his work, the interest in theoretical knowledge is closely linked to the interest in virtuous action and reform of the social and political conditions of his time.[186]

Epilogue

Strauss's dissatisfaction with modernity led him back to the philosophical world of the Middle Ages and antiquity. His restoration of a "classical political philosophy" was based on the insight that the crisis of modernity was essentially a crisis of philosophy. For philosophy had lost the proper form of political interaction with society. Philosophy, according to Strauss, needed religion. The authority of religion was absolutely necessary to control the passionate masses with proper orienting values. The beginnings of the crisis were manifested in the philosophical banishment of religion from the public sphere, a modern reaction to the instrumentalization of philosophy by theology in the Middle Ages. Strauss believed that a socially acceptable emancipation of philosophy could only occur when religion was used to achieve social peace. The difference between the ancients and the moderns lay in their respective assessments of religion. In modernity, religion had become a matter of individual conscience that found its strength in matters of faith. Medieval Jewish and Muslim philosophers, on the other hand, had conceived of religion as a comprehensive form of law, leading to its inviolable authority. Strauss believed that al-Fārābī had invented such an approach to religion based on Plato's political philosophy.

Modernity, in Strauss's eyes, emerged from engaging with ancient thought. Therefore, it could be illuminated through confrontation with the representatives of ancient thought. By interpreting earlier philosophers, he believed he could gain a better understanding of the problems of modernity. Such problems were rooted in the individual's lack of moral orientation, which emerged from a revolt against God. For Strauss, philosophers are the enemies of faith insofar as they search for the nature of beings. Nevertheless, he is of the opinion that atheism does not necessarily imply the removal of religion, as the true must not always be coeval with the useful.[1] In place of the negation of God that characterizes the Enlightenment, Strauss advances an alternative political affirmation of God. In political philosophy, religion should gain new meaning. For Strauss, the compatibility of religion and philosophy was achieved in the concept of divine law, a concept he found in Avicenna and al-Fārābī. A form of religion that has a primarily political function is mandated by human reason and can therefore also be accepted in modernity by philosophy. In this fashion, philosophy can unite the demands of truth with political necessity. Philosophy needs political philosophy, which, in this context, means the political qualification of philosophy as such.

Straussian political philosophy pushes back against political atheism as a modern phenomenon that is incompatible with demanding a stable and just political order.[2] Belief in the immortality of the soul and in divine predestination, beliefs intimately intertwined with the reward of moral behavior and the punishment of sin, ensure proper sociality. Religion can help philosophy achieve a just society. Both imply some form of transcendence. The idea of natural law, according to Strauss, can easily be reconciled with the belief in the existence of divinely revealed law.[3] Furthermore, Strauss believes that the theology of Plato's *Laws* is expressed in its penal code. The religion of the philosophers is therefore identical with the exoteric teachings that constitute political philosophy.[4] It is based on the dialectic of revelation and atheism. The nomistic religion of the atheists must emphasize the existence of God for political purposes, lest the power of law to order society be diluted. The political necessity of religion is based on two premises: An elitist conception of the Enlightenment and the conviction that evil can never be completely banished from the world.[5]

From the ambiguity of the atheistic adherence to religion as a factor of order and a criterion of orientation for those in need of guidance arises the necessity of a twofold form of writing that conceals philosophical views and expresses politically useful doctrines — not only in situations of persecution. Strauss is known for pointing out this mode of writing in the modern period, the necessity of which he sees as rooted in the fundamental antagonism between philosophy and society. For Strauss, philosophy chiefly consists of the genuine appreciation of fundamental and comprehensive problems along with the unending search for wisdom. Philosophy, when conceived in this fashion, is naturally in tension with societies structured by accepted opinions and traditions. In this conception, society, in its essential nature, is set up to oppress philosophy. Philosophers nevertheless remain individuals who in essential ways are dependent on society for their very lives and livelihoods. This places them in a precarious situation. They are convinced of the dangers inherent in a perpetual search for wisdom rooted in uncovering the unwritten laws of nature and the development of their own judgments. Indeed, such judgments do not always conform to social norms, thereby prompting the philosophers to transcend those norms with the argument that they were intended for nonphilosophers. In the interest of philanthropy and prudence, they reveal their true judgments only to those of similar acumen through a double-layered mode of writing. Through noble lies, they can hide philosophical truth between the lines. The double-layered form of writing, according to Strauss, is synonymous with a political philosophy rooted in the proper handling of dangerous ideas.

Strauss's mode of philosophizing is justified by the assumption that the Enlightenment continually fails because of the natural and unbridgeable gap between philosophers and everyday people. His return to the philosophers of the past, whose ideas he sought to uncover and distill, was motivated by the challenges of modernity's self-satisfaction with the universal achievements of reason. Strauss rejects such supposed philosophical achievements as dangerous anthropological strictures. In his view, not all human beings possess the same level of reason, nor are they all guided by it. Therefore, the Enlightenment cannot be seen as a phenomenon applicable to all but must be limited to the few.[6] Strauss is pessimistic about the Enlightenment, convinced that the inhabitant of the cave is incapable of leaving it unless they are a philosopher. The claim to a universalistic form of Enlightenment is an illusion that can be overcome by a political philosophy that contains the necessary orientation to human nature.

Strauss's critique of modernity compelled him to rethink modernity's groundwork and ambitions. In Strauss's alternative, ancient traditions of thought needed to be revived to serve as a yardstick for modernity, against which it could measure itself and thereby correct its course. But while Strauss sought to revive the ideas of these philosophers in order to reinvigorate modernity, he disagreed with them on one important point. For these philosophers had hoped that their own ideas would enlighten society. His own experience taught him that modern rationalism could not overcome religious faith in the hope for a comprehensive form of Enlightenment. In the Bible as well as Greek mythology, the conflict between humans and God (or the gods) points toward the limits of human understanding. The transition from mythos to logos is compelled by a philosophical urge to generalize Prometheus's act. Otherwise, the idea of reason's universality would be considered complete nonsense. Instead, Strauss firmly held to the antagonism between knowledge and faith. This antagonism seems to have emerged as the fulcrum of his thought on the core of the philosophical endeavor. His portrayal of philosophy as constituted by the conflict between knowledge and faith propels him to accord philosophers a monopoly on knowledge. Only they possess the capacity for reason that allows for the recognition of truth. Nonphilosophers can only arrive at an approximation of truth through the knowledge granted to them by the philosophers, a realm of knowledge deliberately delimited due to the danger of philosophical ideas. Such a reliance on mythos prompts an important question — What should be done with the fire of cognition that Prometheus stole from the gods? Must such powers of cognition be conferred only on a small group of philosophers who depict this new world in terms of old gods? Does this form of thought lead to the hopeless conclusion that humanity as a whole has no chance of being enlightened?

Ultimately, and perhaps sadly, Strauss believed that no society could be truly free. This is the obvious conclusion one can derive from a philosophical apparatus built upon an esotericism that posits certain truths as necessarily concealed from the masses out of the philosophers' sense of love and care. This form of elite philosophical truth must survive by propagating false yet useful opinions to counteract the modern condition of an unrestrictedly free society. Truth seems to contradict the necessities of real, existing societies. It is therefore the sole province of the philosophers, who keep it concealed due to the threat it poses to society. This threat lies in the fact that the form of truth Strauss ascribes to the philosophers is predicated upon the atheistic downgrading of religion to a form of political utility. Esoteric truth views religion and morality as necessary tools of deception for humanity. The danger lies in its nihilistic content, which is capable of destroying society.[7]

Strauss's belief in the deep divide between philosophers and their respective societies ultimately proves incommensurate with Socratic wisdom, a form of wisdom conceived in terms of public discourse within society. His depiction of the Socratic method as oriented primarily toward theoretical inquiry, and therefore restricted to the interaction between philosophers and the social elite, ultimately leads to Strauss's division between theory and praxis. Philosophical activity is accordingly restricted to conversations within a small circle of select students. Such a philosophical endeavor rooted in private conversation can be justly accused of being incapable of broader public influence. Furthermore, it can be observed that while Strauss adopts the Aristotelian distinction between theoretical and practical sciences, at the same time he sees philosophy forced to deal not only with theoretical problems in a Platonic way.[8] Philosophy practiced in private discussions by philosophers who feel threatened and estranged from society (and thereby concerned with their own survival) can only lead to a philosophical endeavor incapable of addressing actual and pressing social issues. Moreover, philosophy conceived as a private endeavor justified by persecution cannot be construed as a universal philosophical topos. Rather, courage to change and vigorous resistance to existing conditions characterize the philosophers, without whose prevalent ideas cultural development and social progress cannot be realized. Wisdom cannot only be communicated; it must also be practiced.[9]

The modern critique of religion takes a turn with Strauss, who understands religion as law in order to interpret it politically. Philosophy thus commits itself to conceive of religion as a political force for the establishment of social order. However, behind this theoretical claim, there seems to be a polemical intention to degrade religion to a political instrument of philosophy. However, Strauss's conception of religion as law has two implications. First, the attempt to reduce the value of religion to its lawfulness means casting doubt on the value of religions that, like Christianity, do not take the form of law. Although Strauss tries to establish and save a philosophically justifiable value of religion, the consequence of his interpretation is that religions that cannot be conceived of as laws cannot be saved by philosophy. Strauss's critique of religion thus contains a hidden critique of Christianity.

Strauss's philosophy thematizes the dichotomy of philosophy and law anew. He constructs this conceptual pair in order to render religion more useful for his philosophical critique. However, it seems that his critique remains tangled up in what he intends to criticize. His political philosophy is based on the assumption that divine laws are necessary for the existence of the human community, since neither philosophy nor politics can establish a just social order. God's name is supposed to vouch for justice. He stands for omnipotence and eternal punishment and can therefore give religion a power that philosophy and politics lack. Strauss limits this effect of God only to nonphilosophers; nevertheless, the assumption of a social-existential significance of religion obliges the philosopher, insofar as they are human and thus remain dependent on life in community, to live and philosophize on a religious foundation. Strauss's work itself evinces a clear religious foundation. He wrestled with the problem of law until the end of his life.[10]

Another difficulty arises from the Straussian conception of religion as law. The conceptual politicization of religion posited as an antithesis to modernity betrays a structural similarity with the (Islamist) fundamentalist infusion of politics by religion. Fundamentalism is often perceived simultaneously as both a reaction to modernity and its product. It claims religion and politics are indivisible and mandates a restorative form of crisis management in which the idealization of the past and the emphasis on religion's social role would constitute the negation of modernity's core principles. Muslim fundamentalists would like to erect a religious state ruled by the sharia. Their conception of Islam as fully intertwined with an Islamic state renders religion coeval with political power.[11] Of course, Strauss is not arguing for the political rule of religion. Quite the opposite is the case. He is arguing for the instrumentalization of religion for the purpose of upholding social order as predicated theoretically by political philosophy. Nevertheless, his conceptual utilization of religion reveals functional similarities with religious fundamentalism. His assessment of religion as a political instrument would be appealing to fundamentalists even if their ultimate normative aims differ. The distance Strauss places between philosophy and political action does not play a large role here. Since the philosophers who interpret religion politically provide the politically active religious fundamentalists with important theoretical impulses for their political activities, they run the risk of being misused.

Strauss's restoration of a classical philosophy possessing a Platonic-Aristotelian character ultimately takes the great differences between the two philosophers to be insignificant. Also here, he seems to be influenced by al-Fārābī, who marginalizes the differences in favor of the harmonious intentions of both philosophers and declares them to be purely external.[12] Strauss and al-Fārābī agree that Plato and Aristotle essentially teach the same thing and that the similarities or differences in one matter or another pale in comparison with their common philosophical goals.[13] Al-Fārābī harmonizes the teachings of both philosophers under the strong metaphysical influence of Plotinus's *Enneads*. Al-Fārābī falsely believed that this text contained Aristotle's theology. In his attempt to reconstruct classical political philosophy, Strauss appears to be guided by the same philosophically restorative motivation as al-Fārābī. Yet Strauss's attempt at harmonization was based not on metaphysics but rather on the central place of political thought in the oeuvres of Plato and Aristotle. In addition to this essential difference, the objects of their philosophical contemplation were not the same. While Strauss excluded all metaphysical topics in Plato's philosophy from his own interpretation, al-Fārābī placed metaphysics rather than political writings at the forefront of his.[14]

Arab thought in the Middle Ages drew from an ancient metaphysical repertoire significant components for understanding earthly and extraterrestrial beings and relationships, which were seen as standing in an ordered system of rank. The idea of hierarchy is central to such a conception of order; each being occupies its place in the hierarchical order.[15] Al-Fārābī presented a chain of being whose starting point is God, the First Cause; this chain emerges through emanation and includes the heavenly spheres in descending order. Human beings, composed of souls and bodies, encounter this hierarchy through an ascending hierarchy tied to the four elements: minerals, plants, animals, and finally humans. This hierarchical ontological order includes the scale of ethical postulates, the value of which increases with increasing distance from these materials. The powers of the human soul are also hierarchically arranged in this totalizing conceptualization, with the lower powers serving the higher powers. Such a cosmological order is imbued with harmony. The lower rungs of the chain of being are attracted to the higher rungs and act in their service. All forms of being are oriented toward God, the Supreme Being. He is simple and unique. Multiplicity arises with increasing distance from him. The highest rung of the chain of being is at the same time the final reason for the existence of all other rungs as well as the telos of

Creation. Truth and existence run parallel to each other.[16] Political thinking in Islam translates the metaphysical conception of the cosmic hierarchy into the sphere of political and social order. Following Aristotle, al-Fārābī posits human beings as "social and political animals" inasmuch as human beings must live in community with other humans in accordance with nature.[17] However, human beings need a homogenizing force due to the diversity of their interests. Divine providence expressed through religious laws achieves this goal. Political structures that reflect the cosmic hierarchy are to emerge according to the image of the perfect cosmic order. The connection of religious interests and political needs through the prophet Muhammad is reflected in the political system of the caliphate, where political power is legitimated by God.[18]

According to al-Fārābī, philosophy is the oldest science. The Chaldeans were familiar with it, and it was later transmitted to the ancient Egyptians. Then it came to the Greeks. Muslims became aware of it through the Syrians, who took over its mantle after the Greeks.[19] Philosophy emerges under appropriate preconditions connected to the organization of political community and exists so long as political stability permits it.[20] It migrates from one people to another, enriching itself in the course of its migration with specific elements of the various advanced civilizations in which it flourishes, indicating its heterogeneous character.[21]

Al-Fārābī represents a comprehensive understanding of philosophy whose various parts fit together cohesively. He presupposes a virtuous lifestyle for the study of philosophy, in which theory and practice complement each other.[22] The virtuous composition of the soul presents itself as the ethical basis for understanding mathematics and logic, which enable reason to avoid error and to recognize what is true, even in the moral sense.[23] Al-Fārābī distinguishes the true philosopher from the vain one by the fact that the former is endowed with the intellectual and ethical qualities mentioned in the *Politeia* in order to take up the theoretical sciences. The true philosopher is also educated piously according to the religious laws and beliefs.[24] Furthermore, the true philosopher not only possesses theoretical and practical virtues themselves but also assiduously attempts to facilitate the flourishing of these virtues in the society in which they live.[25] Al-Fārābī's emphasis on the philosophers' obligation to use commonly used terminology in their communal involvement points to a pedagogical relationship between philosophers and nonphilosophers.[26]

Plato and Aristotle occupy a central position in al-Fārābī's reception of the philosophical tradition. His attempt to unite the teachings of both philosophers despite their very real differences is based on the false assumption that Aristotle possessed a theology, an assumption that reflects certain Neoplatonist tendencies.[27] Al-Fārābī's attempt to unify philosophy, which apparently emerged out of debates between philosophers and theologians regarding the world's origin, is primarily aimed at defending philosophy from charges of internal contradictions on certain matters. The harmonization of philosophy is a precondition for harmonizing philosophy and religion and thereby Islamic teachings and Greek philosophy. Accordingly, al-Fārābī mentions that Plato and Aristotle prove the existence and unity of God. Moreover, their teachings save people from confusion and uncertainty in theological matters. The philosophers also prove to be useful in the consolidation of religious doctrines, since philosophy, like theology, ultimately amounts to the confirmation of God's existence and omnipotence through the knowledge of God's works.[28]

Al-Fārābī's emphasis on the usefulness of philosophical teachings for clarifying theological questions not only serves to justify philosophy before the jury of religion by confirming their external complementarity but is meant also to demonstrate their inner harmony. Thus, he states that God's comprehensive care, which grants the solid continuance of the world and all its parts and relations, can be known through knowledge ranging from anatomy to physics and finally to demonstration, politics, and religion. A unified form of knowledge results from both religion and philosophy. Demonstration is entrusted to people with clear minds and straightforward spirits, politics to people with correct insights, and religion to people with spiritual inspiration. Finally, al-Fārābī explains that the subjects dealt with in religion are far-reaching and exceed the capacity of reason. Therefore, they have to be presented by means of imagination. What philosophy shows by means of reason, religion shows by means of imagination.[29] The two do not contradict each other but are ultimately concerned with the same goal: to know God through Creation. Considering that not all people are philosophers and capable of theoretical effort, religious knowledge based on human imagination is addressed to most people, the nonphilosophers.[30]

Al-Fārābī explains that there are two ways to make something understandable. One can render its essential core intellectually conceivable or its representation recognizable by the imagination. As al-Fārābī notes,

> Now when one acquires the knowledge of the beings or receives instruction in them, if he perceives their ideas themselves with his intellect, and his assent to them is by means of certain demonstration, then the science that comprises these cognitions is philosophy. But if they are known by imagining them through similarities that imitate them, and assent to what is imagined of them is caused by persuasive methods, then the ancients call what comprises these cognitions religion. [. . .]. Both comprise the same subjects and both give an account of the ultimate

> principles of the beings. For both supply knowledge about the first principle and the cause of beings., and both give an account of the ultimate end for the sake of which man is made — that is supreme happiness — and the ultimate end of every one of the other beings. In everything of which philosophy gives an account based on intellectual perception or conception, religion gives an account based on imagination. In everything demonstrated by philosophy, religion employs persuasion.[31]

Philosophy and religion are identical with respect to the knowledge of the first principle and the final goal of beings. However, the pedagogical process is different in both. The same content is taught through intellectual perception and understanding in philosophy and through imagination in religion. Everything that is proved in philosophy is the object of belief in religion. Imagination also plays an important role in the teaching of philosophers. For "everything that the soul thinks is mingled with imagination."[32] This is especially true for beings that are difficult or impossible to grasp through theoretical thinking.[33]

Religion is similar to philosophy.[34] Like the latter, it consists of a theoretical and a practical part. The theoretical views, which are accepted in religion without proof, are proved in theoretical philosophy. Religion contains practical doctrines whose universals appear in practical philosophy, while the universals in religion are determined by concrete conditions and are therefore particularized. Since theoretical philosophy provides the necessary proofs for the theoretical doctrines of religion, and practical philosophy explains the reasons and purposes of the religious conditions, both parts of religion can be subordinated to the corresponding parts of philosophy.[35] However, there is a reciprocal relationship of dependence between philosophy and religion when it comes to the communication of truth: the former contains the universally valid theoretical foundations of the latter, while the latter proves to be an indispensable pedagogical tool of the former, addressing a specific people.[36] Al-Fārābī does not reject religion but rather recognizes its great importance in conveying true views and ethical values to humanity. In his view, religion is capable of enlightening people about the principles of existence and true happiness, as long as they do not possess theoretical knowledge in this regard. Philosophy and religion are not in conflict but complement each other when it comes to the appropriate communication of truth, which corresponds to the different receptivity of human beings. Religion surpasses philosophy in that it does not come from reason alone but from reason and revelation together.[37]

In the *Book of Letters*, which is considered al-Fārābī's commentary on Aristotle's *Metaphysics*, al-Fārābī develops an anthropological theory of cultural history in which the emergence of language as well as various arts and science are described.[38] He explains that religion can first emerge in the context of a given people only once philosophy has fully developed. Philosophy is a logical and historical precondition for religion and its pursuant sciences, just as a tree is the precondition for the fruit grown on its branches. Religion arises after philosophy within cultural history because its purpose is "to teach the masses, according to their ability, the theoretical and practical matters that have been discovered in philosophy, by persuasion or imagination, or both together."[39] Fully aware of humans' existence and place in the cosmos, al-Fārābī ascribes to philosophy and religion the right to impart truthful teachings aimed at the knowledge of the One True. He seems to imply a delimitation of spheres of validity when he says that philosophy is limited to what "exists in the world."[40] While religion does not provide philosophers with any theoretical knowledge, it nevertheless infuses ethical norms and social customs within which philosophers are raised. Al-Fārābī posits a qualitative correspondence between philosophy and religion since the nature of religion has its origin subsequent to the existence of philosophy. However, the two become disproportionate to each other when the images used in religion are taken as literally true and taken as the theoretical matters they represent. Since philosophy and its adherents could be harmed by this, philosophers try to clarify the facts.[41] Furthermore, al-Fārābī recognizes the plurality of religions and attributes it not to disagreements in matters of philosophical substance but to differences in matters of imitation.[42]

In the concluding passage of the *Book of Religion*, al-Fārābī shows that the head of the virtuous city must have a complete knowledge of theoretical philosophy in order to recognize and imitate God's ordering of the world. Therefore, it is necessary for a "common religion to exist through which the opinions, articles of faith, and actions" of human beings "are unified and the groups among them harmonized, united, and ordered. Only then can they coordinate their actions and support each other, in order to achieve the goal of attaining the highest form of happiness."[43]

Al-Fārābī assigns philosophy and religion different competencies for ensuring social order. While philosophy provides theoretical knowledge about such order, religion provides coherence for the various concrete parts of society so that order can be realized. Both elements function complementarily in their common quest for felicity. While philosophy provides a necessary theoretical precondition for the emergence of religion, religion, to a similar degree, provides the necessary practical precondition for the communal achievement of felicity and the education of philosophers. The way of life practiced by the true philosopher proceeds, alongside other imperatives, with the fulfillment of religious requirements.[44]

For al-Fārābī, religion and philosophy cohere in a conceptual harmony. Religion is posited as an expression of philosophy conducted through representation and modes of convincing, in which the imagination is stronger than reason. In this fashion, nonphilosophers can apprehend theoretical and practical teachings in the form of comprehensible metaphors. Religion contains the social imitation of philosophical universalities employed in order to convince people of the necessities required for social life.[45] Such an assessment does not reduce religion's importance in the overall schematic. On the basis of Aristotle's interrelationship of thought and perception, it is shown that even a philosopher's thinking is possible only through the use of images that imitate the thing to be thought.[46] An analogy may be useful in order to grasp al-Fārābī's definition of religion as an imitation of philosophy. Religion can be understood as the imprint of a seal. The imprint expresses the value of the seal in a concrete and powerful way.[47]

Another harmonious aspect of al-Fārābī's philosophical project comes to the fore in his conception of the "metaphysical contemplation of beings" (*an-naẓar al-ilāhī fī l-mawjūdāt*)[48] as the basis of the "science of man" (*al-ʿilm al-insānī*) and the "social science" (*al-ʿilm al-madānī*), which together constitute "social philosophy" or practical philosophy (*al-falsafa al-madaniyya* or *al-falsafa al-ʿamaliyya*).[49] The first of these sciences, ethics, contains a theoretical character that explores the nature and character of perfection and thereby achieves an understanding of the purpose of human existence. Ethics also examines everything that leads a person to perfection or is beneficial to them and states that these are the good and noble deeds and the virtues. It distinguishes them from the evils and misdeeds and explains how the former arise, how they are constituted, and how they are conceived.[50] The second science, social science, is oriented practically. It deals with the things by which the people living in the community attain happiness, each according to their natural disposition. Thus, it says that the political community and the totality of people living in a city are similar to the totality of people living in the world, and the structure of governance in the city or nation (*umma*) is analogous to the hierarchical order of the cosmos. The ideal city contains images of what the whole world contains. In al-Fārābī's political thought, politics seems to depend on metaphysics.[51]

Al-Fārābī's conviction that the perfect political structure is analogous to the cosmic order is apparent in the structure of two of his books, *al-Madīna al-fāḍila* and *as-Siyāsa al-madaniyya*. Both books begin with the depiction of the cosmic order and end with the representation of the perfect and deficient political orders. Two orders emerge out of this depiction: a metaphysical, heavenly, and immutable one, along with a political and temporal order, which is to be created on earth in the image of the former. The structure of both writings indicates that politics is dependent on metaphysics because metaphysics provides a theoretical basis for politics. The theoretical part serves as a background against which the political part unfolds. In the metaphysical, static part of the cosmos, the hierarchy descends from the First Cause to the last separate intellect. In contrast, the representation of the natural and human world, determined by continuous becoming and perishing, ascends from the lowest, purely material four elements to the human, the only rational being in the world.

According to al-Fārābī, there is a very first preexistent principle in the world, which is followed by other principles in order of rank. These principles give rise to existents, which are followed by other existents in an infinite order until the last stage of existence. In this structure, each member has a position according to its natural disposition. According to the same pattern, in the ideal state there is a preexistent ruler, who is followed by lower supervisors, who are followed by other, lower supervisors and citizens, until the final stage in the city and humanity in general.[52] In this hierarchy, people occupy the position that best reflects their natural disposition; each does their own. A further analogous order is reflected in the organs of the human body.[53] The powers of the human soul relate to each other according to the same hierarchical pattern of order.[54] Understanding the structural analogy of hierarchically ordered beings presents itself as a "theoretical perfection."[55] A further analogy is manifested in the act of ruling both in the world and in the ideal state. In the city, the ruler fulfills the same function that God fulfills in the world. He was chosen by God for this role.[56] The governance of the state corresponds to God's governance of the world; it aims to establish connection, harmony, and cooperation among the different parts of the community so that they become as one and do the one thing to achieve the one goal of bliss.[57] For political thought, this means that the ideal social order in all its institutions becomes an analogous representation of the cosmic order. The hierarchy of social rule must therefore be built to reflect the hierarchy of the transcendental world. In order to understand the various hierarchical structures of order within nature and the human world, while also identifying the analogous nature of their structures, a perfect theoretical knowledge is required that contains the sum of metaphysics, physics, and psychology. This perfect form of knowledge is employed in order to build the perfect political order. The ideal ruler must therefore be a philosopher, both to understand the divine order and to apply it to the political order. Thereby the heavenly order emerges as a template for the ideal political order. The architecture of the perfect political order is an imitation of the architecture of the metaphysical world.[58]

The philosopher's intellect is at the apex of the hierarchical political community they design. They receive the thought-inspiring imprints of the active intellect, which exists as the final level of the heavenly hierarchy. Both intellects are unified in the theoretical act of thought, which functions as a connective medium between the metaphysical and the political. The metaphysical and the political come into contact within thinking, with the former then emerging as the theoretical side and the latter as the practical side. This grants philosophy the status of the highest science. Al-Fārābī presents philosophy as "royal" (*malakiyya*). Its activity is none other than politics (*siyāsa*), which, according to this understanding, is conceived as the most exalted form of activity, identical with practical philosophy.[59] Consequently, it cannot be claimed that al-Fārābī subordinated theoretical philosophy to politics. Instead, both crystallize as two aspects of perfect thought, thereby reflecting two sides of a medallion. While theoretical knowledge of the harmonious cosmic hierarchy exists as a model for structuring a harmonious political community, its associated political activity aims at erecting harmony in human affairs. Theoretical knowledge is thereby given concrete expression.[60] For al-Fārābī, the world of experience is not grounded in itself but in the order of the transcendent, with which it is not identical but on which it is structurally dependent. The philosophical intellect, both theoretical and political, acts as a sensorium of transcendence and thus as a force for applying the sublime order to social reality. Likewise, it recognizes the truth of revelation because it is convinced that truth and the need for religious education have the same origin (even for philosophers!).[61]

In al-Fārābī's conception, the human being stands in the middle of an image containing analogously constructed structures. The human being is, in and of themselves, a microcosmos. Within them, elements connected to the powers of the soul come together that point to a hierarchical order at whose apex lies the power of mind. The human being represents the summit of composite beings and is characterized by the power of will and reason. Their goal is the achievement of felicity in both this world and the next, which they can pursue through life in the community. In the community, they may find not only the material basis for their existence but also the prospect of attaining theoretical and practical knowledge. The performance of virtue while interacting with fellow human beings is also an important factor in their quest for happiness. Al-Fārābī learned from Aristotle that the theoretical contemplation of being represents the highest form of happiness. He also knew that theoretical science cannot remain without practical effect. Just as logic leads to rational, practical decisions and grammar to correct speaking and writing,[62] theoretical knowledge leads to the development of a practical power of judgment, especially reflected in the act of choice.

Practical experiences tether theoretical knowledge and help it expand. Due to the social preconditions for the emergence of philosophical concepts into the world, these concepts are not bereft of implications for the life of the community. This explains why al-Fārābī assigns the theoretical exploration of felicity to the social sciences.[63]

Al-Fārābī seems to have been aware of the close connection between theory and praxis, a connection that manifested itself to him in music.[64] Like Plato, he must have considered philosophy to be the most perfect music because philosophy understands the cosmic harmony and, through this understanding, strives to establish harmony in human conditions and states.[65] Al-Fārābī, the music theorist and philosopher, who was also considered a master of logic in his time,[66] saw harmony permeating the cosmos, the parts of which attract each other in their mutual sympathy. The best order appeared to him as a symphonic unity in which all organs are directed toward the attainment of harmony. Harmony also pervades the true spiritual world of humans: there is only one true philosophy, whose parts relate to each other in a harmonious hierarchy, and only one true felicity, to which all religions aspire because, despite their differences, they are essentially one and the same.[67] Within this harmonious system, no conflict exists between reason and faith or between will and choice.[68] The rule of reason over all the different human proclivities or drives guarantees a harmonious way of life that does not contradict faith, as reason confirms God's existence through cognition of harmoniously ordered beings. Al-Fārābī is clearly no atheist. His omission of Plato's theory of ideas from the presentation of Platonic philosophy should not indicate a secret atheism but rather the influence of Aristotle, who, according to al-Fārābī, rejected this Platonic teaching.[69]

Al-Fārābī's description of the virtuous city compels the reader to ask the same question that Proclus already posed after reading Plato's *Politeia*, namely, whether this work should be considered a book of ethics or statecraft.[70] Al-Fārābī's perfect political order means the totality of moral views, laws, and hierarchical order established by reason according to the dignity and capacity of its individual members. What we today would call the state is only a subordinate and delimited segment of this totality. There is a vast chasm between the political community thematized by al-Fārābī and the modern differentiation between state and society, between political and religious institutions, and between the state and what we define today as nonpolitical cultural life. This community appears to encompass the totality of the political, social, religious, cultural, and life-world conditions for achieving the perfection of human possibility and the realization of the highest human goal of felicity. In comparison with other, deficient forms of order, the virtuous city is defined *ex negativo* as a community whose first chief is directed by God, whose adherents live ethically by practicing an ethical life in accordance with religion and by striving for true knowledge.[71]

It is extremely difficult to ascribe a political philosophy or political science to al-Fārābī and the other Islamic philosophers without taking into account the heterogeneity of their teaching. Nevertheless, this could be justified if one understands politics as the successful way of dealing with the environment.[72] However, such a form of politics could not be disconnected from ethics. It must also have a theological basis, as it is to some extent dependent on religious content.[73] Whether the introduction of this philosophy into modern discourse is productive or not, one should consider the following: Modernity is defined by an irreversible faculty of judgment that has divided earlier totalities into quite autonomously defined spheres. The employment of premodern methods against modern structures can prove difficult. Indeed, the attempt to revive such totalities as the idea of a divine law regulating state and society seems ill-suited to dealing with a crisis of modernity.

Yet one must not ignore the fact that Strauss's interest in al-Fārābī's philosophy encouraged academic attention to his works over the course of the twentieth century. His interpretation of al-Fārābī significantly impacted many debates regarding Strauss's own legacy.[74] An undeniable merit remains for a thinker who is interested in the great thinkers of the past: they take the continuity of history seriously. As the mind moves into other time periods and cultural spheres, it realizes that the cultures, with their different origins, are connected to each other as though by an umbilical cord. It seems that Leo Strauss was convinced of this, which is why he attempted to find solutions for problems of Western modernity in medieval thinkers from outside Europe. He apparently did not believe in the clash of cultures but rather in a conflict between philosophy and society. His belief in such a meeting of minds compelled him to employ such thinkers (whose books had theretofore been gathering dust) to confront a self-satisfied modern culture. Therefore, his thought also deserves the interest of his critic.

Appendix

ARABIC TEXTS AND THE TEXTS OF ISLAMIC PHILOSOPHERS VIEWED BY STRAUSS

I. Texts by al-Fārābī

1. *Alfarabi's philosophische Abhandlungen*, ed. and trans. Dieterici (Leiden: Brill, 1895). (*PHG*: 103; "QR": 10; *GS* II: 160)
2. *Kitāb al-jam' baina ra'yay al-ḥakīmain*, in *Alfarabi's philosophische Abhandlungen*, ed. and trans. Dieterici (Leiden: Brill, 1895). ("OVAM": 102; "FP": 359, 364)
3. *Kitāb al-milla al-fāḍila*. Manuscript. (*PAW*: 64)
4. *Kitāb as-siyāsa al-madaniyya al-mulaqqab bi-mabādi' al-mawjūdāt*, (Hyderabad: 1346 H). ("QR": 10ff., 23, 28; "VSF": 105; "OVAM": 101; *GS* II: 164, 211; "FP": 381; *PAW*: 64, 117; *WIPP*: 156, 159, 163)
5. *Kitāb at-tanbīh 'alā sabīl as-sa'āda* (Hyderabad: 1346 H). ("QR": 10–11, 13)
6. *Kitāb iḥṣā' al-'ulūm*, ed. O. Amin (Cairo: 1350 H/1931). ("QR": 10–11, 13, 37; "VSF": 97ff., 105; "OVAM": 101, 105; "FP": 363, 371, 374, 389; *PAW*: 40, 77, 99, 119; *WIPP*: 84; *RCPR*: 218, 273)
7. *Kitāb taḥṣīl as-sa'āda*, (Hyderabad: 1345 H). ("QR": 10ff., 22, 26, 31, 36; "VSF": 98ff., 105; *GS* II: 165, 177; "OVAM": 101; "FP": 358–59, 368, 371, 373; *PAW*: 17, 119)
8. *Falsafat Aflāṭūn wa-ajzā'uhā wa-marātib ajzā'ihā min awwalihā ilā ākhirihā* (*De Platonis philosophia*), eds. F. Rosenthal and Walzer (London: Kraus, 1943). ("VSF": 101ff.; "FP": 357–93; *PAW*: 11ff., 137; *WIPP*: 147ff., 167–68; *RCPR*: 159)
9. *Falsafat Arisṭūṭālīs wa-ajzā'u falsafatihi wa-marātibu ajzā'ihā wa-l-mawḍi'u alladhī minhu ibtada'a wa-ilaihi intahā*. Manuscript. ("VSF": 101ff.; "FP": 359)
10. *Mabādi' ārā' ahl al-madīna al-fāḍila* (*The Ideal State*), ed. Dieterici (Leiden: Brill, 1895). (*PHG*: 99ff., 104, 107–8, 115; "QR": 10ff., 16, 25–26, 31; "VSF": 105; "OVAM": 101; *GS* II: 164, 211; "FP": 358, 381; *PAW*: 64, 114; *WIPP*: 159, 163)
11. *Talkhīṣ Nawāmīs Aflāṭūn* (*Compendium Legum Platonis*), ed. Gabrieli (London: Warburg Institute, 1952). (*GS* II: 196; *WIPP*:

134–54; *TM*: 318, 328)

II. Texts by Avicenna

1. *Al-Ishārāt wa-tanbīhāt*, ed. J. Forget (Leiden: Brill, 1892). (*PHG*:112; *PAW*: 50)
2. *An-Najāt*. Manuscript. ("OVAM": 97)
3. *Ash-Shifāʾ* (*Metaphysics*), also as the Berlin manuscript, Minutoli 229. (*PHG*: 103, 112ff.; "OVAM": 97; *GS* II: 424; *PAW*: 139)
4. *De anima*, ed. A. Alpagus (Venice: 1546). (*PHG*: 103–4; "VSF": 97–98; "OVAM": 102; *PAW*: 124)
5. "Die Psychologie des Ibn Sīna," ed. S. Landauer, *Zeitschrift der Deutschen Morgenländischen Gesellschaft* 29 (1875): 335–418. (*PHG*: 103)
6. *Kitāb al-maʿād*, ed. A. Alpagus (Venice: 1546). ("OVAM": 102)
7. *Tisʿ rasāʾil*, ed. (Constantinople: Maṭbaʿat al-Jawāʾib, 1298 H/1881) and Gotha manuscript A1158. (*PHG*: 103–4, 111ff.; "VSF": 97–98, 100; *GS* II: 424ff.; *WIPP*: 161; *RCPR*: 218, 224; *JPCM*: 463)

III. Texts by Averroes

1. Commentary on Aristotle's *De sensu et sensato* (Paris Bibliotheque Nationale, MS hebr., 1009). ("FP": 373)
2. Commentary on Aristotle's *De somniis* (Venice: 1560). (*RKS*: 172n236)
3. Commentary on Aristotle's *Nicomachian Ethics*. Manuscript. (*PAW*: 75, 97)
4. Commentary on Aristotle's *Physics*. (Leo Strauss papers, Department of Special Collections, University of Chicago Library, box 11, folder 2)
5. Commentary on Aristotle's *Rhetoric* (MS Paris, cod. hebr., 1008). ("QR": 37)
6. Commentary on Plato's *Politeia*, in *Opera Aristotelis* (Venice: 1550). ("QR": 2, 20, 35ff.; "OVAM": 99; *GS* II: 162, 164, 196; "FP": 374; *PAW*: 91; *CM*: 26–27; *TM*: 330, 333)
7. *Faṣl al-maqāl wa-taqrīr mā baina ash-sharīʿa wa-l-ḥikma min al-ittiṣāl* and *al-Kashf ʿan manāhij al-adilla fī ʿaqāʾid al-milla*, both in *Philosophie und Theologie* by Averroes, ed. M. J. Müller

(Munich: 1859). (*PHG*: 69ff., 81, 104; "QR": 1, 37; *PAW*: 110–11; *RCPR*: 222)

8. The Great Commentary on the *Metaphysics*. Manuscript. ("VSF": 103–4)
9. The Middle Commentary on Aristotle's *De anima*. (Papers, box 11, folder 4)
10. The Middle Commentary on Aristotle's *Topics*. Manuscript. (MS Munich, cod. hebr. 26). (*PHG*: 84)
11. *Tahāfut at-tahāfut*, ed. M. Bouyges (Beirut: 1930). (*PHG*: 75; "FP": 391; *PAW*: 126)

IV. Further Texts

1. Abū Ḥāmid al-Ghazālī, *Maqāṣid al-falāsifa* (no place of publication or year). (*GS* II: 160)
2. Abū Ḥāmid al-Ghazālī, *Tahāfut al-falāsifa*, ed. M. Bouyges (Beirut: 1927). (*PHG*: 103)
3. Albino Nagy, *Die philosophischen Abhandlungen des Kindi* (Münster: 1897). ("QR": 4)
4. ʿAlī Ibn Muḥammad al-Māwardī, *Aʿlām an-nubūwa* (Cairo: 1315). (*PHG*: 104)
5. ʿAlī Ibn Rabbān aṭ-Ṭabarī, , *Kitāb ad-dīn wa-d-dawla* (Cairo: 1923). (*PHG*: 104)
6. Ibn ar-Rāwandī, *Kitāb az-zumurrud*, ed. P. Kraus, *Rivista degli Studi Orientali* 14 (1934). ("QR": 4; *PAW*: 125)
7. al-Qifṭī, *Taʾrīkh al-ḥukamāʾ*, ed. Julius Lippert (Leipzig: 1903). ("QR": 11; "VSF": 102–3)
8. Ibn Bājja, *Tadbīr al-mutawaḥḥid, Excerpts from the Hebrew von Moses Narboni*, ed. D. Herzog (no year given). (*PAW*: 91)
9. Ibn Khaldūn, *al-Muqaddimah*, ed. Quatremère (Paris: 1858). (*PHG*: 106)
10. Ibn Ṭufail, *Ḥayy Ibn Yaqẓān*, ed. L. Gauthier (Beirut: 1936). (*PHG*: 103; "FP": 372; *PAW*: 14, 111; *RCPR*: 218)
11. Muḥammad Ibn Zakarīyyā ar-Rāzī, *Kitāb as-sīra al-falsafiyya*, ed. P. Kraus, *Orientalia* 4–5 (1935–36). ("QR": 5; *GS* II: 177; "FP": 384; *PAW*: 117)
12. *Rasāʾil Ikhwān aṣ-Ṣafāʾ* (Cairo: 1928). ("QR": 13, 31)

Notes

Introduction to the Translation

1. See, for example, Heinrich Meier, "How Strauss Became Strauss," in *Reorientation: Leo Strauss in the 1930s*, ed. Martin D. Yaffe and Richard S. Ruderman, 13–32 (New York: Palgrave Macmillan, 2014); Daniel Tanguay, *Leo Strauss: An Intellectual Biography*, trans. Christopher Nadon (New Haven, CT: Yale University Press, 2011); Rasoul Namazi, *Leo Strauss and Islamic Political Thought* (Cambridge: Cambridge University Press, 2022).
2. Most recently, Namazi correctly observed that the "limited reception of Strauss's contribution to the study of Muslim philosophers is not consonant with the unique position medieval Islamic political thought occupies in Strauss's intellectual biography" (*Strauss and Islamic Political Thought*, ix). Namazi's book presents previously unpublished materials from Strauss's archive, materials that provide even more proof for Strauss's intensive and decades-long engagement with medieval Arabo-Islamic philosophy.
3. Leo Strauss, *Philosophie und Gesetz — Frühe Schriften*, vol. 2 of *Gesammelte Schriften*, ed. Heinrich Meier with Wiebke Meier (Stuttgart: J. B. Metzler, 1997), 26 (henceforth cited as *GS* II).
4. On July 7, 1973, Leo Strauss wrote to Gershom Scholem, "My favorite citation was and remains the famous saying of Averroes: 'Moriatur anima mea mortem philosophorum.'" Strauss, *Hobbes' politische Wissenschaft und zugehörige Schriften — Briefe*, vol. 3 of *Gesammelte Schriften*, ed. Heinrich Meier with Wiebke Meier (Stuttgart: J. B. Metzler, 2001), 769 (henceforth cited as *GS* III). He repeated the saying in a letter to Scholem on September 30, 1973 (*GS* III, 771), as well as in various earlier letters to other persons.
5. The importance of the Avicennian reference to Plato's *Nomoi* as a classical work on the philosophical interpretation of prophecy and religious law has been acknowledged by many Strauss experts, most notably Heinrich Meier. Therefore, any contention that I overestimate the importance of this reference to Avicenna's remark to the development of Strauss's thought is misplaced. See Markus Kartheininger, *Heterogenität: Politische Philosophie im Frühwerk von Leo Strauss* (Munich: Wilhelm Fink, 2006), 365n34. Kartheininger is interested in the formation of political philosophy in the early works of Leo Strauss, which took place in the Jewish-German context of the 1920s. Of course, in my book I am pursuing a different goal, namely the influence of al-Fārābī, Avicenna, and Averroes on the development of Strauss's thought and Strauss's interpretation of their philosophies of revelation.

6. In a letter to Gerhard Krueger on December 25, 1935, Leo Strauss did not hesitate to praise al-Fārābī. He credited al-Fārābī with revealing to him an aspect of "classical — middle and new — Platonism" (*GS* III, 450). Tanguay, *Strauss: An Intellectual Biography*, speaks of a "Farabian turn" in the thought of Leo Strauss. Also, Joel L. Kraemer acknowledges the influence of al-Fārābī on Strauss's interpretation of Plato. Kraemer, "The Medieval Arabic Enlightenment," in *The Cambridge Companion to Leo Strauss*, ed. Steven Smith (Cambridge: Cambridge University Press, 2009), 137–70 (especially p. 142). For a rich overview of Strauss's treatment of al-Fārābī and its role in inspiring further academic research on al-Fārābī's works, see Steven Harvey, "Leo Strauss's Developing Interest in Alfarabi and Its Reverberations in the Study of Medieval Islamic Philosophy," in *The Pilgrimage of Philosophy: A Festschrift for Charles E. Butterworth*, ed. René M. Paddags, Waseem El-Rayes, and Gregory A. McBrayer, 60–84 (South Bend, IN: St. Augustine's Press, 2019).
7. On this point, see the critique of Strauss's peculiar interpretation of Plato in his essay "Farabi's Plato," in Kraemer, "Medieval Arabic Enlightenment," 158–63, as well as James E. Montgomery, "Leo Strauss and the Alethiometer," in *Renaissance Averroism and Its Aftermath: Arabic Philosophy in Early Modern Europe*, ed. Anna Akasoy and Guido Giglioni, 285–320 (Dordrecht, Netherlands: Springer, 2013).
8. See the critique of Namazi on Strauss's "modeling" of al-Fārābī in Namazi, *Strauss and Islamic Political Thought*, 149.
9. For example, see Muhsin Mahdi, *Alfarabi and the Foundation of Islamic Political Philosophy* (Chicago: University of Chicago Press, 2001); Christopher Colmo, *Breaking with Athens: Alfarabi as Founder* (Lanham, MD: Lexington Books, 2005); Joshua Parens, *Leo Strauss and the Recovery of Medieval Political Philosophy* (Rochester, NY: University of Rochester Press, 2016); Alexander Orwin, *Redefining the Muslim Community: Ethnicity, Religion, and Politics in the Thought of Alfarabi* (Philadelphia: University of Pennsylvania Press, 2017).
10. See chapter 2.
11. *GS* II, 128ff., 136, 142, 150–51, 156ff.
12. Jon McGinnis, *Avicenna* (Oxford: Oxford University Press, 2010), 9, states that "most of the Platonic dialogues were not translated into Arabic, which may perhaps be owing to the high literary and even poetic style of Plato's writings, which makes it often difficult, if nigh impossible, to capture in translation. Instead, most frequently only philosophical synopses of Plato's works were available."
13. Cf. Franz Rosenthal, "On the Knowledge of Plato's Philosophy in the Islamic World," *Islamic Culture* 14 (1940): 387–422, 15 (1941): 396–98; Dimitri Gutas, "The Rebirth of Philosophy and the Translations into Arabic," in *Philosophy in the Islamic World*, ed. Ulrich Rudolph, Rotraud Hansberger, and Peter Adamson, 95–142 (Leiden, Netherlands: Brill, 2017), especially p. 131.
14. *GS* II, 400; Leo Strauss, *The City and Man* (Chicago: University of Chicago Press, 1964), 11 (henceforth cited as *CM*); Leo Strauss, *Natural Right*

and History (Chicago: University of Chicago Press, 1953), 33 (henceforth cited as *NRH*); Leo Strauss, *What Is Political Philosophy? And Other Studies* (Glencoe, IL: Greenwood Press, 1959), 77 (henceforth cited as *WIPP*).

15. Following Leo Strauss, Richard Walzer borrowed the manuscript in 1934 and 1937, as well as Arthur J. Arberry in 1937. Walzer and Paul Kraus were involved in the project "Plato Arabus." It was in this context that al-Fārābī's *Falsafat Aflāṭūn* and his summary of Plato's *Laws* appeared. For this project, see Aileen R. Das, "Paul Kraus, Richard Walzer, and Galen's *Com. Tim.*," *Arabic Sciences and Philosophy* 31 (2021): 225–56. Strauss was also supposed to participate in the project. However, Raymond Klibansky, the editor of *Corpus Platonicum*, was not convinced of his knowledge of Arabic (Das, "Paul Kraus," 239).

16. I am preparing an edition of the Arabic text with an English translation and commentary. It will be published with Brill in 2024.
    In a letter to Charles Kuentz, which was cited in Joel L. Kraemer, "The Death of an Orientalist: Paul Kraus from Prague to Cairo," in *The Jewish Discovery of Islam: Studies in Honor of Bernard Lewis*, ed. Martin Kramer (Tel Aviv: Moshe Dayan Center for Middle Eastern and African Studies, Tel Aviv University, 1999), 209, Strauss writes that he ordered a manuscript of al-Fārābī's summary of Plato's *Laws*, which he examined together with Paul Kraus in Berlin. This must have been in 1931 to 1932, the same time he became aware of the pseudo-Platonic text in question.

17. With this dating, I am following Heinrich Meier. See p. 211n11.

18. In a letter to Gershom Scholem on December 7, 1933, the thirty-four-year-old Leo Strauss wrote (with the aim of securing a possible professorship at the Hebrew University in Jerusalem), "I have been able to read Arabic philosophical texts (which Prof. Gotthold Weil can attest to, and can be confirmed by Schaeder and Kraus, as well). I am not currently working in that area but could be in position to read such texts in a matter of months when I have the chance to dedicate myself to the task." He described his "Hebrew language skills," on the other hand, as "currently minimal" (*GS* III, 709).

19. Obviously, Avicenna believed that the pseudo-Platonic *Kitāb an-Nawāmīs* was authentically written by Plato. Al-Fārābī could have thought the same thing when he wrote his summary of the *Nomoi*. For insight into the controversial topic of whether al-Fārābī had access to Plato's *Laws*, see Steven Harvey, "Did Alfarabi Read Plato's *Laws*?," *Medioevo: Rivista di storia della filosofia medievale* 28 (2003): 51–68, especially 62–63. Harvey agrees with my view that al-Fārābī was not in the position to read Plato's *Laws* in the original (64).

20. Namazi, *Strauss and Islamic Political Thought*, 35.

21. "Voraussetzung hierfür ist die auf den Platonischen Staat zurückgehende Vorstellung." As found in a letter to Gerhard Krüger from June 26, 1930 (*GS* III, 382–83).

22. See p. 42–43 of this book.

23. " . . . the treatment of prophecy and the Divine law in contained in . . . the Laws." Strauss, *The Argument and the Action of Plato's "Laws"* (Chicago: University of Chicago Press, 1975), 1 (henceforth cited as *AAPL*).

24. Namazi, *Strauss and Islamic Political Thought*, 34. Kraemer, "Medieval Arabic Enlightenment," 153n58, states that Muhsin Mahdi "identified the two books as the Republic and the Laws."

25. Gotthard Strohmaier, "Doxography," in *Encyclopaedia of Islam Three Online*, ed. Kate Fleet et al., April 1, 2015, last updated July 19, 2021, http://dx.doi.org/10.1163/1573-3912_ei3_COM_26088. (The third edition of the *Encyclopaedia of Islam* is henceforth cited as *EI3*.)

26. Namazi, *Strauss and Islamic Political Thought*, 34n129.

27. Anna Akasoy, Alexander Fidora, and Douglas Morton Dunlop, eds., *The Arabic Version of the "Nicomachean Ethics"* (Leiden: Brill, 2005), 580.

28. Namazi, *Strauss and Islamic Political Thought*, 134n129.

29. Namazi, *Strauss and Islamic Political Thought*, 35.

30. Abū ʿAlī Aḥmad b. Muḥammad Ibn Miskawaih, *Kitāb Tahdhīb al-Akhlāq wa-Taṭhīr al-Aʿrāq* (Cairo, [1329] 1908), 96; Rémi Brague, *The Law of God: The Philosophical History of an Idea*, trans. Lydia G. Cochrane (Chicago: University of Chicago Press, 2007), 116–17; Namazi, *Strauss and Islamic Political Thought*, 34n129.

31. Unfortunately, Namazi did not profit from my philologically rigorous examination of Leo Strauss's articles on al-Fārābī. Instead, he merely repeats what other previous Straussians have continuously noted. However, his book is proof that Strauss's interpretation of Islamic philosophy remains influential.

32. Namazi, 36.

33. Rémi Brague, "Athens, Jerusalem, Mecca: Leo Strauss's 'Muslim' Understanding of Greek Philosophy," *Poetics Today* 19, no. 2 (1998): 235–59. Brague hits the mark when he notes that "interpreting Strauss is an almost desperate task. One can never tell whether one is probing the depths of his thought or merely blundering about and sliding on its glittering surface" (239). See in particular the illuminating critique of Strauss's esotericism, 242–52.

34. Namazi, *Strauss and Islamic Political Thought*, 38.

35. *GS* III, 545 (letter to Jacob Klein, January 20, 1938). Namazi points to this letter (40n146).

36. Strangely, on p. 40, Namazi seems to have recognized this problem:

> In his [Strauss's] writings, everything seems preliminary. It is often difficult to say who is talking in the text; an idea stated on one page is rejected in the next and it is replaced by another in the next chapter. It is therefore not surprising that there are sharp disagreements among Strauss's readers even about his views on the most prominent aspects of his thought. [. . .] Strauss himself disappears in his commentaries; [. . .]. His

> writings resemble mazes which, once in a while, one believes one has escaped, codes which one believes one has eventually cracked; but in the end it is difficult to find Strauss's own personal views.

A bit later, on p. 43, he writes, "Regardless of what one might think of Strauss's historical claims about the esoteric character of the writings of past philosophers, Strauss himself followed, as we shall see in the commentaries of this book, such a procedure in his writings." See also 38n140.

37. Namazi, 37.
38. As indicated in a letter to Paul Kraus on May 17, 1936 (*GS* III, xxiii). Given that they provide no evidence in their books for this claim, Strauss considered their belief in revelation (*Offenbarungsglaubwürdigkeit*) "highly doubtful" (*völlig zweifelhaft*).
39. This is the accusation made by Kartheininger, *Heterogenität*, 384–86.
40. Kartheininger, 385.
41. For further details on this matter, see Sarah Stroumsa, *Freethinkers of Medieval Islam: Ibn Al-Rawāndī, Abū Bakr Al-Rāzī and Their Impact on Islamic Thought* (Leiden: Brill, 1999).
42. Christian Peltz, *Der Koran des Abū l-ʿAlāʾ* (Wiesbaden: Harrassowitz, 2013).
43. If one were to claim that he was spared persecution because of his blindness, it would have to be countered that his blindness did not help him gain the sympathy and favor of rich patrons in Baghdad. P. Smoor, "al-Maʿarrī," in *Encyclopaedia of Islam New Edition Online*, ed. P. Bearman, April 24, 2012, http://dx.doi.org/10.1163/1573-3912_islam_COM_0599; ʿĀʾishah ʿAbd al-Raḥmān, "Abū ʾl-ʿAlāʾ Al-Maʿarrī," in *Abbasid Belles-Lettres*, ed. Julia Ashtiany et al., 328–38 (Cambridge: Cambridge University Press, 1990). (The second edition ["*New Edition*"] of the *Encyclopaedia of Islam* is henceforth cited as *EI2*.)
44. Patricia Crone, "Dahrīs," in *EI3*, December 1, 2012, last updated July 19, 2021, http://dx.doi.org/10.1163/1573-3912_ei3_COM_25780.
45. Dimitri Gutas, *Greek Thought, Arabic Culture: The Graeco-Arabic Translation Movement in Baghdad and Early ʿAbbāsid Society (2nd–4th / 8th–10th Centuries)* (London: Routledge, 1998).
46. Abū Naṣr al-Fārābī, *Al-Fārābī on the Perfect State: Abū Naṣr al-Fārābī's Mabādiʾ ārāʾ ahl al-madīna al-fāḍila*, trans. and ed. Richard Walzer (Oxford: Clarendon Press, 1985; henceforth cited as *Madīna* [Walzer]); Abū Naṣr al-Fārābī, *Kitāb as-Siyāsa al-madaniyya al-mulaqqab bi-mabādiʾ al-mawjūdāt*, ed. Fauzī M. Najjār (Beirut: al-Maṭbaʿa al-Kāthūlīkiyya, 1964; henceforth cited as *Siyāsa*).
47. The issue of esoterism practiced by medieval Muslim philosophers is discussed at some length in Steven Harvey, "The Story of a Twentieth-Century Jewish Scholar's Discovery of Plato's Political Philosophy in Tenth-Century

Islam: Leo Strauss's Early Interest in the Islamic Falāsifa," in *Modern Jewish Scholarship on Islam in Context: Rationality, European Borders, and the Search for Belonging*, ed. Ottfried Fraisse, 219–44 (Berlin: de Gruyter, 2018), particularly 239–40.

48. Jürgen Habermas's recent monumental work *Auch eine Geschichte der Philosophie* (Frankfurt: Suhrkamp, 2019) proves this fact as it pertains to European thought. Due to the limitations of his academic training, Habermas leaves the history of philosophy in the Islamic world untreated.

49. This leads him to misunderstand my position in many parts of his dissertation. Here is an example: "The difference between my approach and Tamer's is, to repeat, that I believe we must, when engaging with Strauss, ask whether the hermeneutic methods Strauss applies to other thinkers *are to be applied to Strauss himself*" (70, italics in the original). Another example is when he ascribes to me "that Strauss's and Nietzsche's philosophies are fundamentally different insofar as Nietzsche views religion as a 'compensation product for the weak,' while Strauss sees religion as a 'postulate of reason'" (71). Daniel Townsend, "Leo Strauss and Islam" (PhD diss., Deakin University, 2014).

50. Townsend, "Strauss and Islam," 71. Townsend summarizes Strauss's political program and view on religion as follows:

> Strauss considers religion necessary as it serves as a basis for public morality and therefore social and political order. [. . .] This is the position that Strauss constantly attributes to medieval philosophers and one that he does not criticize or dispute. [. . .] Religion preserves differences between human beings [. . .], thus guarding against the conditions that will make the homogeneous world-state possible. The important point here is that, for Strauss, *the survival of philosophy depends upon the survival of religion*: philosophy requires that there are meaningful differences between human beings, and therefore meaningful questions about the right way of life, the best political order, and so on. The homogenous world-state means the death of philosophy insofar as it means, as Strauss writes, "the rule of wisdom," that is, that we collectively believe that "wisdom" has been attained. The world-state presupposes that all fundamental questions have been answered. Relatedly, *human greatness depends, for Strauss, on the possibility of differences being recognized and valued*: if human beings are all considered the same — as would be the case in an egalitarian and homogenous state — there could not be "great" human beings insofar as "greatness" means standing apart from the mass. "Greatness" requires a hierarchy of human types or, in Nietzschean terms, the possibility of rank-ordering. (47–48, italics in the original)

51. Parens, *Strauss and the Recovery of Medieval Political Philosophy*. The substantial weaknesses in Parens's interpretation, as a Strauss devotee, of al-Fārābī's Platonism are explicated by Majid Fakhry in his review of Parens's

book *Metaphysics as Rhetoric: Alfarabi's Summary of Plato's "Laws"* in the *Middle East Journal* 50 (1996): 289–90.

Introduction to the Original Text

1. The most comprehensive list of Strauss's publications to date can be found in Heinrich Meier, *Die Denkbewegung von Leo Strauss: Die Geschichte der Philosophie und Intention der Philosophen* (Stuttgart: J. B. Metzler, 1996), 47–63.
2. To understand Leo Strauss's influence on academic life in North America, see Gordon S. Wood, "The Fundamentalists and the Constitution," *New York Review of Books*, February 18, 1988, 33–40. For Strauss's impact on American politics, see Shadia Drury, *Leo Strauss and the American Right* (New York: Macmillan, 1997). In this book Drury investigates the role Strauss's political ideas have played in the triumph of neoconservatism in America. In Stephen Toulmin's article "The Evolution of Margaret Mead," *New York Review*, December 6, 1984, 4, it is noted that the policy planning unit in the America Foreign Ministry was well versed in Straussian ideas but was not in the position to understand Russian or the cultural diversity of the nations that were affected by its policies. In this regard also see Peter Levine, *Nietzsche and the Modern Crisis of the Humanities* (Albany: State University of New York Press, 1995), 152–53. To understand the breadth of Strauss and his school's affect in the United States, see the following edited volume published to celebrate Strauss's one hundredth birthday, which includes contributions of even third-generation Straussians. Kenneth L. Deutsch and John A. Murley, eds., *Leo Strauss, the Straussians and the American Regime* (Lanham, MD: Rowan and Littlefield, 1999).
3. The German public sphere was made aware of Strauss through the efforts of Heinrich and Wiebke Meier in their editing of Strauss's *Gesammelte Schriften*. Four volumes have been published to date: *Die Religionskritik Spinoza und zugehörige Schriften* (Stuttgart: J. B. Metzler, 1996); *Philosophie und Gesetz — Frühe Schriften* (Stuttgart: J. B. Metzler, 1997); *Hobbes' politische Wissenschaft und zugehörige Schriften — Briefe* (Stuttgart: J. B. Metzler, 2001); and *Naturrecht und Geschichte* (Hamburg: Felix Meiner, 2022). The first three of these are cited as *GS* I, *GS* II, and *GS* III, respectively.
4. From the field of political science, the following examples can be cited: Robert Devigne, *Recasting Conservatism: Ockeshot, Strauss and the Response to Postmodernism* (New Haven, CT: Yale, 1994); Peter Graf Kielmansegg, Horst Mewes, and Elisabeth Glaser Schmidt, eds., *Hannah Arendt and Leo Strauss: German Emigrés and American Political Thought after World War II* (Cambridge: Cambridge University Press, 1995); Ted V. McAllister, *Revolt against Modernity: Leo Strauss, Eric Voegelin, and the Search for a Postliberal Order* (Lawrence: University of Kansas Press, 1996).
5. In a letter to Voegelin on February 13, 1943, Strauss wrote that "Arabic political philosophy […] was once my specialty." Leo Strauss and Eric Voeglin,

Faith and Political Philosophy: The Correspondence between Leo Strauss and Eric Voegelin, ed. and trans. Peter Emberley and Barry Cooper (University Park: Pennsylvania State University Press, 1993; henceforth cited as *FPP*).

6. *GS* II, xviii, 112, 114, 126, 198, 425; Leo Strauss, *Persecution and the Art of Writing* (Chicago: University of Chicago Press, 1988), 10 (henceforth cited as *PAW*); *WIPP*, 161; *AAPL*, 1, 3.
7. Strauss first dealt with Maimonides's most important work in his 1930 text *Die Religionskritik Spinozas*. In 1963 he wrote "How to Begin to Study *The Guide of the Perplexed*" as an introduction to the English translation of the book. Moses Maimonides, *The Guide of the Perplexed*, trans. Shlomo Pines (Chicago: University of Chicago Press, 1963), xi–lvi.
8. Kenneth Hart Green, *Jew and Philosopher: The Return to Maimonides in the Jewish Thought of Leo Strauss* (Albany: State University of New York Press, 1993). The first chapter of that work, which was derived from his dissertation, appeared also in a slightly altered form, "'In the Grip of the Theological-Political Predicament': The Turn to Maimonides in the Jewish Thought of Leo Strauss," in *Leo Strauss's Thought: Toward a Critical Engagement*, ed. Alan Udoff, 41–74 (Boulder, CO: Lynne Rienner, 1991). Additionally, see Green's introduction to Leo Strauss, *Jewish Philosophy and the Crisis of Modernity: Essays and Lectures in Modern Jewish Thought*, 1–84 (Albany: State University of New York Press, 1997; henceforth cited as *JPCM*).
9. Green, *Jew and Philosopher*, xii.
10. Green, 49.
11. Green, 67–68.
12. Cf. Green, 205.
13. Green, 96.
14. Green, 101.
15. Green, 105–6.
16. Green, 111.
17. Green, 115–16.
18. Green, 122ff.
19. Green, "'In the Grip of the Theological-Political Predicament,'" 58–59. Green's remark that Strauss held the Bible and philosophy as constituting the "last antagonists" is reductive and deserves a certain degree of correction. Strauss's position vis-à-vis religion and revelation places (quite self-understandingly given his biography) a tension between the Bible and philosophy. Yet, despite this fact, he viewed this tension as not specifically attributable to Judaism but rather to all religions of revelation per se. Strauss engaged in this more general critique of religion with his investigation of Spinoza's scientific biblical criticism against the combined backdrop of Calvinism and Averroism. This indicates that his interest in the Jewish context was transcended

by his interest in religions of revelation more broadly. Cf. Heinrich Meier's comment in *GS* I, xiii n10.

20. These two volumes are Kenneth L. Deutsch and Walter Nicgorski, eds., *Leo Strauss: Political Philosopher and Jewish Thinker* (Lanham, MD: Rowan and Littlefield, 1994) — most of the contributions to this volume appeared in a special edition of the *Review of Politics*, 53, no. 1 (1991) — and David Novak, ed., *Leo Strauss and Judaism: Jerusalem and Athens Critically Revisited* (Lanham, MD: Rowan and Littlefield, 1996).
21. Hillel Fradkin, "Philosophy and Law: Leo Strauss as a Student of Medieval Jewish Thought," in Deutsch and Nicgorski, *Strauss: Political Philosopher*, 129–42.
22. Hillel Fradkin, "A Word Fitly Spoken: The Interpretation of Maimonides and the Legacy of Leo Strauss," in Novak, *Strauss and Judaism*, 57, 62.
23. Alfred Ivry, "Leo Strauss on Maimonides," in Udoff, *Strauss's Thought*, 78.
24. In this regard, see also Strauss's foreword to the American edition of *Die Religionskritik Spinozas* (henceforth cited as *RKS*) in *GS* I, 5–54; the editor's foreword in *GS* II, xxviii–xxx; David Biale, "Leo Strauss: The Philosopher as Weimar Jew," in Udoff, *Strauss's Thought*, 31–40; Andrew James A. Kent, "Delectation or Poison? Reading Leo Strauss" (BA thesis, Harvard College, 1993), 67–90; John Gunnell, "Strauss before Straussianism: Reason, Revelation, and Nature," in Deutsch and Nicgorski, *Strauss: Political Philosopher*, 107–28; Alfons Söllner, "Leo Strauss: German Origin and American Impact," in Kielmansegg, Mewes, and Glaser-Schmidt, *Hannah Arendt and Leo Strauss*, 121–38; Allan Arkush, "Leo Strauss and Jewish Modernity," in Novak, *Strauss and Judaism*, 111–30.
25. They are reprinted in *GS* II, pt. 2.
26. See also the first passages of *WIPP*, 9–10; Leo Strauss, *An Introduction to Political Philosophy: Ten Essays by Leo Strauss*, ed. Hilail Gilden (Detroit, MI: Wayne State University Press, 1989), 2; Leo Strauss, "Why We Remain Jews," in *JPCM*, 311–56; foreword to the American edition of *RKS* in *GS* I, 5–54. Cf. Emil L. Fackenheim, *Jewish Philosophers and Jewish Philosophy*, ed. Michael Morgan (Bloomington: University of Indiana Press, 1996), 97–105.
27. Hadley Arkes, "Athens and Jerusalem: The Legacy of Leo Strauss," in Novak, *Strauss and Judaism*, 1–23. The same with Deutsch and Murley, *Strauss, the Straussians*, 87–88. Regarding the relationship between Strauss and Hermann Cohen, see Udoff, *Strauss's Thought*, 1–27; see also Thomas Pangle's introduction to Leo Strauss, *Studies in Platonic Political Philosophy* (Chicago: University of Chicago Press, 1980), 26 (henceforth cited as *SPPP*); Green in *JPCM*, 17–25.
28. Cf. Pines, "Translator's Introduction: The Philosophic Sources of *The Guide of the Perplexed*," in Maimonides, *Guide*, especially pp. lxxviii–xcii.
29. Frederick G. Lawrence, "Leo Strauss and the Fourth Wave of Modernity," in Novak, *Strauss and Judaism*, 131.

30. David Novak claims that Strauss believed that philosophy was incompatible with Judaism and therefore could not be called a "Jewish philosopher . . . for that is an oxymoron pure and simple." Novak, *Strauss and Judaism*, viii. See also Michael M. Morgan, "Teaching Leo Strauss as a Jewish and General Philosopher," in *Jewish Philosophy and the Academy*, ed. Emil L. Fackenheim and Raphael Jospe, 174–88 (Cranbury, NJ: Fairleigh Dickinson University Press, 1996), 186–87.
31. Steven B. Smith, "Leo Strauss: Between Athens and Jerusalem," in Deutsch and Nicgorski, *Strauss: Political Philosopher*, 81–105.
32. Smith, "Leo Strauss: Between Athens and Jerusalem," 82. The same could be said in Laurence V. Berns, "Leo Strauss 1889–1973," *Independent Journal of Philosophy* 2 (1978): 2. Cf. Strauss, *JPCM*, xvi–xvii. Green relativizes the characterization of Strauss as a Jewish philosopher given the fact that Strauss himself contested the very notion of Jewish philosophy. See *JPCM*, 247ff.
33. Similar in Smith, "Leo Strauss: Between Athens and Jerusalem," 89ff., 105; Drury, *Strauss and the American Right*, 38ff.
34. Green, "'In the Grip of the Theological-Political Predicament,'" 59.
35. Cf. Laurence Lampert, *Leo Strauss and Nietzsche* (Chicago: University of Chicago Press, 1996), 133ff.
36. This stance becomes clear in Rémi Brague, "Leo Strauss and Maimonides," in Udoff, *Strauss's Thought*, 94, 98; Fradkin, "A Word Fitly Spoken," 79–80.
37. Leo Strauss, "Eine vermißte Schrift Fārābī's," *Monatsschrift für Geschichte und Wissenschaft des Judentums* 80 (1936): 96–106 (henceforth cited as "VSF"), in *GS* II, 175–76; Leo Strauss, "Quelques remarques sur la science politique de Maïmonide et de Fārābī," *Revue des Etudes Juives* 100 (1936): 1–37 (henceforth cited as "QR") in *GS* II, 128; *FPP*, 1.
38. Ivry, "Strauss on Maimonides," 78, claims that Strauss could only connect to Plato via al-Fārābī, whose "emphasis upon the political dimension of Plato's thought establishes for Strauss the dominant perspective of Maimonides' own approach." In this context, it can be observed that most of the interpreters listed above see al-Fārābī as Strauss's stepchild because they apparently feel that recognizing al-Fārābī's philosophic worth would reduce the standing of Maimonides in Strauss's oeuvre. Therefore, they attempt to prioritize Maimonides against any sort of comparative examination with al-Fārābī. These efforts, however, unfairly reduce the recognition of al-Fārābī's impact on Strauss's work.
39. Brague, "Strauss and Maimonides," 93, 98. The points above should be seen as correcting Ivry's remarks in Udoff where he notes that since 1939 Maimonides's predecessors "have receded in significance in Strauss' mind and he appears completely taken with the profundity and subtlety of Maimonides' genius."
40. From this first period, the following texts emerge: "Maimunis Lehre von der Prophetie und ihre Quellen," pt. 3 of Leo Strauss, *Philosophie und Gesetz: Beiträge zum Verständnis Maimunis und seiner Vorläufer* (Berlin: Schocker, 1935; henceforth cited as *PHG*); "QR" (1936); "VSF" (1936); and Leo

Strauss, "Der Ort der Vorsehungslehre nach der Ansicht Maimunis," *Monatsschrift für Geschichte und Wissenschaft des Judentums* 81 (1937): 93–105 (with marginalia in *GS* II, 179–94; henceforth cited as "OVAM").

41. Meier, *Die Denkbewegung*, 42.

42. Leo Strauss, "Farabi's Plato," in *Louis Ginzberg Jubilee Volume on the Occasion of His Seventieth Birthday*, ed. Alexander Marx et al., 357–93 (New York: American Academy for Jewish Research, 1945; hereafter cited as "FP"). An edited version can be found reprinted as the foreword to *PAW*. Cf. Lampert, *Strauss and Nietzsche*, 137.

43. *AAPL*.

44. Muhsin Mahdi, a student and longtime Strauss research assistant, reported that in 1931 to 1932 Strauss and Paul Kraus in Berlin translated part of al-Fārābī's summary of Plato's *Nomoi* from Arabic into German. Apparently, Strauss dealt multiple times with this Farabian text. See Mahdi, "The Editio Princeps of Fārābī's *Compendium Legum Platonis*," *Journal of Near Eastern Studies* 20 (1961): 1, 15; *GS* II, 196n4. Mahdi's remark confirms the view articulated above about the importance of al-Fārābī's text for Strauss. It was probably philological difficulties that prevented him from bringing this translation to a successful conclusion.

45. Cropsey's confirmation is printed on the reverse side of the book cover (Strauss, *WIPP*, 1988 reprint).

46. These texts are "How Farabi Read Plato's *Laws*," in *WIPP*; and "Maimonides' Statement on Political Science." In the final essay, Strauss heavily emphasizes al-Fārābī's influence on Maimonides's political science, just as he did in the essay "QR" twenty years prior.

47. Green, "'In the Grip of the Theological-Political Predicament,'" 41.

48. See Pangle's introduction in *SPPP*, 4ff.; Meier, *Die Denkbewegung*, 94ff.; David Bolotin, "Leo Strauss on Classical Political Philosophy," *Interpretation* 22 (1994): 130ff.

49. Allan Bloom, "Leo Strauss: September 20, 1889 – October 18, 1973," *Political Theory* 2 (1974): 376; Nathan Tarcov and Thomas Pangle, "Epilogue: Leo Strauss and His History of Political Philosophy," in *History of Political Philosophy*, ed. Leo Strauss and Joseph Cropsey (Chicago: University of Chicago Press, 1963), 907; Nathan Tarcov, "On a Certain Critique of 'Straussianism,'" in Deutsch and Nicgorski, *Strauss: Political Philosopher*, 259; Christopher Bruell, "A Return to Classical Political Philosophy and the Understanding of the American Founding," in Deutsch and Nicgorski, *Strauss: Political Philosopher*, 331.

50. Pangle, introduction to *SPPP*, 1–26, as well as the same in Thomas L. Pangle, "The Platonism of Leo Strauss: A Reply to Henry Jaffa," *Claremont Review of Books* 4 (1985): 19–20. Also see Thomas L. Pangle, "Introduction to the Thought of Leo Strauss," in *The Rebirth of Classical Political Rationalism: Essays and Lectures of Leo Strauss*, ed. Pangle, vii–xxxviii (Chicago: University of Chicago Press, 1989; henceforth cited as *RCPR*).

51. Pangle, "Introduction to the Thought," in *RCPR*, viii; same as in Tarcov and Pangle, "Epilogue," 910–12.
52. Pangle, "Introduction to the Thought," in *RCPR*, xiv; David Lowenthal, "Leo Strauss's Studies in Platonic Political Philosophy," *Interpretation* 13 (1985): 297.
53. Pangle, introduction to *SPPP*, 2ff.
54. Strauss, *CM*, 29. See also *AAPL*, 1; *WIPP*, 29.
55. Pangle, introduction to *SPPP*, 8ff.
56. Pangle, 13ff.; Strauss, *WIPP*, 31ff.; Strauss, *AAPL*, 2. Also see in this regard Lowenthal, "Strauss's Studies," 311.
57. Pangle, introduction to *SPPP*, 17–18.
58. Pangle, "Introduction to the Thought," in *RCPR*, xvii; introduction to *SPPP*, 20.
59. Bloom, "Leo Strauss," 378. See also H. Ritter in the *Frankfurter Allgemeine Zeitung*, September 18, 1999.
60. Bloom, "Leo Strauss," 380ff.
61. Bloom, 383–86. In his depiction of Strauss's development, Bloom misses Strauss's treatment of Plato's political philosophy in *Philosophie und Gesetz*. This leads him to the false assumption that Strauss had not found himself on Platonic ground in the first period of his intellectual development and therefore was unfamiliar with Plato's understanding of religion. One may surmise from a remark by Bloom that he has not read that book given the fact that it was only later translated into American English: Leo Strauss, *Philosophy and Law: Essays Toward the Understanding of Maimonides and His Predecessors*, trans. Fred Baumann (Philadelphia: Jewish Publication Society, 1987). A further translation was completed by Eve Adler in 1995. See Bloom, "Leo Strauss," 383.
62. Lampert, *Strauss and Nietzsche*, 129ff.
63. Lampert, 159ff. Cf. Leo Strauss, "On Plato's Republic," in *CM*, 50–138.
64. Lampert, *Strauss and Nietzsche*, 162ff.
65. Susan Orr, *Jerusalem and Athens: Reason and Revelation in the Work of Leo Strauss* (Lanham, MD: Rowan and Littlefield, 1995). See also Harry V. Jaffa, "Leo Strauss, the Bible, and Political Philosophy," in Deutsch and Nicgorski, *Strauss: Political Philosopher*, 195–210.
66. Orr, *Jerusalem and Athens*, 15.
67. Orr, 49.
68. Orr, 68ff.
69. Orr, 18.
70. Heinrich Meier, *Die Denkbewegung von Leo Strauss. Die Geschichte der Philosophie und Intention der Philosophen* (Stuttgart: J.B. Metzler, 1996), 19–20.

71. H. Meier, *Die Denkbewegung*, 14–15. Against this approach, Hadley Arkes ascribes to Strauss a "Talmudic style" in the interpretation of texts in Arkes, "Strauss on Our Minds," in Deutsch and Murley, *Strauss, the Straussians*, 69. Cf. Drury's last point in *Strauss and the American Right*, 59.

72. H. Meier, *Die Denkbewegung*, 22. This is similar to Tarcov, "On a Certain Critique," 262, 269–70, as well as Hiram Caton, "Der hermeneutische Weg von Leo Strauss," *Philosophisches Jahrbuch* 80 (1973): 172. Caton believes that Strauss represented a "provocative historicism . . . that attempted to emerge through the historical discovery of an 'eternal truth.'" Against this position, Holmes is convinced that Strauss is not a philosopher, but rather a historian of political ideas. See Stephan Holmes, "Wahrheit für Wenige: Leo Strauss und die Gefährlichkeit der Philosophie," *Merkur* 44 (1990): 554, 569.

73. H. Meier, *Die Denkbewegung*, 32ff. Harald Bluhm opposes Meier's "anointing of Leo Strauss as *the* political philosopher of the twentieth century." He characterizes Strauss' work accurately as a form of "political philosophizing" that "does not contain any type of systematicity in terms of an ordered totality of observation and analyses." Harald Bluhm, "Variationen des Höhlengleichnisses — Kritik und Restitution politischer Philosophie bei Hannah Arendt und Leo Strauss," *Deutsche Zeitschrift für Philosophie* 47 (1999): 913.

74. H. Meier, *Die Denkbewegung*, 34, 42–43. Similarly, see Heinrich Meier, *Carl Schmitt, Leo Strauss und der "Begriff des Politischen": Zu einem Dialog unter Abwesenden* (Stuttgart: J. B. Metzer, 1988), 95–96; Strauss, "FP," 377.

75. Clemens Kauffmann, *Leo Strauss zur Einführung* (Hamburg: Junius, 1997). Cf. Harald Bluhm, "Besprechung von Leo Strauss, *Philosophie und Gesetz*," in *GS* II, 411–12.

76. Kauffmann, *Leo Strauss zur Einführung*, 195ff.

77. Kauffmann, 16ff, 140–45, 184–85.

78. Bloom, "Leo Strauss," 392.

79. H. Meier, *Die Denkbewegung*, 31.

80. *GS* II, 47.

81. Regarding Lessing's influence on the development of Strauss's teachings on double meaning in writing, see *RCPR*, 63–71; *JPCM*, 462. The two studies mentioned above are found in *PAW*. Cf. Friedrich Niewöhner, "Die zweifache Schrift der Weisen," *Die Zeit*, November 8, 1996; Drury, *Strauss and the American Right*, 43–48.

82. This is exemplified in the Jaffa – Pangle controversy that led the Straussians to split into two camps. See Harry Jaffa's discussion of Thomas Pangle's introduction to *SPPP* in Jaffa, "The Legacy of Leo Strauss," *Claremont Review* 3 (1984): 14–21, and Pangle's response in "The Platonism of Leo Strauss," 18–20. Also see Shadia Drury, *The Political Ideas of Leo Strauss* (New York: Palgrave Macmillan, 1988), 182–92; and Deutsch and Nicgorski, *Strauss: Political Philosopher*, 1ff.

83. Burnyeat, "Sphinx without a Secret," *New York Review of Books* 32, no. 9 (May 1985): 30–36. Replies by Joseph Cropsey, Harry V. Jaffa, Allan Bloom,

Thomas L. Pangle et al. and a rebuttal by Burnyeat follow in "The Studies of Leo Strauss: An Exchange," *New York Review of Books* 32, no. 15 (October 10, 1985): 41–44. Cf. D. Levine's discussion with Burnyeat, "Without Malice but with Forethought: A Response to Burnyeat," in Deutsch and Nicgorski, *Strauss: Political Philosopher*, 353–72.

84. Anastaplo and Jaffa compare Strauss with the figure of a prophet or Jesus. George Anastaplo, "Leo Strauss at the University of Chicago," in Deutsch and Murley, *Strauss, the Straussians*, 3; Harry V. Jaffa, "Strauss at One Hundred," in Deutsch and Murley, 41.

85. Burnyeat, "Sphinx without a Secret," 30–31. Allan Bloom admits that Strauss's personal charm often hindered his students from understanding his books properly. "Only a tiny number of men who did not fall under the spell of his personal charm were profoundly affected by his books." Bloom, "Leo Strauss," 387. The positive impressions of Strauss's teaching on a student are relayed in Werner Dannhauser, "Leo Strauss: Becoming Naïve Again," *American Scholar* 44 (1975): 636–42. Enthusiastic memories of Strauss's students are also contained in Deutsch and Murley, *Strauss, the Straussians*.

86. Burnyeat, "Sphinx without a Secret," 31ff.

87. Burnyeat, 33–34.

88. Burnyeat, 36.

89. Burnyeat; cf. Charles Larmore, *The Morals of Modernity* (Cambridge: Cambridge University Press, 1996), 71n16.

90. Drury, *Political Ideas*, 3. Dietmar Herz advances a similar thesis in Herz, "Der Philosoph als Verführer: Überlegungen zur Philosophie des Leo Strauss," *Archiv für Rechts-und Sozialphilosophie* 79 (1993): 544–49.

91. Shadia Drury, "The Esoteric Philosophy of Leo Strauss," *Political Theory* 15 (1985): 315ff.; as well as her "Strauss, Leo (1899–1973)," in *Routledge Encyclopedia of Philosophy*, ed. Edward Craig (London: Routledge, 1998), 9:167–68.

92. Drury, *Political Ideas*, 15.

93. Drury, "Esoteric Philosophy," 315.

94. Drury, *Political Ideas*, 18–36, 182–92. See also Larmore, *Morals of Modernity*, 65–76.

95. Drury, "Esoteric Philosophy," 316ff. Cf. Drury, *Strauss and the American Right*.

96. Drury, "Esoteric Philosophy," 322–23.

97. Drury, 332–24.

98. Drury, *Political Ideas*, 19–20, 23–24, 114ff.

99. Drury, "Esoteric Philosophy," 417ff., 333–34.

100. Strauss, *PAW*, 144.

101. Kent, "Delectation or Poison?"

102. Kent, 26ff., 31.

103. Kent, 39–40. The accusation of deception described above coalesces with the following evidence: "Even the best regime [. . .] demands a belief in a founding myth, a binding set of salutary delusions, a noble lie. A philosopher may well argue for the necessity of lying, but he will be constitutionally unable to believe in lies whether they prove to be necessary or not." Werner Dannhauser, "Leo Strauss as Citizen and Jew," *Interpretation* 17 (1990): 435.

104. Kent, "Decletation or Poison?," 46–50.

105. Kent, 63.

106. Kent, 88.

107. Rüdiger Bubner, "Verfolgung und die Kunst des Schreibens. Die Moderne ist antiker als sie glaubt: Eine Renaissance von Leo Strauss?," *Frankfurter Allgemeine Zeitung*, December 3, 1996.

108. Not to mention accounts of Strauss's philosophy that completely overlook this relationship. See, for example, Alfons Söllner, "Leo Strauss," in *Politische Philosophie des 20. Jahrhunderts*, ed. K. G. Ballestrem and H. Ottmann, 105–21 (Munich: De Gruyter Oldenburg, 1990).

109. Lawrence, "Strauss and the Fourth Wave of Modernity," 138ff.

110. Same as in Bolotin, "Strauss on Classical Political Philosophy," 130.

111. Also see Orr, *Jerusalem and Athens*, 148; Lawrence, "Strauss and the Fourth Wave of Modernity," 142ff.; H. Meier, *Die Denkbewegung*, 41ff.; the same as in H. Meier, *Carl Schmitt, Leo Strauss*, 184–85. In addition to the observations of Heinrich Meier, Clemens Kauffmann, and Lawrence Lampert pertaining to Strauss's affinity with al-Fārābī that we have already discussed, it is important to discuss the views of Hiram Caton. Caton believes that Strauss's primary achievement consists of "rediscovering political philosophy as the modern philosopher who most deeply understood Socrates, thereby clarifying the main purpose of modern philosophy. In this fashion, Strauss rediscovers the forgotten horizon of classical philosophy." He nevertheless claims that Strauss's achievements "were not recognized by his contemporary colleagues," which "[reminds] one of a remark made by Alfarabi that the disorders of his time are very serious." He continues by noting that "Alfarabi was not clueless as he learned from Plato the ways in which it was possible to revive philosophy following its disappearance." Caton, "Der hermeneutische Weg," 182. Beiner notes that Strauss's reproduction of the political philosophy of antiquity was substantially influenced by al-Fārābī's valuations. Roland Beiner, "Hannah Arendt and Leo Strauss: The Uncommenced Dialogue," *Political Theory* 18 (1990): 253, n33.

Chapter One

1. *Das Erkenntnisproblem in der philosophischen Lehre Fr. H. Jacobis* (Hamburg: Schröder, 1921), in Strauss, *GS* II, 237–92.

2. Like Norbert Elias and Hans Jonas, Strauss was part of a small, elite circle within the Zionist youth movement Blau-Weiß (Blue-White) and of the Jewish Students' Association. See Raphael Gross, "Zwischen Athen und Jerusalem: Zum ersten Band der gesammelten Schriften von Leo Strauss," *Neue Zürcher Zeitung*, October 1, 1996. The two articles Strauss published in Martin Buber's journal *Der Jude* (the Jew) and in the *Jüdische Rundschau* (Jewish review) between 1923 and 1925 testify to a strong political commitment. See Heinrich Meier's introduction to the early writings of Strauss in *GS* II, xxviii ff.
3. Leo Strauss, "Cohens Analyse der Bibelwissenschaft Spinozas," *Der Jude* 8 (1924): 295–314; "Zur Bibelwissenschaft Spinozas und seiner Vorläufer," *Korrespondenzblatt des Vereins zur Gründung und Erhaltung einer Akademie für die Wissenschaft des Judentums* 7 (1926): 1–22. Both essays are reprinted in Strauss, *GS* I, 363–414.
4. *GS* I, 5. The book appeared first in 1930 in Berlin and is included within the first volume of the *Gesammelte Schriften* (*GS*; collected works) of Leo Strauss. Edited by Heinrich Meier, the book now appears alongside the written commentary by Strauss on the margins of the original text and other associated texts. The page number citations in the current study reflect the pagination of the new edition. For the difficult conditions Strauss endured at the Akademie für die Wissenschaft des Judentums, the institution under whose auspices this book was written and published, see the editor's introduction in *GS* I, xiii.
5. Leo Strauss, *Hobbes' Politische Wissenschaft* (Neuwied, Germany: Luchterhand, 1965), 7 (henceforth cited as *HPW*).
6. *GS* I, 28. For more on the topic see *GS* I, 33–50, where Strauss once again engages with Cohen's critique of Spinoza. Compare this with Hermann Cohen, "Spinoza über Staat und Religion, Judentum und Christentum," first in the *Jahrbuch für jüdische Geschichte und Literatur* 18 (1915). It has been reprinted in *Jüdische Schriften*, ed. Hermann Cohen (Berlin: Schwetschke, 1924), 3:290–372.
7. *GS* I, 63.
8. *GS* I, 78–79, 239.
9. As mentioned previously, existing research has hitherto neglected the influence of Averroes on Leo Strauss and the origins of his thought. Compare this with Udoff, *Strauss's Thought*; Green, "'In the Grip of the Theological-Political Predicament,'" 41–49; Gunnell, "Strauss before Straussianism," 112–17; Walter Soffer, "Modern Rationalism, Miracles, and Revelation: Strauss's Critique of Spinoza," in Deutsch and Nicgorski, *Strauss: Political Philosopher*, 143–73; Arkes, "Athens and Jerusalem," 1–23; Susan Orr, "Strauss, Reason, and Revelation: Unraveling the Essential Question," in Novak, *Strauss and Judaism*, 28–30. In this context, the question may arise of whether and to what extent Spinoza himself was familiar with Averroes's ouevre and whether Strauss's interpretation of Spinoza was justified. However, answering these questions would be too far of a deviation from the central research question of this book.

10. For more on the Epicurean critique of religion, see Lukrez, *Von der Natur*, trans. Hermann Diels (Munich: Deutscher Taschenbuch-Verlag, 1991). This text includes an introduction and several important thematic elucidations by Ernst G. Schmidt; Marcus Tullius Cicero, *Über die Ziele des menschlichen Handelns: De finibus bonorum et malorum*, ed. and trans. Olof Gigon and Laila Straume-Zimmermann (Darmstadt, Germany: Wissenschaftliche Buchgesellschaft, 1988); A. J. Festugière, *Epicure et ses dieux* (Paris: Presses Universitaires de France, 1946); Phillip Mitsis, *Epicurus' Ethical Theory* (Ithaca, NY: Cornell University Press, 1988); H. Jones, *The Epicurean Tradition* (London: Routledge, 1989).

11. See *GS* II, 145, where Strauss opines that the search for the secret origin of the Torah would lead either to theosophy or to Epicureanism.

12. Leo Strauss, papers, box 11, folder 4, Department of Special Collections, University of Chicago Library.

13. Friedrich Niewöhner, "Epikureer sind Atheisten: Zur Geschichte des Wortes apikuros in der jüdischen Philosophie," in *Atheismus im Mittelalter und in der Renaissance*, ed. Friedrich Niewöhner and Olaf Pluta (Wiesbaden, Germany: Harrassowitz, 1999), 15–16; also see Mūsā Ibn Maimūn, *Dalālat al-ḥā'irīn*, ed. Ḥusain Atai (Cairo: Maktabat ath-Thaqāfa ad-Dīniyya, ca. 1980), pt. 2, ch. 13, p. 308 and pt. 3, ch. 17, pp. 520–21 (henceforth cited as *Dalālat*).

14. *GS* I, 51.

15. *GS* I, 76.

16. After reading al-Fārābī's writings, Strauss corrects his abovementioned view and declares him to be the founder of the post-revelation critique of religion (*GS* II, 115ff., 126ff., 176; *PAW*, 11–12).

17. *GS* I, 76–77. See also Stanislaus von Dunin-Borkowski, *Der junge De Spinoza* (Münster: Aschendorff, 1910), 475–91; Harry A. Wolfson, *The Philosophy of Spinoza* (Cambridge, MA: Harvard University Press, 1934), 1:9–11, 1:30; 2:151. Leo Strauss's papers, now archived in the Department of Special Collections of the University of Chicago Library, bear witness to the extent of Strauss's preoccupation with the writings of Averroes while he worked on *Spinoza's Critique of Religion*. He excerpted extended passages of Averroes's commentaries on Aristotle's *Physics* and of those passages in *Tahāfut at-tahāfut* (*Destructio Destructuinis*) that pertain to physics, comparing them to the relevant passages in Aristotle's writings (Strauss, papers, box 11, folder 2). Averroes's conception of religion, which we cannot dwell on in this study, has been discussed controversially and continues to divide the research community. See Ernest Renan, *Averroès et l'Averroïsm* (Paris: Calmann and Lévi, 1861); Etienne Gilson, *Reason and Revelation in the Middle Ages* (New York: Scribner, 1938); Averroes, *Averroes on Plato's "Republic,"* trans. Ralph Lerner (Ithaca, NY: Cornell University Press, 1974); Averroes, *On the Harmony of Religion and Philosophy*, ed. and trans. George F. Hourani (London: Luzac, 1976); Oliver Leaman, *Averroes and His Philosophy* (Oxford: Clarendon Press, 1988); Iysa A. Bello, *The Medieval Islamic Controversy between Philosophy and Orthodoxy: Ijmāʿ and taʾwīl in the Conflict between al-Ghazālī and Ibn Rushd* (Leiden: Brill, 1989); Majid Fakhry, *Ibn Rushd:*

Failasūf Qurṭubah (Beirut: al-Maṭbaʿa al-Kāthūlīkiyya, 1992); Muḥammad ʿĀbid al-Jābirī, *Ibn Rushd: Sīra wa-fikr* (Beirut: Markaz Dirāsāt al-Waḥda al-ʿArabiyya, 1998).

18. The following thinkers are, among others, considered "Latin Averroists." They include the Parisians Siger of Brabant and his followers as well as John of Jandun, Thomas Wilton and Walter Burleigh in Oxford, and Theodericus Erfordia in Erfurt. In Italy, the centers of Averroism were Bologna and Padua. Representatives are the scholastics Gentile de Cingulo, Angelus Aretius, Matthaeus Agubiensis, Taddeo da Parma, Anselmus Guittus, and Cambiolus Bononiensis as well as Petrus Abanus Patvinus, Paulus Venetus, Cajetanus Thienaeus, and Nicoletto Vernia in Padua. For further reading, see Renan, *Averroès*; Martin Grabmann, *Der lateinische Averroismus des 13. Jahrhunderts und seine Stellung zur christlichen Weltanschauung* (Munich: Verlag der Bayerische Akademie der Wissenschaften, 1931), 607–87; Fernand van Steenberghen, *Aristotle in the West: The Origins of Latin Aristotelianism*, trans. Leonard Johnston (Louvain-la-Neuve, Belgium: Nauwelaerts, 1955); Steenberghen, *La philosophie au 13e siècle* (Louvain: Publ. Universitaires 1966); Maurice-Ruben Hayoun and Alain de Liberia, *Averroès et l'Averroïsme: Que sais-je?* (Paris: Presses Universitaires de France, 1991); and also Friedrich Niewöhner and Loris Sturlese, eds., *Averroismus im Mittelalter und in der Renaissance* (Zürich: Spur, 1994), particularly the contributions by Alain de Libera (51–80), Henrik Wels (85–100), Zdzislaw Kuksewicz (101–13), Loris Sturlese (114–31), Burkhard Mojsisch (180–86), and M. H. Markowski (187–200).
19. *GS* I, 77.
20. *GS* I, 77–78, 306–7.
21. *GS* I, 78. For the history of this "catch-phrase of the three impostors" see Friedrich Niewöhner, *Veritas sive Varietas: Lessings Toleranzparabel und das Buch von den drei Betrügern* (Heidelberg: Schneider, 1988).
22. *GS* I, 78–79. See Strauss, *SPPP*, 226: "The substance of what Machiavelli says or suggests regarding religion is not original. As indicated by his use of the term 'sect' for religion, he follows in the path of Averroism, namely those medieval Aristotelians who as philosophers refused to make any concessions to revealed religion." For the relationship of Bruno and Averroes, see Rita Sturlese, "Averroè quantumque arabo et ignorante di lingua greca: Note sull'averroismo di Giordano Bruno," in Niewöhner and L. Sturlese, *Averroismus*, 319–50.
23. *SPPP*, 267, 281–82. See also Benedictus de Spinoza, *Tractatus theologico-politicus*, ed. Günter Gawlick and Friedrich Niewöhner (Darmstadt, Germany: Wissenschaftliche Buchgesellschaft, 1989), 7–9.
24. Indeed, Strauss's papers (box 11, folder 2) show that he had excerpted pp. 329–39 (vol. 10) of Averroes's *Destructio Destructionis* (the Latin edition that was published in Venice in 1560) at that time.
25. Averroes, *Tahafut al-Tahafut* (*The Incoherence of Incoherence*), trans. Simon Van Den Bergh (London: Luzac, 1954), 1:359–60. See also the passage in

Spinoza, *Tractatus theologico-politicus*, 432, which reads, “fidem non per se, sed tantum ratione obedientiae salutiferam esse.”

26. *GS* I, 298–99. See Spinoza, 489ff.
27. *GS* I, 299ff.
28. *GS* I, 306.
29. *GS* I, 145.
30. *GS* I, 306.
31. *GS* I, 307ff.
32. *GS* I, 311.
33. Averroes, *Faṣl al-maqāl wa-taqrīr mā baina ash-sharīʿa wa-l-ḥikma min al-ittiṣāl*, ed. A. N. Nādir (Beirut: Dār al-Mashriq, 1995), 27 (henceforth cited as *Faṣl*); German translation in Averroes, *Philosophie und Theologie von Averroes*, trans. Marcus Joseph Müller (Munich, 1875), 1.
34. *GS* I, 164.
35. Averroes, *Faṣl*, 27ff.; *Philosophie*, 1–2.
36. *GS* I, 165.
37. See also Oliver Leaman, “Introduction: The Jewish Philosophical Tradition in the Islamic Cultural World,” and Arthur Hyman, “Jewish Philosophy in the Islamic World,” in Seyyed Hossein Nasr and Oliver Leaman, eds., *History of Islamic Philosophy* (London: Routledge, 1996), 673–76 and 677–95. Regarding Yaḥyā, see Gerhard Endress, *The Works of Yahia Ibn ʿAdi: An Analytical Inventory* (Wiesbaden, Germany: Reichert, 1977); Shams Inati, “Ibn ʿAdi, Yahya (893–974),” in *Routledge Encyclopedia of Philosophy*, 4:599–601.
38. *GS* I, 195–247.
39. *GS* I, 199–200.
40. *GS* I, 358; this can be found in the marginalia of the handwritten text of Leo Strauss on p. 139 of the first edition. Strauss wrote the word *sharīʿā* in Arabic. In dealing with the contentious question of whether the world is eternal or created, Averroes reacted to al-Ghazālī’s critique of the philosophers. As a consequence, Averroes relativizes the importance of the controversial question of whether the world is eternal or created. He further sees no reason to accuse the philosophers of atheism if they thought that the world was eternal, insofar as they would by no means equate the eternity of the world with the eternity of God. See Averroes, *Faṣl*, 42–44; *Philosophie*, 11–12. It appears that Strauss adopts Averroes’s thought in this regard, relegating the question of the createdness or eternity of the world to a secondary concern following the primary question of the rational knowledge of social phenomena: “By becoming aware of the dignity of the mind, we realize the true ground of the dignity of man and therewith, the goodness of the world, whether we understand it as created or as uncreated, which is the home of man because it is the home of the human mind” (Strauss qtd. in Tarcov and Pangle, “Epilogue,” 934).

41. *GS* I, 221–22.
42. See Wolfson, *Philosophy of Spinoza*, 2:326–30.
43. Leon Roth, *Spinoza, Descartes, and Maimonides* (Oxford: Clarendon Press, 1924).
44. "The philosophers" (Arabic: *al-falāsifa*) is the common name of the Arab philosophers. Strauss often uses the transcribed Arabic word.
45. *GS* I, 239n238.
46. See Dunin-Borkowski, *Der junge De Spinoza*, 224–40; Carl Gebhardt, "Spinoza und der Platonismus," in *Chronicon Spinozanum* (the Hague: Hagae Comitis, 1921), 1:178–234, especially 202–16.
47. Strauss, *RKS*, 207–8. See Spinoza, *Tractatus de intellectus emendatione: Ethica*, ed. Konrad Blumenstock (Darmstadt, Germany: Wissenschaftliche Buchgesellschaft, 1989), 3:256ff.
48. *RKS*, 244–45.
49. *RKS*, 245–46. See also Spinoza, *Tractatus theologico-politicus*, 461.
50. See also David R. Lachterman, "Laying Down the Law: The Theological-Political Matrix of Spinoza's Physics," in Udoff, *Strauss's Thought*, 131–41.

Chapter Two

1. This is Oliver Leaman's assessment in "Is Averroes an Averroist?," in Niewöhner and L. Sturlese, *Averroismus*, 15, 18.
2. This is particularly relevant in the *Faṣl al-maqāl wa-taqrīr mā baina ash-sharīʿa wa-l-ḥikma min al-ittiṣāl* (in English known as *On the Harmony of Religions and Philosophy*), which Strauss knew well.
3. *GS* I, 49–50.
4. *GS* I, 54.
5. Hildegard Korth, *Guide to the Leo Strauss Papers* (Department of Special Collections, University of Chicago Library, 1978), 5. This is similar to what is mentioned in a letter to Gerhard Krüger on June 26, 1930, in *GS* II, xviii n14; *JPCM*, 462–63.
6. In 1935, Erwin I. J. Rosenthal reported in a paper that eight years prior, Leo Strauss had drawn his attention to Averroes's commentary on Plato's *Politeia* and to Plato's influence on Islamic political philosophy. A few months before this paper appeared, Rosenthal had announced his plan to edit the Hebrew version of Averroes's commentary, followed by an English translation. He also mentioned that he had learned from Strauss about preserved Hebrew and Latin translations of the commentary. It was actually Strauss who had encouraged him to work on this edition. According to Rosenthal, his conversation with Strauss occurred in the context of Albert Brackmann's seminar on political opinions in the era of Frederick II of Hohenstaufen, which took

place in the winter term of 1927–28. It was at this time that Strauss finished his analysis of Spinoza. Erwin Rosenthal, "Averroes' Paraphrase on Plato's 'Politeia,'" *Journal of the Royal Asiatic Society* (1934): 737–44; Erwin Rosenthal, "Maimonides' Conception of State and Society," in *Moses Maimonides*, ed. I. Epstein (London: Soncino Press, 1935), 191. See also Strauss, *GS* II, 196n4; Friedrich Niewöhner, "Einleitung zur deutschen Ausgabe," in *Kommentar des Averroes zu Platons Politeia*, by Averroes, ed. Erwin I. J. Rosenthal (Zürich: Spur, 1996), 7 (henceforth cited as *KPP*).

7. "Cohen und Maimuni" was first published in *GS* II, 393–436. "Maimunis Lehre von der Prophetie und ihre Quellen" constitutes part 4 of *Philosophie und Gesetz*. The chronology of these texts was assembled by Heinrich Meier in *GS* II, xvi.

8. Strauss, *GS* II, 113n58. On p. 104n40, Strauss writes: "I have consulted the original of the Greater Metaphysics [by Avicenna] in a manuscript in Berlin (Minutoli 229, f. 165b–166a)." In the same remark, he mentions Avicenna's *Tisʿ rasāʾil* and "Ghazzâli's Tahāfut." He also mentions multiple Arabic texts he read, which include Ibn Ṭufail's *Ḥayy Ibn Yaqẓān* (*GS* II, 103n38) and Avicenna's *Ishārāt wa-tanbīhāt* (113n58).

9. In *Tisʿ rasāʾil* (Constantinople: Maṭbaʿat al-Jawāʾib, 1298 H/1881), 71–80. A newer edition has been prepared by Ḥasan ʿĀṣī (Beirut: Dār Qābis, 1986).

10. *GS* II, 112. Strauss quotes passages from Avicenna's *Tisʿ rasāʾil* (1298 H/1881), 73–74, and from a manuscript that can be consulted in the Forschungs- und Landesbibliothek Gotha (fol. 160a, n1158).

11. Heinrich Meier's description of Strauss's discovery of Avicenna's text and the subsequent philosophical turn hits the mark:

> It came as a great surprise to Strauss when, in 1929 or 1930, he read in Avicenna's *Treatise on the Divisions of Rational Sciences* that Plato's *Nomoi* contained a discussion of prophecy and divine law. Overnight, this finding opened up a new access not only to the Arabic philosophers al-Fārābī, Avicenna, and Averroes, but also to Maimonides and Plato himself. More than four decades later, Strauss would use this hint from Avicenna as the motto which would proceed his final book, a commentary on the *Nomoi*, which should be considered simultaneously the most "pious" and most "ironic" among Plato's works. This discovery in the Berlin State Library augured Strauss's preoccupations in *Philosophy and Law*. While Strauss's interest in this subject matter was historical in nature, this subject turned out to be of great philosophical interest." (*GS* II, xviii)

The numerous quotations here from Avicenna's text testify to its enormous importance for Strauss (*GS* II, 112, 114, 126, 198, 425; *AAPL*, 1, 3; Leo Strauss with Jacob Klein, "A Giving of Accounts," *The College* 22, no. 1 [April 1970]: 1–5; reprinted in *JPCM*, 457–66, here 463 [henceforth cited as "GA"]).

12. Avicenna, *Tisʿ rasāʾil* (1298 H/1881), 71–72.
13. Avicenna, 72–73.
14. Avicenna, 73–74.
15. Avicenna, 74–79.
16. Avicenna, 79–80.
17. In the Gotha manuscript, the correct book by Bryson is mentioned. See Martin Plessner, *Der OIKONOMIKOC des Neupythagoreers "Bryson"* (Heidelberg: Winter, 1928).
18. Strauss names his source as the collection *Tisʿ rasāʾil* (1298 H/1881), 73–74. The following is a translation of the cited text:

> What we identify with the concept of kingship (*mulk*) is to be found in Plato's and Aristotles' books on politics (*siyāsa*). What we identify with prophecy (*nubūwwa*) and the religious law (*sharīʿa*) is to be found in the two books about the law (*nawāmīs*). With the word nāmūs, the philosophers do not wish to express what the crowd associates with the term, namely deception and cunning. When philosophers use the term, they wish to discuss the proper and ideal way of life (*sunna*) as well as revelation (*waḥī*). The Arabs also associate the term *nāmūs* with the angel who descended from heaven with revelation. This section of practical philosophy posits the existence of prophecy in terms of the need of humankind for such prophecy as reflected through its content and the variations inherent in multiple revelations. A part of philosophy concerns itself with the common perception of the general laws (*sharāʾiʿ*) as well as individual religious laws that are contingent on the people to whom these laws are revealed and the era in which these people live. The difference between divine prophecy and all pretentions thereto can be perceived.

In *ʿUyūn al-ḥikma* (Latin: *Fontes Sapientiae*), ed. ʿAbd al-Raḥmān Badawī (Kuwait: Wakālat al-Maṭbūʿāt, 1980), 16, Avicenna defines the three parts of practical philosophy and their relationship with religious law somewhat differently. (Parts of *ʿUyūn al-ḥikma* were included in the 1298 H/1881 edition of *Tisʿ rasāʾil*, where the respective definitions can be found on page 2.) This treatise contains a summary of Avicenna's philosophical teachings. According to Badawī, who edited *ʿUyūn al-ḥikma* in 1980, this is one of Avicenna's last writings. Shams Inati translated this passage as follows:

> Practical philosophy [. . .] is concerned with learning one of the following: (1) the principles on which public sharing among people is based, (2) the principles on which personal sharing among people is based, or (3) the principles on which the affairs of the individual are based. The first is the management of the city, referred to as political science; the second is home

> management; and the third is management of the individual, referred to as ethics. The principles of practical philosophy are derived from the divine Sharīah, and its complete definitions are made clear by the divine *Sharīah*. The benefit of the science of management of the city is to make known the manner in which sharing among people occurs for the purpose of the well-being of the human body and of the preservation of humanity. The benefit of the science of home management is to make known the type of sharing that must take place among the members of the same home in order to ensure their well-being. Such sharing occurs between husband and wife, parent and child, and master and slave. The science of management of the individual yields a twofold benefit – to make known the virtues and the manner of acquiring them in order to refine the soul, and to make known the vices and the manner of avoiding them in order to refine the soul, and to make known the vices and the manner of avoiding them in order to purify the soul. ("Ibn Sīnā," in Nasr and Leaman, *History of Islamic Philosophy*, 234)

In this passage, all three principles of practical philosophy are considered to be derived from religious law, which is viewed as the measure of their perfection.

19. *GS* II, 112, n57.
20. This sentence contains a grammatical error. The attribute must take the dual form and should read *al-mawḍū ʿān*.
21. Moritz Steinschneider, *Die arabischen Übersetzungen aus dem Griechischen* (Graz, Austria: Akademische Druck- und Verlags-Anstalt, 1960); Manfred Ullmann, *Die Natur- und Geheimwissenschaften im Islam* (Leiden, Netherlands: Brill, 1972). Mahdi provides an incorrect explanation of this matter in Ralph Lerner and Muhsin Mahdi, *Medieval Political Philosophy: A Sourcebook* (Glencoe, IL: Free Press of Glencoe, 1963), 97n2.
22. Dimitri Gutas, "Galen's *Synopsis* of Plato's *Laws* and Fārābī's *Talḫīṣ*," in *The Ancient Tradition in Christian and Islamic Hellenism: Studies on the Transmission of Greek Philosophy and Sciences dedicated to H. J. Drossaart Lulofs on his ninetieth birthday*, ed. Gerhard Endress and Remke Kruk, 101–19 (Leiden: Research School CNWS, 1997), contends that Plato's *Nomoi* was ever present in Arabic translation. He presents convincing arguments that al-Fārābī was only following Galen's summary, which al-Fārābī himself then summarized.
23. In this regard, see also Harry A. Wolfson, "Additional Notes," *Hebrew Union College Annual* 3 (1926): 374–75.
24. Philologists have long since provided evidence for the multiple meanings of *nāmūs*. Moritz Steinschneider demonstrated on the basis of multiple studies the ambiguity of *nawāmīs*, which could mean either laws or tricks (in the sense of fraud). Steinschneider, *Zur pseudepigraphischen Literatur des*

Mittelalters, insbesondere der geheimen Wissenschaften (Berlin, 1862), 52 (reprinted in Amsterdam: Philo Press, 1965); Steinschneider, "Gauberi's 'entdeckte Geheimnisse': Eine Quelle für orientalische Sittenschilderung," *Zeitschrift der Deutschen Morgenländischen Gesellschaft* 19 (1865): 564. Regarding etymology, Heinrich Leberecht Fleischer (1801 to 1888) assumed that the word was the result of a convergence of two entirely different roots. To Fleischer, one source was the Greek word *νόμος* (also Manfred Ullmann, *Die Medizin im Islam* [Leiden: Brill, 1970], 33), while the other word was genuinely Arabic and derived from the radical "*namasa, namisa*." Combined with a direct object that is a person, *namasa* means "to unveil his or her secret." Combined with a direct object that is a thing, it means "to buzz, to mumble, to whisper in an ear, smell, aspirate or to speak secretly." *Nāmūs* therefore means, "and here we can see the full semantic power of the verb root," (1) summer, i.e., the summer mosquito; (2) the whisperer in an ear; (3) a confidant who retains a deep secret, or who is the expert at a topic; (4) secret, cunning behavior; (5) a hiding place, or that which is hidden; (6) cunning with which one operates behind the scenes or behind someone's back. Fleischer also stipulates that the notions *an-Nāmūs* or *an-Nāmūs al-Akbar*, notions originally used by Arabic-speaking Christians and Jews for the archangel Gabriel, are translated as "God's supreme confidant." This reflects the meaning of "someone's confidence." Theodor Nöldeke, "Hatte Muhammad christliche Lehrer?," *Zeitschrift der Deutschen Morgenländischen Gesellschaft* 12 (1858): 701–2 n3; Heinrich L. Fleischer, "Bemerkungen zu Gaubari's 'entdeckten Geheimnissen' u. a.," *Zeitschrift der Deutschen Morgenländischen Gesellschaft* 21 (1867): 275. As an example of this emphasis on "confidence," Fleischer cites Ibn Qutayba, who himself is citing a saying of Waraqa Ibn Nawfals (the uncle of Khadīja, Muhammad's first wife) that the angel (*an-Nāmūs al-Akbar*) who came to Muhammad was the same angel who used to come to Moses. In a subsequent study that bases itself upon these insights, Fleischer contradicts the claim that the *Nawāmīs Aflāṭūn* (*Nomoi*) renders the meaning of the term *nawāmīs* into "the art of secrecy" and that due to the "many imagistic and mysterious elements in the text" it should be considered the same as the "*mysterious sayings* of Plato." Rather, he insists that the word *nāmūs* has "a hybrid, double meaning" (Fleischer, "Bemerkungen," 275). See also Martin Plessner, "Nāmūs," in *Enzyklopaedie des Islam*, ed. M. Th. Houtsma et al. (Leiden: Brill, 1913–36), 3:911–14. (The first edition of the *Encyclopedia of Islam* is henceforth cited as *EI1*.) *Νόμος* is also the title of an Arabic work translated from the Greek that provides instructions for young doctors; see Ullmann, *Die Medizin im Islam*, 33.

25. For proof of the philosophic usage of the word *nāmūs* in Arabic, see Soheil M. Afnan, *A Philosophical Lexicon in Persian and Arabic* (Beirut: Dār al-Mashriq, 1969), 287. Unfortunately, Afnan does not refer to Avicenna's use of the term.

26. Moritz Steinschneider, *Al-Fārābī (Alpharabius): Des arabischen Philosophen Leben und Schriften mit besonderer Rücksicht auf die Geschichte der griechischen Wissenschaft unter den Arabern* (St. Petersburg: n.p., 1869), 78, reprinted in Amsterdam: Philo Press, 1966; as well as Steinschneider, *Die arabischen Übersetzungen*, 56ff.; Ullmann, *Die Natur- und*

Geheimwissenschaften, 364. Steinschneider, *Zur pseudepigraphischen Literatur*, 51–56, assumes that Petrus Alfonsi's quotation from Plato referring to "de prophetiis" is actually derived from this pseudo-Platonic text, as do many references to Plato in the works of Christian authors in the thirteenth century. Steinschneider believes that it is possible Ḥunayn b. Isḥāq (ca. 808 to 873) served as the "translator" or did some other work on the text due to the fact that he "also translated a similar work by Apollonius." Furthermore, he relays that this work contains two books, one "big" the other "small," wherein "things are contained, which the wise, those that deeply desire God, those called the prophets, or those similar to them, understand. Some examples include viewing the moon in the last three nights, and recognizing the dark absence of the moon occurring at an irregular time, that trees walk and to those men who are called the prophets , etc . . . etc . . . , which have all been described in the previous chapters. The small book has many names and chapters, as many have engaged in this art form. . . . Its effect on those that do not understand it is wonderous." It is best to bring an additional confirmation for the existence of pseudo-Platonic *nawāmīs*-book that deals with topics of magic. At the beginning of a book from the thirteenth century written by a Damascene named Jawbarī that contained magical secrets and astrology, which was probably finished around 650 H/1252–53, the author listed all the previous books he read on the same topic. These books include all works discussing the various "arts of *nawāmīs*," such as the *Nawāmīs Aflāṭūn*. In the first part of the book dealing with decrying false prophets, Jawbarī posits Abū Saʿīd al-Qirmiṭī as a pseudo-prophet who deeply understood the *Nawāmīs Aflaṭūn* and thereby was well respected by many people. The *Nawāmīs* is mentioned throughout the book in connection with charlatans, astrologers, alchemists, and kabbalists. Many researchers consider Jawbarī connected to these art forms. Steinschneider refers to this text in the *Zeitschrift der Deutschen Morgenländischen Gesellschaft* 19 (1865): 562–77. Following this study, M. J. de Goeje's article appeared regarding Jawbarī's "discovered secrets": "Gaubari's 'entdeckte Geheimnisse,'" *Zeitschrift der Deutschen Morgenländischen Gesellschaft* 20 (1866): 485–510. The full title of the work is *Kitāb al-mukhtār fī kashf al-asrār wa-hatk al-astār* (Selections for uncovering the secrets and dispensing with the masks). In another source, the text is called *Kashf asrār al-muḥtalīn wa-nawāmīs al-khayyālīn* (Revealing the secrets of the deceitful and the secret arts of the charlatans).

27. This pseudo-Platonic *nawāmīs*-book came out in 1973 as part of an edited collection of Platonic and pseudo-Platonic texts translated into Arabic: *Kitāb an-nawāmīs li-Aflāṭūn* in ʿAbd ar-Raḥmān Badawī, *Aflāṭūn fī l-Islām* (*Plato in Islam*), 2nd ed. (Beirut: Dār al-Andalus, 1980), 197–234. This book has been largely neglected in the scholarly literature. According to Gutas, "Galen's *Synopsis*," 102, there exist many handwritten manuscripts of it. Alongside Badawī's edition, I am in possession of photocopies from the Bodleian Library (MS Ouseley 95) and the British Museum (Or. 12070). [Author's addition: in the meantime, I acquired many other manuscripts. An annotated edition of the text combined with an English translation and a commentary will appear soon.] In the Sachau's and Ethe's catalogue of 1889, 873, no. 1422, the Bodleian handwritten manuscript is described in the following fashion: "*Kitāb-al nawāmīs* [. . .] Arabic, on ff. 150b–152b and ff. 133–37.

Ff 150–52 are damaged at the top. Plato's 'De legibus' in Arabic translation, made by Ḥunayn bin Isḥāq, according to another version by Abū 'Alī Ibn Miskawayh. Comp. Wüstenfeld, Geschichte der arabischen Aerzte, pp 26 and 64. Ḥunayn died A. H. 260 = A. D. 873, 874, and Ibn Miskawayh 421 = A.D. 1030." It has been reported that the second and third tractates (*maqāla*) contain the handwritten manuscript of the three tractates dealing with prophecy. This manuscript was damaged in multiple places, especially at the top and bottom. The three tractates in the MS British Museum Or. 12070, 17–32b, are in a better condition. The second and third tractates are dedicated in the title to prophecy (*fī n-nubūwat*). Additionally, a manuscript to be found in Tehran (university library collection "kitābkhanah markazī," no. 2110) contains, in addition to *Kitāb an-Nawāmīs*, two treatises by al-Fārābī, namely *Mabādi' ārā' ahl al-madīna al-fāḍila* and *Kitāb taḥṣīl as-sa'āda*, as is also mentioned by Ja'far Āl Yāsīn in his edition of the latter book (Beirut: Dār al-Andalus, 1401 H/1981), 29–30 (cited here as *Taḥṣīl*). Cf. Shlomo Pines, "Shī'ite Terms and Conceptions in Judah Halevi's *Kuzari*," *Jerusalem Studies in Arabic and Islam* 2 (1980): 236–39. The results presented here, in which the existence of three *nawāmīs*-books is substantiated, have happily been confirmed in a letter by Prof. Dimitri Gutas dated April 26, 1999.

28. Badawī, *Aflāṭūn fī l-Islām*, 199. This rather odd combination probably designates the social and political order contained in the revealed law. Joel L. Kraemer, "Maimonides on the Philosophic Sciences in his Treatise on the Art of Logic," in *Perspectives on Maimonides: Philosophical and Historical Studies*, ed. Joel L. Kraemer (Oxford: Oxford University Press, 1991), 101.

29. The idea that prophets deal with humans as humans deal with animals can also be found in Abū Ya'qūb Isḥāq as-Sijistānī, *Kitāb ithbāt an-nubū'āt*, ed. 'Ārif Tāmir (Beirut: al-Maṭba'a al-Kāthūlīkiyya, 1966), 68–69.

30. Thoughts similar to those expressed in this *nawāmīs*-book can be found in writings by Shiite authors such as as-Sijistānī's *Kitāb Ithbāt an-nubū'āt* and in *Rasā'il ikhwān aṣ-ṣafā'*. The resemblance with Sufi literature that I highlight here does not exclude other contexts or meanings. My intention behind referring to the Sufi context is to demonstrate that this pseudo-Platonic text stems from an Islamic context and does not have anything in common with Plato's *Nomoi* (Pines, "Shī'ite Terms," 238).

31. See Abū 'Abd Allāh Muḥammad b. Alī l-Ḥakīm at-Tirmidhī, *Adab al-mulūk: Ein Handbuch zur islamischen Mystik aus dem 4./10. Jahrhundert*, ed. Bernd Radtke (Beirut: Steiner, 1991), 23, 3–14. The work was translated into German along with an introduction and commentary by Richard Gramlich: al-Ḥakīm at-Tirmidhī, *Die Lebensweise der Könige: Adab al-mulūk: Ein Handbuch zur islamischen Mystik* (Stuttgart: Steiner, 1993), 53.

32. For more, see al-Ḥakīm at-Tirmidhī, *Drei Schriften des Theosophen von Tirmidh*, ed. and trans. Bernd Radtke (Beirut: Steiner, 1992 and 1996), 1:188, line 12 (original) / 2:227 (German trans.).

33. See also in this regard al-Ḥakīm at-Tirmidhī, *Adab al-mulūk*, 16, line 3 / 39.

34. See also al-Ḥakīm at-Tirmidhī, 13, line 19 / 34.

35. Regarding *jashiyā*, see Richard Gramlich, *Schlaglichter über das Sufitum* (Stuttgart: Steiner, 1990), 477.

36. See also al-Ḥakīm at-Tirmidhī, *Adab al-mulūk*, 8, line 23 / 25.

37. It is common to compare the life of a Sufi to a spiritual journey that is unfortunately burdened by material concerns. This is why Sufis are encouraged to rid themselves of these material sorrows and to lead a life in poverty. Doing so, they have to "rely on God," which is the classical Sufi concept of *tawakkul*. The text above equally argues along these lines. The first of the *nawāmīs*-treatises reports that there were several ascetics, people who renounced breadwinning, who consorted with the prophet. Bernd Radtke, "The Concept of wilāya in Early Sufism," in *Classical Persian Sufism from Its Origins to Rumi (700–1300)*, vol. 1 of *The Heritage of Sufism*, ed. Leonard Lewisohn (London: Khaniqahi Nimatullahi Publications, 1993), 489; Benedikt Reinert, *Die Lehre vom* tawakkul *in der klassischen Sufik* (Berlin: de Gruyter, 1968).

38. See al-Ḥakīm at-Tirmidhī, *Adab al-mulūk*, 9, 18ff./27.

39. Al-Ḥakīm at-Tirmidhī, 51/75–76. The text goes on to describe the "inspired" as those who, by means of the law, "raise the call to God and directs the people to the Divine. What comes to his tongue from God relates to the legal order and that means good tidings, support and admonition. This is not a message which contradicts the law. It is, rather, completely concordant with the law." Those who reject God's messengers or the prophets are to be considered nonbelievers. Those who reject the inspired lose their "blessings and light" (52/76–77). The characteristics of those three types of divine messengers are briefly described in the following manner: "The Inspired possess inspiration, the clarity of vision, and utter honesty. The prophet possessed these characteristics in addition to the capacity for prophecy as the highly perfected bearer of the divine message. The friends of God possess in this capacity only clarity of vision, inspiration and ultra-honesty" (4/79). In this context it is noteworthy that the Qur᾽ān mentions prophets, some of whom are already included in the Old Testament (Abraham, Isaac, Jacob, Aaron, and Job). However, others, like Idrīs, are not. These prophets can, as in the case of Hūds, be sent to a small community (sura 26:123–40; 9; 7:63–70; 46:20) or prophesy on their own like Elias (sura 26:85; 27:123ff.). *Der Koran*, trans. Rudi Paret, 5th ed. (Stuttgart: Kohlhammer, 1989). See also J. Horovitz, "Nabī," in *EI1*, 3:867; A. J. Wensinck, "Rasūl," in *EI2*, 8:454–55; T. Nagel, "Kiṣaṣ al-anbiyā'," in *EI2*, 5:180–81.

40. Plato's proximity to mysticism is basically in line with the image Arabic speakers had of Plato in the Middle Ages.

41. A common Islamic quotation concisely sums up the difference between God's envoy (*rasūl*) and a prophet (*nabī*): Every envoy from God is a prophet, but not every prophet is God's envoy.

42. See also Josef van Ess, *Theologie und Gesellschaft im 2. und 3. Jahrhundert Hidschra: Eine Geschichte des religiösen Denkens im frühen Islam* (Berlin: de Gruyter, 1997), 4:591–604.

43. It seems that al-Fārābī adopted this distinction between God's envoys and prophets. He recognizes six law-giving prophets (Adam, Noah, Abraham, Moses, Jesus, and Muhammad) and enumerates many other biblical and non-biblical prophets, among them even Alexander the Great. Al-Fārābī, *Kitāb al-milla wa-nuṣūṣ ukhrā* (*Book of Religion and Related Texts*), ed. Muhsin Mahdi (Beirut: Dār al-Mashriq, 1991), 97–115 (henceforth cited as *Milla*).

44. It is noteworthy that the understanding of prophecy in the pseudo-Platonic book appears to be very close to the understanding of prophecy in early Islam inasmuch as both clearly differentiate between prophecy and divination (*kihāna*). This is evocative of the debate on the differentiation between Muhammad's prophecy and the widespread divinatory rites in early Islam. In the pseudo-Platonic book, the prophet stresses that his knowledge had been imparted to him in its final form, which he did not change. This statement must have been convenient for the Muslim orthodox belief in Muhammad's verbal inspiration. For the understanding of prophecy in Islam, see T. Fahd, "Nubuwwa," in *EI2*, 8:93–97; Aziz al-Azmeh, *Arabic Thought and Islamic Societies* (London: Croom Helm, 1986), 56ff.

45. According to the aforementioned conception, prophethood can be divided into several parts or criteria. Muhammad, the seal of the prophets, fulfills all of them. Nonetheless, there are individuals such as those attracted to God along with the inspired who partially fulfill the criteria of prophethood. A Sufi master quoted the prophet Muhammed in response to a worried comment made by a student as to how anybody could achieve even a fraction of what made Muhammed worthy of prophecy. The quoted Ḥadīth reads as follows: "Moderation, pious instruction and good behavior are one part of the 24 constituent parts of prophethood." Furthermore, he notes that "if he who is thrifty already possesses a characteristic of prophethood," then of course those that find themselves at advanced stages on the mystical path and who stand close to God also possess the qualities of a prophet. (*Al-iqtiṣādu wa-l-hudā ṣ-ṣāliḥu wa-s-samtu l-ḥasanu juzʾun min arbaʿatin wa-ʿishrīna juzʾan mina n-nubūwa.*) From this Ḥadīth it becomes clear that the qualities the prophet Muhammad had in mind were of an ethical nature possessed by those who had foresight in their dealings. Al-Ḥakīm at-Tirmidhī, *Drei Schriften*, 51/75–76, §§ 61, 69.

46. Avicenna, *Tisʿ rasāʾil* (1298 H/1881), 85.

47. See also Felix Klein-Franke, "Zur Überlieferung der platonischen Schriften im Islam," *Israel Oriental Studies* 3 (1973): 120–39, especially 127–28, 134, 139. Avicenna also wrote a commentary on the pseudepigraphal *Theology of Aristotle*, which suggests that he did not doubt its authenticity. ʿAbd ar-Raḥmān Badawī, *Arisṭū ʿinda al-ʿarab* (Cairo: Maktabat an-Nahḍa al-Miṣriyya, 1947), 35–74, 121. However, the *Theology of Aristotle* is a summary of the fourth, fifth, and sixth books of Plotinus's *Enneads*, which was translated into Arabic in the ninth century and falsely ascribed to Aristotle. Majid Fakhry, *Dirāsāt fī l-fikr al-ʿarabī* (Beirut: Dār an-Nahār, 1982), 63ff.; Oliver Leaman, *An Introduction to Medieval Islamic Philosophy* (Cambridge: Cambridge University Press, 1992), 5; Gotthard Strohmaier, *Avicenna* (Munich: Beck, 1999), 60–61.

48. Avicenna, *An-Najāt*, ed. M. al-Kurdī (Cairo: Matbaʿat as-Saʿāda, 1357 H/1938), 303–8 (henceforth cited as *Najāt*); "*Risāla fī ithbāt an-nubūwāt*," in *Tisʿ rasāʾil*, 82–90.

49. There were Arabic translations of Alexander's *De Intellectu* and of Themistius's paraphrasing of Aristotle's *De Anima* (3.4–8). Frederic M Schroeder and Robert B. Todd, trans. and ed., *Two Greek Aristotelian Commentators on the Intellect: The "De Intellectu" Attributed to Alexander of Aphrodisias and Themistius' Paraphrase of Aristotle "De Anima" 3.4–8* (Toronto: Pontifical Institute of Mediaeval Studies, 1990), 2, 31. For Avicenna's psychology, see the English translation of his *Kitāb an-Najāt* — Avicenna, *Avicenna's Psychology*, ed. F. Rahman (London: Oxford University Press, 1952, reprint 1981) — and also S. Landauer, ed., "Die Psychologie des Ibn Sīnā," *Zeitschrift der Deutschen Morgenländischen Gesellschaft* 29 (1875): 335–418; F. Rahman, *Prophecy in Islam: Philosophy and Orthodoxy* (London: Allen and Unwin, 1958), 14–20; Majid Fakhry, *Tarīkh al-falsafa al-islāmiyya*, trans. Kamāl al-Yāzijī (Beirut: ad-Dār al-Muttaḥida li-n-Nashr, 1979), 190–97; Lenn E. Goodmann, *Avicenna* (London: Routledge, 1992), 149–63; Inati, "Ibn Sīnā," 236–39.

50. Cf. Richard Walzer, "Alfārābi's Theory of Prophecy and Divination," *Journal of Hellenic Studies* 77 (1957): 142–48; Rahman, *Prophecy in Islam*, 14–91.

51. Rahman, *Prophecy in Islam*, 31ff.

52. Avicenna, *Najāt*, 300ff.

53. Rahman, *Prophecy in Islam*, 36.

54. Rahman, *Prophecy in Islam*, 36–39. As is generally known, Avicenna authored several writings on mysticism. See Avicenna's autobiography, which was completed by one of his students, al-Juzjānī: Avicenna, *The Life of Ibn Sina*, trans. and ed. William E. Gohlman (Albany: State University of New York Press, 1974). Avicenna was considered to be one of the original figures to introduce Aristotelian-Neoplatonic thought into mysticism. Annemarie Schimmel, *Mystical Dimensions of Islam* (Chapel Hill: University of North Carolina Press, 1975), 19, 293, 307; al-Ḥakīm at-Tirmidhī, *Drei Schriften*, 32; Bernd Radtke, "How Can We Reach the Mystical Union? Ibn Ṭufayl and the Divine Spark," in *The World of Ibn Ṭufayl: Interdisciplinary Perspectives on Ḥayy ibn Yaqẓān*, ed. Lawrence I. Conrad (Leiden: Brill, 1996), 166; Sayyid H. Nasr, "Ibn Sīnā's 'Oriental Philosophy,'" in Nasr and Leaman, *History of Islamic Philosophy*, 247–51. The pseudo-Platonic *nawāmīs*-book, whose proximity to Sufi thought is apparent, would likely have been attractive to Avicenna due to his own mystical tendencies. Therefore, the designation of Plato as a mystic is imaginable.

55. Alongside prophecy, which is demonstrable through the utterance of truth and prediction of the future, law-giving prophecy emerges in the case of Moses and Muhammad with the emergence of legal religions. An additional feature of prophethood is on display in both the Old Testament and the Qurʾān and is associated with legal religions in periods of religious decline and collapse. This feature is that of moral judgement in the service of ethical rectitude that comes of adherence to the law. See Ibn Maimūn, *Dalālat*, II, Ch.36: 404–5,

Ch.39: 411, Ch. 45: 432–33 (the Arabic edition by H. Atai). Avicenna mentions "the great philosophers and prophets of the Greeks" (*ajillat falāsifat yūnān wa-anbiyā'uhum*) who together used symbols and signs in their books in order to communicate secrets. He names Pythagoras, Socrates, and Plato as examples. Yet it is difficult in the context of this text to discern whether he considered these philosophers to be prophets (*Tisʿ rasā'il*, 85). A text from the eleventh century mentions Socrates as a figure who in prophetic fashion rejects idolatry and calls for belief in a single, rational God who created the world; see Franz Rosenthal, "On the Knowledge of Plato's Philosophy in the Islamic World," *Islamic Culture* 14 (1940): 389. Finally, it is notable that al-Ghazālī, perhaps the most vehement Islamic critic of Greek peripatetic philosophy, accepted and further developed Avicenna's prophetology: Abū Ḥāmid al-Ghazālī, *Tahāfut al-falāsifa*, ed. Maurice Bouyges (Beirut: Imprimerie Catholique, 1927), 192ff., 199ff. Regarding al-Ghazālī's conflict with the philosophers, see the nuanced treatment in Frank Griffel, *Apostasie und Toleranz: Voraussetzungen und Entwicklung von al-Ġazālis Urteil gegen die Philosophie und die Reaktionen der Philosophen* (Leiden: Brill, 2000).

56. *Najāt*, 301; Rahman, *Prophecy in Islam*, 45–51. Richard Gramlich, *Die Wunder der Freunde Gottes: Theologien und Erscheinungsformen des Islamischen Heiligenwunders* (Wiesbaden: Steiner, 1987), 133, had already noticed that Avicenna in *Al-Ishārāt wa-t-tanbīhāt* discovered "an unusually strong capacity of the soul" that enabled it to transcend the body and "simultaneously become a soul of the world. Therein the wonderworker and the magician become the same, yet it is only in the wonderworker where the inner spiritual capacities are intensified though ascetic living. In the magician his evil behavior weakens these capacities." Avicenna's differentiation between good and evil wonderworking is curiously reflected in "Nawāmīs Aflātūn," in Badawī, *Aflāṭūn fī l-Islām*, 222–23, where the good, faithful, and ascetic wonderworker, whose attention is directed to the heavens, is paralleled by the recidivist ascetic who deceives the people.

57. *Najāt*, 302, 306ff.; Rahman, *Prophecy in Islam*, 58. It appears that Avicenna, on the one hand, acknowledges the universal nature of religion yet, on the other hand, holds Islam to be the best religion (Rahman, 41, 77–78). Avicenna follows the previously depicted distinction between the divine messenger *rasūl* and the prophet (*Tisʿ rasā'il*, 85).

58. *GS* II, 128ff., 136, 142, 150–51, 156ff.

59. Cf., for example, Pangle in *SPPP*, 10ff.

60. In his study on Halevi's *Kuzari*, Strauss refers to Steinschneider's report on the dubious *nawāmīs*-text and remarks that the connection of Plato's *Nomoi* with magical writings was common for the Arabic reception of philosophy in the Middle Ages (*PAW*, 123n86).

61. Authentic statements can be found in Ullmann, *Die Natur- und Geheimwissenschaften*, 154ff., 287, 341, 362, 387. In the book *Placita Philosophorum*, Plato and the Stoics profess their belief in the art of truth telling and root its possibility in the divinity of the soul. This book was quite early on falsely attributed to Plutarch and later translated into Arabic by Qusṭā b. Lūqā (~205 H/820 to 300 H/912), as claimed by Ibn an-Nadīm in *al-Fihrist*, written in

377 H/987. Hans Daiber, *Aetius Arabus: Die Vorsokratiker in arabischer Überlieferung* (Wiesbaden: Steiner, 1980), 216.

62. F. Rosenthal, "On the Knowledge," 387–422, especially 388–89; Klein-Franke, "Zur Überlieferung der platonischen Schriften," 134ff.

63. Walzer, "Aflāṭūn," in *EI2*, 1:234–36; F. Rosenthal, "On the Knowledge," 387–422; Ullmann, *Die Natur- und Geheimwissenschaften*, especially 154ff., 365–66; Klein-Franke, "Zur Überlieferung der platonischen Schriften," 134ff. References to the pseudo-Platonic sources can be found in Hans Daiber, *Bibliography of Islamic Philosophy* (Leiden: Brill, 1999), 1:730–31.

64. Walzer, "Aflāṭūn," in *EI2*, 1:234–36; F. Rosenthal, "On the Knowledge," 395–96; Paul Kraus, "Plotin chez les Arabes," *Bulletin de l'Institut d'Égypte* 23 (1941): 263–95; Klein-Franke, "Zur Überlieferung der platonischen Schriften," 124–25; F. E. Peters, "The Greek and Syriac Background," in Nasr and Leaman, *History of Islamic Philosophy*, 40–51.

65. Walzer, "Aflāṭūn," in *EI2*, 1:235.

66. See Steinschneider, *Die arabischen Übersetzungen*; A. J. Arberry, "Some Plato in an Arabic Epitome," *Islamic Quarterly* 2 (1955): 86–99; Richard Walzer, "Arabische Übersetzungen aus dem Griechischen," *Miscellanea Medievalia* 9 (1962): 179–95; also the English translation, Richard Walzer, *Greek into Arabic: Essays on Islamic Philosophy* (Oxford: Cassirer, 1962); Klein-Franke, "Zur Überlieferung der platonischen Schriften," 124–25; Franz Rosenthal, *Greek Philosophy in the Arab World* (Aldershot: Variorum, 1990); Gutas, *Greek Thought, Arabic Culture*.

67. See also Erwin Rosenthal, "The Place of Politics in the Philosophy of Ibn Rushd," *Bulletin of the School of Oriental and African Studies* 15 (1953): 246–78, especially 247–48, reprinted in E. Rosenthal, *Studia Semitica*, 2:60–92; Niewöhner, "Einleitung zur deutschen Ausgabe," 10–11; "Madkhal: Jadīd fī l-fikr as-sīyāsī bi-t-turāth al-ʿarabī" and "Muqaddima taḥlīliyya: Muwājahat as-siyāsa bi-khiṭāb siyāsī," in Averroes, *Aḍ-Ḍarūrī fī s-siyāsa: Mukhtaṣar kitāb as-siyāsa li-Aflāṭūn*, introduction and explanatory remarks by Muḥammad ʿĀbid al-Jābirī (Beirut: Markaz Dirāsāt al-Waḥda al-ʿArabiyya, 1998), 13–68.

68. Strauss, *GS* II, 400; *CM*, 11; *NRH*, 33; *WIPP*, 77; Joseph Cropsey, ed., *Ancients and Moderns: Essays on the Tradition of Political Philosophy in Honor of Leo Strauss* (New York: Basic Books, 1964), viii; Caton, "Der hermeneutische Weg von Leo Strauss," 172.

69. This appears to be much more confusing, as Strauss states in another section that the discussions in Plato's *Nomoi* upon which Avicenna bases his concept of prophecy (in order to justify its esoteric character) are actually "pseudo-Platonic." One can only conclude that Strauss was likely aware that Avicenna was working with a pseudo-Platonic *Book of Laws* but he didn't really care to acknowledge it. *GS* II, 425. Cf. Avicenna, *Tisʿ rasāʾil* (1298 H/1881), 85.

70. Gutas, "Galen's *Synopsis*," 118.

71. Strauss, "FP," 376–77.

Chapter Three

1. The article first appeared in the *Archiv für Sozialwissenschaft und Sozialpolitik* 67, no. 6 (1932): 732–49 and was edited anew by Heinrich Meier; see Meier, *Carl Schmitt, Leo Strauss*. Our pagination follows Meier's edition.
2. Strauss, *Spinoza's Critique of Religion*, trans. E. M. Sinclair (New York: Schocken, 1965), 329–51 (hereafter cited as *SCR*).
3. *GS* I, 54.
4. See H. Meier, *Carl Schmitt, Leo Strauss* (1988), 11–96; Heinrich Meier, *Carl Schmitt and Leo Strauss: The Hidden Dialogue*, trans. J. Harvey Lomax (Chicago: University of Chicago Press, 1995); Heinrich Meier, *Carl Schmitt, Leo Strauss und der "Begriff des Politischen": Zu einem Dialog unter Abwesenden*, expanded ed. (Stuttgart: J. B. Metzler, 1998), 155–90. Meier brilliantly unveiled and analyzed the "hidden dialogue" between Strauss and Schmitt. Important indications for this dialogue were the modifications Schmitt applied to his *Concept of the Political*. See also Shell, "Meier on Strauss," 219–23; Shell, "Taking Evil Seriously: Schmitt's 'Concept of the Political' and Strauss's 'True Politics,'" in Deutsch and Nicgorski, *Leo Strauss: Political Philosopher*, 175–93; Mark Lilla, "The Enemy of Liberalism," *New York Review of Books* 44, no. 8 (May 1997): 38–44. Evidently, Schmitt realized that Strauss had seen through him. H. Meier, *Carl Schmitt, Leo Strauss* (1998), 16, 158.
5. H. Meier, *Carl Schmitt, Leo Strauss* (1988), 99–100. Cf. Carl Schmitt, *Der Begriff des Politischen* (Berlin: Duncker and Humblot, [1932] 1963), 20, 65ff., 95.
6. H. Meier, *Carl Schmitt, Leo Strauss* (1988), 102ff. Cf. Schmitt, *Der Begriff des Politischen*, 26, 33, 39.
7. H. Meier, 109. Cf. Schmitt, 37, 52–53.
8. H. Meier, 113. Cf. Schmitt, 59ff.
9. H. Meier, 115. Cf. Schmitt, 60. Italics are from Strauss.
10. H. Meier, 119. Cf. Schmitt, 35–36, 54.
11. H. Meier, 121. Cf. Schmitt, 95.
12. H. Meier, 122. Cf. Schmitt, 49, 80ff. Compare the rest of this with Larmore, *Morals of Modernity*, 68.
13. H. Meier, 123ff. Cf. Schmitt, 31, 52, 70.
14. *GS* I, 54.
15. While Strauss initially considered Hobbes to be the founder of modernity, he admits in *HPW*, 9, that "not Hobbes, but Machiavelli, deserves this honor." A letter addressed to Gerschom Sholem on October 2, 1935, attests that Strauss meant Islamic philosophy when he spoke of the horizon within which Hobbes had laid the foundations for liberalism. *GS* II, xxii ff.
16. *GS* II, 30–31 n2.

17. H. Meier, *Carl Schmitt, Leo Strauss*, 106.

18. *AAPL*, 1, 3.

19. Avicenna, *Ash-Shifā'*, ed. G. C. Anawati and S. Zayed (Cairo: Organisme General des Imprimeries Gouvernementales, 1975), 441–42; German translation: *Das Buch der Genesung der Seele: Die Metaphysik Avicennas*, trans. Max Horten (Frankfurt am Main: Minerva, 1960), 622–23. Henceforth cited as *Shifā'*.

20. *GS* II, 30–31 n2. See also H. Meier, *Carl Schmitt, Leo Strauss* (1998), 182ff. Susan Shell's study in "Taking Evil Seriously," 191–92, of Schmitt's influence on the development of Strauss's thought interprets both *Spinoza's Critique of Religion* and *Philosophy and Law*, which appeared before and after Strauss's "Notes on Carl Schmitt's *Concept of the Political*." She concludes that while working on Schmitt, Strauss became convinced that the transcendence of liberalism required "a recognition of the primacy of duty for political life, and hence an understanding of the significance of Law in its original pre-modern sense." To Shell, Strauss had noticed the Kantian connection between morality and politics along with the political importance of religious law. However, Shell overlooks the fact that it was Islamic philosophy that had drawn his attention to this connection in the first place.

    Furthermore, it is noteworthy that Strauss's affirmation of a de-theologized basis of the political does not entail a blending of political theology and political philosophy. While political theology looks for the foundations of the political in faith, the concept of the political claims to be self-determined and thus makes use of the idea of God for the foundation of the political. Heinrich Meier, *Die Lehre Carl Schmitts: Vier Kapitel zur Unterscheidung Politischer Theologie und Politischer Philosophie* (Stuttgart: J. B. Metzler, 1994). It was Meier's intention to explain the discrepancy between Schmitt and Strauss, which had become central to his work, as a result of the difference between political theology and political philosophy. Herfried Münkler, in "Carl Schmitt als Politischer Theologe," *Neue Politische Literatur* 41 (1996): 273–75, criticized this approach as insufficient. However, Meier's position seems to have changed as well. In a new edition of his book on Schmitt and Strauss (originally published in 1988), he contends that all of Strauss's writings are in fact theologico-political treatises. In these treatises, the discussion of the theologico-political problem forms the centerpiece of political philosophy. This statement cautiously indicates an abandoning of the sharp differentiation between political theology and political philosophy that Meier previously emphasized. H. Meier, *Carl Schmitt, Leo Strauss* (1998), 187.

21. Letter from Strauss to Schmitt on July 10, 1933, in H. Meier, 134.

22. *GS* I, xiii.

23. Julius Guttmann, *Die Philosophie des Judentums* (Munich: Reinhardt, 1933). In reaction to Strauss's critique, Guttmann wrote a paper that Shlomo Pines published after Guttmann's death: Julius Guttmann, *Philosophie der Religion oder Philosophie des Gesetzes?* (Jerusalem: Israel Academy of Sciences and Humanities, 1974).

24. See Eve Adler's complete representation of the contents in "Leo Strauss's *Philosophie und Gesetz*," in Udoff, *Strauss's Thought*, 183–226.
25. See Meier's representation of the origins of this book in *GS* II, x–xx.
26. *GS* II, 13–14 n2. The image of a "second highpoint" comes forth in the 1930 lecture "Religiöse Lage der Gegenwart" and the 1931 treatment of Julius Ebbinghaus's *Über die Fortschritte der Metaphysik* (*GS* II, 439). See also *PAW*, 155–56; Bluhm, "Variationen des Höhlengleichnisses," 919ff.
27. *GS* II, 26.
28. *GS* II, 145.
29. *GS* II, 9, 68, 395.
30. *GS* II, 56–57. Maimonides's reliance on the Islamic masters is unchallenged by scholars. See Pines, "Translator's Introduction," lxxviii–cxxxii; Oliver Leaman, *Moses Maimonides* (London: Routledge, 1990). For an overall discussion of Maimonides's philosophy, see Friedrich Niewöhner, *Maimonides: Aufklärung und Toleranz im Mittelalter* (Wolfenbüttel: Lessing-Akademie, 1988); Alexander Broadie, "Maimonides," in Nasr and Leaman, *History of Islamic Philosophy*, 725–38; Ralph Lerner, *Maimonides' Vorbilder menschlicher Vollkommenheit* (Munich: Carl Friedrich von Siemens Stiftung, 1996).
31. *GS* II, 64. H. Meier, *Carl Schmitt, Leo Strauss* (1998), 187, accurately refers to *Philosophy and Law* as Strauss's first theologico-political treatise where Strauss replicates the discussion of the foundation of the ideal state (which Arabic philosophers had undertaken before him); he subsequently applies these insights to his entire oeuvre.
32. *GS* II, 60 n24.
33. *GS* II, 116–17.
34. Hermann Cohen, "Charakteristik der Ethik Maimunis," in *Jüdische Schriften*, by Hermann Cohen (Berlin: Schwetschke, 1924), 3:221–89.
35. *GS* II, 119–20.
36. *GS* II, 128, 175–76; "FP," 1.
37. H. Meier comes to a similar conclusion in *GS* II, xx.
38. Strauss, "QR," 1–37 (with marginalia in *GS* II, 125–66).
39. *GS* II, 125–26. Strauss's conclusion that medieval Islamic philosophy included a political science became widely accepted and employed by his adherents and students.
40. *GS* II, 128ff.; 134ff.; 139; 144ff.; 148ff.; 156n120.
41. *GS* II, 128ff.; 136, 142, 150–51, 156ff.
42. *GS* II, 130.
43. The complete title is *Mabādiʾ ārāʾ ahl al-madīna al-fāḍila* (translated as *The Principles of the Opinions Belonging to the Inhabitants of the Virtuous City*).
44. *GS* II, 129.

45. *GS* II, 141ff.

46. *GS* II, 51–52, 55, 77, 82.

47. Strauss's interpretation of the *Iḥṣāʾ al-ʿulūm* (*On the Enumeration of Sciences*) illustrates this procedure. To Strauss, this book offers a critical introduction to the different sciences, which subordinates religious studies to political science. What is more, he deems *Kitāb taḥṣīl as-saʿāda* (*The Attainment of Happiness*) more important than *Kitāb at-tanbīh ʿālā sabīl as-saʿāda* (*Remarks concerning the Path of Happiness*), as the former constituted an introduction to a book on Plato's and Aristotle's philosophy, while the latter was merely a grammar book. GS II, 134 n25, n28.

48. Most striking is one passage from al-Fārābī, *Iḥṣāʾ al-ʿulūm*, ed. ʿUthmān Amīn (Cairo: Maktabat al-Anjlū al-Miṣriyya, 1931), 64 (henceforth cited as *Iḥṣāʾ*), which Strauss shortened considerably. This is how he translated this passage into French:

> La science politique examine les espèces des actions et des manières de vivre qui dependent de la volonté, et les habitudes . . . dont dérivent ces actions et ces manières de vivre, et les fins pour lesquelles on fait ces actions . . . Et elle distingue entre les fins pour lesquelles les actions sont faites et les manières de vivre sont suivies; et elle explique qu'il y a une fin qui est la félicité veritable . . . et elle distingue entre les actions et les manières de vivre, et elle explique que celles par lesquelles on attaint la félicité veritable, sont les biens louables et les vertus . . . .et que la condition de leur existence dans l'homme est que les actions parfaites et les manières de vivre parfaits soient fixes dans les cites et les nations d'une manière hiérarchique et qu'elles soient pratiquées en commun. (*GS* II, 133n22)

The extent and the tendency of Strauss's excisions are illustrated by a comparison to Fauzī M. Najjār's English translation of al-Fārābī's original text:

> Political science investigates the various kinds of voluntary actions and ways of life; the positive dispositions, morals, inclinations, and states of character that lead to these actions and ways of life; the ends for the sake of which they are performed; how they must exist in man; how to order them in man in the manner in which they must exist in him; and the way to preserve them for him. It distinguishes among the ends for the sake of which actions are performed and ways of life are practiced. It explains that some of them are true happiness, while others are presumed to be happiness although they are not. That which is true happiness cannot possibly be of this life, but of another life after this, which is the life to come; while that which is presumed to be happiness consists of such things as wealth, honor, and the pleasures, when these are made the only ends in this life. Distinguishing the actions and ways of life, it explains that

> the ones through which true happiness is attained are the goods, the noble things, and the virtues, while the rest are the evils, the base things, and the imperfections; and that they [must] exist in man in such a way that the virtuous actions and ways of life are distributed in the cities and nations according to a certain order and are practiced in common. (*Iḥṣā'*, 24)

49. Most importantly, see the marginalia in *GS* II, 160ff.
50. See the English translation of the remarks in Leo Strauss, "Some Remarks on the Political Science of Maimonides and Farabi," trans. Robert Bartlett, *Interpretation* 18, no. 1 (Fall 1990): 3.
51. *GS* II, 164.
52. It appeared in "VSF" (with marginalia in *GS* II, 167–78).
53. Steinschneider, *Al-Fārābī (Alpharabius)*, 176.
54. *GS* II, 167. Cf. Isarel Efros, "Falquera's Reshit Hokmah and al-Fārābī's Iḥṣa al-ʿulum," *Jewish Quarterly Review*, n.s., 25 (1934–35): 227–35. Strauss did not mention the title of Efros's paper. Strauss used O. Amin's edition of the *Iḥṣā' al-ʿulūm* (Cairo 1350 H/1931). The fifth chapter of this book, which is the chapter of relevance to Strauss' paper, was translated by F. M. Najjār and is included in Lerner and Mahdi, *Medieval Political Philosophy*, 22–31.
55. *GS* II, 168. Strauss wrongly read this word as "*Iqsām*," while it should read "*Aqsām*" (plural of *qism* = part). He used the Latin translation by Andrea Alpago (Venice, 1546) as a reference to provide evidence for the origin of those passages.
56. *GS* II, 168–69. Strauss knew al-Fārābī's *Kitāb taḥṣīl as-saʿāda* from the Hyderabad edition of 1345 H. More recently, the book was reedited by Jaʿfar Āl Yāsīn (Beirut: Dār al-Andalus, 1981; henceforth cited as *Taḥṣīl*). An English translation can be found in Lerner and Mahdi, *Medieval Political Philosophy*, 59–82, and Mahdi, *Alfarabi's Philosophy of Plato and Aristotle* (New York: Free Press of Glencoe, 1969).
57. *GS* II, 169, 175.
58. *GS* II, 170. Cf. Steinschneider, *Al-Fārābī (Alpharabius)*, 176ff.
59. Cf. "FP," 359–60. Like Strauss, Walzer, F. Rosenthal, and Mahdi advance the view that al-Fārābī's *Kitāb taḥṣīl as-saʿāda* formed the first of the three parts of this book, which also contains accounts of Plato's and Aristotle's philosophy. Āl Yāsīn, on the contrary, holds the view that this first treatise on the attainment of happiness is independent and separate from al-Fārābī's other works and that Strauss was misguided by a mistake on Falaquera's side (*Taḥṣīl*, 17–18).
60. Strauss refers to Averroes's great *Commentary on Aristotle's "Metaphysics,"* bk. 12 (comm. 18, fol. 143, col. 2, 1.27–39). As a matter of fact, it cannot be ruled out that Averroes was referring to al-Fārābī's book *al-Jamʿ bayna ra'yay al-ḥakīmayn*, ed. A. N. Nādir (Beirut: Dār al-Mashriq, 1960; henceforth cited as *Jamʿ*). An English version of the book, *The Harmonization of*

the Two Opinions of the Two Sages: Plato the Divine and Aristotle, was published by Charles Butterworth (Ithaca, NY: Cornell University Press, 2001), 115–68.

61. *GS* II, 172ff. Strauss cites Jamāl ad-Dīn Abū l-Ḥasan ʿAlī b. Yūsuf al-Qifṭī, *Taʾrīkh al-ḥukamāʾ*, on the basis of previous work done by August Müller that was edited by Julius Lippert (Leipzig: Dieterich, 1903).

62. *GS* II, 176.

63. *GS* II, 173–74, 176.

64. *GS* II, 177. Cf. *GS* II, 160, marginalia to p. 11n 28: "Plato's practical philosophy] is exoteric preliminary, whereas Ar.' [Aristotle's] practical philos.[ophy] is not exoteric."

65. Today, there are editions of the respective treatises on Plato's and Aristotle's philosophy: *De Platonis philosophia* (*Falsafat Aflāṭūn wa-ajzāʾuhā wa-marātub ajzāʾihā min awwalihā ilā ākhirihā*), edited by Franz Rosenthal and Richard Walzer (London: Kraus, 1943; henceforth cited as *Falsafat Aflāṭūn*). The Arabic text is on pp. 3–23. A more recent edition was published in Badawī, *Aflāṭūn fī l-Islām*, 5–27. Pages 28 to 32 of Badawī's edition contain critical remarks on the earlier edition by Rosenthal and Walzer. The book on Aristotle (*Falsafat Arisṭūṭālīs wa-ajzāʾu falsafatihi wa-marātibu ajzāʾihā wa-l-mawḍiʿ al-ladhī minhu ibtadaʾa wa-ilaihi intahā*) was edited (1961) and translated (1969) by Muhsin Mahdi (henceforth cited as *Falsafat Arisṭū*).

66. *GS* II, 153–56, 187–88 n29.

67. *GS* II, 182, 184, 187–88, 191. The paper was first published as Strauss, "Der Ort der Vorsehungslehre nach der Ansicht Maimunis," *Monatsschrift für Geschichte und Wissenschaft des Judentums* 81 (1937): 93–105 (henceforth cited as "OVAM"). H. Meier, who included the paper together with Strauss's marginalia notes in the second volume of his complete edition (*GS* II, 179–94), assumes that the paper was composed in August 1936 (*GS* II, xvi). Apart from one much more recent article, this is Strauss's last German-language publication. In 1962, twenty-five years later, he wrote a last German paper for the Festschrift of his friend Gerhard Krüger. Oddly enough, this paper also deals with the doctrine of providence. "Zu Mendelssohns 'Sache Gottes oder die gerettete Vorsehung,'" in *Einsichten: Gerhard Krüger zum 60. Geburtstag*, ed. Klaus Oehler and Richard Schaeffler, 361–75 (Frankfurt am Main: Klostermann, 1962). English translations of "OVAM" have been published by Bartlett and Minkov (2004) and in Kenneth Hart Green's recent book, Leo Strauss, *Leo Strauss on Maimonides: The Complete Writings*, ed. Kenneth Hart Green (Chicago: University of Chicago Press, 2013), 314–28.

68. *GS* II, 180ff.

69. See also the reference to Spinoza and Thomas Aquinas in the marginalia (*GS* II, 192).

70. *GS* II, 183–84. At this point, Strauss ties in Pines, who had ascertained the prominent influence of Islamic *kalām* on Jewish philosophy of religion. Shlomo Pines, "Besprechung: Ventura, M.: La Philosophie de Saadia Gaon,

Paris 1934 und ders.: Le Kalām et le Péripatétisme d'après le Kuzari, ebda 1934," *Orientalische Literaturzeitung*, no. 10 (1935): column 623.

71. *GS* II, 185.

72. *GS* II, 185–86 n20. This is the first time Strauss applies his method of "reading between the lines," which he later elaborates upon in *Persecution and the Art of Writing* (*PAW*). Strauss argues that Maimonides foregrounds the doctrine of the law by enumerating the different opinions on providence twice, thereby hiding this own opinion.

73. *GS* II, 186–87. Emphasis in original.

74. *GS* II, 189.

75. *GS* II, 190. Quite consequentially, Strauss writes the word "Religion" in quotation marks. In *Philosophie und Gesetz*, he had already replaced the word *religion* with *law*. In the marginalia, he includes the following remark regarding the characterization of the *Guide* as a political book: "This is correct, as the comparison of the Moreh with both 'political books' of al-Fārābī (*al-Madīna al-fāḍila* and *as-Siyāsa al-madaniyya*) teaches." *GS* II, 193. Compare this with *GS* II, 200.

76. *GS* II, 193, marginalia to p. 103.

77. Strauss, "FP." Strauss draws on this paper for his introduction to *PAW*.

78. "FP," 357, 393. These rather inaccessible writings have meanwhile been edited by two of his students: Fauzī M. Najjār edited *Kitāb as-siyāsa al-madaniyya al-mulaqqab bi-mabādi' al-mawjūdāt* (*The Political Regime*, also known as the *Treatise on the Principles of Beings*, 1964), while Muhsin Mahdi edited *Kitāb al-Milla wa-Nuṣūṣ Ukhrā* (*Book of Religion and Related Texts*, 1991).

79. Strauss, *PAW*, 12.

80. Strauss, "FP," 359–60.

81. "FP," 374–75. In a side note, Strauss characterizes al-Fārābī's account of Plato's thought as "esoteric philosophy" and his treatise on Aristotle's philosophy as "exoteric" philosophy (*GS* II, 177, marginalia to p. 103).

82. "FP," 376–77.

83. "FP," 363ff., 371ff., 376ff., 382ff.

84. Cf. H. Meier, *Die Denkbewegung*, 42.

85. "FP," 363ff., 382ff.

86. "FP," 376–77.

87. "FP," 357. "Eben derselbe Gedanke kann, an einem anderen Orte, einen ganz anderen Wert haben" ("The very same thought, but in a different place, can have an entirely different value"). Gotthold Ephraim Lessing, *Lessings Werke*, ed. Kurt Wölfel (Frankfurt am Main: Insel-Verlag, 1967), 3:279; Heinrich Mettler, "Lessing und Leibniz: Bemerkungen zur Exoterik anhand dreier Abschnitte aus 'Leibniz von den ewigen Strafen,'" in *Esoterik und Exoterik der Philosophie: Beiträge zu Geschichte und Sinn philosophischer*

Selbstbestimmung, ed. Helmut Holzhey and Walther Ch. Zimmerli, 207–17 (Basel: Schwabe, 1977).

88. "FP," 376–77.

89. *GS* II, 128–29.

90. "FP," 363ff.

91. "FP," 385ff.

92. "FP," 375. Christopher Colmo, "Theory and Practice: Alfarabi's *Plato* Revisited," *American Political Science Review* 86 (1992): 974–75, rightly points to the fact that Strauss himself did not comply with this rule.

93. See for example "FP," 379–80 n53, 392.

94. "FP," 361n12; *Flasafat Aflāṭūn*, p. 14, lines 11, 14; p. 15, lines 3, 7, 11–12, 18; p. 16, line 2.

95. "FP," 372n40; *Falsafat Aflāṭūn*: §25.

96. The respective passages read as follows: "al-insān al-faylasūf wa-l-insān al-malik shayʾ wāḥid" (*Falsafat Aflāṭūn*, p. 13, line 7) and "an-takūn al-mihna al-malakiyya allatī fīhā al-iṭlāq" (p. 20, line 9).

97. "FP," 372n40; *Falsafat Aflāṭūn*, p. 6, line 6; p. 5, lines 2–3; p. 15, line 5.

98. "FP," 382n62; *Falsafat Aflāṭūn*, p. 12, line 10; p. 23, line 2.

99. "FP," 385–86; *Falsafat Aflāṭūn*, 3. Cf. p. 3, line 14; p. 4, lines 11–12. The translation of the passage on p. 3, line 8, by Rosenthal and Walzer, which Strauss believed to be wrong, seems to be correct ("FP," 370n32).

100. *Falsafat Aflāṭūn*, p. 14, line 16; p. 15, lines 4–5, 8, 12–13.

101. *Falsafat Aflāṭūn*, p. 15, lines 2–8.

102. *Falsafat Aflāṭūn*, p. 15, lines 6, 8–11; p. 17, lines 7–14.

103. "FP," 391–92.

104. Leo Strauss, "How Fārābī Read Plato's *Laws*" was first published in *Mélanges Louis Massignon* (Damascus: Institut Français de Damas, 1957) and republished in *What Is Political Philosophy?* (*WIPP*, 134–54). To the author's knowledge, there are two editions of al-Fārābī's *Talkhīṣ Nawāmīs Aflāṭūn*. It was published and translated by Franciscus Gabrieli in his *Compendium Legum Platonis* (London: Warburg Institute, 1952; henceforth cited as *Talkhīṣ*). A more recent edition can be found in Avicenna, *ʿUyūn al-ḥikma*, 34–83.

105. The last sentence reads, "We admire the ease with which Fārābī invented Platonic speeches" (Strauss, *WIPP*, 154).

106. Mahdi, "Editio Princeps," 1, 15. See *GS* II, 196n4.

107. *WIPP*, 140.

108. *WIPP*, 134.

109. *WIPP*, 134ff.

110. *WIPP*, 137.

111. *WIPP*, 138, 147.

112. *WIPP*, 138–39. The Arabic verb *takallama* means "spoke." To interpret its frequent use as a hint towards *kalām* studies (theology) seems to be a rather far-fetched construction given the Arabic-language semantics.

113. *WIPP*, 139; *Iḥṣā'*, 131ff., in the translation by Lerner and Mahdi, *Medieval Political Philosophy*, 27ff. For further reading on the *kalam*, see M. Abdel Haleem, "Early kalām," in Nasr and Leaman, *History of Islamic Philosophy*, 71–88; James Pavlin, "Sunni kalām and Theological Controversies," in Nasr and Leaman, 105–18.

114. *WIPP*, 134.

115. *WIPP*, 140.

116. *WIPP*, 140ff.

117. *WIPP*, 144–45.

118. *WIPP*, 145–46. The passage Strauss quotes as alluding to universal laws (al-Fārābī, *Talkhīṣ*, p. 39, lines 3–7) quite obviously fails to achieve this move. It is, for the large part, a paired enumeration of eight notions: the evil and the slackers, the bees and the beekeeper, the free and the slaves, the path of the lawgiver and the righteous path. The text (lines 7–11) goes on to state that there are politicians who are capable of guiding a certain people whose customs and manners they know, while they are not able to guide another people (even if it is a less numerous one) because they lack any knowledge about such people.

119. *WIPP*, 146–47.

120. *Talkhīṣ*, p. 27, lines 3–7; Plato, *Nomoi*, 732c7.

121. *WIPP*, 147–50. The paragraph alleging that al-Fārābī is an atheist constitutes the longest paragraph of the entire paper.

122. Cf. the critique of Strauss's interpretation of the matter in Oliver Leaman, "Does the Interpretation of Islamic Philosophy Rest on a Mistake?," *International Journal for Middle East Studies* 12 (1980): 531–35. Gutas, "Galen's *Synopsis*," 101ff., to mention just one skeptic, conjectures that al-Fārābī had to rely on Galen's synopsis of Plato's *Nomoi*. The same critique applies to Joshua Parens's attempt to refute Heidegger's view of Plato as the founder of metaphysics on the basis of his own interpretation of al-Fārābī's *Talkhīṣ Nawāmīs Aflāṭūn*. Parens also claims to have demonstrated that al-Fārābī's Plato "does not ground his account of politics on metaphysical presuppositions" but that he regards his "metaphysica specialis" (i.e., theology) only as rhetoric for defense of the law. Furthermore, he holds that al-Fārābī demonstrates that Plato's political analyses are a phenomenological analysis of the needs of the human soul as they appear in political psychology. Joshua Parens, *Metaphysics as Rhetoric: Alfarabi's "Summary" of Plato's "Laws"* (Albany: State University of New York Press, 1995), xii–xvi, 143–44. Parens's argumentation is based on the assumption that al-Fārābī knew Plato's complete works and, in particular, an unabridged version of the *Nomoi*. The justified doubts of this knowledge turn Parens's investigation into a form

of speculation without a solid foundation. Eventually, Parens's attempt to refute Heidegger's interpretation of Plato's philosophy using al-Fārābī's interpretation of Plato amounts to declaring the research on Plato during the past millennium null and void. The same critique is voiced by Gutas, *Greek Thought, Arabic Culture*, 410–16.

Chapter Four

1. Cf. Tarcov and Pangle, "Epilogue," 907ff.; McAllister, *Revolt against Modernity*, 24ff.
2. Robert B. Pippin, "The Modern World of Leo Strauss," *Political Theory* 20 (1992): 448.
3. Cf. Strauss, *CM*, 2–3; Strauss, *An Introduction to Political Philosophy: Ten Essays by Leo Strauss*, ed. Hilail Gildin (Detroit, MI: Wayne State University Press, 1989), 81 (henceforth cited as *IPP*); Jürgen Gebhardt, "Leo Strauss: The Quest for Truth in Times of Perplexity," in Kielmansegg et al., *Hannah Arendt and Leo Strauss*, 90ff.
4. *CM*, 1–12; Leo Strauss, "The Crisis of Our Time" and "The Crisis of Political Philosophy," in *The Predicament of Modern Politics*, ed. Harold J. Spaeth, 41–54 and 91–103, respectively (Detroit, MI: University of Detroit Press, 1964; henceforth cited as "COT" and "CPP," respectively); Strauss, "The Mutual Influence of Theology and Philosophy," *Independent Journal of Philosophy* 3 (1979): 111–18 (henceforth cited as "MITP"); Strauss, "Progress or Return? The Contemporary Crisis in Western Civilization," *Modern Judaism* 1 (1981): 17–45 (henceforth cited as "PRC"); *IPP*, 249–310.
5. "COT," 44.
6. Pippin, "Modern World," 448; Robb McDaniel, "The Philosopher's Jeremiad: Prophecy and Political Philosophy in Leo Strauss and Emmanuel Levinas" (PhD diss., Vanderbilt University, 1998), 36–37, 58–64. Cf. Anastaplo, "Strauss at the University of Chicago," 3; Jaffa, "Strauss at One Hundred," 41.
7. *IPP*, 81–98. Cf. Drury, *Political Ideas*, 151–58; McAllister, *Revolt against Modernity*, 31ff.; Kauffmann, *Strauss zur Einführung*, 47–55.
8. "PRC," 25ff.; *CM*, 3–4.
9. "PRC," 31ff.; *IPP*, 81.
10. *CM*, 7.
11. "PRC," 28–29. Cf. "MITP," 111ff.
12. *CM*, 241.
13. "PRC," 45.
14. "PRC"; "MITP," 111. See additionally Morgan, "Teaching Leo Strauss," 186–87.

15. "MITP," 113–18.

16. *GS* I, 5–54; Biale, "Leo Strauss," 31–40; Green in *JPCM*, 3–15, 17–36. Strauss wrote to Voegelin on February 25, 1951, that he was "basically still on the same ground" as *Philosophy and Law*, although he believed he had "learned something in the last fifteen years" and would therefore "express many things differently." Eric Voegelin et al., *Briefwechsel über "Die Neue Wissenschaft der Politik,"* ed. Peter J. Opitz (Freiburg: Alber, 1993); Shlomo Pines, "On Leo Strauss," *Independent Journal of Philosophy* 5/6 (1988): 169.

17. Strauss, *SCR*, 6. Also see Tarcov and Pangle, "Epilogue," 909; Orr, *Jerusalem and Athens*, 17; J. Gebhardt, "Leo Strauss: The Quest," 95; Morgan, "Teaching Leo Strauss," 179ff.

18. *GS* II, 26. Orr undertook a study of the problem of reason and revelation in Strauss's work. Her conclusion is that his "endeavor may be considered a bit impious, but it is nonetheless undertaken with pious intentions and pious results" (Orr, *Jerusalem and Athens*, 158). Such a conclusion is untenable when the abovementioned argumentation is taken into account. It should also be added here that Orr underrates Strauss's strongly political interpretation of religion.

19. From the letter just cited written by Strauss to Voegelin, in Voegelin et al., *Briefwechsel*, 30. Cf. Orr, *Jerusalem and Athens*, 148–49.

20. *GS* II, 26.

21. Leo Strauss, "Correspondence concerning Modernity: Karl Löwith and Leo Strauss," *Independent Journal of Philosophy* 4 (1983): 114 (henceforth cited as "CCM"); *CM*, 1, 9–10.

22. McAllister, *Revolt against Modernity*, 33.

23. See also H. Meier, *Die Denkbewegung*, 19ff., 29ff.

24. *IPP*, 93.

25. "The Middle Ages witnessed the first, and certainly the first adequate, discussion between these two most important forces of the Western world: [. . .] between religion as such and science or philosophy as such: between the way of life based on faith and obedience and a way of life based on true insight, on human wisdom, alone" (Strauss, *RCPR*, 214).

26. Strauss asserts that the "situation of philosophy in the Islamic-Jewish world resembles [. . .] its situation in classical Greece" (*RCPR*, 223; *PAW*, 8ff., 18ff.). This leads to the conclusion that Strauss's understanding of classical philosophy was "intrinsically bound up with the medieval Jewish and Islamic interpretation of classical philosophy" (J. Gebhardt, "Leo Strauss: The Quest," 97). On the contrary, Laurence Lampert in *Leo Strauss and Nietzsche*, 136–45, holds the view that, although resorting to the medieval proponents of enlightenment, Strauss failed to find a permanent solution to the problem of political philosophy. These philosophers had only led him to Plato. According to Strauss there are permanent, insolvable problems in human existence. Lampert's claim that Strauss had sought permanent solutions is therefore questionable. Furthermore, a tendency to view Strauss's

thought in the light of Nietzsche causes Lampert to understate the importance of the conflict between disbelief and belief in Strauss's work. Contrary to Nietzsche, Strauss adopts an atheist position that is based on the Bible, thereby remaining committed to the critique of religion in the post-revelation tradition.

27. *GS* II, 27, 39.

28. *GS* II, 44–45.

29. *GS* II, 395.

30. Equally pertinent to Harald Bluhm, "Leo Strauss' politische Philosophie und das 'einfache Denken,'" in *Bürgerreligion und Bürgertugend: Debatten über die vorpolitischen Grundlagen politischer Ordnung*, ed. Herfreid Münkler (Baden-Baden: Nomos, 1996), 215. Kauffmann, *Strauss zur Einführung*, 66, in line with H. Meier, *Die Denkbewegung*, 20, 31, holds the view that Heidegger was the natural starting point for Strauss's turn to Platonic political philosophy. This opinion seems valid as long as it concerns the beginning of *The City and Man*. However, the present work argues that the roots of Strauss's Platonic philosophizing cannot be found in his engagement with Heidegger but in his reading of Avicenna's tractate on the divisions of the sciences in 1928 or 1929. In *The City and Man* (*CM*, 1), Strauss asserts that his turn to the texts of classical antiquity is not at all a kind of antiquity-related self-obliviousness but that he made this move out of a passionate interest and an unrestricted desire to learn. In my opinion, this statement, which contrasts starkly with Heidegger's approach, illustrates the mode and the intentions behind his philosophical return to the antiquity but defines neither its course nor its outcome. See the report on the testimony of Hans Jonas in Udoff, *Strauss's Thought*, 26–27 n61.

31. *GS* II, 90. Cf. *GS* II, 138, where Strauss quotes Maimonides's remark that had prophets not existed, there would be no law. *Dalālat*, III, K. 45:658.

32. *GS* II, 87–123.

33. Cf. Badawī, *Arisṭū ʿinda al-ʿarab*, 253–77.

34. *GS* II, 66, 120. My account of Strauss's study of Maimonides here mainly relies on his examination of Maimonides's prophetology in *Philosophie und Gesetz* and in "Quelques remarques sur la science politique de Maïmonide et de Fârâbî." Passages that can already be found in Strauss's lecture "Cohen and Maimuni" from 1931 are neither quoted nor referred to. This lecture was apparently given when Strauss was working on the last part of *Philosophie und Gesetz*, which was the part Strauss wrote first. Compared to the third chapter of *Philosophy and Law*, this lecture adds nothing new to our understanding (*GS* II, xvi, xxx).

35. *GS* II, 394. Strauss's and Cohen's interpretation of Maimonides is discussed in the following publications: Udoff, *Strauss's Thought*, 2–3; Adler, "Strauss's *Philosophie und Gesetz*," 195; Novak, *Strauss and Judaism*, xii–xiii; Green, *Jew and Philosopher*, 12, 53–54, 56ff., 100–101, 151n11, 168n3; Green, introduction to *JPCM*, 17–25.

36. *GS* II, 87–88, 99, 105–6, 424. See especially *Dalālat*, II, K. 32–40; III, K. 27–28. Cf. Rahman, *Prophecy in Islam*, 11–29.

37. *GS* II, 91ff., 97ff.

38. *GS* II, 99–100.

39. al-Fārābī, *Alfārābī's Abhandlung: Der Musterstaat*, ed. and trans. Friedrich Dieterici (Leiden: Brill, 1895), reprinted in Hildesheim: Olms, 1985, 47–52 (henceforth cited as *Madīna* [Dieterici]); GS II, 100–101.

40. *Madīna* [Dieterici], 57–59; *GS* II, 101–2.

41. *GS* II, 102–3. Cf. *GS* II, 58, 23; Ibn Ṭufail, *Ḥayy Ibn Yaqẓān*, ed. A. N. Nādir (Beirut: al-Maṭbaʿa al-Kāthūlīkiyya, 1986), 21–22; Lawrence I. Conrad, ed., *The World of Ibn Ṭufayl: Interdisciplinary Perspectives on Ḥayy ibn Yaqẓān* (Leiden: Brill, 1996). In a lengthy note to chapter 3 (147–48 n34), the chapter of *Philosophy and Law* that contains the most detailed discussion of Maimonides and his Islamic predecessors, Strauss aims to clarify the hitherto unanswered question of "whether and in what sense Maimonides claims that the active intellect directly influences the imaginative faculty." He starts by drawing a parallel between Maimonides's and al-Fārābī's ideas of prophetic knowledge. Both taught that the active intellect first influenced the intellect of the prophet and "after that" his imaginative faculty. Hence, as regards prophetic knowledge, neither Maimonides nor al-Fārābī assumed that the active intellect directly influenced the imaginative faculty. In this regard, it does not matter if the imaginative faculty adopts an imaginative perception of the forms of meaning derived from reason or the knowledge of future events. Whereas al-Fārābī leaves the door open for a potential direct influence of the active intellect on the imaginative faculty in the case of divinatory knowledge, such an influence is categorically ruled out by Maimonides. In this context, Strauss finds Maimonides inconsistent. See *Madīna* [Dieterici], 47, 58–59; *Dalālat*, II, K. 36–38.

42. *GS* II, 103.

43. *GS* II, 104. For his reconstruction of Avicenna's prophetology, Strauss mainly used the following publications and manuscripts: Avicenna, *De Anima* (Venice, 1508); *Tisʿ rasāʾil* (Constantinople, 1298 H); "Die Psychologie des Ibn Sīnā," 335–418; *Avicennae Metaphysices Compendium*, ex. ar. lat. redd. Carame (Rome, 1927); *an-Najāt*, manuscript in the Staatsbibliothek Berlin (Manuscripts' Collection Minutoli 229). Furthermore, Strauss points to the account of Avicenna's prophecy in al-Ghazālī's *Tahāfut al-falāsifa*, 272–75.

44. *GS* II, 106–7, 141. Cf. Rahman, *Prophecy in Islam*, 45–52. Strauss closely follows the account in Ibn Khaldūn's *Muqqadima* describing two opposed conceptions of miracles in Islamic philosophy. According to this account, the Islamic *kalām* contends that only God's power can perform miracles. The prophet announces these miracles but does not have any influence upon their realization. However, the realization of the miracles that he previously announced represents a divine confirmation of his prophecy. The Islamic philosophers, on the other hand, hold the view that it is the prophet who performs miracles. Obviously, this view originates in their opinion that not everything on earth goes back to God's will. Under certain circumstances,

events can have other causes and this leaves room for human freedom and responsibility. According to Strauss, Maimonides held the view that miracles resulted from the power that God put into nature when creating the world in order to make wonders happen at a predetermined time. See Ibn Khaldūn, *The Muqaddimah: An Introduction to History*, trans. from the Arabic by Franz Rosenthal in three volumes (London: Routledge / K. Paul, 1967), 1:188–91.

Strauss mentions three further elements of Maimonides's prophetology that seem to contradict the teachings of his Islamic predecessors without undermining the groundwork the latter had laid. The first element consists of the lessons and studies that the prophet, according to Maimonides, needs to accomplish for the perfection of his intellect. Such a condition clearly contradicts the idea of the prophet propagated by the Islamic philosophers, according to which the prophet did not need to acquire direct knowledge and therefore did not need to make an effort to learn. This latter opinion has its roots in the traditional Islamic conviction that Muhammad was illiterate. For Strauss, there is therefore reason to assume that Maimonides's focus on learning as a precondition for prophecy can be understood as form of polemic against Islam and a hidden attempt to refute Muhammad's claim to be a prophet.

Maimonides's second deviation from the Islamic philosophers concerns the prophecy of Moses, which, as Maimonides saw it, was not comparable to any other instantiation of prophecy. For Moses did not require the medium of imaginative faculty and therefore prophesied without allegory. Strauss argues that Maimonides adds another reservation regarding the prophetology of the Islamic philosophers. Apart from admitting that God may deny prophecy to someone who is basically apt, which is the third deviation of Maimonides from his Islamic predecessors, he seems to exclude the imaginative faculty from the prophecy of Moses, a figure whom he held in high esteem. However, Strauss considered this suggestion to be refuted by a hint from Maimonides himself that stated that Moses's exemption from "the ban on the imaginative faculty" only took place when he was in a state of elated prophetic emotion. Therefore, such a temporary exemption did not prevent Moses from disposing of the same imaginative faculty as the other prophets and from using it in order to make his speeches to the crowd understandable. Eventually, the postulated harmony between Maimonides and the Islamic philosophers remained untouched. For the exact references to the respective passages in the *Guide*, see *GS* II, 105–6 n44.

At this point, Strauss does not fail to refer to Narboni, Maimonides's disciple, translator, and commentator, in order to confirm the foregrounding of this harmony. Narboni bore witness to the fact that Maimonides had taken his prophetology from al-Fārābī and Ibn Bājja. The conclusion of Salomon Munk in his edition of the *More Nevukhim* (1856; II, 288) is similar in this regard and is said to coincide with a remark by Ephodis. Furthermore, Strauss refers to two other Arabic writings that give an account of the orthodox Islamic doctrine regarding Muhammad's prophecy: ʿAlī b. Rabbān aṭ-Ṭabarī, *Kitāb ad-Dīn wa-d-Dawla* (Cairo, 1923), 48–50; and ʿAlī b. Muḥammad al-Māwardī, *Aʿlām an-Nubūwa* (Cairo, 1315).

45. *GS* II, 108–9. Cf. *Madīna* [Dieterici], 50, lines 18–51, 2.

46. Maimonides illustrates the superiority of the prophet over the philosopher through an allegory that portrays only Moses as capable of remaining in a permanent state of illumination. Light, in this allegory, stands for knowledge. Only the prophets have direct access to this knowledge, but they differ with regard to the perfection of their knowledge. The philosophers, represented by Aristotle, rank below the prophet inasmuch as they dispose themselves of indirect knowledge of the heavenly spheres. The rabble of the ignorant ranks lowest. Strauss mentions that, according to Ibn Falaquera, Maimonides had appropriated this allegory from al-Fārābī. Additionally, Strauss claims that al-Fārābī had divided humanity into three subsections: On the first level, there exists a populace who is only capable of understanding the material elements among the apprehensible things and hereby resembles the inhabitants of Plato's cave who never see the sunlight and only know the shadows of the things. The next level is the level of the philosophers, who recognized the apprehensible things only indirectly. In allegorical terms, they can be compared to those who see the sun but only as reflected on the surface of the water. However, philosophers consist of those individuals who have left the cave and have seen the light. On the absolute highest level, there are those individuals who can see the natural things themselves as well as the light itself. As far as I know, there exists no such passage in al-Fārābī's writings (*GS* II, 94–95, 117).

47. *GS* II, 51–52, 55, 77, 82, 111, 143.

48. *GS* II, 109, 423. In al-Fārābī's *al-Madīna al-Fāḍila* (*Madīna* [Dieterici], 58, lines 23–59, 1), he presents a concept of prophecy combining philosophy and divination.

49. Aristotle, *Politik*, trans. Eugen Rolfes (Hamburg: Meiner, 1981), III.6.1278b19ff., here p. 88.

50. Avicenna, *Shifāʾ*, 441–42; 663–64 in Horten's translation.

51. Cf. al-Fārābī, *Kitāb as-siyāsa al-madaniyya al-mulaqqab bi-mabādiʾ al-mawjūdāt*, ed. Fauzī M. Najjār (Beirut: Dār al-Mashriq, 1964), 78; English translation by Najjār in Lerner and Mahdi, *Medieval Political Philosophy*, 35–36 (henceforth cited as *Siyāsa*).

52. *GS* II, 110, 423–24.

53. *GS* II, 111.

54. *GS* II, 111, 422.

55. *GS* II, 112–13. Written in italics by Strauss. See note 58 for the passages in Avicenna's writings that Strauss uses for the reconstruction of Avicenna's thought. See also *GS* II, 145–46. The quoted passage is taken from the treatise *ʿUyūn al-Ḥikma* (*Sources of Wisdom*), itself a part of the compendium *Tisʿ rasāʾil*, 2, which I have already mentioned earlier in this book. In this treatise, Avicenna discusses the use of *al-ḥikma al-madaniyya* (social philosophy), which he considers the third part of practical philosophy after ethics (part 1) and domestic economy (part 2). It is similar to the respective passage in *On the Divisions of Science*. Avicenna adds that the principles of all three divisions of practical philosophy stem from divine law. Strauss disregards

this dependence of all parts of practical philosophy, politics included, on religious law.

56. *GS* II, 114, Strauss's italics. Strauss quotes Avicenna's treatise on prophecy, which forms a part of the *Tisʿ rasāʾil*, 85. His translation is noteworthy, for Strauss translates the Arabic word *waḥī* as "inspiration" (Arabic: *ilhām*) although he is clearly referring to the revelation received by the prophet. As is commonly known, Avicenna distinguishes between the revelation (*waḥī*) that the prophet obtains through the active intellect and the inspiration (*ilhām*) that conveys knowledge about the future to mystics and soothsayers through the influence of the heavenly bodies (Rahman, *Prophecy in Islam*, 36, 38–39). In addition, Strauss translates the Arabic word *ʿilm* as "science" (*Wissenschaft*), although the context suggests "knowledge" or "insight" as more appropriate translations. It seems that Strauss's word choice is meant to support the claim of a philosophical-theoretical dimension of prophecy through Avicenna's argumentation. Strauss clearly overemphasizes this dimension in Avicenna's prophetology.
    In this context, it is noteworthy that Avicenna's understanding of prophecy betrays a strong Sufi influence. In the context of the passage quoted in the text, he presents the idea of prophecy through the allegorical interpretation of the following Qurʾānic verse: "God is the Light of the heavens and the earth; The likeness of His Light is a niche wherein is a lamp (the lamp in a glass, the glass as it were a glittering star) kindled from a Blessed Tree, an olive that is neither of the East nor of the West whose oil wellnigh would shine, even if no fire touched it; Light upon Light; (God guides to His Light whom He will.) (And God strikes similitudes for men, and God has knowledge of everything.)" (sura 24:35, Arberry's trans.) Avicenna interprets this light as an allusion to God, with the heaven and earth serving as hints at the cosmos. The niche stands for the passive intellect, the lamp for the active intellect, and the glittering star for pure transparence. The olive tree, eventually, is interpreted by Avicenna as representing practical thinking, while "neither of the East nor of the West" means that this form of thinking is neither purely intellectual nor a part of the animalistic drives in man. As a consequence, this practical reasoning is neither the place where the light, in its absolute sense, rises nor the place where the light, in its absolute sense, sets (*Tisʿ rasāʾil*, 85ff.).

57. *GS* II, 114, 117. Avicenna is manifestly of the opinion that prophets and Sufis attain a higher degree (*ittiṣāl*) of understanding regarding the active intellect than the philosophers. According to him, a permanent connection between ordinary people and the active intellect is only possible after death. However, the prophet seems to be able to maintain such a connection in his lifetime. Avicenna, *De Anima*, 247–48, 249–50; Pines, "Shīʿite Terms," 211ff.

58. *GS* II, 117–18.

59. *GS* II, 119.

60. *GS* II, 115–16, 126. Cf. Walzer, "Alfārābi's Theory," 142–48; Rahman, *Prophecy in Islam*, 30–91; Erwin Rosenthal, *Studia Semitica* (Cambridge: Cambridge University Press, 1971), 136–44. Hans Daiber's reading of al-Fārābī contrasts sharply with Strauss's interpretation: "Der Prophet ist

[. . .] für Fārābī keine Alternative zum Philsophenherrscher" ("For Al-Fārābī, the prophet is [. . .] no alternative to the philosopher-king"). Daiber, *The Ruler as Philosopher: A New Interpretation of al-Fārābī's View* (Amsterdam: North-Holland, 1986), 738–39.

61. *GS* II, 120; *FPP*, 16. Cf. Fakhry, *Tarīkh al-falsafa*, 43–55; Leaman, *An Introduction*, 4–20; Nasr and Leaman, *History of Islamic Philosophy*, 7.

62. *PAW*, 9.

63. *GS* II, 63.

64. *GS* II, 123. See also *Politeia* 519d–520c. Fazlur Rahman, on the contrary, observes that the doctrine of the internal compulsion of philosophers to found a state is Aristotelian (*Prophecy in Islam*, 88n89). Miriam Galston equally opposes Strauss's tendency to Platonize medieval philosophy. Galston, "Realism and Idealism in Avicenna's Political Philosophy," *Review of Politics* 41 (1979): 562ff.

65. *GS* II, 47, 122.

66. *GS* II, 122–23. Strauss probably had the structures of al-Fārābī's *Ideal State* and his *Principles of Beings* as well as Avicenna's *Metaphysics* in mind.

67. *GS* II, 118–19, 129.

68. In this regard see also Averroes, *KPP*, 73/36–37; Oliver Leaman, "Averroes' Commentary on Plato's *Republic*, and the Missing Politics," in *Across the Mediterranean Frontiers: Trade, Politics and Religion, 650–1450*, ed. D. A. Agius and I. R. Netton (Turnhout: Brepols, 1997), 195–203; Gutas, "Galen's *Synopsis*," 101–19.

69. *GS* II, 119.

70. al-Fārābī, *Siyāsa*, 80 (Najjār trans. 36–37), and *Sharḥ risālat Zaynūn al-kabīr al-yūnānī* (Hyderabad: Maṭbaʿat Majlis Dāʾirat al-Maʿārif, 1349 H/1930), 8 (henceforth cited as *Zaynūn*).

71. *GS* II, 114.

72. *GS* II, 111, 114.

73. *GS* II, 424.

74. In Arabic: "al-madīna al-fāḍila . . . al-madīna al-ḥasanat as-sīra" (Avicenna, *Shifāʾ*, 453, line 4; Horten trans. 680–81, line 13).

75. *GS* II, 111, 114, 127–28. Pines holds the view that the Arabs knew at least fragments of Aristotle's *Politics*. Shlomo Pines, "Aristotle's Politics in Arabic Philosophy," *Israel Oriental Studies* 5 (1975): 150–60. Brague agrees with him ("Strauss and Maimonides," 107n15).

76. *GS* II, 115. In this context, Strauss draws a parallel between Avicenna's *Metaphysics* (*Shifāʾ*, X.4:447, lines 4–5; Horten trans. 671), where the first postulation pertaining to the city involves the regulation of marriage necessary for securing procreation, and a passage in Plato's *Nomoi* that deals with the same matter: Plato, *Werke in acht Bänden: Griechisch und Deutsch*, ed. Gunther Eigler (Darmstadt: Wissenschaftliche Buchgesellschaft, 1977), 720e–721a.

However, an absolute compatibility between Avicenna's and Plato's teachings seems impossible in this regard. Erwin Rosenthal observed that the Muslim philosopher, contrary to Plato, compels care for the sick and the invalid. E. Rosenthal, *Political Thought in Medieval Islam* (Cambridge: Cambridge University Press, 1958), 152.

77. *GS* II, 119–20.

78. al-Fārābī, *Taḥṣīl*, 93; Mahdi trans. 79.

79. Al-Fārābī is referring here to his commentary on the *Nichomachean Ethics*, of which only a Hebrew translation was preserved (Leaman, *Averroes and His Philosophy*, 132ff.).

80. Averroes, *KPP*, 135ff./87–88. (I have examined Lauer's translation in light of the new Arabic translation from Hebrew and thereby observed small modifications.)

81. See also, further afield, Averroes, *Al-Kashf ʿan manāhij al-adilla fī ʿaqāʾid al-milla*, ed. Muḥammad ʿĀbid al-Jābirī (Beirut: Markaz Dirāsāt al-Waḥda al-ʿArabiyya, 1998), 173–85 / German translation in Müller, *Philosophie und Theologie von Averroes*, 86–96 (henceforth cited as *Kashf*); Leaman, *Averroes and His Philosophy*, 129–30.

82. *KPP*, 139/89.

83. *KPP*, 120, 125, 140–41 / 67, 70, 90–91. In this regard, see also E. Rosenthal, "Place of Politics," 247; E. Rosenthal, *Political Thought*, 176; Leaman, *Averroes and His Philosophy*, 130ff.

84. *GS* II, 143.

85. *GS* II, 116ff.

86. *GS* II, 119–20. In this regard, see also Erwin R. Goodenough, "The Political Philosophy of Hellenistic Kingship," *Yale Classical Studies* 1 (1928): 55–102. It would go beyond the scope of this book to investigate to what extent the philosophical-historical connections Strauss draws through such bold assertions are actually valid. However, it is noteworthy that Strauss does not consider the important question of whether the Islamic philosophers and Maimonides were actually aware of these connections derived by Strauss.

87. *GS* II, 125. With this statement, Strauss is explicitly referring to Averroes (*Kashf*, 98, lines 15–18, and 102, lines 2–3). The examination of the respective passage shows that Averroes is only concerned with prophetical lawgiving through divine revelation. Neither the philosopher nor the king are mentioned in this context.

88. *GS* II, 100ff., 115–16, 142.

89. Cf. Brague, "Strauss and Maimonides," 96.

90. *GS* II, 143.

91. Hans Daiber, "Political Philosophy," in Nasr and Leaman, *History of Islamic Philosophy*, 835, on the contrary, holds that Avicenna considers the prophet to be a Sufi who regards the divine law as a vehicle leading to the mystical path and, therefore, ranks higher than the philosopher and is not identical

with al-Fārābī's *ra'īs*. Erwin Rosenthal's view is similar (*Political Thought*, 146–47).

92. *GS* II, 101, 108, 116.

93. *GS* II, 126.

94. *GS* II, 136.

95. *GS* II, 140ff., 156ff., 206. Strauss also notes that al-Fārābī's and Averroes's appraisal of the rhetorical arts of the prophet went beyond Plato's assertions in this regard. The same holds true for Maimonides's positions, which came along after theirs. Rhetoric and courage were supposed to put the prophet into a position to implement his mission either by discourse or by force. Strauss interprets this characterization as the philosophical politicization of prophecy. Muhammad Shahjahan, "The Concept of Courage in the Philosophy of Al-Farabi," *Islamic Quarterly* 29 (1985): 234–39. Miriam Galston, in "Philosopher-King v. Prophet," *Israel Oriental Studies* 8 (1978): 214–15, 217–18, subtly contradicts Strauss when she argues that in Maimonides's writings, the true prophets were not philosopher-kings. She continues by arguing that the prophetic figure of Moses, whom Maimonides regards as the perfect political guide, seems to be the only authority figure in whose personhood philosophical and political perfection are united. As such, his prophecy is excluded from the examination of prophecy in the *Guide of the Perplexed*.

96. Again, Daiber raises objections against Strauss's interpretation through his insistence that al-Fārābī's prophetology be considered against the backdrop of the Aristotelian model of theory and practice. Daiber, *Ruler as Philosopher*, 5, 15ff., and "Prophetie und Ethik bei Fārābī (gest. 339/950)," in *L'homme et son Univers au moyen Âge*, ed. Christian Wenin (Louvain-la-Neuve: Editions de l'Institut Supérieur de Philosophie, 1986), 730. Daiber, in turn, was criticized by Joep Lameer in *Al-Fārābī and Aristotelian Syllogistics: Greek Theory and Islamic Practice* (Leiden: Brill, 1994), 271–72.

97. al-Fārābī, *Madīna* [Walzer], 246ff. Cf. *KPP*: 137–38/88–89; Walzer, ed., *Al-Fārābī on the Perfect State*, 445–46.

98. Cf. Muhsin Mahdi, "al-Fārābī," in Leo Strauss and Joseph Cropsey, eds., *History of Political Philosophy* (Chicago: University of Chicago Press, 1963), 195ff.; A. J. Arberry, "An Arabic Treatise on Politics," *Islamic Quarterly* 2 (1955): 15–16.

99. al-Fārābī, *Fuṣūl al-madanī: Aphorisms of the Statesman*, ed. D. M. Dunlop (Cambridge: Cambridge University Press, 1961), §58, 66–67 (henceforth cited as *Fuṣūl* [Dunlop]); *KPP*, 169/114.

100. al-Fārābī, *Siyāsa*, 79–80 (Najjār trans. 36–37). Cf. Rosenthal, *Political Thought*, 162.

101. al-Fārābī, *Milla*, 66. The *ra'īs al-awwal* needs to have command of theoretical philosophy in order to be able to discern the effects of God's providence in the world (Averroes, *Faṣl*, 27; Müller trans. 69–70).

102. al-Fārābī, *Taḥṣīl*, 93–94 (Mahdi trans. 79). On multiple occasions, Mahdi's translation lacks precision. "Ar-raʾīs al-awwal" is translated as "Supreme ruler," and "malik" (= king) as "prince."

103. Cf. Fauzī M. Najjār, "Fārābī's Political Philosophy and Shiʿism," *Studia Islamica* 14 (1961): 70.

104. al-Fārābī, *Milla*, 50.

105. Walzer, ed., *Al-Fārābī on the Perfect State*, 423–46; Daiber, "Prophetie," 133ff.

106. "Plato's philosopher-king in Islamic disguise" or "Plato in Muhammad's prophet dress" are images one finds in the stylings of those scholars. Quotations from Michael Marmura and Tjitze J. de Boer in Bassam Tibi, *Der Wahre Imam: Der Islam von Muhammed bis zur Gegenwart* (Munich: Piper, 1996), 147; cf. Muhammad S. H. al-Maʿsumi, "Al-Fārābī," in *History of Muslim Philosophy*, ed. M. M. Sharif (Wiesbaden: Harrassowitz, 1963), 716–17.

107. Rahman, *Prophecy in Islam*, 63–64; Ibrahim Madkour, "Al-Fārābi," in Sharif, *History of Muslim Philosophy*, 465; Walzer, ed., *Al-Fārābī on the Perfect State*, 423.

108. Najjār, "Fārābī's Political Philosophy and Shiʿism," 62ff. Walzer holds that al-Fārābī adheres to the doctrine of the Shiite Imāmiyya (*Al-Fārābī on the Perfect State*, 5–6, 17–18, 441–42, 447–48). Mahdi, on the other hand, is of the view that al-Fārābī's *raʾīs* refers to the Islamic prophet. Muhsin Mahdi, "Al-Fārābī's Imperfect State," *Journal of the American Oriental Society* 110 (1990): 705–13. An overlap between al-Fārābī's terminology in *Al-Madīna al-Fāḍila* and the doctrines of the Ismāʿīliyya is identified by Daiber (*Ruler as Philosopher*, 740–41). A more recent study by Daiber attempts to unveil the *ismāʿīlī* background of al-Fārābī's political philosophy on the basis of a comparison between *Al-Madīna al-Fāḍila* and the *Kitāb aʿlām an-nubūwa*, authored by the Ismaili Abū Ḥātim ar-Rāzī around 320 H/932–33 CE: Hans Daiber, "The Ismaili Background of Fārābī's Political Philosophy — Abū Ḥātim ar-Rāzī as a Forerunner of Fārābī," in *Gottes ist der Orient – Gottes ist der Okzident: Festschrift für Abdoljavad Falaturi zum 65. Gebutstag*, ed. Udo Tworuschka (Vienna: Orientalisches Institut der Universität Wien, 1991), 143–50. He comes to the conclusion that the *ismāʿīlī* conception of the universal validity of thought enabled al-Fārābī to combine Greek and Islamic ideas. Cf. Daiber, "Ismaili Background," 149. Lameer, in *Al-Fārābī and Aristotelian Syllogistics*, 286–87, questions this interpretation but does not offer an alternative. Hamid Enayat, "An Outline of the Political Philosophy of the Rasāʾil of the Ikhwān al-Ṣafāʾ," in *Ismāʿīlī Contributions to Islamic Culture*, ed. Seyyed Hossein Nasr (Tehran: Imperial Iranian Academy of Philosophy, 1977), 25–49; Pines, "Shīʿite Terms," 179–83.

109. Ann Lambton, *State and Government in Medieval Islam* (Oxford: Oxford University Press, 1981), 72, 121. Regarding the depiction of the caliphs, see Patricia Crone and Martin Hinds, *God's Caliph: Religious Authority in the First Centuries of Islam* (Cambridge: Cambridge University Press, 1986).

110. Al-Fārābī underpins the outstanding position of the *ra'īs al-awwal* in the virtuous city by highlighting his excellence in the arts (*Taḥṣīl*, 86–87 / Mahdi trans. 75; Walzer, ed., *Al-Fārābī on the Perfect State*, 430).

111. Mahdi, "Al-Fārābī's Imperfect State," 712–13; Tibi, *Der Wahre Imam*, 127.

112. E. Rosenthal in *Political Thought*, 128–29, and Madkour in "Al-Fārābi," 463, argue in a similar vein, although Madkour's description of a virtuous city inhabited by saints and ruled by the prophet is rather difficult to follow. Muhsin Mahdi, "Alfarabi," in Strauss and Cropsey, *History of Political Philosophy*, 190ff. Galston's interpretation differs considerably from the aforementioned accounts. She holds that "the dominant portrait of the supreme ruler in Alfarabi's writings is of a person who combines philosophy and the experiential faculty equated variously with practical reason or a part of practical reason." Miriam Galston, *Politics and Excellence: The Political Philosophy of Alfarabi* (Princeton, NJ: Princeton University Press, 1990), 126. It seems that she exempts the reception of revelation from the elements constituting the *ra'īs*, thereby dropping the only element that actually distinguishes al-Fārābī's *ra'īs* from Plato's philosopher-king. Furthermore, it is noteworthy that Galston's translation of al-Fārābī's *Al-Madīna al-Fāḍila* as "city of excellence" is not accurate. The attribute *fāḍil(a)* means "virtuous," as in Mahdi's translation.

113. Similar to Daiber, "Prophetie," 11ff., 15ff.; and *Ruler as Philosopher*, 740.

114. Similar to Madkour, "Al-Fārābi," 466.

115. In al-Fārābī's *Siyāsa*, 32 (Najjār trans. 33–34), the active intellect is called "ar-rūḥ al-amīn wa-rūḥ al-quds" (the loyal spirit, the spirit of the saint).

116. Cf. Mahdi, "Alfarabi," 194–95. Mahdi notices that "the only qualification that Alfarabi is willing to drop in the *Virtuous City* is prophecy" and that "unlike prophecy, philosophy cannot be dispensed with, and nothing can take its place." These conclusions give the impression that al-Fārābī deems philosophy more important than prophecy. However, Mahdi's statements fail to take into account al-Fārābī's realistic approach: Given the rarity of instantiations of prophecy in the history of humanity, he does not rule out excellent leadership without prophecy (Mahdi, "Alfarabi," 194–95).

117. *GS* II, 116.

118. Muhsin Mahdi, "Science, Philosophy, and Religion in Alfarabi's *Enumeration of the Sciences*," in *The Cultural Context of Medieval Learning*, ed. J. E. Murdoch and E. D. Sylla (Boston: Reidel, 1975), 113.

119. McDaniel assumes that Heidegger's sympathizing with National Socialism was the trigger for Strauss's search for the roots of philosophy, "tracking them from the medieval Jewish and Islamic thinkers to their source in the Greek Polis" ("Philosopher's Jeremiad," 11). However, Strauss's interest in medieval theories of prophecy began before Heidegger turned to National Socialism and was independent of this latter event. On the contrary, it seems that the political ideas that Strauss adopted from his studies in medieval prophetology were used later on to criticize Heidegger.

120. James W. Morris is in line with Strauss when he argues that the Islamic philosophers regarded political achievements as the most important miracles of the prophets. Morris, "The Philosopher-Prophet in Avicenna's Political Philosophy," in *The Political Aspects of Islamic Philosophy: Essays in Honor of Muhsin S. Mahdi*, ed. Charles Butterworth (Cambridge, MA: Harvard University Press, 1992), 152–98. Morris's argumentation clearly betrays a strong Straussian influence. (See also Morris, "Philosopher-Prophet," 159, 161, and 163.) Although we cannot go into detail here, it has to be noted that he entirely misunderstands Avicenna's philosophy.

121. *GS* II, 116–17.

Chapter Five

1. Strauss, *GS* II, 47, 60ff.; *RCPR*, 223.
2. "PRC," 35. Cf. Voegelin et al., *Briefwechsel*, 31.
3. *GS* II, 63–64. Cf. Voegelin et al., *Briefwechsel*, 31.
4. In his early works, Strauss made only cautious attempts to define the relationship between the sharia and nomos. In an earlier statement, Strauss argued that Plato had provided the medieval Islamic philosophers only with a "starting point from which they could understand the revelation philosophically" (*GS* II, 76). Furthermore, he finds that the "*Laws* point to the revelation, but only point to it" (76). Later on, Strauss found this relationship to be much stronger: The medieval philosophers were Platonists because they considered sharia and nomos as essentially identical inasmuch as both originated from basic human needs and targeted the perfection of the individual with respect to both body and spirit. Strauss even went so far as to advise Shlomo Pines to translate the word "sharia" in Maimonides's *Guide of the Perplexed* as "law" instead of "religious law." Pines did not follow this advice. Letter from Strauss to Pines, July 15, 1959; see Joel L. Kraemer and Josef Stern, "Shlomo Pines on the Translation of Maimonides' *Guide of the Perplexed*," *Journal of Jewish Thought and Philosophy* 8 (1998): 15–16.
5. In this context I disregard the previously mentioned concerns of recent research regarding the specific *Nomoi* text that al-Fārābī was working on. I am interested here in Strauss's own self-understanding and the way it was tied to his analysis of al-Fārābī.
6. Strauss, *WIPP*, 29; *AAPL*, 1.
7. *WIPP*, 144.
8. *RCPR*, 223.
9. *WIPP*, 14.
10. Cf. *GS* II, 129.
11. *WIPP*, 145.
12. *WIPP*, 150ff.

13. "FP," 392; *WIPP*, 149. Cf. *NRH*, 178: "The goal was lowered in order to increase the probability of its attainment."

14. *WIPP*, 152ff.; "FP," 380–81.

15. *WIPP*, 163.

16. *WIPP*. Cf. *NRH*, 144–45, 152; *Siyāsa*, 80–81 (Najjār trans. 37); *Madīna* [Dieterici], 60.

17. *NRH*, 90.

18. In this regard, see Seth Benardete, "Leo Strauss's *The City and Man*," *Political Science Reviewer* 8 (1978): 3. R. Hepp, "Nomos," in *Historisches Wörterbuch der Philosophie*, ed. Karlfried Gründer, Joachim Ritter, and Gottfried Gabriel (Basel: Schwabe AG Verlag, 1971–2007), 6:893–95; Felix Heinimann, *Nomos und Physis: Herkunft und Bedeutung einer Antithese im griechischen Denken des 5. Jahrhunderts* (Darmstadt: Wissenschaftliche Buchgesellschaft, 1965); Ada B. Hentschke, *Politik und Philosophie bei Plato und Aristoteles: Die Stellung der "NOMOI" im Platonischen Gesamtwerk und die politische Theorie des Aristoteles* (Frankfurt am Main: Klostermann, 1971); Francisco L. Lisi, *Einheit und Vielheit des platonischen Nomosbegriffs: Eine Untersuchung zur Beziehung von Philosophie und Politik bei Platon* (Königstein: Hain, 1985). An in-depth treatment of Strauss's concept of nomos, which would essentially constitute a comparison with Carl Schmitt's concept of nomos, must remain outside our purview. The juxtaposition of philosophy and nomos recalls Karl Reinhardt's thesis that the pair of opposites represented by nomos/physis is a reformulation of "the fundamental antithesis in the thought of Parmenides between δόξα and ἀλήθεια." Cited by Heinimann, *Nomos und Physis*, 10.

19. *PAW*, 112, 116. Cf. 10–11.

20. *PAW*, 115–16.

21. *PAW*, 117. Cf. *WIPP*, 152ff. Strauss refers to ar-Rāzī's *Kitāb as-sīra al-falsafiyya* [The philosophical way of life]; Paul Kraus, "Raziana I," *Orientalia* 4 (1935): 300–21, and "Raziana II," *Orientalia* 5 (1936): 35–56, 358–78.

22. *PAW*, 133.

23. *PAW*, 119ff., 137n133.

24. *PAW*, 136–37. Cf. *NRH*, 206. See also Ibn Bājja, *Tadbīr al-mutawaḥḥid*, ed. Maʿan Ziyade (Beirut: Dār al-Fikr, 1398 H/1978), along with the respective part in Strauss (*PAW*, 117n66).

25. *WIPP*, 164–65.

26. *WIPP*, 11.

27. See also in this regard Mahdi, "Editio Princeps," 6ff.; Parens, *Metaphysics as Rhetoric*, xxviii–xxxiv; Gutas, "Galen's *Synopsis*," 103ff.; Gutas, "Fārābī's Knowledge of Plato's *Laws*," *International Journal of the Classical Tradition* 4 (1999): 413ff.

28. Harry Wolfson, "The Amphibolous Terms in Aristotle, Arabic Philosophy and Maimonides," *Harvard Theological Review* 31 (1938): 155ff. Evidence is to be found there.

29. See *Talkhīṣ*, "Prefatio," ix–xii. For discussions of Galen's synopses of Plato's works, see Gutas, "Galen's *Synopsis*," 116ff.

30. *Talkhīṣ*, p. 4, line 10ff.; p. 5, line 15ff.; p. 43, lines 5–13; p. 22, lines 2–10.

31. *Talkhīṣ*, p. 5, lines 3–4.

32. *Talkhīṣ*, p. 37, lines 2–5.

33. *Talkhīṣ*, p. 5, line 5; p. 7, line 13. Most of al-Fārābī's discussion refers to *nawāmīs* (= nomoi).

34. *Talkhīṣ*, p. 8, lines 18–20.

35. *Talkhīṣ*, p. 6, line 17ff.; p. 7, lines 5–9; p. 10, line 10ff.; p. 11, line 19; p. 12, line 1; p. 38, lines 7–21.

36. *Talkhīṣ*, p. 8, line 8ff.; p. 36, line 20; p. 38, line 7; p. 38, line 22; p. 39, line 2; p. 40, lines 10–15; p. 41, lines 5–6.

37. *Talkhīṣ*, p. 16, line 21; p. 17, line 22; p. 18, line 15ff.; p. 22, lines 2–10; p. 26, lines 12–13.

38. *Talkhīṣ*, p. 12, line 11ff.; p. 14, line 13ff.; p. 16, lines 1–11; p. 18, lines 5–9; p. 20, lines 23–24; p. 21, line 3ff.; p. 24, line 5; p.30, lines 19–20; p. 31, line 11ff.; p. 33, line 8ff.; p. 34, lines 2–10.

39. Kraemer holds a similar view with regard to Maimonides's interpretation of the Torah ("Maimonides on the Philosophic Sciences," 79).

40. *Talkhīṣ*, p. 6, lines 5–8; p. 12, line 16; p. 13, line 13; p. 33, line 19; p. 34, line 2; p. 39, lines 2–20; p. 41, line 21; p. 43, line 4.

41. *Talkhīṣ*, p. 27, lines 3–11; p. 36, line 20; p. 37, line 14.

42. In this regard, see Pavlin, "Sunni kalām and Theological Controversies," 105–18; Fahmī Jidʿān, "Al-Fārābī: Madkhal ilā tajribat al-ʿilm wa-l-fiʿl ʿindahu," in *al-Māḍī fī l-ḥāḍir*, ed. Fahmī Jidʿān (Beirut: al-Muʾassasa al-ʿArabiyya li-d-Dirāsāt wa-n-Nashr, 1997), 210ff. Erwin Rosenthal (*Political Thought*, 116–17) holds that the Muslim philosophers saw a fundamental difference between religious law (sharia) and nomos. Whereas the sharia was based on revelation and focused on God, the Platonic nomos originated from myth and was centered around the rational human being. Furthermore, the sharia mainly aims at preparing humanity for eternal life in the world hereafter. The main purpose of Plato's nomos, on the other hand, was to allow humankind to reach intellectual perfection in this world (Leaman, *An Introduction*, 175–76).

43. *Milla*, p. 46, line 22; p. 47, line 17; *Talkhīṣ*, p. 41, line 21; p. 42, line 3. Cf. Averroes, *Averroes' Commentary on Plato's Republic*, ed. Erwin Rosenthal (Cambridge: Cambridge University Press, 1956), 265, 272, 298. Maimonides, *Dalālat*, II, K. 40:416–17. In his *Guide of the Perplexed*, Maimonides clearly distinguishes between divine law (sharia) and human laws (*nawāmīs*). If al-Fārābī had regarded both laws

as belonging to one and the same category, Maimonides would probably not have admired al-Fārābī to the extent that Strauss himself highlights on several occasions (Leaman, *An Introduction*, 156–57, 161–62).

In his *Treatise on Logic* — Mūsā b. Maimūn, "Maqāla fī ṣināʿat al-manṭiq," *Ankara Üniversitesi Dil ve Tarih-Coğrafya Fakültesi Dergisi* 18 (1960): 9–64 — in which Strauss claims to have found "Maimonides' statement on political science" (*WIPP*, 155), Maimonides clearly distinguishes between the divine laws (*al-awāmir al-ilāhiyya*) and those human laws (*nawāmīs*). Maimonides held that the latter have been established by the scholars of past religious communities (*ʿulamāʾ al-umam al-khāliya*) according to their individual perfection (*ḥasab kamāl kull shakhṣ minhum*) in order to enable the kings to rule their peoples. Furthermore, Maimonides states that the philosophers had written many books on those laws, some of which were translated into Arabic, with even more of them remaining untranslated. He also argues that in those times (*hādhihi al-azmina*) human affairs were regulated by divine laws only (*tadabbara an-nās bi-l-awāmir al-ilāhiyya*), whereas one dispensed with all those (*istughniya ʿan jamīʿ dhālik*) regimes and laws (*as-sīyāsāt wa-n-nawāmīs*). In his interpretation of this treatise, Kraemer stresses definitively that Maimonides followed al-Fārābī and criticizes Strauss's identification of sharia and nomos ("Maimonides on the Philosophic Sciences," 77–104).

44. *Tisʿ rasāʾil*, 85.
45. *PAW*, 9–10; *GS* II, 30–31 n2. Cf. Udoff, *Strauss's Thought*, 3–4, 15–16.
46. *GS* II, 126, 131–32; *WIPP*, 156–57. Cf. Kraemer, "Maimonides on the Philosophic Sciences," 101ff.
47. *GS* II, 137. Cf. *WIPP*, 159–60.
48. *GS* II, 145ff.
49. *GS* II, 152–53. Cf. ibid., 152n98.
50. Cf. *Taḥsīl*, 91 (Mahdi trans. 77).
51. *GS* II, 153. Cf. *Taḥsīl*, 109ff., 156ff.
52. *GS* II, 58, 112–13.
53. *GS* II, 153.
54. *GS* II, 156.
55. Strauss tries to demonstrate that Maimonides, following al-Fārābī, was aware of the political effects of the doctrine of providence when he excluded this topic from the subject area of metaphysics and assigned it to politics, as demonstrated by his *Guide of the Perplexed*. As Strauss saw it, this happened in accordance with the aforementioned "so-called Islamic Aristotelians" who had, from the very outset, assigned prophecy as well as religious law to the realm of politics. Furthermore, this was in accordance with Plato's teachings in the *Nomoi* (Strauss, *Strauss on Maimonides*, 321; *SPPP*, 166).
56. "FP," 371–72. At this point, Strauss refers to the critical statements of Ibn Ṭufayl in *Ḥayy Ibn Yaqẓān*, ed. A. N. Nādir (Beirut: al-Maṭbaʿa

al-Kāthūlīkiyya, 1986, 21–22). The aforementioned commentary by al-Fārābī is believed to be lost.

57. "FP," 372ff.

58. "FP," 374–75.

59. *PAW*, 15ff.

60. "FP," 378; *NRH*, 153.

61. *GS* II, 66. Strauss is probably referring to the statement by Avicenna discussed earlier in this book.

62. *GS* II, 60n24. It seems that Strauss considers philosophy and unbelief to be identical. Cf. *GS* II, 67; *PAW*, 107, especially n35.

63. *GS* II, 59.

64. See also Drury, *Political Ideas*, 52ff., 121ff. Cf. Pines, "On Leo Strauss," 169–70.

65. Strauss in Leo Strauss and Joseph Cropsey, eds., *History of Political Philosophy* (Chicago: University of Chicago Press, 1963), 297 (henceforth cited as *HPP*).

66. *GS* II, 58–59. Cf. *PAW*, 122ff.

67. Strauss in Voegelin et al., *Briefwechsel*, 31. See also "MITP," 116; Smith, "Leo Strauss: Between Athens and Jerusalem," 85–86; Orr, *Jerusalem and Athens*, 29.

68. *NRH*, 74.

69. See also Thomas Pangle, "Platonic Political Science in Strauss and Voegelin," in *FPP*, 322.

70. *NRH*, 86; *AAPL*, 3.

71. Cf. Drury, *Political Ideas*, 37–52.

72. *NRH*, 101.

73. *NRH*, 107, 151.

74. *NRH*, 85.

75. *NRH*, 164.

76. *NRH*, 169.

77. *SPPP*, 61ff., 96.

78. *NRH*, 86; Strauss in Voegelin et al., *Briefwechsel*, 31.

79. *NRH*, 95.

80. It was Avicenna who brought this thought to its fullest expression (*Shifā'*, 441ff./661ff.).

81. *NRH*, 204–5.

82. *SPPP*, 147; Thomas J. J. Altizer, "The Theological Conflict between Strauss and Voegelin," in *FPP*, 267. Cf. Bluhm, "Leo Strauss' politische Philosophie und das 'einfache Denken,'" 216–17.
83. In this regard, see also Smith, "Leo Strauss: Between Athens and Jerusalem," 84–89.
84. *RKS*, 215.
85. "CCM," 112; *GS* II, 54–55.
86. *PAW*, 119–20. Cf. *WIPP*, 156.
87. Leo Strauss, *The Political Philosophy of Hobbes: Its Basis and Its Genesis*, trans. Elsa M. Sinclair (Chicago: University of Chicago Press, 1952) 74ff. (henceforth cited as *PPH*).
88. *PAW*, 10, 134–35; *WIPP*, 160–61.
89. Christopher A. Colmo interprets the hyphen between "theological" and "political" as a sign for the joint need of both fields for practical decision-making in the face of opposing values. Colmo, "Reason and Revelation in the Thought of Leo Strauss," *Interpretation* 18 (1990): 151. In my opinion, this explanation fails to grasp the magnitude of the connection between religion and politics in Strauss's conceptual schematic.
90. *PAW*, 114–15.
91. Rosen, *Hermeneutics as Politics* (Oxford: Oxford University Press, 1987), 112.
92. Leo Strauss, *On Tyranny*: *Including the Strauss-Kojève Correspondence*, rev. ed., ed. Victor Gourevitch and Michael S. Roth (New York: Free Press, 1991), 86ff., 125n58–59 (henceforth cited as *OT*).
93. *NRH*, 139–40; Rosen, *Hermeneutics as Politics*, 110.
94. *SPPP*, 61ff.; *RCPR*, 203–4. Cf. Kojève in *HPP*, 98ff.
95. *OT*, 103.
96. *AAPL*, 1, 3–4. Pangle, "Platonic Political Science," 347.
97. *GS* II, 123n80. It seems that Strauss is referring to Averroes, who held the position of grand qadi.
98. *GS* II, 67–68. Strauss believes that the prophet is also called a philosopher due to philosophy's attempt to justify itself before revealed law. *PAW*, 10.
99. *GS* II, 68. At this point, Strauss refers to the treatise *Faṣl al-maqāl*. He used the Arabic edition of Averroes's treatise edited by M. J. Müller, published under the title *Philosophie und Theologie des Averroes* (Munich, 1859). The passages Strauss quotes were translated by Strauss himself. Fred Baumann argues in his English translation of *Philosophy and Law* that Strauss clearly resorted to Müller's translation of the treatise of 1875 without mentioning him as a reference. Leo Strauss, *Philosophy and Law: Essays toward the Understanding of Maimonides and His Predecessors*, trans. Fred Baumann (Philadelphia: Jewish Publication Society, 1987), 121. Strauss's translation

sometimes deviates from Müller's translation. Most importantly, Strauss always translates *sharia* with "law," while Müller translates it with "religion."

100. *GS* II, 75–86. For the reception of Averroes in Jewish intellectual history, see Leaman, *Averroes and His Philosophy*, 175ff.; Leaman, "Jewish Averroism," in Nasr and Leaman, *History of Islamic Philosophy*, 769–80; Leaman, "Jewish Averroism," in *Routledge Encyclopedia of Philosophy*, 1:598–602.

101. This characterization deviates somewhat from the manner in which Averroes described the intention behind his treatise. According to a statement at the beginning of the treatise, Averroes announces that he intends to legally (Arabic: *ash-shar'ī*) speculate whether reflection upon philosophy and the sciences of logic was permitted, forbidden, or demanded by religious law. To take the arguments of religious law into account when analyzing the possibility of philosophizing does not seem to be identical with conducting an investigation that has the character of legal speculation. However, Averroes's attempt to justify philosophy out of religious law may fall into the category of philosophical apologetics. When Strauss describes Averroes's investigation as "legal speculation," he runs the risk of understating its philosophical nature.

102. *GS* II, 69–70. Cf. Averroes, *Faṣl*, 27–32 (Müller trans. 1–4).

103. *GS* II, 70. Cf. *Faṣl*, 34–35 (6–7).

104. *Faṣl*, 45 (15).

105. *GS* II, 71. Cf. *Faṣl*, 35–36, 38–39, 45, 52–53 (7–8, 9–10, 14–15, 20–21).

106. *GS* II, 71.

107. *Faṣl*, 35–36 (7).

108. *GS* II, 71.

109. *Faṣl*, 36 (7–8).

110. *Faṣl*, 37–38 (8–9).

111. *Faṣl*, 45ff. (14ff.).

112. *Faṣl*, 48 (16–17).

113. *GS* II, 71ff.

114. *GS* II, 73–74.

115. *GS* II, 74.

116. *GS* II, 74–75.

117. *GS* II, 76–77. In a footnote, Strauss quotes the following statement by Averroes in Arabic: "only God and the men of demonstration know its interpretation" (*JPCM*, 142n15). See also Niewöhner in Niewöhner and L. Sturlese, *Averroismus*, 29ff.

118. *GS* II, 77–78, 84. With this observation, Strauss opposes the thesis held by both Léon Gauthier and G. M. Manser that Averroes's denial of supernatural truths reflected the lack of a clerical magisterium. Cf. Léon Gauthier, *La thèorie d'Ibn Rochd (Averroès) sur les rapports de la religion et de*

la philosophie (Paris: Leroux, 1909); G. M. Manser, "Das Verhältnis von Glaube und Wissen bei Averroës," in *Jahrbuch für Philosophie und spekulative Theologie* (Paderborn: Schöning, 1910, 1911), 24:398–408, 25:9–34, 163–179.

119. *GS* II, 78.

120. On this matter, see Leaman, *An Introduction*, 169ff., 177–78.

121. *GS* II, 42. When Averroes states that the Qurʾān obliges the philosophers to philosophize and to interpret apparently irrational passages of the Qurʾān in a way that lends them rational meaning, Strauss takes this as a confirmation of his view that the Islamic medieval philosophers were Platonists. It seems that he equates the philosophers who are obliged to philosophize by means of examining religious laws with Plato's philosophers who have duties with regard to the city. However, it has to be noted that the religious obligation to philosophize as conceived by Averroes actually served the justification of philosophy and is henceforth of an apologetic nature. Plato, on the other hand, wants to oblige the theory-prone philosophers to participate in political life for the benefit of the community. Therefore, there are fundamental differences between Plato and Averroes with regard to both the intentions behind philosophizing and the nature of the duties assigned to the philosopher (*GS* II: 46–47, 69–70).

122. Rosen, *Hermeneutics as Politics*, 17.

123. Colmo, "Reason and Revelation," 145.

124. Orr, *Jerusalem and Athens*, 18.

125. Orr, 149, 158.

126. Drury, *Political Ideas*, 37, 215. Strauss strongly objected when Karl Löwith called him an "Orthodox Jew." Leo Strauss, "Correspondence: Karl Löwith and Leo Strauss," *Independent Journal of Philosophy* 5/6 (1988): 185 (henceforth cited as "CLS"). As gleaned from the correspondence between Karl Jasper and Hannah Arendt, Jasper also considered him an "Orthodox Jew," whereas Arendt described him as an orthodox atheist by conviction. Lotte Köhler and Hans Saner, eds., *Hannah Arendt, Karl Jaspers: Briefwechsel 1926–1969* (Munich: Piper, 1987), 277, 281–82. Drury in *Strauss and the American Right*, 40, argues that Strauss was a "Jewish nationalist" who had wrongly been mistaken for an "Orthodox Jew." This seems to mesh very well with the political character of Strauss's Jewish identity.

127. *GS* II, 26; *GS* I, 53.

128. *JCPM*, 459–60.

129. Leo Strauss, *Thoughts on Machiavelli* (Glencoe, IL: Free Press, 1958), 49, 111, 218n63 (henceforth cited as *TM*); Pines, "On Leo Strauss," 169.

130. *WIPP*, 159ff.; *AAPL*, 3, 6–7; Harry Neumann, "Civic Piety and Socratic Atheism: An Interpretation of Strauss's Socrates and Aristophanes," *Independent Journal of Philosophy* 2 (1978): 34–35.

131. Colmo, in "Reason and Revelation," 146, fails to grasp the core point of Strauss's argumentation. It is exactly because religion relies on belief that it is important for his political philosophy.

132. See Averroes, *Tahāfut at-tahāfut*, ed. Maurice Bouyges (Beirut: Dār al-Mashriq, 1992), 866ff. (henceforth cited as *TT*); Frederick D. Wilhelmsen, *Christianity and Political Philosophy* (Athens: University of Georgia Press, 1978), 211; as well as the pertinent critique in Drury, *Political Ideas*, 54; Brague, "Leo Strauss and Maimonides,"103.

133. "CLS," 185.

Chapter Six

1. Leo Strauss, "COT," 41–42; "CPP," 91; *NRH*, 34; Drury, *Political Ideas*, 165.

2. *NRH*, 35–80; *WIPP*, 17–27; Leo Strauss, *Liberalism, Ancient and Modern* (Ithaca, NY: Basic Books, 1968), 26–64 (henceforth cited as *LAM*); "CPP," 91; *SPPP*, 29ff.; *RCPR*, 13–46. We will leave aside the investigations referred to above as they do not touch on our core subject matter. Compare John G. Gunnell, "Political Theory and Politics: The Case of Leo Strauss," *Political Theory* 13 (1985): 347–59; Drury, *Political Ideas*, 163–69; Laurence Berns, "The Prescientific World and Historicism: Some Reflections on Strauss, Heidegger, and Husserl," in Udoff, *Strauss's Thought*, 169–81; Stanley Rosen, "Politics or Transcendence? Responding to Historicism," in *FPP*, 261–66; H. Meier, *Die Denkbewegung*, 19–31; Kauffmann, *Leo Strauss zur Einführung*, 55–84.

3. Leo Strauss, "On a New Interpretation of Plato's Political Philosophy," *Social Research* 13 (1956): 328ff. (henceforth cited as "ONI"); "COT," 54; Victor Gourevitch, "Philosophy and Politics," *Review of Metaphysics* 22 (1968): 59–60; Gunnell, "Political Theory and Politics," 339. Strauss designates political philosophy as "rhetorical" in that it, at least implicitly, places the conditions and boundaries of academic political theory in question.

4. For more, see Pippin, "Modern World," 450–51.

5. Strauss declares ("FP," 359n4) al-Fārābī's text *al-Jamʿ bayna raʾyay al-ḥakīmayn* (The Harmonization of the Opinions of Both Wise Men) to be exoteric because its title holds the word *raʾy* (opinion). Due to a similar reason, *Mabādiʾ ārāʾ ahl al-madīna al-fāḍila* is considered more exoteric than *as-Siyāsa al-madaniyya* ("FP," 358). If Strauss's interpretation were correct, al-Fārābī's view that the city is the ideal political unit (*GS* II, 135) would be in question. Therefore, the implied central meaning of the city would not count as one of al-Fārābī's true teachings. Cf. Galston, *Politics and Excellence*, 151n17.

6. *GS* II, 176; "FP," 358–59; *PAW*, 9. Cf. Bolotin, *Strauss on Classical Political Philosophy*, 130–31, 142. Strauss's thesis that al-Fārābī subsumed the theoretical within the political is based primarily the title *as-Siyāsa al-madaniyya*, which he translates as "The Political Regime" and with which he

characterizes the content of the work. He also applies this interpretation to *Mabādiʾ al-mawjūdāt* (The Principles of Beings), a text whose first section contains metaphysical discussions. Strauss also bases this position on the classification of *Mabādiʾ ārāʾ ahl al-madīna al-fāḍila* in the Bodleian library as a political text] (*GS* II, 136n38). Maimonides's decision to name the same text *Mabādiʾ al-mawjūdāt* stands as a rejection of this view of the text as "political" due to its title (*GS* II, 128, 175–76; "FP," 1). The thought process in both texts not only points to the fact that "theoretical philosophy [is presented] alongside political philosophy," as Galston (*Politics and Excellence*, 181–82 n5) claims, but also is due to the dependency of politics on metaphysics. See the epilogue below.

7. *GS* II, 125.

8. *GS* II, 127–28, 197; *RCPR*, 223.

9. *GS* II, 128. Cf. Madkour, "Al-Fārābi," 465.

10. "FP," 379.

11. See ch. 3, note 48 in the present volume.

12. al-Fārābi, *Iḥṣāʾ*, 125–26; *GS* II, 133, especially n22, 187. See a detailed analysis of this text in Mahdi, "Science, Philosophy, and Religion," 113–47. Strauss translates the expression "al-ʿilm al-madanī" to "Politikwissenschaft / science politique / Political Science" and uses the expressions "political science / political philosophy / practical philosophy" as synonyms. Cf. *GS* II, 125ff.; "FP," 366; *WIPP*, 155, 168; Mahdi, "Science, Philosophy, and Religion," 131. See also al-Fārābi on the harmony of religion and philosophy as discussed in the epilogue of the present volume.

13. "FP," 362–63. Cf. *WIPP*, 140.

14. "FP," 365–66; "ONI," 348–49. Strauss's crediting of al-Fārābī with the interpretation of Plato's judgment of theoretical life as existing on a higher plane than practical life constitutes the core of Strauss's refutation of John Wild's interpretation of Plato's political philosophy. See "ONI," 346ff.

15. *Falsafat Aflāṭūn*, §18. Cf. "FP," 367–68.

16. "FP," 379, 381. In contrast, compare medieval Jewish and Islamic interpretations of the eudaimonia concept as presented by Erwin Rosenthal, "The Concept of Eudaimonia in Medieval Islamic and Jewish Philosophy," in *Storia della filosofia antica e medievale* (Florence: Sansoni, 1960), 145–52. Rosenthal concludes that Averroes and his predecessors consider felicity to be relative. It does not mean the same thing to philosophers as it does to nonphilosophers. For philosophers, felicity is constituted through perfection in practical abilities as well as ethical, intellectual, and speculative virtues. From the vantage point of God, they can be considered perfect.

17. "FP," 378.

18. "FP," 370. Compare this with Galston's critique in *Politics and Excellence*, 91n69.

19. "FP," 382. Strauss ascribes to al-Fārābī a similar process for summarizing Plato's *Nomoi*. Galston (*Politics and Excellence*, 172ff.) criticizes Strauss's

thesis that al-Fārābī's twofold presentation of this issue stems from a fear of persecution and states that there is simply no proof for this.

20. "FP," 379ff. Against this view, see al-Maʿsumi, "Al-Fārābī," 705ff.; Galston, *Politics and Excellence*, 55–94; and the same in Charles Butterworth, *The Political Aspects of Islamic Philosophy: Essays in Honor of Muhsin S. Mahdi* (Cambridge, MA: Harvard University Press, 1992), 95–151. Galston's thorough treatment of the topic of felicity in al-Fārābī's philosophy makes it plain that he rejects a narrow understanding of theoretical perfection and instead attempts to expand it to include practical philosophy. "Knowledge of human things finds its completion in the realization of their best state," and therefore only a theoretical *and* practical perfection of the individual can bring them to the true goal of felicity (Galston, *Politics and Excellence*, 94).
21. "FP," 379ff., especially n55, where Strauss explains that al-Fārābī's interpretation of Plato's *Nomoi* differs from Plato's own interpretation. In Strauss's view, al-Fārābī is cognizant of the reality of revelation. The Arabic text does not give any indication that al-Fārābī believed in a possible multiplicity of virtuous cities, a view that Strauss ascribes to him. See *Falsafat Aflāṭūn*, §§2, 25, 29; "FP," 381 and n56.
22. Galston (*Politics and Excellence*, 175ff.) is of the opinion that given the aforementioned evidence, al-Fārābī held out the possibility that felicity could be achieved in deficient political circumstances.
23. Strauss ascribes to al-Fārābī the position that justice is to be separated from the other virtues. *WIPP*, 167n21. Cf. *Falsafat Aflāṭūn*, p. 22, line 5.
24. *GS* II, 148–49. Cf. *Falsafat Aflāṭūn*, 19.
25. "FP," 383; *RCPR*, 159. See also Benardete, "Leo Strauss's *The City and Man*," 9ff.
26. *WIPP*, 153–54.
27. *WIPP*, 154.
28. "FP," 384. Cf. *WIPP*, 126: "philosophy and philosophic education are possible in all kinds of more or less imperfect regimes."
29. Daiber ("Political Philosophy," 845) argues against this position in that "politics became a part of ethics."
30. *WIPP*, 166–67.
31. *GS* II, 133–34. Cf. *WIPP*, 155–56. Strauss attempts to prove his thesis of the primacy of politics over ethics in al-Fārābī's oeuvre by assigning different values to different texts in which this topic is presented. This renders the text *at-Tanbīh ʿalā sabīl a-saʿāda* (*Indicating the Path to Felicity*), in which ethics and politics are separated from one another, less important than the text *Taḥṣīl as-saʿāda* (*The Attainment of Happiness*), in which ethics and politics are presented as part of the *ʿilm al-madanī* (*GS* II, 134n28). See Fauzī M. Najjār, "Al-Fārābī on Political Science," *Muslim World* 48 (1958): 94ff.; Mahdi, "Science, Philosophy, and Religion," 137. In more nuanced fashion than Strauss, Najjār identifies the relationship between politics and ethics in the following manner: "Politics and ethics are not separate sciences treating

independent subject matters, but different approaches to common problems" ("Al-Fārābī on Political Science," 94).

32. *WIPP*, 164. Also Najjār, "Al-Fārābī on Political Science," 97.

33. *GS* II, 129. Strauss plays with the title of al-Fārābī's text *Mabādiʾ ārāʾ ahl al-madīna al-fāḍila* (*The Principles of the Opinions of the Residents of the Virtuous City*). He could have been thinking about their common identification in Arabic philosophy with *al-ilāhiyyāt* or *al-ʿilm al-ilāhī* in the way he describes metaphysics, as introduced above.

34. *GS* II, 153, 211. See also Najjār, "Al-Fārābī on Political Science," 99–100; Mahdi, "Science, Philosophy, and Religion," 130–31.

35. *GS* II, 136–37. Cf. Galston's critique of Strauss (*Politics and Excellence*, 164–65).

36. "FP," 373, 388.

37. Against Strauss's interpretation, the fact that al-Fārābī uses the verb *yanbaghī* as a predicate in the singular tense in conjunction with philosopher, king, and lawgiver is significant. *Falsafat Aflāṭūn*, p. 22, line 6–7.

38. Colmo, "Theory and Practice," 966ff. See also Colmo, "Reason and Revelation," 158.

39. "FP," 385ff.; *Falsafat Aflāṭūn*, 3–4. The Arabic text does not say that the virtuous way of life grants false felicity. The phrase "this bliss" (*hādhihi as-saʿāda*) indicates in context both "the true felicity" and "that which is thought to be felicity but is not" but may be more contextually related to "the true felicity." Strauss's conclusion that al-Fārābī does not name the desired way of life and, by denying that it is the virtuous one, "tacitly affirms that the contemplative way of life is the desired one" is an imposition on al-Fārābī's text. Al-Fārābī's following remarks leave no doubt that the virtuous way of life is the desired one that leads to happiness. *Falsafat Aflāṭūn*, p. 4, lines 6–9.

40. "FP," 387ff.

41. Cf. the critique of Galston, *Politics and Excellence*, 172ff.

42. Cf. J. G. A. Pocock, "Prophet and Inquisitor; or, A Church Built upon Bayonets Cannot Stand: A Comment on Mansfield's 'Strauss's Machiavelli,'" *Political Theory* 3 (1975): 388.

43. "FP," 392–93.

44. "FP," 390. See Mahdi, "Science, Philosophy, and Religion," 128.

45. Cf. *WIPP*, 150.

46. "FP," 372–73, 389, 392; *WIPP*, 147ff.

47. "CCM," 111. See *NRH*, 124–25; *CM*, 240; Gourevitch, "Philosophy and Politics," 284ff.

48. *WIPP*, 11, 39–40. Cf. Ernst R. Sandvoss, "Was ist Philosophie?," *Independent Journal of Philosophy* 1 (1977): 22–28; and the critique in Pippin, "Modern World," 457ff.

49. *WIPP*, 10; *PAW*, 37. Cf. Benardete, "Leo Strauss's *The City and Man*," 4–5; Biale, "Leo Strauss," 34–35.

50. *RCPR*, 134. See Strauss's treatment of Max Weber. *NRH*, 35–80; *WIPP*, 18–25.

51. *WIPP*, 14ff.; *AAPL*, 39–40.

52. *WIPP*, 73–74, 26. See *WIPP*, 56–77; H. Meier, *Die Denkbewegung*, 19ff.; Kauffmann, *Leo Strauss zur Einführung*, 156ff.

53. *WIPP*, 12–13.

54. *WIPP*, 13; *HPP*, 5.

55. *WIPP*, 13–14, 17, 79, 81–82; *HPP*, 1.

56. *WIPP*, 27–28, 78–79; *CM*, 12; *HPP*, 1ff. See also Gourevitch, "Philosophy and Politics," 60–61; Pippin, "Modern World," 451–52.

57. *RCPR*, 146. See *WIPP*, 34–35, 80–81; *NRH*, 135ff.; *HPP*, 35; *CM*, 45–46; Bolotin, *Strauss on Classical Political Philosophy*, 131ff.

58. *NRH*, 138–39; *AAPL*, 38.

59. *HPP*, 48; *AAPL*, 46–47; Gourevitch, "Philosophy and Politics," 300ff. See *WPP*, 163: "According to Fārābī, [. . .] the unchangeable divine law (*sharīʿa*) is only a substitute for the government of a perfect ruler who governs without written laws and who changes his ordinances in accordance with the change of times as he sees fit."

60. *NRH*, 141ff.; *RCPR*, 144ff. Cf. Plato, *Politikos* 296e–301e.

61. *WIPP*, 83.

62. *AAPL*, 8–9. In the course of Strauss's presentation of the utterly complex Aristotelian conception of natural law, Strauss presents Thomas Aquinas's and Averroes's interpretations of this conception. Aristotle does not seem to accept a fundamental separation between natural law and the requirements of political society and therefore to justify law within political life. Aquinas is of the opinion that the principles of natural law are unchangeable and applicable universally, and that the change only affects specific rules. Averroes, on the other hand, sees natural law as a matter of legal natural law, a position shared by other Muslim philosophers and Marsilius of Padua in the Christian world. Such natural law is semi-naturally dependent on human composition and general convention. Through his attempt to thread the needle between these two differing interpretations, Strauss deems natural law to be applicable only in certain concrete situations in which concrete consequential decisions must be made. Thereby, general and ostensibly unchangeable principles are required and made applicable, with intelligence assuming an important role in highlighting the situations requiring exceptions and creative maliciousness. Strauss's interpretation appears to come closest to that of Averroes as it is dependent on specific situations and the flexibility of natural law in the hands of those possessing political intelligence. *NRH*, 156–61; *PAW*, 95–141, especially 97n5; *RCPR*, 157 including references.

63. *WIPP*, 84, 87. Strauss refers to al-Fārābī's *Iḥṣā'* on this point (ch. 5). There it becomes apparent that religious jurisprudence (*fiqh*) is connected with the social sciences (*al-'ilm al-madanī*). In light of this, Strauss considers legislation less important than politics. See *GS* II, 129; "FP," 372–73, 377–81. Galston, *Politics and Excellence*, 5ff., offers a portrait of the different interpretations regarding this controversial teaching of al-Fārābī.

64. *WIPP*, 52.

65. *WIPP*, 29ff.; *AAPL*, 17, 21ff., 26–27.

66. *PAW*, 37.

67. *WIPP*, 36–37. Similarly, see Laurence V. Berns, "Political Philosophy and the Right to Rebellion," *Interpretation* 5 (1975/6): 313–14. Compare the representation of the critique on Strauss by Burnyeat, Drury, and Kent in the introduction to this work.

68. *RCPR*, 131.

69. *WIPP*, 93–94. Cf. Pippin, "Modern World," 454.

70. Gunnell, "Political Theory and Politics," 340.

71. *WIPP*, 93.

72. See Gourevitch, "Philosophy and Politics," 84, in this regard.

73. *WIPP*, 38.

74. Compare this with Kauffmann, *Leo Strauss zur Einführung*, 101ff.

75. "CPP," 92–93; *AAPL*, 102.

76. *NRH*, 82, 120ff.

77. *WIPP*, 34. Cf. Leo Strauss, *Socrates and Aristophanes* (New York: Basic Books, 1966), 314 (henceforth cited as *SA*).

78. *GS* II, 153, 211; *NRH*, 92; *AAPL*, 8; Gourevitch, "Philosophy and Politics," 287.

79. *NRH*, 167; *LAM*, 256; *HPP*, 296–97.

80. *RCPR*, 118; *NRH*, 143. Cf. the critique in Kent, "Delectation or Poison?," 45–46.

81. *NRH*, 112; *JPCM*, 464–65.

82. *RCPR*, 157–58, 162–63.

83. *NRH*, 113.

84. *RCPR*, 134.

85. *WIPP*, 91.

86. *OT*, 78ff.; Gourevitch, "Philosophy and Politics," 68ff.

87. *RCPR*, 161–62. Berns ("Political Philosophy," 309ff.) attempts to apply an emancipatory moment that he identifies in Strauss's political philosophy. However, this is not possible because Strauss's attention is not centered on the *vita activa*.

88. *NRH*, 145; *RCPR*, 132–33, 148, 159; *AAPL*, 1.

89. *CM*, 29.

90. *NRH*, 152–53.

91. Similar to Drury, *Political Ideas*, viii.

92. *RCPR*, 142.

93. *CM*, 20.

94. *WIPP*, 81–82.

95. Compare this to Kauffmann, *Leo Strauss zur Einführung*, 111ff.

96. *NRH*, 129.

97. *NRH*, 125ff., 262–63.

98. *RCPR*, 133.

99. *CM*, 1; *WIPP*, 9.

100. *RCPR*, 133.

101. *PAW*, 9–10; *GS* II, 197–98; "FP," 387ff.; *RCPR*, 222–23; *WIPP*, 29ff.; *AAPL*, 17ff.

102. *PAW*, 133. Similarly, see Bolotin, *Strauss on Classical Political Philosophy*, 137–38.

103. See *GS* II, 168–69, 177, marginalia to 98n1a.

104. *RCPR*, 158–59; "FP," 383.

105. H. Meier, *Die Denkbewegung*, 27. See Kauffmann, *Leo Strauss zur Einführung*, 15, 27–47; "Politik" and "Politisch, das Politische" in *Historisches Wörterbuch der Philosophie*, ed. Karlfried Gründer, Joachim Ritter, and Gottfried Gabriel (Basel: Schwabe AG Verlag, 1971–2007), 7:1038–72, 1072–75.

106. Cf. Berns, "Political Philosophy," 312–13.

107. *RCPR*, 132. Cf. *WIPP*, 148; "COT," 32. That the meaning of *siyāsa* was known to Strauss is evidenced by the following note on Halewi's designation of religion as *siyāsī*: "*Siyāsī*, derived from *siyāsa* (government or rule). *Siyāsa* may mean πολιτεία [. . .] as well as the rule of reason over passion [. . .]. Accordingly, *siyāsī* can sometimes be rendered by 'political' [. . .]. — The Arabic translation of πολιτεία in the sense of πολίτευμα seems to be *riyāsa*" (*PAW*, 119n72). See *PAW*, 137n133.

108. Fauzī M. Najjār, "Siyasa in Islamic Political Philosophy," in *Islamic Theology and Philosophy: Studies in Honor of George F. Hourani*, ed. Michael E. Marmura (Albany: State University of New York Press, 1984), 92; Bernard Lewis, "Siyāsa," in *In Quest of an Islamic Humanism: Arabic and Islamic Studies in Memory of Mohamed al-Nowaihi*, ed. A. H. Green (Cairo: American University in Cairo Press, 1984), 3; Lewis, *The Political Language of Islam* (Chicago: University of Chicago Press, 1988), 11.

109. Cf. Afnan, *A Philosophical Lexicon*, 131–32; *NRH*, 127, 132–33.

110. Cf. *NRH*, 135.

111. Najjār, "Siyasa in Islamic Political Philosophy," 92.

112. Najjār, 92–93.

113. Rosenthal, *Studia Semitica*, 20.

114. The other three are farming, building, and weaving.

115. Najjār, "Siyasa in Islamic Political Philosophy," 93–101.

116. Najjār, 102.

117. Lewis, "Siyāsah," 3–14; Lewis, *Political Language of Islam*, 19. As an example, two titles are named *Siyāsat an-nafs* (*Treatment of the Soul*), assumed to have been written by al-Qāsim b. Ibrahīm al-Ḥasanī (d. 860 H/246), and *Kitāb as-siyāsa fī tadbīr ar-riʾāsa*, the famous so-called *Secretum Secretorum* that was ascribed to Aristotle in the Middle Ages. See Lewis, "Siyāsah," n31; Badawī, *al-Uṣūl al-yūnāniyya li-n-naẓariyyāt as-sīyāsiyya fī l-Islām* (Cairo: Maṭbaʿat Dār al-Kutub al-Miṣriyya, 1954), introduction (32–75) and text (67–71).

118. Also Najjār, "Siyasa in Islamic Political Philosophy," 93–101.

119. al-Fārābī, *Iḥṣāʾ*, 124; *Fuṣūl*, no. 88 (Dunlop no. 83). Dunlop interprets this point a bit differently.

120. al-Fārābī, *Iḥṣāʾ*, 124ff.; *Fuṣūl*, nos. 889–92 (Dunlop nos. 84–87).

121. al-Fārābī, "Kitāb at-tanbīh ʿalā sabīl as-saʿāda," in *al-Aʿmāl al-falsafiyya*, ed. Jaʿfar Āl Yāsīn (Beirut: Dār al-Manāhil, 1413 H/1992), 237 (henceforth cited as *Tanbīh*).

122. al-Fārābī, *Tanbīh*, 256–57.

123. al-Fārābī, "Risāla fī s-siyāsa," *Al-Mashriq* 4, ed. L. Cheikho (1901): 648–53, 689–700. German translation by Georg Graf, "Farabis Traktat 'Über die Leitung,'" *Jahrbuch für Philosophie und spekulative Theologie* 16 (1902): 385–406.

124. Avicenna, *Tisʿ rasāʾil*, 73.

125. Avicenna, *Tisʿ rasāʾil*, 85.

126. Averroes, *KPP*, 135–36, 142, 150, 153, 167ff. (87, 91, 97, 99, 113ff.). The meaning of the word *siyāsa* is difficult to decipher in the context of Averroes's commentary given that the Arabic original has been lost.

127. See *Tisʿ rasāʾil*, 2–3.

128. *PAW*, 7–8, 21.

129. *PAW*, 8. Drury ("Esoteric Philosophy," 317) points to the fact that *falsafa*, the Arabic word for philosophy, "still carries a derogatory connotation, indicating empty talk, full of false human pride, setting itself above divine wisdom."

130. *PAW*; *RCPR*, 222–23.

131. *PAW*, 17.

132. *PAW*, 14; "FP," 372–75.

133. *WIPP*, 138. Cf. the analogy between the leader and the team of animals in Plato's *Phaedrus* 246a ff. Against Strauss's characterization of al-Fārābī's discussion as esoteric, see Leaman, *An Introduction*, 195ff.; Daiber, *Ruler as Philosopher*, 17–18. Galston also differs from Strauss. Cf. Galston, *Politics and Excellence*, 52. Al-Fārābī's mode of writing is essentially dialectical, given that his primary wish was to educate. The fear of persecution played a secondary role at most.

134. Mahdi, "Editio Princeps," 1, 15. Cf. *GS* II, 196n4.

135. *GS* II, 47.

136. *WIPP*, 134–37.

137. *Talkhīṣ*, p. 3, lines 1–20; *WIPP*, 134–35.

138. *Talkhīṣ*, p. 4, lines 1–9; *WIPP*, 135.

139. *WIPP*, 135–36.

140. *WIPP*, 136. See here Drury, *Political Ideas*, 24ff.

141. The concept of the nation was probably completely foreign to Plato. Thus, Strauss's usage of this term constitutes an anachronism.

142. *WIPP*, 137, 139.

143. "FP," 374. Strauss alludes here to the teaching attributed to Averroes and his school of a double-layered truth. He distances himself as well as al-Fārābī from this notion. Cf. Drury's incorrect interpretation (*Political Ideas*, 30).

144. "FP," 376–77.

145. See Rainer Marten, "'Esoterik und Exoterik' oder 'Die philosophische Bestimmung wahrheitsfähiger Öffentlichkeit,' demonstriert an Platon und Aristoteles," in Holzhey and Zimmerli, *Esoterik und Exoterik der Philosophie*, 13–31.

146. "FP," 377. Translation by H. Meier, *Die Denkbewegung*, 42. Relatedly, Meier deems Strauss's aforementioned characterization of al-Fārābī's philosophy as self-explicative.

147. "FP," 376; *WIPP*, 153. See also Drury, "Esoteric Philosophy," 317ff., in this regard.

148. "FP," 384; *PAW*, 17, 35; Drury, "Esoteric Philosophy," 317ff.

149. *PAW*, 15. Cf. Drury, "Esoteric Philosophy," 29.

150. *RCPR*, 222–23; *PAW*, 9–10. Strauss demonstrates that Islam and Judaism are distinguishable from Christianity in that they do not profess revealed theology but rather divine law as holy doctrine. This has subsequently influenced the relationship between philosophy in all faiths. Thus, Aquinas was able to enjoy a level of authority in his church that was not accessible to Maimonides and al-Fārābī in their respective communities given the need of the latter to justify philosophy in the forum of religion. The official recognition of philosophy in the Christian world leads Strauss to devalue it in many ways. The precarious situation of philosophy in the Islamic and Jewish world, on the other hand, grants it a private character and inner freedom. Since Strauss is of

the opinion that the philosopher cannot belong to any of the three monotheistic religions in their identity as a philosopher, his commentary must be seen as an implicit critique of Christianity and the so-called Christian philosophy. He is apparently of the opinion that because of the intertwined nature of philosophy and theology in the Christian world, philosophy not only loses its independence but allows for the illusion of philosophy's compatibility with religion to take hold. Cf. *RCPR*, 222; *PAW*, 8ff., 21; Drury, *Political Ideas*, 32ff.; Joseph Carpino, "Review of Frederick D. Wilhelmsen's Christianity and Political Philosophy," *Interpretation* 8 (1980): 217.

151. *GS* II, 197–98; *RCPR*, 187–206. See also Neumann, "Civic Piety and Socratic Atheism," 33ff.; Smith, "Leo Strauss: Between Athens and Jerusalem," 88–89.

152. "FP," 388.

153. *WIPP*, 221–22.

154. Gourevitch, "Philosophy and Politics," 318–19. Strauss's antidemocratic position is based on conviction. Cf. Gunnell, "Political Theory and Politics," 343.

155. *PAW*, 21.

156. See Drury, "Esoteric Philosophy," 315ff., in this regard. Stanley Rosen writes that Strauss, as opposed to Kojève, could express the eccentricity of his philosophy from behind the mask of a rabbi from the Middle Ages. Rosen, *Hermeneutics as Politics*, 107

157. Cf. Walther Ch. Zimmerli, "Esoterik und Exoterik in den Selbstdarstellungsbegriffen der Gegenwartsphilosophie: Eine historische Analyse in systematischer Absicht," in Holzhey and Zimmerli, *Esoterik und Exoterik der Philosophie*, 253–88.

158. *RCPR*, 69ff.

159. "CCM," 112.

160. Rosen (*Hermeneutics as Politics*, 113ff.) discusses Strauss's interpretation of esoteric teachings and comes to the conclusion that this method is, in and of itself, exoteric. In this context, Ellis Sandoz's remarks in Sandoz, "Medieval Rationalism or Mystic Philosophy? Reflections on the Strauss-Voegelin Correspondence," in *FPP*, 297–319, are relevant given that they thematize the influence of Averroes on Strauss's conception of political philosophy. Cf. Larmore, *Morals of Modernity*, 69–70.

161. *PAW*, 18.

162. See *GS* II, 160, marginalia to 11n28, 172ff.

163. *PAW*, 15; "FP," 387–88; *NRH*, 6; Gourevitch, "Philosophy and Politics," 65.

164. *PAW*, 15. Strauss's remark that, in the last three paragraphs of the treatise, al-Fārābī treats "philosopher," "king," "perfect man," and "researcher," on the one hand, and "legislator" and "virtuous man," on the other, as "interchangeable" does not coincide with the Arabic text: *Falsafat Aflāṭūn*, p. 22, lines 6–7, 9–10, 11–12, 15.

165. "FP," 377–78.

166. *PAW*, 22–37, especially 32ff.; *OT*, 26: "Society will always try to tyrannize thought."

167. *WIPP*, 126–27; *OT*, 205–6. Cf. *GS* II, 128–29.

168. Motzkin, Rosen, and H. Meier all identify similarities between Strauss's and al-Fārābī's writing styles: Aryeh Leo Motzkin, "On the Interpretation of Maimonides," *Independent Journal of Philosophy* 2 (1978): 41; Rosen, *Hermeneutics as Politics*, 117; H. Meier, *Die Denkbewegung*, 42–43.

169. *GS* II, 198ff.; Laurence V. Berns, "The Relation between Philosophy and Religion: Reflections on Leo Strauss's Suggestion concerning the Source and Sources of Modern Philosophy," *Interpretation* 19 (1991): 49–50, 52–53; Fradkin, "A Word Fitly Spoken," 66ff.

170. *WIPP*, 78–94; *IPP*, 125–55.

171. *TM*, 295.

172. This is Jung's judgment. Cf. Hwa Yol Jung, "Leo Strauss's Conception of Political Philosophy: A Critique," *Review of Politics* 29 (1967): 511–12.

173. Cf. Berns, "Political Philosophy," 309.

174. al-Fārābī, *Kitāb al-jamʿ baina raʾyai al-ḥakīmain*, ed. A. N. Nādir (Beirut: Dār al-Mashriq, 1960), 84–85 (henceforth cited as *Jamʿ*). German translation from Friedrich Dieterici, *Alfārābī's philosophische Abhandlungen* (Leiden: Brill, 1892), 9ff.; *Talkhīṣ*, 4.

175. *Dalālat*, 3–4.

176. Dimitri Gutas, *Avicenna and the Aristotelian Tradition: Introduction to Reading Avicenna's Philosophical Works* (Leiden: Brill, 1988), 225ff. Cf. Leaman, *An Introduction*, 18–19.

177. al-Fārābī, *Mā yanbaghī an yuqaddam qabla taʿallum falsafat Arisṭū*, in *Mabādiʾ al-falsafa al-qadīma*, 14. (Cairo: Maṭbaʿat al-Muʾayyid, 1328 H/1910). German translation by F. Dieterici in al-Fārābī, *Alfārābī's philosophische Abhandlungen* (Leiden: Brill, 1892), 89. Cf. Galston, *Politics and Excellence*, 27–35.

178. Galston, *Politics and Excellence*, 42.

179. See al-Azmeh, *Arabic Thought*, 201–11, in this regard.

180. Strauss writes Voegelin on December 10, 1950, that "the Islamic Shiʿah [. . .] has a connection with Plato's *Statesman*" (*FPP*, 75). Cf. *FPP*, 343–44; Fakhry, *Tarīkh al-falsafa*, 226ff.; Pines, "Shīʿite Terms," 189 and n168. Regarding *taqiyya* (caution, dissimulation) in Islam, see R. Strothmann, "Taḳīya," in *EI1*, 4:680–81; Etan Kohlberg, "Some Imāmī-Shīʿī Views on Taqiyya," *Journal of the American Oriental Society* 95 (1975): 395–402; Tilman Nagel, *Staat und Glaubensgemeinschaft im Islam: Geschichte der politischen Ordnungsvorstellungen der Muslime* (Zürich: Artemis, 1981), 1:206ff., 1:213, 1:216ff., 2:327ff.; Heinz Halm, *Die Schia* (Darmstadt: Wissenschaftliche Buchgesellschaft, 1988), 54–55.

181. Cf. "FP," 376; *WIPP*, 154.

182. Jung, "Strauss's Conception of Political Philosophy," 500–501.

183. Fred R. Dallmayr, "Politics against Philosophy: Strauss and Drury," *Political Theory* 15 (1987): 332.

184. According to Kent, "Delectation or Poison?," 41ff.

185. Letter to Voegelin from April 7, 1951, in Voegelin et al., *Briefwechsel*, 49–50.

186. al-Fārābī, *Falsafat Aflāṭūn*, p. 9, line 17; p. 18, line 8ff. This position is also taken by Richard Walzer, "Aspects of Islamic Political Thought: Al-Fārābī and Ibn Xaldūn," *Oriens* 16 (1963): 40ff.; and Galston, *Politics and Excellence*, 90ff. The relationship between theory and praxis in al-Fārābī's philosophy is convincingly presented by Daiber, *Ruler as Philosopher*, 1–18, especially 6, 11–15. Cf. Mahdi, "Science, Philosophy, and Religion," 145.

Epilogue

1. Strauss, *NRH*, 6.
2. *NRH*, 169.
3. *NRH*, 15, 85.
4. *PAW*, 121. Strauss apparently culled the identification of religion with exoteric philosophy from al-Fārābī, *Taḥsīl*, 90 (Mahdi trans. 77).
5. *TM*, 318, 328.
6. See Averroes, *Faṣl*, 52–53 (Müller trans. 20–21). Wilhelm Keller, "Innen und Außen als anthropologisches Problem," in Holzhey and Zimmerli, *Esoterik und Exoterik der Philosophie*, 289–314.
7. See also Drury, *Strauss and the American Right*, 20–21; P. Levine, *Nietzsche and the Modern Crisis of the Humanities*, 152ff. Cf. the debate between H. C. Mansfield Jr. and J. G. A. Pocock regarding Strauss's exoteric interpretation of Machiavelli in Harvey C. Mansfield Jr., "Strauss's Machiavelli," *Political Theory* 3 (1975): 372–84, and "Reply to Pocock," *Political Theory* 3 (1975): 402–5.
8. *GS* II, 120ff.; Victor Gourevitch, "Philosophy and Politics," 313ff.
9. Xenophon, *Memorabilia* IV.4.10. Citation in Gourevitch, "Philosophy and Politics," 310n65.
10. *FPP*, 77–78. In Leo Strauss, papers, box 11, folder 6, one can find a plan penned on October 22, 1935, for a book with the title "The Philosophy of Law (from Plato to Mendelssohn)." This plan from 1946, published by Green in *JPCM*, 467–72, is part of this earlier plan for a book.
11. William Montgomery Watt, *Islamic Philosophy and Theology* (Edinburgh: Edinburgh University Press, 1962), 88ff. Cf. Andreas Meier, *Der politische Auftrag des Islam: Programme und Kritik zwischen Fundamentalismus und Reformen; Originalstimmen aus der islamischen Welt* (Wuppertal: Hammer,

1994); Friedemann Büttner, "Der fundamentalistische Impuls und die Herausforderung der Moderne," *Leviathan* 24 (1996): 469–92.

12. al-Fārābī, *Jam*ʾ, 79–80 (Dieterici trans. 1–2).

13. *PAW*, 12.

14. In the context of this work, which explores Strauss's relationship to the Islamic philosophy of the Middle Ages, we cannot engage in an in-depth discussion of al-Fārābī's political philosophy. For this, one should turn to Galston, *Politics and Excellence*, and the various studies of Muhsin Mahdi and Hans Daiber. Walzer's commentary for *al-Madīna al-fāḍila* remains important for researching the relationship between Arabic philosophy and antiquity/Hellenism. Nevertheless, it does not offer an analysis of the internal conceptual constitution of the work. See the critique of Walzer by Ralph Lerner, "Beating the Neoplatonic Bushes," *Journal of Religion* 67 (1987): 510–17; Mahdi, "Al-Fārābī's Imperfect State."

15. al-Azmeh, *Arabic Thought and Islamic Societies*, 1–2.

16. al-Azmeh, 5.

17. "*Al-ḥayawān al-insī wa-l-ḥayawān al-madanī.*" *Taḥṣīl*, 61–62 (Mahdi trans. 60).

18. al-Azmeh, *Arabic Thought and Islamic Societies*, 38–39; Daiber, "Political Philosophy," 841. Cf. E. Rosenthal, *Political Thought*, 21ff.; Crone and Hinds, *God's Caliph*.

19. al-Fārābī, *Taḥṣīl*, 88 (Mahdi trans. 76). In this fashion, the historical priority of philosophy to religion is explained. *Taḥṣīl*, 91 (78).

20. The historian Ibn Abī Uṣaibiʿa refers to a passage from a lost manuscript by al-Fārābī regarding the origins of philosophy, which he claims blossomed in Alexandria following the death of Aristotle and from there expanded to Rome through the Roman conquest of Egypt by the emperor Augustus. It remained taught there until its suppression by Christianity, while Alexandria survived as a city of philosophy. In Majid Fakhry, *A History of Islamic Philosophy* (New York: Columbia University Press, 1970), 158. Cf. al-Fārābī, "FP," 379n52.

21. In this regard, see also al-Azmeh, *Arabic Thought and Islamic Societies*, 184, and *Muslim Kingship: Power and the Sacred in Muslim, Christian and Pagan Politics* (London: Tauris, 1997), 209ff.
    Al-Fārābī's biographers are united in their position that he studied in the northern Mesopotamian city of Ḥarrān, in which adherents of the Sabean religion, still tolerated by Islam, still lived. These Sabeans were most likely an ethnic mix of Greeks and Chaldeans. They believed in one God and at the same time worshipped the stars, which they regarded as animated and as mediators between God and humans. See Hans Lewy, *Chaldean Oracles and Theugry* (Paris: Institut des Etudes Augustiniennes, 1987); G. Fehérvári, "Ḥarrān," in *EI*², 3:227–39. Before the persecution of the Sabeans and the destruction of their last temple in the eleventh century, Ḥarrān was the site of an important school for philosophy, medicine, and astronomy in which many mathematical and astronomical texts were translated from Greek into Arabic.

The Sabeans recognized many prophets, of which the majority were philosophers. On the basis of this symbiosis between prophets and philosophers, al-Fārābī could construct the figure of the *raʾīs al-awwal* of the virtuous city. Regarding the cultural importance of Ḥarrān in Islam, see Fakhry, *A History of Islamic Philosophy*, 3–4, 25; Abū Rida in al-Kindī, *Rasāʾil al-Kindī al-falsafiyya*, ed. M. ʿA. Abū Rīda (Cairo: Dār al-Fikr, 1369 H/1950), 38–42.

In Muhsin Mahdi and Owen Wright, "Al-Fārābī," in *Dictionary of Scientific Biography*, ed. Charles Gillispie (New York: Charles Scribner's Sons, 1971), 4:523–24, Mahdi claims that al-Fārābī studied for eight years in Constantinople. In the absence of closer reference, Mahdi refers to al-Khaṭṭābī. This means that al-Fārābī understood Greek and had direct access to the sources of antiquity. Against this interpretation stands his incorrect explanation of the word *safasṭa* (Sophism) as "*ḥikma mumawwaha*" (fake wisdom): *Iḥṣāʾ*, 81; *Kitāb al-alfāẓ al-mustaʿmala fī al-mantiq*, ed. Muhsin Mahdi (Beirut: Dār al-Mashriq, 1968), 105, 10–20. See also Madkour, "Al-Fārābi," 451. A further indication against al-Fārābī's knowing Greek can be found in the intellectual confrontation in Baghdad in 932 between al-Fārābī's teacher, the translator and logician Abū Bishr Mattā bin Yūnis (ca. 870 to 940), and the grammarian and theologian Abū Saʿīd as-Sīrafī (893 to 979). While Abū Bishr defended the position of the philosophers and explained the transfer of logic and philosophical doctrines from Greek to Arabic, Abū Saʿīd accused his philosophical contemporaries of being able to read the Greek philosophers only "third hand" through faulty translations from Syriac. Al-Fārābī's knowledge of Greek would have been emphasized in the debate if he had been an exception among the philosophers criticized. See also Gerhard Endress, "Grammatik und Logik: Arabische Philologie und griechische Philosophie im Widerstreit," in *Sprachphilosophie in Antike und Mittelalte*r, ed. Burkhard Mojsisch, 163–299 (Amsterdam: Grüner, 1986).

22. al-Fārābī, *Alfārābī's philosophische Abhandlungen*, 88. See also Galston, *Politics and Excellence*, 109–27.

23. al-Fārābī, *Tanbīh*, 257–58.

24. al-Fārābī, *Taḥṣīl*, 94–95 (Mahdi trans. 80). Cf. Erwin Rosenthal, "The Place of Politics in the Philosophy of Al-Farabi," *Islamic Culture* 29 (1955): 171–72.

25. al-Fārābī, *Taḥṣīl*, 89–90 (Mahdi trans. 76).

26. al-Fārābī, *Kitāb al-ḥurūf* (*Alfarabi's Book of Letters*), ed. Muhsin Mahdi (Beirut: Dār al-Mashriq, 1990), 157–58 (henceforth cited as *Ḥurūf*).

27. al-Fārābī, *Jamʿ*, 101, 105, 109 (38, 44, 50). In *Jamʿ*, al-Fārābī refers to a similar text by Ammonius. He refers to page 95 (27) in the commentary of Porphyry to the *Nicomachean Ethics*. Porphyry also might be credited with a book that sought to portray a unity between Plato's and Aristotle's ideas: Fakhry, *Dirāsāt fī l-fikr al-ʿarabī*, 66, 74.

28. *Jamʿ*, 103 (41). See also *Jamʿ*, 80 (3); Farouk Sankari, "Plato and al-Fārābī: A Comparison of Some Aspects of Their Political Philosophy," *Muslim World* 60 (1970), 218, 222–23; Oliver Leaman, *Introduction to Medieval Islamic Philosophy*, 142.

29. *Jamʿ*, 103–4 (41–42).

30. Same as with Averroes in *TT*, 582–83 (Van Den Berg trans. 358–59).

31. In *Taḥṣīl*, 90 (Mahdi trans. 77):

> *Wa-matā ḥaṣala ʿilmu al-mawjudāt aw tuʾullimat; fa-in ʿuqilat maʾānīhā anfusuhā wa-ūqiʾa at-taṣdīqu bihā ʿan al-barāhīn al-yaqīniyya; kāna al-ʿilmu al-mushtamilu ʿalā tilka al-maʿlūmati falsafa. Wa-matā ʿulimat bi-an tukhuyilat bi-mithālātihā allatī tuḥākīhā wa-ḥaṣala at-taṣdiqu bi-mā khuyila minhā ʿan aṭ-ṭuruqi al-iqnāʾiiya, kāna al-mushtamilu ʿalā tilka al-maʿlūmāti tasmiyat al-qudamāʾ milla [. . .] Wa-humā yashtamilān ʿalā mawḍūʿāt bi-aʿyānihā, wa-kiltāhumā tuʾṭiyān al-mabādiʾ al-quṣwā li-l-mawjūdāt. Fa-innahumā tuʾṭīyān ʿilma al-mabdaʾ al-awwal wa-s-sabab al-awwal li-l mawjūdāt, wa-tuʾṭiyān al-ghaya al-quṣwā allatī li-ajlihā kūwina al-insān wa-hiya as-saʿāda al-quṣwā, wa-l-ghāya al-quṣwā fi kull wāḥid min al-mawjūdāt al-ukhar. Wa-kull mā tuʾṭīhi al-falsafa min hādhihi maʾqulān aw mutaṣawwaran; fa-inna al-milla tuʾṭīhi mutakhayyalan, wa-kull mā tubarhinuhu al-falsafa min hādhihi fa-inna al-milla tuqniʾ.*

Cf. *Madīna* [Walzer], 278, lines 8–10.

32. "*Kull mā taʾqiluhu an-nafs maṣḥūb bi-t-takhayyul.*" *Taʿliqāt*. 66, in al-Fārābī, *al-Aʿmāl al-falsafiyya*, vol. 1, ed. Jaʿfar Āl Yāsīn (Beirut: Dār al-Manāhil, 1413 H/1992), 391.

33. *Taḥṣīl*, 78–79 (Mahdi trans. 70).

34. "*Fa-l-milla muḥākiya li-l-falsafa*" (*Taḥsīl*, 90 [77]); "Fa-l-milla al-fāḍila shabīha bi-l-falsafa" (*Milla*, 46, line 22).

35. *Milla*, 46–47.

36. *Siyāsa*, 85–86 (Najjār trans. 40–41); *Milla*, 43, lines 3–4: "*Al-milla hiya ārāʾ wa-afʿāl muqaddara muqay-yada bisharāʾiṭ yarsumuhā li-l-jamʿ raʾīsuhum al-awwal yaltamis an yanāl bi-stiʿmālihim lahā gharḍan lahu fīhim aw bihim maḥdūdan.*"

37. Averroes, *TT*, 584 (Van Den Berg trans. 361). In this regard, see also Leaman, *Introduction to Medieval Islamic Philosophy*, 144–45; Lameer, *Al-Fārābī and Aristotelian Syllogistics*, 259ff.

38. Mahdi in the foreword of his edition of the text (*Hurūf*, 27, 30–34).

39. *Ḥurūf*, 131, lines 6–9, 10; *Taḥsīl*, 90–91 (Mahdi trans. 77–78). Cf. *Ḥurūf*, 132, line 9. This explains why al-Fārābī discusses religious jurisprudence (*fiqh*) and theology (*kalām*) only at the end of his list of the various sciences. *Iḥṣāʾ*, 130ff. (Najjār trans. 27ff.).

40. *Jamʿ*, 80 (3).

41. *Ḥurūf*, 153ff.

42. *Madīna* [Walzer], 280, lines 1–9. *Siyāsa*, p. 85, line 17–p.86, line 4 / 40–41. See also Leaman, *Introduction to Medieval Islamic Philosophy*, 67, 143–44.

43. "*Wa-tabayyana maʿa dhālika anna hādhihi kullahā lā tumkinu illā an takūna fī l-muduni millatun mushtarakatun tajtamiʿu bihā ārāʾuhum wa-ʿtiqādātuhum wa-afʿāluhum wa-taʾtalifu bihā aqsāmuhum wa-tartabiṭu wa-tantaẓimu, wa-ʿinda dhālika tataʿāḍadu afʿāluhum wa-tataʿāwanu ḥattā yablughū l-gharaḍa al-multamasa wa-huwa as-sʿādatu al-quṣwā.*" *Milla*, 66, lines 10–13. See also *Milla*, p. 64, line 19–p. 66, line 10.

44. al-Fārābī, *Zainūn*, 8–9. See E. Rosenthal, "Place of Politics in the Philosophy of Al-Farabi," 178; Leaman, *Introduction to Medieval Islamic Philosophy*, 147ff., 166ff.

45. al-Fārābī, *Taḥṣīl*, 90 (Mahdi trans. 77). See also in this regard Gilson, *Reason and Revelation*, 43. Regarding al-Fārābī's assessment of the dialectic, see Deborah Black, "Al-Fārābī," in Nasr and Leaman, *History of Islamic Philosophy*, 182.

46. Daiber, *Ruler as Philosopher*, 11ff. Same as in Daiber, "Political Philosophy," 848–49; Galston, *Politics and Excellence*, 90–91.

47. Al-Fārābī's conception of religion and its relationship to philosophy was not considered by al-Ghazālī, the greatest critic of philosophy, to be heterodox. If so, al-Fārābī would have received a rebuke. Al-Ghazālī's critique in *Tahāfut al-falāsifa* was aimed against philosophic interpretation of speculative religious themes. Al-Fārābī avoided the employment of religious terminology. This could perhaps be traced to his distinguishing of philosophy, which he considered universally applicable, from dialectical theology (*kalām*). Furthermore, his intellectual relationship with Christian sages could have contributed to this. See Walzer, "Aspects of Islamic Political Thought," 46ff.

48. Literally, "The Divine Viewing of the Beings." According to al-Fārābī, metaphysics deals with the principles and characteristics of being. Due to God's existing as "the absolute being" (*al-wujūd al-muṭlaq*), metaphysics and theology are closely related. See Black, "Al-Fārābī," 188.

49. *Taḥṣīl*, 63 (Mahdi trans. 61); *Tanbīh*, 256–57; *Iḥṣāʾ*, 127 (Najjār trans. 25). In *Tanbīh*, 257, al-Fārābī explains that social philosophy (*al-falsafa al-madaniyya*) includes ethics (*as-ṣināʾa al-khuluqiyya*) and political philosophy (*al-falsafa as-siyāsiyya*) within it. In *Iḥṣāʾ*, 124–25 (24–25), *al-ʿilm al-madanī* (social sciences) appears as practical philosophy within which ethics and politics are united. It is not only restricted to political science, as Strauss and his students understood. It includes practical questions and matters pertaining to social life insomuch as these matters are viewed from the perspective of human happiness or affliction. Therefore, the practically oriented religious sciences of *kalām* and *fiqh* are attributed to it, disciplines that stand at the bottom of the scientific hierarchy due to their status as historically late-arriving apparitions of the political sciences and their logical deployment of philosophical arguments. See *Milla*, 52, lines 5–6; al-Azmeh, *Arabic Thought and Islamic Societies*, 206; Galston, *Politics and Excellence*, 55ff.; Leaman, *Introduction to Medieval Islamic Philosophy*, 143–44.

50. Regarding ethics in Islamic philosophy, see Majid Fakhry, *Ethical Theories in Islam* (Leiden: Brill, 1991) and "Ethics in Islamic Philosophy," in *Routledge Encyclopedia of Philosophy*, 3:438–42; Charles Butterworth, "Ethics in Medieval Islamic Philosophy," *Journal of Religious Ethics* 11 (1983): 224–39; Richard Hovannisian, *Ethics in Islam* (Malibu, CA: Undena Publications, 1985), 17–45, 221–50; Daniel H. Frank, "Ethics," in Nasr and Leaman, *History of Islamic Philosophy*, 959–68; Leaman, "Averroes' Commentary," 195–203.

51. *Taḥṣīl*, 63–64 (Mahdi trans. 61). See *Iḥṣā'*, 127–28 (Najjār trans. 25–26); E. Rosenthal, "Place of Politics in the Philosophy of Al-Farabi," 158ff.

52. *Taḥṣīl*, 63–64 (61).

53. *Fuṣūl* [Dunlop §§], 22–23; *Milla*, 65, lines 13–14.

54. *Madīna* [Walzer], 164–74.

55. *Taḥsīl*, 64 (Mahdi trans. 61).

56. al-Azmeh, *Muslim Kingship*, 190.

57. *Milla*, 65–66. See also the analogy made between the statesman and the doctor in *Fuṣūl* [Dunlop §§], 3–4, 23–24. See also Galston, *Politics and Excellence*, 10ff., in this regard.

58. See the elucidation of the various types of systems of rulership in Galston, *Politics and Excellence*, 127–42.

59. *Iḥṣā'*, 125 (Najjār trans. 24). Cf. Galston, *Politics and Excellence*, 95ff.; al-Azmeh, *Muslim Kingship*, 213. Galston's interpretation of the concept of *siyāsa* as a "regime [. . .] in the sense of the structure and the character of a community" is not appropriate for this context (*Politics and Excellence*, 109).

60. *Milla*, 58–59.

61. See Averroes, *KPP*, 139, 144 (89, 93); Leaman, *Introduction to Medieval Islamic Philosophy*, 147–48.

62. *Iḥṣā'*, 72ff. See Black, "Al-Fārābī," 180.

63. *Fuṣūl* [Dunlop §§], 8. *Talkhīṣ*, 3, lines 1–14. Compare this with Galston, *Politics and Excellence*, 117ff.

64. Al-Fārābī composed books regarding music, the most important of which is the *Kitāb al-mūsīqā l-kabīr* (*The Large Book of Music*), in Steinschneider, *Al-Fārābī (Alpharabius)*, 79ff.; al-Fākhūrī and al-Jurr, *Tārīkh al-falsafa al-ʿarabiyya*, 376.

65. The Neoplatonic idea of cosmic musicality resembles the notion put forth in Johann Wolfgang von Goethe, *Faust*, ed. Erich Trunz (Munich: Beck, 1989), "Prologue in Heaven," lines 243–44.

66. al-Fākhūrī and al-Jurr, *Tārīkh al-falsafa al-ʿarabiyya*, 374–75; Black, "Al-Fārābī," 179; al-Azmeh, *Arabic Thought and Islamic Societies*, 116.

67. In this regard, see Black, "Al-Fārābī," 181, 190ff.

68. Similar to al-Azmeh, *Arabic Thought and Islamic Societies*, 207–8.

69. *Jam'*, 105 (43). See Black, "Al-Fārābī," 188.

70. Proclus Diadochus, *Procli Diadochi in Platonis rem publicam commentarii*, ed. Wilhelm Kroll (Leipzig: Teubner, 1899), 1:7ff.

71. al-Fārābī, *Madīna* [Walzer], 252–58, 268–78, 286–328; *Siyāsa*, 87–104 (Najjār trans. 41–53); E. Rosenthal, "The Place of Politics in the Philosophy of Al-Farabi," 168ff.; E. Rosenthal, *Political Thought*, 134ff.; Walzer, "Aspects of Islamic Political Thought," 50ff.

72. Cf. Strauss, *PAW*, 18; Gourevitch, "Philosophy and Politics," 65n23.

73. Daiber, "Political Philosophy," 844ff., 849, 858–59.

74. See Galston, *Politics and Excellence*, 7–8, in this regard.

BIBLIOGRAPHY

Abbreviations

Works frequently cited have been identified by the following abbreviations:

AAPL: Leo Strauss. *The Argument and the Action of Plato's "Laws."* Chicago: University of Chicago Press, 1975.

"CCM": Leo Strauss. "Correspondence concerning Modernity: Karl Löwith and Leo Strauss." *Independent Journal of Philosophy* 4 (1983): 105–19.

"CLS": Leo Strauss. "Correspondence: Karl Löwith and Leo Strauss." *Independent Journal of Philosophy* 5/6 (1988): 177–92.

CM: Leo Strauss. *The City and Man*. Chicago: University of Chicago Press, 1964.

"COT": Leo Strauss. "The Crisis of Our Time." In *The Predicament of Modern Politics*, ed. Harold J. Spaeth, 41–54. Detroit, MI: University of Detroit Press, 1964.

"CPP": Leo Strauss. "The Crisis of Political Philosophy." In Spaeth, *Predicament of Modern Politics*, 91–103.

Dalālat: Mūsā Ibn Maimūn [Maimonides]. *Dalālat al-ḥāʾirīn*. Ed. Ḥusain Atai. Cairo: Maktabat ath-Thaqāfa ad-Dīniyya, ca. 1980.

EI1: *Enzyklopaedie des Islam*. Ed. M. Th. Houtsma et al. Leiden: Brill, 1913–36.

EI2: *Encyclopaedia of Islam New Edition Online*. Ed. P. Bearman. Brill, 1960–2004. Published online 2012.

EI3: *Encyclopaedia of Islam Three Online*. Ed. Kate Fleet, Gudrun Krämer, Denis Matringe, John Nawas, and Devin J. Stewart. Brill, 2007–.

Falsafat Aflāṭūn: al-Fārābī. *Falsafat Aflāṭūn wa-ajzāʾuhā wa-marātib ajzāʾihā min awwalihā ilā ākhirihā* (*De Platonis philosophia*). Ed. Franz Rosenthal and Richard Walzer (*Corpus Platonicum medii alevi, Plato Arabus* 2). London: Kraus, 1943.

Falsafat Arisṭū: al-Fārābī. *Falsafat Arisṭūṭālīs wa-ajzāʾu falsafatihi wa-marātibu ajzāʾihā wa-l-mawḍiʿ alladhī minhu ibtadaʾa wa-ilaihi intahā*. Ed. Muhsin Mahdi. Beirut: 1961.

Faṣl: Averroes. *Faṣl al-maqāl wa-taqrīr mā baina ash-sharīʿa wa-l-ḥikma min al-ittiṣāl*. Ed. A. N. Nādir. Beirut: Dār al-Mashriq, 1995.

"FP": Leo Strauss. "Farabi's *Plato*." In *Louis Ginzberg Jubilee Volume on the Occasion of His Seventieth Birthday*, ed. Alexander Marx et al., 357–93. New York: American Academy for Jewish Research, 1945.

FPP: Leo Strauss and Eric Voegelin. *Faith and Political Philosophy: The Correspondence between Leo Strauss and Eric Voegelin, 1934–1964*. Ed. and trans. Peter Emberley and Barry Cooper. University Park: Pennsylvania State University Press, 1993.

Fuṣūl [Dunlop]*:* al-Fārābī. *Fuṣūl al-madanī: Aphorisms of the Statesman*. Ed. and trans. D. M. Dunlop. Cambridge: Cambridge University Press, 1961.

"GA": Leo Strauss with Jacob Klein. "A Giving of Accounts." *The College* 22, no. 1 (April 1970): 1–5.

GS I: Leo Strauss. *Die Religionskritik Spinozas und zugehörige Schriften*. Vol. 1 of *Gesammelte Schriften*, ed. Heinrich Meier. Stuttgart: J. B. Metzler, 1996.

GS II: Leo Strauss. *Philosophie und Gesetz — Frühe Schriften*. Vol. 2 of *Gesammelte Schriften*, ed. Heinrich Meier. Stuttgart: J. B. Metzler, 1997.

GS III: Leo Strauss. *Hobbes' politische Wissenschaft und zugehörige Schriften — Briefe*. Vol. 3 of *Gesammelte Schriften*, ed. Heinrich Meier. Stuttgart: J. B. Metzler, 2001.

HPP: Leo Strauss and Joseph Cropsey, eds. *History of Political Philosophy*. Chicago: University of Chicago Press, 1963.

HPW: Leo Strauss. *Hobbes' politische Wissenschaft*. Neuwied, Germany: Luchterhand, 1965.

Ḥurūf: al-Fārābī. *Kitāb al-ḥurūf* (*Alfarabi's Book of Letters*). Ed. Muhsin Mahdi. Beirut: Dār al-Mashriq, 1990.

Iḥṣāʾ: al-Fārābī. *Iḥṣāʾ al-ʿulūm*. Ed. ʿUthmān Amīn. Cairo: Maktabat al-Anjlū al-Miṣriyya, 1350 H/1931.

IPP: Leo Strauss. *An Introduction to Political Philosophy: Ten Essays by Leo Strauss*. Ed. Hilail Gildin. Detroit, MI: Wayne State University Press, 1989.

Jamʿ: al-Fārābī. *Al-Jamʿ baina raʾyai al-ḥakīmain*. Ed. A. N. Nādir. Beirut: Dār al-Mashriq 1960.

JPCM: Leo Strauss. *Jewish Philosophy and the Crisis of Modernity: Essays and Lectures in Modern Jewish Thought*. Ed. Kenneth Hart Green. Albany: State University of New York Press, 1997.

Kashf: Averroes. *Al-Kashf ʿan manāhij al-adilla fī ʿaqāʾid al-milla*. Ed. Muḥammad ʿĀbid al-Jābirī. Beirut: Markaz Dirāsāt al-Waḥda al-ʿArabiyya, 1998.

KPP: Averroes. *Kommentar des Averroes zu Platons "Politeia."* Ed. Erwin I. J. Rosenthal, trans. into German by Simon Lauer. Zürich: Spur, 1996.

LAM: Leo Strauss. *Liberalism, Ancient and Modern*. Ithaca, NY: Basic Books, 1968.

Madīna [Dieterici]: al-Fārābī. *Alfārābī's Abhandlung: Der Musterstaat*. Ed. and trans. Friedrich Dieterici. Leiden: Brill, 1895. Reprinted in Hildesheim: Olms, 1985.

Madīna [Walzer]: al-Fārābī. *Al-Fārābī on the Perfect State: Abū Naṣr al-Fārābī's Mabādiʾ ārāʾ ahl al-madīna al-fāḍila*. Ed. and trans. Richard Walzer. Oxford: Clarendon Press, 1985.

Milla: al-Fārābī. *Kitāb al-milla wa-nuṣūṣ ukhrā* (*Book of Religion and Related Texts*). Ed. Muhsin Mahdi. Beirut: Dār al-Mashriq, 1991.

"MITP": Leo Strauss. "The Mutual Influence of Theology and Philosophy." *Independent Journal of Philosophy* 3 (1979): 111–18.

Najāt: Avicenna. *An-Najāt*. Ed. M. al-Kurdī. Cairo: Matbaʿat as-Saʿāda, 1357 H/1938.

NRG: Leo Strauss. *Naturrecht und Geschichte*. German translation by Horst Boog. Stuttgart: Koehler, 1956.

NRH: Leo Strauss. *Natural Right and History*. Chicago: University of Chicago Press, 1953.

"ONI": Leo Strauss. "On a New Interpretation of Plato's Political Philosophy." *Social Research* 13 (1956): 326–67.

OT: Leo Strauss. *On Tyranny: Including the Strauss-Kojève Correspondence*. Revised and expanded ed., ed. Victor Gourevitch and Michael S. Roth. New York: Free Press, 1991.

"OVAM": Leo Strauss. "Der Ort der Vorsehungslehre nach der Ansicht Maimunis." *Monatsschrift für Geschichte und Wissenschaft des Judentums* 81 (1937): 93–105.

PAW: Leo Strauss. *Persecution and the Art of Writing*. Chicago: University of Chicago Press, 1988. Originally published in 1952.

PHG: Leo Strauss. *Philosophie und Gesetz: Beiträge zum Verständnis Maimunis und seiner Vorläufer*. Berlin: Schocker, 1935.

PPH: Leo Strauss. *The Political Philosophy of Hobbes: Its Basis and Its Genesis*. Trans. Elsa M. Sinclair. Chicago: University of Chicago Press, 1952.

"PRC": Leo Strauss. "Progress or Return? The Contemporary Crisis in Western Civilization." *Modern Judaism* 1 (1981): 17–45.

"QR": Leo Strauss. "Quelques remarques sur la science politique de Maïmonide et de Fārābī." *Revue des Etudes Juives* 100 (1936): 1–37.

RCPR: Leo Strauss. *The Rebirth of Classical Political Rationalism: An Introduction to the Thought of Leo Strauss*. Ed. Thomas L. Pangle. Chicago: University of Chicago Press, 1989.

RKS: Leo Strauss. *Die Religionskritik Spinozas als Grundlage seiner Bibelwissenschaft: Untersuchungen zu Spinozas Theologisch-Politischem Traktat.* Berlin: Akademie-Verlag, 1930.
SA: Leo Strauss. *Socrates and Aristophanes.* New York: Basic Books, 1966.
SCR: Leo Strauss. *Spinoza's Critique of Religion.* Trans. E. M. Sinclair. New York: Schocken, 1965.
Shifāʾ: Avicenna. *Ash-Shifāʾ.* Ed. G. C. Anawati and S. Zayed. Cairo: Organisme General des Imprimeries Gouvernementales, 1975.
Siyāsa: al-Fārābī. *Kitāb as-siyāsa al-madaniyya al-mulaqqab bi-mabādiʾ al-mawjūdāt.* Ed. Fauzī Mitrī Najjār. Beirut: Dār al-Mashriq, 1964.
SPPP: Leo Strauss. *Studies in Platonic Political Philosophy.* With an introduction by Thomas L. Pangle. Chicago: University of Chicago Press, 1983.
Taḥṣīl: al-Fārābī. *Kitāb taḥṣīl as-saʿāda.* Ed. Jaʿfar Āl Yāsīn. Beirut: Dār al-Andalus, 1401 H/1981.
Talkhīṣ: al-Fārābī. *Talkhīṣ Nawāmīs Aflāṭūn* (*Compendium Legum Platonis*). Ed. and trans. into Latin by Franciscus Gabrieli. London: Warburg Institute, 1952.
Tanbīh: al-Fārābī. *Kitāb at-tanbīh ʿalā sabīl as-saʿāda.* In *al-Aʿmāl al-falsafiyya,* ed. Jaʿfar Āl Yāsīn, 227–65. Beirut: Dār al-Manāhil, 1413 H/1992.
TM: Leo Strauss. *Thoughts on Machiavelli.* Glencoe, IL: Free Press, 1958.
TT: Averroes. *Tahāfut at-tahāfut.* Ed. Maurice Bouyges. Beirut: Dār al-Mashriq, 1992.
"VSF": Leo Strauss. "Eine vermißte Schrift Fārābī's." *Monatsschrift für Geschichte und Wissenschaft des Judentums* 80 (1936): 96–106.
WIPP: Leo Strauss. *What Is Political Philosophy? And Other Studies.* Glencoe, IL: Greenwood Press, 1959.
Zaynūn: al-Fārābī. *Sharḥ risālat Zaynūn al-kabīr al-yūnānī.* Hyderabad: Maṭbaʿat Majlis Dāʾirat al-Maʿārif, 1349 H/1930.

I. Primary Sources

Writings of Leo Strauss

Strauss, Leo. "Anmerkungen zu Carl Schmitt, Der Begriff des Politischen." *Archiv für Sozialwissenschaft und Sozialpolitik* 67, no. 6 (1932): 732–49. Reprinted in H. Meier, *Carl Schmitt, Leo Strauss,* 99–125.
———. *The Argument and the Action of Plato's "Laws."* Chicago: University of Chicago Press, 1975. (*AAPL*)
———. *The City and Man.* Chicago: University of Chicago Press, 1964. (*CM*)

———. "Cohens Analyse der Bibelwissenschaft Spinozas." *Der Jude* 8 (1924): 295–314.

———. "Correspondence concerning Modernity: Karl Löwith and Leo Strauss." *Independent Journal of Philosophy* 4 (1983): 105–19. ("CCM")

———. "Correspondence concerning Wahrheit und Methode: Leo Strauss and Hans-Georg Gadamer." *Independent Journal of Philosophy* 2 (1978): 5–12.

———. "Correspondence: Karl Löwith and Leo Strauss." *Independent Journal of Philosophy* 5/6 (1988): 177–92. ("CLS")

———. "The Crisis of Our Time." In *The Predicament of Modern Politics*, edited by Harold J. Spaeth, 41–54. Detroit, MI: University of Detroit Press, 1964. ("COT")

———. "The Crisis of Political Philosophy." In *The Predicament of Modern Politics*, edited by Harold J. Spaeth, 91–103. Detroit, MI: University of Detroit Press, 1964. ("CPP")

———. *Das Erkenntnisproblem in der philosophischen Lehre Fr. H. Jacobis*. PhD dissertation, University of Hamburg. Hamburg: Schröder, 1921. In Strauss, *GS* II, 237–92.

———. "Der Ort der Vorsehungslehre nach der Ansicht Maimunis." *Monatsschrift für Geschichte und Wissenschaft des Judentums* 81 (1937): 93–105. With marginalia in *GS* II, 179–94. ("OVAM")

———. *Die Religionskritik Spinozas als Grundlage seiner Bibelwissenschaft: Untersuchungen zu Spinozas Theologisch-Politischem Traktat*. Berlin: Akademie-Verlag, 1930. (*RKS*)

———. *Die Religionskritik Spinozas und zugehörige Schriften*. Vol. 1 of *Gesammelte Schriften*, edited by Heinrich Meier with the participation of Wiebke Meier. Stuttgart: J. B. Metzler, 1996. (*GS* I)

———. "Eine vermißte Schrift Fārābī's." *Monatsschrift für Geschichte und Wissenschaft des Judentums* 80 (1936): 96–106. With marginalia in *GS* II, 167–78. ("VSF")

———. "Exoteric Teaching." In *RCPR*: 63–71 and *Interpretation* 14, no. 1 (January 1986): 51–59.

———. "Farabi's *Plato*." In *Louis Ginzberg Jubilee Volume on the Occasion of His Seventieth Birthday*, edited by Alexander Marx, Saul Lieberman, Shalom Spiegel, and Solomon Zeitlin, 357–93. New York: American Academy for Jewish Research, 1945. ("FP")

———. *Hobbes' politische Wissenschaft*. Neuwied, Germany: Luchterhand, 1965. (*HPW*)

———. *Hobbes' politische Wissenschaft und zugehörige Schriften — Briefe*. Vol. 3 of *Gesammelte Schriften*, edited by Heinrich Meier with the participation of Wiebke Meier. Stuttgart: J. B. Metzler, 2001. (*GS* III)

———. "How Fārābī Read Plato's *Laws*." In *Mélanges Louis Massignon*, vol. 3, 319–44. Damascus: Institut Français de Damas, 1957. Reprinted in *WIPP*, 134–54.

———. "How to Begin to Study *The Guide of the Perplexed*." In Maimonides, *Guide*, xi–lvi.

———. *An Introduction to Political Philosophy: Ten Essays by Leo Strauss*. Edited and with an introduction by Hilail Gildin. Detroit, MI: Wayne State University Press, 1989. (*IPP*)

———. *Jewish Philosophy and the Crisis of Modernity: Essays and Lectures in Modern Jewish Thought*. Edited and with an introduction by Kenneth Hart Green. Albany: State University of New York Press, 1997. (*JPCM*)

———. *Leo Strauss on Maimonides: The Complete Writings*. Edited by Kenneth Hart Green. Chicago: University of Chicago Press, 2013.

———. "Letter to Helmut Kuhn." *Independent Journal of Philosophy* 2 (1978): 23–26.

———. *Liberalism, Ancient and Modern*. Ithaca, NY: Basic Books, 1968. (*LAM*)

———. "The Mutual Influence of Theology and Philosophy." *Independent Journal of Philosophy* 3 (1979): 111–18. ("MITP")

———. *Natural Right and History*. Chicago: University of Chicago Press, 1953. 7th ed. published in 1971. (*NRH*)

———. *Naturrecht und Geschichte*. German translation by Horst Boog. Stuttgart: Koehler, 1956. (*NRG*)

———. "On Abravanel's Philosophical Tendency and Political Teaching." With marginalia in *GS* II: 195–232.

———. "On a New Interpretation of Plato's Political Philosophy." *Social Research* 13 (1956): 326–67. ("ONI")

———. "On Collingwood's Philosophy of History." *The Review of Metaphysics* 5, no. 4 (June 1952): 559–86.

———. "On the Intention of Rousseau." *Social Research* 14 (1947): 455–87.

———. *On Tyranny: Including the Strauss-Kojève Correspondence*. Revised and expanded ed., edited by Victor Gourevitch and Michael S. Roth. New York: Free Press, 1991. (*OT*)

———. Papers, Department of Special Collections, University of Chicago Library.

———. *Persecution and the Art of Writing*. Chicago: University of Chicago Press, 1988. Originally published in 1952. (*PAW*)

———. *Philosophie und Gesetz: Beiträge zum Verständnis Maimunis und seiner Vorläufer*. Berlin: Schocker, 1935. (*PHG*)

———. *Philosophie und Gesetz — Frühe Schriften*. Vol. 2 of *Gesammelte Schriften*, edited by Heinrich Meier with the participation of Wiebke Meier. Stuttgart: J. B. Metzler, 1997. (*GS* II)

———. *Philosophy and Law: Contributions to the Understanding of Maimonides and His Predecessors*. Translated by Eve Adler. Albany: State University of New York Press, 1995.

———. *Philosophy and Law: Essays toward the Understanding of Maimonides and His Predecessors*. Translated by Fred Baumann. Philadelphia: Jewish Publication Society, 1987.

———. *The Political Philosophy of Hobbes: Its Basis and Its Genesis*. Translated by Elsa M. Sinclair. Chicago: University of Chicago Press, 1952. (*PPH*)

———. "Progress or Return? The Contemporary Crisis in Western Civilization." *Modern Judaism* 1 (1981): 17–45. ("PRC")

———. "Quelques remarques sur la science politique de Maïmonide et de Fārābī." *Revue des Etudes Juives* 100 (1936): 1–37. With marginalia in *GS* II, 125–66. ("QR")

———. *The Rebirth of Classical Political Rationalism: An Introduction to the Thought of Leo Strauss*. Selected and edited with an introduction by Thomas L. Pangle. Chicago: University of Chicago Press, 1989. (*RCPR*)

———. "Social Science and Humanism." In *The State of the Social Sciences*, edited by Leonard D. White, 415– 25. Chicago: University of Chicago Press, 1956.

———. *Socrates and Aristophanes*. New York: Basic Books, 1966. (*SA*)

———. "Some Remarks on the Political Science of Maimonides and Farabi." Translated by Robert Bartlett. *Interpretation* 18, no. 1 (Fall 1990): 3–30.

———. *Spinoza's Critique of Religion*. Translated by E. M. Sinclair. New York: Schocken, 1965. (*SCR*)

———. "The Spirit of Sparta or the Taste of Xenophon." *Social Research* 6 (1939): 502–36.

———. *Studies in Platonic Political Philosophy*. With an introduction by Thomas L. Pangle. Chicago: University of Chicago Press, 1983. (*SPPP*)

———. *Thoughts on Machiavelli*. Glencoe, IL: Free Press, 1958. (*TM*)

———. *What Is Political Philosophy? And Other Studies*. Glencoe, IL: Greenwood Press, 1959. Reprinted in Chicago: University of Chicago Press, 1988. (*WIPP*)

———. *Xenophon's Socrates*. Ithaca, NY: Cornell University Press, 1972.

———. "Zu Mendelssohns 'Sache Gottes oder die gerettete Vorsehung.'" In *Einsichten: Gerhard Krüger zum 60. Geburtstag*, edited by Klaus Oehler and Richard Schaeffler, 361–75. Frankfurt am Main: Klostermann, 1962.

———. "Zur Bibelwissenschaft Spinozas und seiner Vorläufer." *Korrespondenzblatt des Vereins zur Gründung und Erhaltung einer Akademie für die Wissenschaft des Judentums* 7 (1926): 1–22.

Strauss, Leo, and Joseph Cropsey, editors. *History of Political Philosophy*. Chicago: University of Chicago Press, 1963 (3rd ed., 1987). (*HPP*)

Strauss, Leo, with Jacob Klein. "A Giving of Accounts." *The College* 22, no. 1 (April 1970): 1–5. Reprinted in *JPCM*, 457–66. ("GA")

Strauss, Leo, and Eric Voegelin. *Faith and Political Philosophy: The Correspondence between Leo Strauss and Eric Voegelin, 1934–1964*. Edited and translated by Peter Emberley and Barry Cooper. University Park: Pennsylvania State University Press, 1993. (*FPP*)

Writings of Arab Philosophers
Writings of al-Fārābī

al-Fārābī, Abū Naṣr. *Al-Aʿmāl al-falsafiyya*. Vol. 1, edited by Jaʿfar Āl Yāsīn. Beirut: Dār al-Manāhil, 1413 H/1992.

———. *Al-Fārābī on the Perfect State: Abū Naṣr al-Fārābī's Mabādiʾ ārāʾ ahl al-madīna al-fāḍila*. Edited and translated by Richard Walzer. Oxford: Clarendon Press, 1985. (*Madīna* [Walzer])

———. *Alfārābī's Abhandlung: Der Musterstaat*. Edited and translated by Friedrich Dieterici. Leiden, Netherlands: Brill, 1895. Reprinted in Hildesheim: Olms, 1985. (*Madīna* [Dieterici])

———. *Alfarabi's Commentary and Short Treatise on Aristotle's "De Interpretatione."* Translated with an introduction and notes by F. W. Zimmermann. London: Oxford University Press, 1981.

———. *Alfarabi's philosophische Abhandlungen*. Edited by Friedrich Dieterici. Leiden, Netherlands: Brill, 1895.

———. *Alfārābī's philosophische Abhandlungen*. Translated by Friedrich Dieterici. Leiden, Netherlands: Brill, 1892. Reprinted in Frankfurt am Main: Minerva, 1976.

———. *Alfarabi's Philosophy of Plato and Aristotle*. Translated and with an introduction by Muhsin Mahdi. New York: Free Press of Glencoe, 1969.

———. *Falsafat Aflāṭūn wa-ajzā'uhā wa-marātib ajzā'ihā min awwalihā ilā ākhirihā* (*De Platonis philosophia*). Edited by Franz Rosenthal and Richard Walzer (*Corpus Platonicum medii alevi, Plato Arabus* 2). London: Kraus, 1943. (*Falsafat Aflāṭū*)

———. *Falsafat Arisṭūṭālīs wa-ajzā'u falsafatihi wa-marātibu ajzā'ihā wa-l-mawḍi' alladhī minhu ibtada'a wa-ilaihi intahā*. Edited by Muhsin Mahdi. Beirut: 1961. (*Falsafat Arisṭū*)

———. *Fuṣūl al-madanī: Aphorisms of the Statesman*. Edited with an English translation, introduction, and notes by D. M. Dunlop. Cambridge: Cambridge University Press, 1961. (*Fuṣūl* [Dunlop])

———. *Fuṣūl muntaza'a* (*Selected aphorisms*). Edited by Fauzī M. Najjār. Beirut: Dār al-Mashriq, 1971. 2nd ed., 1993.

———. *Fuṣūṣ al-ḥikam*. Edited by Ja'far Āl Yāsīn. Baghdad: Maṭba'at al-Ma'ārif, 1396 H/1976.

———. *Iḥṣā' al-'ulūm*. Edited by 'Uthmān Amīn. Cairo: Maktabat al-Anjlū al-Miṣriyya, 1350 H/1931. Third ed., 1968. An English translation of the fifth chapter by F. M. Najjār can be found in Lerner and Mahdi, *Medieval Political Philosophy*, 24–30. (*Iḥṣā'*)

———. *Kitāb al-alfāẓ al-musta'mala fī al-manṭiq*. Edited by Muhsin Mahdi. Beirut: Dār al-Mashriq, 1968.

———. *Kitāb al-burhān wa-kitāb sharā'iṭ al-yaqīn ma'a ta'ālīq Ibn Bājja 'alā al-burhān*. In *al-Manṭiq 'inda al-Fārābī*, edited by Majid Fakhry. Beirut: Dār al-Mashriq, 1987.

———. *Kitāb al-ḥurūf* (*Alfarabi's Book of Letters*). Edited by Muhsin Mahdi. Beirut: Dār al-Mashriq, 1990. (*Ḥurūf*)

———. *Al-Jam' baina ra'yai al-ḥakīmain*. Edited by A. N. Nādir. Beirut: Dār al-Mashriq 1960. German translation by Dieterici, *Alfārābī's philosophische Abhandlungen*, 1–53. English translation by Butterworth, *The Harmonization of the Two Opinions of the Two Sages: Plato the Divine and Aristotle*, 115–68 (Ithaca, NY: Cornell University Press, 2001). (*Jam'*)

———. *Kitāb al-milla wa-nuṣūṣ ukhrā* (*Book of Religion and Related Texts*). Edited by Muhsin Mahdi. Beirut: Dār al-Mashriq, 1991. (*Milla*)

———. *Kitāb al-mūsīqā al-kabīr*. Edited by Gh. A. M. Khashaba and M. A. Ḥifnī. Cairo: Dār al-Kātib al-ʿArabī li-ṭ-Ṭibāʿa wa-n-Nashr, 1966.

———. *Kitāb al-wāḥid wa-l-waḥda* (*On One and Unity*). Edited by Muhsin Mahdi. Casablanca: Les Editions Toubkal, 1989.

———. *Kitāb as-siyāsa al-madaniyya al-mulaqqab bi-mabādiʾ al-mawjūdāt*. Edited by Fauzī Mitrī Najjār. Beirut: Dār al-Mashriq, 1964. English translation by Najjār in Lerner and Mahdi, *Medieval Political Philosophy*, 32–57. (*Siyāsa*)

———. *Kitāb at-tanbīh ʿalā sabīl as-saʿāda*. In *al-Aʿmāl al-falsafiyya*, edited by Jaʿfar Āl Yāsīn, 227–65. Beirut: Dār al-Manāhil, 1413 H/1992. (*Tanbīh*)

———. *Kitāb taḥṣīl as-saʿāda*. Edited by Jaʿfar Āl Yāsīn. Beirut: Dār al-Andalus, 1401 H/1981. English partial translation by Muhsin Mahdi in Lerner and Mahdi, *Medieval Political Philosophy*, 59–83. (*Taḥṣīl*)

———. *Maqāla fī aghrāḍ mā baʿda aṭ-ṭabīʿa*. Hyderabad: Maṭbaʿat Majlis Dāʾirat al-Maʿārif, 1349 H/1930.

———. *Mā yanbaghī an yuqaddam qabla taʿallum falsafat Arisṭū*. In *Mabādiʾ al-falsafa al-qadīma*, 1–17. Cairo: Maṭbaʿat al-Muʾayyid, 1328 H/1910. German translation by F. Dieterici, *Alfārābī's philosophische Abhandlungen*, 82–91.

———. *Philosophy of Plato and Aristotle*. Revised ed., translated and with an introduction by Muhsin Mahdi. Ithaca, NY: Cornell University Press, 1969.

———. *Risāla fī faḍīlat al-ʿulūm wa-ṣ-ṣināʿāt*. Hyderabad: Maṭbaʿat Majlis Dāʾirat al-Maʿārif, 1340 H/1921.

———. *Risāla fī ithbāt al-mufāriqāt*. Hyderabad: Maṭbaʿat Majlis Dāʾirat al-Maʿārif, 1345 H/1927.

———. *Risāla fī l-ʿaql*. Edited by Maurice Bouyges. Beirut: Imprimerie Catholique, 1938.

———. "Risāla fī s-siyāsa." *Al-Mashriq* 4, edited by L. Cheikho (1901): 648–53, 689–700. German translation by Georg Graf, "Farabis Traktat 'Über die Leitung,'" *Jahrbuch für Philosophie und spekulative Theologie* 16 (1902): 385–406.

———. *Risālat ad-daʿāwī al-qalbiyya*. Hyderabad: Maṭbaʿat Majlis Dāʾirat al-Maʿārif, 1349 H/1930.

———. *Sharḥ risālat Zaynūn al-kabīr al-yūnānī*. Hyderabad: Maṭbaʿat Majlis Dāʾirat al-Maʿārif, 1349 H/1930. (*Zaynūn*)

———. *Talkhīṣ Nawāmīs Aflāṭūn* (*Compendium Legum Platonis*). Edited and translated into Latin by Franciscus Gabrieli. London: Warburg Institute, 1952. English translation by Muhsin Mahdi in Lerner and Mahdi, *Medieval Political Philosophy*, 83–94. (*Talkhīṣ*)

Writings of Avicenna

Avicenna. *Al-Ishārāt wa-t-tanbīhāt, maʿ sharḥ Naṣīr ad-Dīn aṭ-Ṭūsī*. Edited by Sulaimān Dunyā. Cairo: Dār al-Maʿārif, 1957.

———. *An-Najāt*. Edited by M. al-Kurdī. Cairo: Matbaʿat as-Saʿāda, 1357 H/1938. (*Najāt*)

———. *Ash-Shifā'*. Edited by G. C. Anawati and S. Zayed. Cairo: Organisme General des Imprimeries Gouvernementales, 1975. German translation: *Das Buch der Genesung der Seele: Die Metaphysik Avicennas*, translated and with an explanation by Max Horten (Frankfurt am Main: Minerva, 1960). (*Shifā'*)

———. *Avicenna's Psychology*. English translation of *Kitāb an-Najāt*, book 2, chapter 6, with historical-philosophical notes and textual improvements on the Cairo ed. by F. Rahman. London: Oxford University Press, 1952. Reprinted 1981.

———. *De Anima*. Edited by F. Rahman. Oxford: Oxford University Press, 1959.

———."Die Psychologie des Ibn Sīnā." ed. S. Landauer, *Zeitschrift der Deutschen Morgenländischen Gesellschaft* 29 (1875): 335–418.

———. *The Life of Ibn Sina*. Critical ed., Arabic text and English translation of the author's autobiography, translated by William E. Gohlman. Albany: State University of New York Press, 1974.

———. *Tis' rasā'il*. Constantinople: Maṭba'at al-Jawā'ib, 1298 H/1881.

———. *Tis' rasā'il*. Edited by Hasan 'Āṣī. Beirut: Dār Qābis, 1986.

———. *'Uyūn al-ḥikma* (*Fontes Sapientiae*). Edited by 'Abd ar-Raḥmān Badawī. Kuwait: Wakālat al-Maṭbū'āt, 1980.

Writings of Averroes

Averroes. *Aḍ-Ḍarūrī fī as-siyāsa: Mukhtaṣar kitāb as-siyasa li-Aflāṭūn*. Translated from Hebrew by Aḥmad Shaḥlān. Introduction and explanatory remarks by Muḥammad 'Ābid al-Jābirī: Beirut: Markaz Dirāsāt al-Waḥda al-'Arabiyya, 1998.

———. *Al-Kashf 'an manāhij al-adilla fī 'aqā'id al-milla*. Edited by Muḥammad 'Ābid al-Jābirī. Beirut: Markaz Dirāsāt al-Waḥda al-'Arabiyya, 1998. German translation in Müller, *Philosophie und Theologie von Averroes*, 26–122. (*Kashf*)

———. *Averroes' Commentry on Plato's Republic*. Edited and translated by Erwin I. J. Rosenthal. Cambridge: Cambridge University Press, 1956.

———. *Averroes on Plato's "Republic."* Translated and with an introduction and notes by Ralph Lerner. Ithaca, NY: Cornell University Press, 1974.

———. *Faṣl al-maqāl wa-taqrīr mā baina ash-sharī'a wa-l-ḥikma min al-ittiṣāl*. Edited by A. N. Nādir. Beirut: Dār al-Mashriq, 1995. German translation in Averroes, *Philosophie und Theologie von Averroes*, trans. Müller, 1–25. (*Faṣl*)

———. *Kommentar des Averroes zu Platons "Politeia."* Edited by Erwin I. J. Rosenthal, translated into German by Simon Lauer. Zürich: Spur, 1996. (*KPP*)

———. *On the Harmony of Religion and Philosophy*. Translation, with introduction and notes, of Ibn Rushd's *Kitāb faṣl al-maqāl*, with its appendix (Ḍamīma) and an extract from *Kitāb al-kashf 'an manāhij al-adilla*, by George F. Hourani. London: Luzac, 1976.

———. *Philosophie und Theologie von Averroes*. Translated by Marcus Joseph Müller. From the estate of the same, edited by Königlichen Bayarischen Akademie der Wissenschaften. Munich, 1875. Reprinted in 1974.

———. *Tahāfut at-tahāfut*. Edited by Maurice Bouyges. Beirut: Dār al-Mashriq, 1992. (*TT*)

———. *Tahafut al-Tahafut* (*The Incoherence of the Incoherence*). Translated from the Arabic with introduction and notes by Simon Van Den Bergh. London: Luzac, 1954.

———. *Talkhīṣ kitāb al-burhān* (*Middle Commentary on Aristotle's Posterior Analytics*). Critical ed. by M. M. Kassem, completed, revised, and annotated by Charles E. Butterworth and Ahmad Abd al-Magid Haridi. Cairo: al-Haiʾa al-Miṣriyya al-ʿĀmma li-l-Kitāb, 1982.

Further Primary Sources and Reference Works

Alexander Aphrodisiensis. *Praeter commentaria Scripta minora*. 1: *De anima liber cum mantissa*. 2: *Quaestiones. De fato. De mixtione*. Edited by Ivo Bruns (Supplementum Aristotelicum, 2). Berolini: Reimer, 1887–92.

al-ʿĀmirī, Abū al-Ḥasan. *As-Saʿāda wa-l-isʿād*. Edited by Mojtaba Minovi. Wiesbaden: Steiner, 1957–58.

Aristotle. *Nikomachische Ethik*. Based on the translation by Eugen Rolfes, edited by Günther Bien. Hamburg: Meiner, 1985.

———. *Politik*. Translated and annotated by Eugen Rolfes, with an introduction by Günther Bien. Hamburg: Meiner, 1981.

Cicero, Marcus Tullius. *Über die Ziele des menschlichen Handelns: De finibus bonorum et malorum*. Edited, translated, and with commentary by Olof Gigon and Laila Straume-Zimmermann. Darmstadt, Germany: Wissenschaftliche Buchgesellschaft, 1988.

Der Koran. Translation by Rudi Paret. 5th ed. Stuttgart: Kohlhammer, 1989.

Enzyklopaedie des Islam. Edited by M. Th. Houtsma et al. Leiden, Netherlands: Brill, 1913–36. (*EI1*)

Encyclopaedia of Islam New Edition Online. Edited by P. Bearman. Brill, 1960–2004. Published online 2012. (*EI2*)

Encyclopaedia of Islam Three Online. Edited by Kate Fleet, Gudrun Krämer, Denis Matringe, John Nawas, and Devin J. Stewart. Brill, 2007–. (*EI3*)

al-Ghazālī, Abū Ḥāmid. *Tahāfut al-falāsifa*. Edited by Maurice Bouyges. Beirut: Imprimerie Catholique, 1927. New ed. with an introduction by Majid Fakhry (Beirut: Dār al-Mashriq, 1990).

Goethe, Johann Wolfgang von. *Faust*. Edited and commented upon by Erich Trunz. Munich: Beck, 1989.

al-Ḥakīm at-Tirmidhī, Abū ʿAbd Allāh Muḥammad b. Alī. *Adab al-mulūk fī ḥaqāʾiq at-taṣawwuf: Ein Handbuch zur islamischen Mystik aus dem 4./10. Jahrhundert*. Edited with an introduction by Bernd Radtke. Beirut: Steiner, 1991.

———. *Die Lebensweise der Könige: Adab al-mulūk: Ein Handbuch zur islamischen Mystik*. Translated with an introduction and commentary by Richard Gramlich. Stuttgart: Steiner, 1993.

———. *Drei Schriften des Theosophen von Tirmiḏ*. Edited and translated by Bernd Radtke. Beirut: Steiner, 1992 and 1996. 2 vols.

Historisches Wörterbuch der Philosophie. Edited by Karlfried Gründer, Joachim Ritter, and Gottfried Gabriel. Basel: Schwabe AG Verlag, 1971–2007.

Ibn Bājja, Abū Bakr. *Tadbīr al-mutawaḥḥid*. Edited by Maʿan Ziade. Beirut: Dār al-Fikr, 1398 H/1978.

Ibn Khaldūn, ʿAbd ar-Raḥmān b. Muḥammad. *Al-Muqaddima*. Beirut: Manshūrāt al-Ādāb ash-Sharqiyya, 1950.

———. *The Muqaddimah: An Introduction to History*. Translated from the Arabic by Franz Rosenthal. London: Routledge / K. Paul, 1967. 3 vols.

Ibn Maimūn, Mūsā [Maimonides]. *Dalālat al-ḥāʾirīn*. Edited by Ḥusain Atai. Cairo: Maktabat ath-Thaqāfa ad-Dīniyya, ca. 1980. (*Dalālat*)

———. *The Guide of the Perplexed*. Translated by Shlomo Pines. Chicago: University of Chicago Press, 1963.

———. "Maqāla fī ṣināʿat al-manṭiq." *Ankara Üniversitesi Dil ve Tarih-Coğrafya Fakültesi Dergisi* 18 (1960): 9–64. Edited with an introduction and Turkish translation by Mubahat Türker.

Ibn Miskawaih, Abū ʿAlī Aḥmad b. Muḥammad. *Kitāb Tahdhīb al-Akhlāq wa-Taṭhīr al-Aʿrāq*. Cairo, (1329) 1908.

Ibn Ṭufail, Abū Bakr. *Ḥayy Ibn Yaqẓān*. Edited by A. N. Nādir. Beirut: al-Maṭbaʿa al-Kāthūlīkiyya, 1986.

al-Kindī. *Rasāʾil al-Kindī al-falsafiyya*. Edited by M. ʿA. Abū Rīda. Cairo: Dār al-Fikr, 1369 H/1950.

Lessing, Gotthold Ephraim. *Lessings Werke*. Edited by Kurt Wölfel. Frankfurt am Main: Insel-Verlag, 1967.

Lukrez. *Von der Natur*. Translated by Hermann Diels, with an introduction and explanation by Ernst G. Schmidt. Munich: Deutscher Taschenbuch-Verlag, 1991.

Al-Mawsūʿa al-falsafiyya al-ʿarabiyya. Edited by Maʿan Ziade. Beirut: Maʿhad al-Inmāʾ al-ʿArabī, 1986–1997.

Mawsūʿat as-siyāsa. Edited by ʿAbd al-Wahhāb al-Kaiyyālī and Kāmil Zuhairī. Beirut: al-Muʾassasa al-ʿArabiyya li-d-Dirāsāt wa-n-Nashr, 1995.

Plato. *Werke in acht Bänden*: *Griechisch und Deutsch*. Edited by Gunther Eigler. Darmstadt, Germany: Wissenschaftliche Buchgesellschaft, 1977.

Proclus Diadochus. *Procli Diadochi in Platonis rem publicam commentarii*. Vol. 1, edited by Wilhelm Kroll. Leipzig: Teubner, 1899.

al-Qifṭī, Jamāl ad-Dīn Abū al-Ḥasan ʿAlī b. Yūsuf. *Taʾrīkh al-ḥukamāʾ*. Based on the preparatory work of August Müller, edited by Julius Lippert. Leipzig: Dieterich, 1903.

Rasāʾil Ikhwān aṣ-Ṣafāʾ. Edited by Buṭrus al-Bustānī. Beirut: Dār Ṣādir, 1376 H/1957. 4 vols.

ar-Rāzī, Abū Bakr Muḥammad b. Zakariyyā. *Kitāb as-sīra al-falsafiyya*. (v.i. Kraus, "Raziana I" and "Raziana II").

ar-Rāzī, Abū Ḥātim. *Aʿlām an-nubuwwa* (*The Peaks of Prophecy*). Edited with introduction and notes by Salah al-Sawy and Ghulamriḍa Aʿwānī. English introduction by Seyyed Hossein Nasr. Tehran: Imperial Iranian Academy of Philosophy, 1977.

"Risālat Dāmistiyūs [Themistius] fī s-siyāsa." *al-Mašriq* 11 (1920): 881–89. Edited by L. Cheikho. (More recent edition in Daiber, *Bibliography*, 1:887.)

Routledge Encyclopedia of Philosophy. Edward Craig, general editor. London: Routledge, 1998. 10 vols.

Schmitt, Carl. *Der Begriff des Politischen*. Berlin: Duncker and Humblot, 1963. Originally published in 1932.

———. *Politische Theologie: Vier Kapitel zur Lehre von der Souveränität*. Munich: Duncker and Humblot, 1922.

ash-Shahrastānī, Abū al-Fatḥ Muḥammad. *Al-Milal wa-n-niḥal*. Edited by Aḥmad Fahmī Muḥammad. Cairo: al-Maktaba al-Ḥusain at-Tijāriyya, 1368 H/1949.

as-Sijistānī, Abū Yaʿqūb Isḥāq. *Kitāb ithbāt an-nubūʾāt*. Edited by ʿĀrif Tāmir. Beirut: al-Maṭbaʿa al-Kāthūlīkiyya, 1966.

Spinoza, Benedictus de. *Tractatus de intellectus emendatione: Ethica*. Edited by Konrad Blumenstock. Darmstadt, Germany: Wissenschaftliche Buchgesellschaft, 1989.

———. *Tractatus theologico-politicus*. Edited by Günter Gawlick and Friedrich Niewöhner. Darmstadt, Germany: Wissenschaftliche Buchgesellschaft, 1989.

Voegelin, Eric, Alfred Schütz, Leo Strauss, and Aron Gurwitsch. *Briefwechsel über "Die Neue Wissenschaft der Politik."* Edited by Peter J. Opitz in cooperation with the Eric Voegelin. Archive of the Ludwig Maximilian University of Munich. Freiburg, Germany: Alber, 1993.

II. Secondary Literature

Abdel Haleem, M. "Early kalām." In Nasr and Leaman, *History of Islamic Philosophy*, 71–88.

Abed, Shukri B. *Aristotelian Logic and the Arabic Language in Alfārābī*. Albany: State University of New York Press, 1991.

Achtenberg, Deborah. "Human Being, Beast and Good: The Place of Human Happiness According to Aristotle and some Twentieth-Century Philosophers." In *The Crossroads of Norm and Nature. Essays on Aristotle's "Ethics" and "Metaphysics,"* edited by May Sim, 29–50. Lanham: Rowan and Littlefield, 1995.

Adler, Eve. "Leo Strauss's *Philosophie und Gesetz*." In Udoff, *Strauss's Thought*, 183–226.

Afnan, Soheil M. *A Philosophical Lexicon in Persian and Arabic*. Beirut: Dār al-Mashriq, 1969.

Akasoy, Anna, Alexander Fidora, and Douglas M. Dunlop, editors. *The Arabic Version of the "Nicomachean Ethics."* Leiden: Brill, 2005.

al-Aʿsam, ʿAbd al-Amīr. *Al-Muṣṭalaḥ al-falsafī ʿinda al-ʿarab: nuṣūṣ min at-turāth al-falsafī fī ḥudūd al-ashyāʾ wa-rusūmihā*. Cairo: al-Haiʾa al-Miṣriyya al-ʿĀmma li-l-Kitāb, 1989.

al-Azmeh, Aziz. *Arabic Thought and Islamic Societies*. London: Croom Helm, 1986.

———. *Muslim Kingship: Power and the Sacred in Muslim, Christian and Pagan Politics*. London: Tauris, 1997.

al-Maʿsumi, Muhammad Saghir Hasan. "Al-Fārābī." In Sharif, *A History of Muslim Philosophy*, 704–17.

al-Miṣbāḥī, Muḥammad. *Min al-ma'rifa ilā al-'aql: Buḥūth fī naẓariyyat al-'aql 'inda al-'arab*. Beirut: Dār aṭ-Ṭalī'a li-ṭ-Ṭibā'a wa-n-Nashr, 1990.

al-Miskīnī, Fatḥī. *Falsafat an-nawābit*. Beirut: Dār aṭ-Ṭalī'a li-ṭ-Ṭibā'a wa-n-Nashr, 1997.

Alon, Ilai. "Fārābī's Funny Flora: Al-Nawābit as 'Opposition'." *Arabica* 37 (1990): 56–90.

Altizer, Thomas J. J. "The Theological Conflict between Strauss and Voegelin." In Strauss and Voegelin, *FPP*, 267–77.

Anastaplo, George. "Leo Strauss at the University of Chicago." In Deutsch and Murley, *Strauss, the Straussians*, 3–30.

Anderson, Abraham. "Descartes Contra Averroes? The Problem of Faith and Reason in the Letter of Dedication to the Meditationes." *Interpretation* 23 (1996): 209–21.

Anṭūn, Faraḥ. *Ibn Rushd wa-falsafatuhu*. Beirut: Dār al-Fārābī, 1988.

Arberry, A. J. "An Arabic Treatise on Politics." *Islamic Quarterly* 2 (1955): 9–21.

———. "Some Plato in an Arabic Epitome." *Islamic Quarterly* 2 (1955): 86–99.

Arkes, Hadley. "Athens and Jerusalem: The Legacy of Leo Strauss." In Novak, *Strauss and Judaism*, 1–23.

———. "Strauss on Our Minds." In Deutsch and Murley, *Strauss, the Straussians and the American Regime*, 69–89.

Arkush, Allan. "Leo Strauss and Jewish Modernity." In Novak, *Strauss and Judaism*, 111–30.

Assheuer, Thomas. "Frohe Botschaft für Höhlenbewohner: Die frühen Schriften von Leo Strauss, dem unsterblichen Kronzeugen der konservativen Kulturkritik." *Die Zeit* 7 (February 1998).

Assmann, Jan. *Politische Theologie zwischen Ägypten und Israel*. Munich: Carl Friedrich von Siemens Stiftung, 1995.

Badawī, 'Abd ar-Raḥmān. *Aflāṭūn fī l-Islām*. 2nd ed. Beirut: Dār al-Andalus, 1980.

———. *Arisṭū 'inda al-'arab*. Cairo: Maktabat an-Nahḍa al-Miṣriyya, 1947.

———. *Al-Uṣūl al-yūnāniyya li-n-naẓariyyāt as-sīyāsiyya fī l-Islām*. Cairo: Maṭba'at Dār al-Kutub al-Miṣriyya, 1954.

Bagley, Paul J. "Harris, Strauss, and Esoterism in Spinoza's Tractatus theologico-politicus." *Interpretation* 23 (1996): 387–415.

Beiner, Roland. "Hannah Arendt and Leo Strauss: The Uncommenced Dialogue." *Political Theory* 18 (1990): 238–54.

Belaval, Yvon. "Pour une sociologie de la philosophie." *Critique* 9 (1953): 852–66.

Bello, Iysa A. *The Medieval Islamic Controversy between Philosophy and Theology: Ijmā' and ta'wīl in the Conflict between al-Ghazālī and Ibn Rushd*. Leiden, Netherlands: Brill, 1989.

Benardete, Seth. "Leo Strauss's *The City and Man*." *Political Science Reviewer* 8 (1978): 1–20.

———. *On Plato's* Symposium/*Über Platons* Symposion. Munich: Carl Friedrich von Siemens Stiftung, 1994.

Berman, Lawrence V. "The Broken Mirror: Ibn Rushd's Aristotle on Ethics." In *L'homme et son Univers au moyen Âge*, edited by Christian Wenin, 763–68. Louvain la Neuve, Belgium: Editions de l'Institut Supérieur de Philosophie, 1986.

———. "Maimonides, the Disciple of Alfārābi." *Israel Oriental Studies* 4 (1974): 154–78.

———. "The Political Interpretation of the Maxim: The Purpose of Philosophy is the Imitation of God." *Studia Islamica* 15 (1961): 53–61.

Berns, Laurence V. "Leo Strauss 1899–1973." *Independent Journal of Philosophy* 2 (1978): 1–3.

———. "Political Philosophy and the Right to Rebellion." *Interpretation* 5 (1975/6): 309–15.

———. "The Prescientific World and Historicism: Some Reflections on Strauss, Heidegger, and Husserl." In Udoff, *Strauss's Thought*, 169–81.

———. "The Relation between Philosophy and Religion: Reflections on Leo Strauss's Suggestion concerning the Source and Sources of Modern Philosophy." *Interpretation* 19 (1991): 43–60.

Bertman, Martin A. "Alfarabi and the Concept of Happiness in Medieval Islamic Philosophy." *Islamic Quarterly* 14 (1970): 122–25.

———. "Hobbes' Science of Politics and Plato's Laws." *Independent Journal of Philosophy* 2 (1978): 47–53.

Biale, David. "Leo Strauss: The Philosopher as Weimar Jew." In Udoff, *Strauss's Thought*, 31–40.

Black, Deborah. "Al-Fārābī." In Nasr and Leaman, *History of Islamic Philosophy*, 178–97.

Bloom, Allan. "Leo Strauss: September 20, 1899 – October 18, 1973." *Political Theory* 2 (1974): 373–92.

Bluhm, Harald. "Besprechung von Leo Strauss, Die Religionskritik Spinozas und zugehörige Schriften, unter Mitwirkung von Wiebke Meier herausgegeben Heinrich Meier, Stuttgart, Weimar 1996." *Politische Vierteljahresschrift* 38 (1997): 389–91.

———. "Besprechung von Leo Strauss, *Philosophie und Gesetz — Frühe Schriften*, unter Mitwirkung von Wiebke Meier herausgegeben Heinrich Meier, Stuttgart, Weimar 1996 und Clemens Kauffmann, *Leo Strauss zur Einführung*." *Politische Vierteljahresschrift* 39 (1998): 411–12.

———. "Leo Strauss' politische Philosophie und das 'einfache Denken.'" In *Bürgerreligion und Bürgertugend: Debatten über die vorpolitischen Grundlagen politischer Ordnung*, edited by Herfreid Münkler, 203–27. Baden-Baden, Germany: Nomos, 1996.

———. "Philosophie, jüdische Identität und Intellektuellenkritik bei Franz Rosenzweig und Leo Strauss." In *Intellektuelle in der Weimarer Republik*, edited by Wolfgang Bialas and Georg G. Iggers, 233–52. Frankfurt am Main: Lang, 1996.

———. "Variationen des Höhlengleichnisses — Kritik und Restitution politischer Philosophie bei Hannah Arendt und Leo Strauss." *Deutsche Zeitschrift für Philosophie* 47 (1999): 911–33.

Bolotin, David. "Leo Strauss on Classical Political Philosophy." *Interpretation* 22 (1994): 129–42.

Brague, Rémi. "Athens, Jerusalem, Mecca: Leo Strauss's 'Muslim' Understanding of Greek Philosophy." *Poetics Today* 19, no. 2 (1998): 235–59.

———. *The Law of God: The Philosophical History of an Idea*. Translated by Lydia G. Cochrane. Chicago: University of Chicago Press, 2007.
———. "Leo Strauss and Maimonides." In Udoff, *Strauss's Thought*, 93–114.
Broadie, Alexander. "Maimonides." In Nasr and Leaman, *History of Islamic Philosophy*, 725–38.
Bruell, Christopher. "A Return to Classical Political Philosophy and the Understanding of the American Founding." In Deutsch and Nicgorski, *Strauss: Political Philosopher*, 325–38.
———. *Xenophons Politische Philosophie*. Translated from the American by Friedrich Griese and Heinrich Meier. Munich: Carl Friedrich von Siemens Stiftung, 1994.
Bubner, Rüdiger. "Verfolgung und die Kunst des Schreibens. Die Moderne ist antiker, als sie glaubt: Eine Renaissance von Leo Strauss?" *Frankfurter Allgemeine Zeitung*, December 3, 1996.
Burns, J. H., editor. *The Cambridge History of Medieval Political Thought c. 350 – c. 1450*. Cambridge: Cambridge University Press, 1988.
Burnyeat, M. F. "Sphinx without a Secret." *New York Review of Books* 32, no. 9 (May 1985): 30–36.
Busche, Jürgen. "Eine neue Form der Tapferkeit, die jede Flucht in den Wahn verbietet." *Der Tagesspiegel* (December 1997).
Butterworth, Charles E. "Die politischen Lehren von Avicenna und Averroës." In *Pipers Handbuch der Politischen Ideen*, vol. 2, edited by Iring Fetscher and Herfried Münkler, 141–74. Munich: Piper, 1993.
———. "Ethics and Classical Islamic Philosophy: A Study of Averroes' Commentary on Plato's Republic." In Hovannisian, *Ethics in Islam*, 17–45.
———. "Ethics in Medieval Islamic Philosophy." *Journal of Religious Ethics* 11 (1983): 224–39.
———. "Medieval Islamic Philosophy and the Virtue of Ethics." *Arabica* 34 (1987): 221–50.
———. "New Light on the Political Philosophy of Averroès." In Hourani, *Essays on Islamic Philosophy and Science*, 118–27.
———. "On Paul Sigmund's 'Review of Ralph Lerner's *Averroes on Plato's Republic*.'" *Political Theory* 4 (1976): 505–6.
———. "The Origins of al-Rāzī's Political Philosophy." *Interpretation* 20 (1993): 237–57.
———. *Philosophy, Ethics and Virtuous Rule: A Study of Averroes' Commentary on Plato's* "Republic." Cairo: American University in Cairo, 1986.
———. *The Political Aspects of Islamic Philosophy: Essays in Honor of Muhsin S. Mahdi*. Cambridge, MA: Harvard University Press, 1992.
———. "Rhetoric and Islamic Political Philosophy." *International Journal of Middle East Studies* 3 (1972): 187–98.
———. "What Is Political Averroism?" In Niewöhner and L. Sturlese, *Averroismus*, 239–250.
Büttner, Friedemann. "Der fundamentalistische Impuls und die Herausforderung der Moderne." *Leviathan* 24 (1996): 469–92.

Calder, Norman. "Philosophy of Islamic Law." In *Routledge Encyclopedia of Philosophy*, 5:457–60.

Cantor, Paul A. "Leo Strauss and Contemporary Hermeneutics." In Udoff, *Strauss's Thought*, 267–314.

Carpino, Joseph. "Review of Frederick D. Wilhelmsen's Christianity and Political Philosophy." *Interpretation* 8 (1980): 204–22.

Caton, Hiram. "Der hermeneutische Weg von Leo Strauss." *Philosophisches Jahrbuch* 80 (1973): 171–82.

Choueiri, Youssef. "Islamic Fundamentalism." In *Routledge Encyclopedia of Philosophy*, 5:9–12.

Clay, Diskin. "On a Forgotten Kind of Reading." In Udoff, *Strauss's Thought*, 253–66.

Cohen, Hermann. "Charakteristik der Ethik Maimunis." In *Jüdische Schriften*, by Hermann Cohen, 3:221–89. Berlin: Schwetschke, 1924.

———. "Spinoza über Staat und Religion, Judentum und Christentum." In *Jüdische Schriften*, by Hermann Cohen, 3:290–372. Berlin: Schwetschke, 1924.

Colmo, Christopher A. *Breaking with Athens: Alfarabi as Founder*. Lanham, MD: Lexington Books, 2005.

———. "Reason and Revelation in the Thought of Leo Strauss." *Interpretation* 18 (1990): 145–60.

———. "Reply to Lowenthal." *Interpretation* 18 (1990–91): 313–15.

———. "Theory and Practice: Alfarabi's *Plato* Revisited." *American Political Science Review* 86 (1992): 966–76.

Conrad, Lawrence I., editor. *The World of Ibn Ṭufayl: Interdisciplinary Perspectives on Ḥayy ibn Yaqẓān*. Leiden, Netherlands: Brill, 1996.

Crone, Patricia. "Dahrīs." In *EI3*. Published December 1, 2012, last updated July 19, 2021. http://dx.doi.org/10.1163/1573-3912_ei3_COM_25780.

Crone, Patricia, and Martin Hinds. *God's Caliph: Religious Authority in the First Centuries of Islam*. Cambridge: Cambridge University Press, 1986.

Cropsey, Joseph, editor. *Ancients and Moderns: Essays on the Tradition of Political Philosophy in Honor of Leo Strauss*. New York: Basic Books, 1964.

Cropsey, Joseph, Harry V. Jaffa, Allan Bloom, Ernest J. Weinrib, Thomas L. Pangle, Robert Gordis, and M. F. Burnyeat. "The Studies of Leo Strauss: An Exchange." Letters to the editor, *New York Review of Books* 32, no. 15 (October 1985): 41–44.

Daiber, Hans. *Aetius Arabus: Die Vorsokratiker in arabischer Überlieferung*. Wiesbaden, Germany: Steiner, 1980.

———. *Bibliography of Islamic Philosophy*. Leiden, Netherlands: Brill, 1999. 2 vols.

———. "The Ismaili Background of Fārābī's Political Philosophy — Abū Ḥātim ar-Rāzī as a Forerunner of Fārābī." In *Gottes ist der Orient – Gottes ist der Okzident: Festschrift für Abdoljavad Falaturi zum 65. Gebutstag*, edited by Udo Tworuschka, 143–150. Vienna: Orientalisches Institut der Universität Wien, 1991.

———. *Neuplatonische Pythagorica in arabischem Gewande: Der Kommentar des Iamblichus zu den Carmina aurea. Ein verlorener griechischer Text in arabischer Überlieferung*. Amsterdam: North-Holland, 1995.

———. "Political Philosophy." In Nasr and Leaman, *History of Islamic Philosophy*, 841–85.

———. "Prophetie und Ethik bei Fārābī (gest. 339/950)." In *L'homme et son Univers au moyen Âge, edited by Christian Wenin*, 729–53. Louvain-la-Neuve, Belgium: Editions de l'Institut Supérieur de Philosophie, 1986.

———. *The Ruler as Philosopher: A New Interpretation of al-Fārābī's View*. Amsterdam: North-Holland, 1986.

Dallmayr, Fred R. "Politics against Philosophy: Strauss and Drury." *Political Theory* 15 (1987): 326–37.

Dannhauser, Werner J. "Athens and Jerusalem or Jerusalem and Athens?" In *Leo Strauss and Judaism: Jerusalem and Athens Critically Revisited*, edited by David Novak, 155–71. Lanham: Rowan and Littlefield, 1996.

———. "Leo Strauss as Citizen and Jew." *Interpretation* 17 (1990): 433–47.

———. "Leo Strauss: Becoming Naïve Again." *American Scholar* 44 (1975): 636–42.

Das, Aileen R. "Paul Kraus, Richard Walzer, and Galen's *Com. Tim.*" *Arabic Sciences and Philosophy* 31 (2021): 225–56.

Davidson, Herbert Alan. "Alfarabi and Avicenna on the Active Intellect." *Viator* 3 (1972): 109–78.

———. *Alfarabi, Avicenna, and Averroes, on Intellect: Their Cosmologies, Theories of the Active Intellect, and Theories of Human Intellect*. Oxford: Oxford University Press, 1992.

———. *Proofs for Etemity, Creation and the Existence of God in Medieval Islamic and Jewish Philosophy*. Oxford: Oxford University Press, 1987.

Deutsch, Kenneth L., and John A. Murley, editors. *Leo Strauss, the Straussians and the American Regime*. Lanham, MD: Rowan and Littlefield, 1999.

Deutsch, Kenneth L., and Walter Nicgorski, editors. *Leo Strauss: Political Philosopher and Jewish Thinker*. Lanham, MD: Rowan and Littlefield, 1994.

Deutsch, Kenneth L. and Walter Soffer, editors. *The Crisis of Liberal Democracy: A Straussian Perspective*. Albany: State University of New York Press, 1987.

Devigne, Robert. *Recasting Conservatism: Oekeshot, Strauss, and the Response to Postmodernism*. New Haven, CT: Yale, 1994.

Diesendruck, Z. "Maimonides' Lehre von der Prophetie." In *Jewish Studies in Memory of Israel Abrahams*, edited by George Alexander Kohut, 74–134. New York: Press of the Jewish Institut of Religion, 1927.

Drury, Shadia. "The Esoteric Philosophy of Leo Strauss." *Political Theory* 13 (1985): 315–37.

———. *Leo Strauss and the American Right*. New York: Palgrave Macmillan, 1997.

———. "Leo Strauss's Classic Natural Right Teaching." *Political Theory* 15 (1987): 299–315.

———. *The Political Ideas of Leo Strauss*. New York: Palgrave Macmillan, 1988.

———. "Strauss, Leo (1899–1973)." In *Routledge Encyclopedia of Philosophy*, 9:167–68.

Dunin-Borkowski, Stanislaus von. *Der junge De Spinoza*. Münster: Aschendorff, 1910.

Efros, Isarel. "Palquera's Reshit Hokmah and Alfarabi's Iḥṣa al-ʿulum." *Jewish Quarterly Review*, n.s., 25 (1934–1935): 227–35.

Enayat, Hamid. "An Outline of the Political Philosophy of the Rasāʾil of the Ikhwān al-Ṣafāʾ." In *Ismāʿīlī Contributions to Islamic Culture*, edited by Seyyed Hossein Nasr, 25–49. Tehran: Imperial Iranian Academy of Philosophy, 1977.
Endress, Gerhard."'Der erste Lehrer': Der arabische Aristoteles und das Konzept der Philosophie im Islam." In *Gottes ist der Orient – Gottes ist der Okzident: Festschrift für Abdoljavad Falaturi zum 65. Gebutstag*, edited by Udo Tworuschka, 151–81. Vienna: Orientalisches Institut der Universität Wien, 1991.
———. "Die wissenschaftliche Literatur." In *Grundriß der Arabischen Philologie: Literaturwissenschaft*, vol. 2, edited by Helmut Gätje, 400–506. Wiesbaden: Reichert, 1987.
———. "Grammatik und Logik: Arabische Philologie und griechische Philosophie im Widerstreit." In *Sprachphilosophie in Antike und Mittelalter*, edited by Burkhard Mojsisch, 163–299. Amsterdam: Grüner, 1986.
———. "Wissen und Gesellschaft in der islamischen Philosophie des Mittelalters." In *Pragmatik: Handbuch pragmatischen Denkens*. Vol. 1, *Pragmatisches Denken von den Ursprüngen bis zum 18. Jahrhnudert*, edited by Herbert Stachowiak, 219–45. Hamburg: Meiner, 1986.
———. *The Works of Yahia Ibn ʿAdi: An Analytical Inventory*. Wiesbaden, Germany: Reichert, 1977.
Ess, Josef van. *Theologie und Gesellschaft im 2. und 3. Jahrhundert Hidschra: Eine Geschichte des religiösen Denkens im frühen Islam*. Vol. 4. Berlin: de Gruyter, 1997.
Fackenheim, Emil L. *Jewish Philosophers and Jewish Philosophy*. Edited by Michael L. Morgan. Bloomington: University of Indiana Press, 1996.
Fahd, T. "Nubuwwa." In *EI2*, 8:93–97. 1998.
Fakhry, Majid. *Dirāsāt fī l-fikr al-ʿarabī*. Beirut: Dār an-Nahār, 1982.
———. *Ethical Theories in Islam*. Leiden, Netherlands: Brill, 1991.
———. "Ethics in Islamic Philosophy." In *Routledge Encyclopedia of Philosophy*, 3:438–42.
———. "Al-Fārābī and the Reconciliation of Plato and Aristotle." *Journal of the History of Ideas* 26 (1965): 469–78.
———. "Greek Philosophy: Impact on Islamic Philosophy." In *Routledge Encyclopedia of Philosophy*, 4:155–59.
———. *A History of Islamic Philosophy*. New York: Columbia University Press, 1970. Arabic translation: *Tarīkh al-falsafa al-islāmiyya*, trans. Kamāl al-Yāzijī (Beirut: ad-Dār al-Muttaḥida li-n-Nashr, 1979).
———. *Ibn Rushd: Failasūf Qurṭuba*. Beirut: al-Maṭbaʿa al-Kāthūlīkiyya, 1992.
———. *Tarīkh al-falsafa al-islāmiyya* [*A History of Islamic Philosophy*]. Translated to Arabic by Kamāl al-Yāzijī. Beirut: ad-Dār al-Muttaḥida li-n-Nashr, 1979.
al-Fākhūrī, Ḥannā, and Khalīl al-Jurr. *Tārīkh al-falsafa al-ʿarabiyya*. Beirut: Muʾassasat Badrān wa-Šurakāh, 1966.
Festugière, A. J. *Epicure et ses dieux*. Paris: Presses Universitaires de France, 1946.
Fleischer, Heinrich Leberecht. "Bemerkungen zu Gaubari's 'entdeckten Geheimnissen' u. a." *Zeitschrift der Deutschen Morgenländischen Gesellschaft* 21 (1867): 274–76.

Fradkin, Hillel. "Philosophy and Law: Leo Strauss as a Student of Medieval Jewish Thought." In Deutsch and Nicgorski, *Strauss: Political Philosopher*, 129–42.
———. "A Word Fitly Spoken: The Interpretation of Maimonides and the Legacy of Leo Strauss." In Novak, *Strauss and Judaism*, 55–85.
Frank, Daniel H. "Ethics." In Nasr and Leaman, *History of Islamic Philosophy*, 959–68.
Frank, Richard Macdonough. "Reason and Revealed Law: A Sample of Parallels and Divergences in Kalam and Falsafa." In *Recherches d'islamologie: Recueil d'articles offert a Georges C. Anawati et Louis Gardet par leurs collegues et amis*, edited by Olivier Lacombe, 123–38. Louvain: Peeters, 1977.
Fuller, Timothy. "Philosophy, Faith, and the Question of Progress." In *Faith and Political Philosophy: The Correspondence between Leo Strauss and Eric Voegelin, 1934–1964*, edited by Peter Emberley and Barry Cooper, 279–95. University Park: Pennsylvania State University Press, 1993.
Gadamer, Hans-Georg. *Die Idee des Guten zwischen Plato und Aristoteles*. Heidelberg: Winter, 1978.
———. "Interview on Leo Strauss." *Interpretation* 12 (1984): 1–13.
———. "Philosophizing in Opposition: Strauss and Voegelin on Communication and Science." In *Faith and Political Philosophy: The Correspondence between Leo Strauss and Eric Voegelin, 1934–1964*, edited by Peter Emberley and Barry Cooper, 249–59. University Park: Pennsylvania State University Press, 1993.
———. *Wahrheit und Methode: Grundzüge einer philosophischen Hermeneutik*. Tübingen: Mohr, 1960.
Galston, Miriam. "Philosopher-King v. Prophet." *Israel Oriental Studies* 8 (1978): 204–18.
———. *Politics and Excellence: The Political Philosophy of Alfarabi*. Princeton, NJ: Princeton University Press, 1990.
———. "Realism and Idealism in Avicenna's Political Philosophy." *Review of Politics* 41 (1979): 561–77.
Gauthier, Léon. *La thèorie d'Ibn Rochd (Averroès) sur les rapports de la religion et de la philosophie*. Paris: Leroux, 1909.
Gebhardt, Carl. "Spinoza und der Platonismus." In *Chronicon Spinozanum*. The Hague: Hagae Comitis, 1921. 5 vols.
Gebhardt, Jürgen. "Leo Strauss: The Quest for Truth in Times of Perplexity." In Kielmansegg et al., *Hannah Arendt and Leo Strauss*, 81–104.
Ghaussy, Abdul Aziz. "Aufbau und System der Philosophie und der Wissenschaften im Islam nach al-Kindī, al-Fārābī und Ibn Sīnā in ihren systematischen Werken." PhD dissertation, Universität Hamburg, 1961.
Gildin, Hilail. "The First Crisis of Modernity: Leo Strauss on the Thought of Rousseau." *Interpretation* 20 (1992–93): 157–64.
———. Introduction. In Strauss, *IPP*, vii–xxiv.
Gilson, Etienne. *Reason and Revelation in the Middle Ages*. New York: Scribner, 1938.
Goeje, M. J. de. "Gaubari's 'entdeckte Geheimnisse.'" *Zeitschrift der Deutschen Morgenländischen Gesellschaft* 20 (1866): 485–510.
Goodenough, Erwin R. "The Political Philosophy of Hellenistic Kingship." *Yale Classical Studies* 1 (1928): 55–102.

Goodmann, Lenn E. *Avicenna*. London: Routledge, 1992.

Gourevitch, Victor. "Philosophy and Politics." *Review of Metaphysics* 22 (1968): 58–84, 281–328.

Grabmann, Martin. *Der Lateinische Averroismus des 13. Jahrhunderts und seine Stellung zur christlichen Weltanschauung*. Sitzungsberichte der Bayerischen Akademie der Wissenschaften, Philosophisch-historische Abteilung, 609–87. Munich: Verlag der Bayerische Akademie der Wissenschaften, 1931.

Gramlich, Richard. *Die Wunder der Freunde Gottes: Theologien und Erscheinungsformen des Islamischen Heiligenwunders*. Wiesbaden, Germany: Steiner, 1987.

———. *Schlaglichter über das Sufitum*. Stuttgart: Steiner, 1990.

Green, Kenneth Hart. "'In the Grip of the Theological-Political Predicament': The Turn to Maimonides in the Jewish Thought of Leo Strauss." In Udoff, *Strauss's Thought*, 41–74.

———. Introduction. In Strauss, *JPCM*, 1–84.

———. *Jew and Philosopher: The Return to Maimonides in the Jewish Thought of Leo Strauss*. Albany: State University of New York Press, 1993.

Griffel, Frank. *Apostasie und Toleranz: Voraussetzungen und Entwicklung von al-Ġazālis Urteil gegen die Philosophie und die Reaktionen der Philosophen*. Leiden, Netherlands: Brill, 2000.

Gross, Raphael. "Zwischen Athen und Jerusalem: Zum ersten Band der gesammelten Schriften von Leo Strauss." *Neue Zürcher Zeitung*, October 1, 1996.

Gunnell, John G. "Political Theory and Politics: The Case of Leo Strauss." *Political Theory* 13 (1985): 339–61.

———. *Political Theory: Tradition and Interpretation*. Cambridge: Winthrop, 1979.

———. "Strauss before Straussianism: Reason, Revelation, and Nature." In Deutsch and Nicgorski, *Strauss: Political Philosopher*, 107–28.

Gutas, Dimitri. *Avicenna and the Aristotelian Tradition: Introduction to Reading Avicenna's Philosophical Works*. Leiden, Netherlands: Brill, 1988.

———. "Fārābī's Knowledge of Plato's *Laws*." *International Journal of the Classical Tradition* 4 (1999): 410–16.

———. "Galen's *Synopsis* of Plato's *Laws* and Fārābī's *Talḫīṣ*." In *The Ancient Tradition in Christian and Islamic Hellenism: Studies on the Transmission of Greek Philosophy and Sciences Dedicated to H. J. Drossaart Lulofs on His Ninetieth Birthday*, edited by Gerhard Endress and Remke Kruk, 101–19. Leiden, Netherlands: Research School CNWS, 1997.

———. *Greek Thought, Arabic Culture: The Graeco-Arabic Translation Movement in Baghdad and Early ʿAbbāsid Society (2nd–4th / 8th–10th Centuries)*. London: Routledge, 1998.

———. "Paul the Persian on the Classification of the Parts of Aristotle's Philosophy: A Milestone between Alexandria and Baġdād." *Der Islam* 60 (1983): 231–67.

———. "The Rebirth of Philosophy and the Translations into Arabic." In *Philosophy in the Islamic World*, edited by Ulrich Rudolph, Rotraud Hansberger, and Peter Adamson, 95–142. Leiden, Netherlands: Brill, 2017.

Guttmann, Julius. *Die Philosophie des Judentums*. Munich: Reinhardt, 1933.

———. "Elia del Medigos Verhältnis zu Averroës in seinem Bechinat ha-dat." In *Jewish Studies in Memory of Israel Abrahams*, edited by George Alexander Kohut, 192–208. New York: Press of the Jewish Institute of Religion, 1927. Reprinted 1980.

———. *Philosophie der Religion oder Philosophie des Gesetzes?* Jerusalem: Israel Academy of Sciences and Humanities, 1974.

———. *Religion und Wissenschaft im mittelalterlichen und im modernen Denken.* Berlin: Philo-Verlag, 1922.

———. "Zur Kritik der Offenbarungsreligion in der islamischen und jüdischen Philosophie." *Monatsschrift für Geschichte und Wissenschaft des Judentums* 78 (1934): 456–64.

Habermas, Jürgen. *Auch eine Geschichte der Philosophie*. Frankfurt: Suhrkamp, 2019. 2 vols.

Haddad, Fuad Sayyid. *Alfarabi's Theory of Communication*. Beirut: American University of Beirut, 1989.

Hallowell, John. "Review of Natural Right and History." *American Political Science Review* 48 (1954): 538–41.

———. "Review of Thoughts on Machiavelli." *Journal of Politics* 3 (1959): 300–3.

Halm, Heinz. *Die Schia*. Darmstadt, Germany: Wissenschaftliche Buchgesellschaft, 1988.

Harbison, Warren. "Irony and Deception." *Independent Journal of Philosophy* 2 (1978): 89–94.

Harvey, Steven. "Did Alfarabi Read Plato's *Laws*?" *Medioevo: Rivista di storia della filosofia medievale* 28 (2003): 51–68.

———. "Leo Strauss's Developing Interest in Alfarabi and Its Reverberations in the Study of Medieval Islamic Philosophy." In *The Pilgrimage of Philosophy: A Festschrift for Charles E. Butterworth*, edited by René M. Paddags, Waseem El-Rayes, and Gregory A. McBrayer, 60–84. South Bend, IN: St. Augustine's Press, 2019.

———. "The Story of a Twentieth-Century Jewish Scholar's Discovery of Plato's Political Philosophy in Tenth-Century Islam: Leo Strauss' Early Interest in the Islamic Falāsifa." In *Modern Jewish Scholarship on Islam in Context: Rationality, European Borders, and the Search for Belonging*, edited by Ottfried Fraisse, 219–44. Berlin: de Gruyter, 2018.

Hayoun, Maurice-Ruben and Alain de Libera. *Averroès et l'Averroïsme: Que sais-je?* Paris: Presses Universitaires de France, 1991.

Heinimann, Felix. *Nomos und Physis: Herkunft und Bedeutung einer Antithese im griechischen Denken des 5. Jahrhunderts*. Darmstadt, Germany: Wissenschaftliche Buchgesellschaft, 1965.

Heinrichs, Wolfhart. "Die antike Verknüpfung von phantasia und Dichtung bei den Arabern." *Zeitschrift der Deutschen Morgenländischen Gesellschaft* 128 (1978): 252–98.

Heller, Erdmute and Hassouna Mosbahi. *Islam, Demokratie, Moderne: Aktuelle Antworten arabischer Denker*. Munich: Beck, 1998.

Hentschke, Ada Babette. *Politik und Philosophie bei Plato und Aristoteles: Die Stellung der "NOMOI" im Platonischen Gesamtwerk und die politische Theorie des Aristoteles*. Frankfurt am Main: Klostermann, 1971.

Herz, Dietmar. "Besprechung von Shadia Drury, the Political Ideas of Leo Strauss." *Philosophisches Jahrbuch* 98 (1991): 430–32.

———. "Der Philosoph als Verführer: Überlegungen zur Philosophie des Leo Strauss." *Archiv für Rechts- und Sozialphilosophie* 79 (1993): 544–49.

Himmelfarb, Milton. "On Leo Strauss." *Commentary* 58 (1974): 60–66. Replies to the article and the author's response in *Commentary* 59 (1975): 14, 16.

Holmes, Stephan. "Truths for Philosophers Alone?" *Times Literary Supplement*, December 1–7, 1989, 1319–24.

———. "Wahrheit für Wenige: Leo Strauss und die Gefährlichkeit der Philosophie." *Merkur* 44 (1990): 554–69.

Holzhey, Helmut, and Walther Ch. Zimmerli, editors. *Esoterik und Exoterik der Philosophie: Beiträge zu Geschichte und Sinn philosophischer Selbstbestimmung*. Basel: Schwabe, 1977.

Horovitz, J. "Nabī." In *EI1*, 3:867. 1936.

Hourani, George F. "Averroes on Good and Evil." *Studia Islamica* 16 (1962): 13–40.

———, editor. *Essays on Islamic Philosophy and Science*. Albany: State University of New York Press, 1975.

Hovannisian, Richard G. *Ethics in Islam*. Malibu, CA: Undena Publications, 1985.

Hübener, Wolfgang. "Unvorgreifliche Überlegungen zum möglichen Sinn des Topos 'politischer Averroismus'." In Niewöhner and L. Sturlese, *Averroismus*, 222–38.

Hyman, Arthur. "Jewish Philosophy in the Islamic World." In Nasr and Leaman, *History of Islamic Philosophy*, 677–95.

Inati, Shams. "Ibn ʿAdi, Yahya (893–974)." In *Routledge Encyclopedia of Philosophy*, 4:599–601.

———. "Ibn Sīnā." In Nasr and Leaman, *History of Islamic Philosophy*, 231–46.

Iqbal, Muḥammad. *Tajdīd al-fikr ad-dīnī fī l-Islām*. Translated by ʿAbbās Maḥmūd. Cairo: Maṭbaʿat Lajnat at-Taʾalif wa-t-Tarjama, 1968.

Irwin, Terence. "Review of Xenophon's Socrates." *Philosophical Review* 83 (1974): 409–13.

Ivry, Alfred. "Leo Strauss on Maimonides." In Udoff, *Strauss's Thought*, 75–91.

———. "Towards a Unified View of Averroes' Philosophy." *Philosophical Forum* 4 (1972): 87–113.

al-Jābirī, Muḥammad ʿĀbid. *Ibn Rushd: Sīra wa-fikr*. Beirut: Markaz Dirāsāt al-Waḥda al-ʿArabiyya, 1998.

———, editor. "Madkhal: Jadīd fī l-fikr as-sīyāsī bi-t-turāth al-ʿarabī" and "Muqaddima taḥlīliyya: Muwājahat as-siyāsa bi-khiṭāb siyāsī." In *Aḍ-Ḍarūrī fī s-siyāsa: Mukhtaṣar kitāb as-siyāsa li-Aflāṭūn*, by Ibn Rushd, Abū al-Walīd Muḥammad b. Aḥmad b. Muḥammad al-Andalusī al-Mālikī, naqalahu min al-ʿibriyya ilā al-ʿarabiyya Aḥmad Shaḥlān, maʿa madkhal wa-muqaddima taḥlīliyya wa-shurūḥ lil-mushrif ʿala al-mashrūʿ Muḥammad ʿĀbid al-Jābirī, 13–68. Beirut: Markaz Dirāsāt al-Waḥda al-ʿArabiyya, 1998.

Jackson, Michael Peter. "Leo Strauss's Teaching: A Study of Thoughts on Machiavelli." PhD dissertation, Georgetown University, 1985.
Jaffa, Harry V. "Dear Professor Drury." *Political Theory* 15 (1987): 316–25.
———. "The Legacy of Leo Strauss." *Claremont Review* 3 (1984): 14–21.
———. "Leo Strauss, the Bible, and Political Philosophy." In Deutsch and Nicgorski, *Strauss: Political Philosopher*, 195–210.
———. "Strauss at One Hundred." In Deutsch and Murley, *Strauss, the Straussians*, 41–48.
Jidʿān, Fahmī. "Al-Fārābī: Madkhal ilā tajribat al-ʿilm wa-l-fiʿl ʿindahu." In *al-Māḍī fī l-ḥāḍir*, edited by Fahmī Jidʿān, 259–308. Beirut: al-Muʾassasa al-ʿArabiyya li-d-Dirāsāt wa-n-Nashr, 1997.
Jones, H. *The Epicurean Tradition*. London: Routledge, 1989.
Jung, Hwa Yol. "Leo Strauss's Conception of Political Philosophy: A Critique." *Review of Politics* 29 (1967): 492–517.
———. "Two Critics of Scientism: Leo Strauss and Edmund Husserl." *Independent Journal of Philosophy* 2 (1978): 81–88.
Kamp, Andreas. *Die politische Philosophie des Aristoteles und ihre metaphysischen Grundlagen*. Freiburg: Alber, 1985.
Kartheininger, Markus. *Heterogenität: Politische Philosophie im Frühwerk von Leo Strauss*. Munich: Wilhelm Fink, 2006.
Kauffmann, Clemens. *Leo Strauss zur Einführung*. Hamburg: Junius, 1997.
Keller, Wilhelm. "Innen und Außen als anthropologisches Problem." In Holzhey and Zimmerli, *Esoterik und Exoterik der Philosophie*, 289–314.
Kendall, Willmoore. "Review of Thoughts on Machiavelli." *Philosophical Review* 75 (1966): 247–54.
Kennington, Richard H. "Strauss's *Natural Right and History*." In Udoff, *Strauss's Thought*, 227–52.
Kent, James Andrew. "Delectation or Poison? Reading Leo Strauss." BA thesis, Harvard College, 1993.
Kerr, Malcolm H., editor. *Islamic Studies: A Tradition and Its Problems*. Malibu, CA: Undena Publications, 1980.
Kielmansegg, Peter Graf, Horst Mewes, and Elisabeth Glaser-Schmidt, editors. *Hannah Arendt and Leo Strauss: German Émigrés and American Political Thought after World War II*. Cambridge: Cambridge University Press, 1995.
Klein-Franke, Felix. *Die klassische Antike in der Tradition des Islam*. Darmstadt: Wissenschaftliche Buchgesellschaft, 1980.
———. "Zur Überlieferung der platonischen Schriften im Islam." *Israel Oriental Studies* 3 (1973): 120–39.
Klosko, George. "The 'Straussian' Interpretation of Plato's Republic." *History of Politcal Thought* 7 (1986): 275–93.
Köhler, Lotte, editor. *Hannah Arendt, Heinrich Blücher: Briefe 1936–1968*. Munich: Piper, 1996.
Köhler, Lotte, and Hans Saner, editors. *Hannah Arendt, Karl Jaspers: Briefwechsel 1926–1969*. Munich: Piper, 1987.

Kohlberg, Etan. "Some Imāmī-Shīʿī Views on Taqiyya." *Journal of the American Oriental Society* 95 (1975): 395–402.

Korth, Hildegard. *Guide to the Leo Strauss Papers*. Department of Special Collections, University of Chicago Library, 1978.

Kraemer, Joel L. "The Death of an Orientalist: Paul Kraus from Prague to Cairo." In *The Jewish Discovery of Islam: Studies in Honor of Bernard Lewis*, edited by Martin Kramer. Tel Aviv: Moshe Dayan Center for Middle Eastern and African Studies, Tel Aviv University, 1999.

———. "Maimonides on the Philosophic Sciences in His Treatise on the Art of Logic." In *Perspectives on Maimonides: Philosophical and Historical Studies*, edited by Joel L. Kraemer, 77–104. Oxford: Oxford University Press, 1991.

———. "The Medieval Arabic Enlightenment." In *The Cambridge Companion to Leo Strauss*, edited by Steven Smith. Cambridge: Cambridge University Press, 2009.

Kraemer, Joel L., and Josef Stern. "Shlomo Pines on the Translation of Maimonides' *Guide of the Perplexed*." *Journal of Jewish Thought and Philosophy* 8 (1998): 13–24.

Kraus, Paul. "Beiträge zur Islamischen Ketzergeschichte." *Rivista degli Studi Orientali* 14 (1934): 93–129, 335–379.

———. "Plotin chez les Arabes." *Bulletin de l'Institut d'Égypte* 23 (1941): 263–95.

———. "Raziana I." *Orientalia* 4 (1935): 300–21.

———. "Raziana II." *Orientalia* 5 (1936): 335–56, 358–78.

Kraut, Richard, editor. *The Cambridge Companion to Plato*. Cambridge: Cambridge University Press, 1995.

Krüger, Gerhard. "Besprechung von Die Religionskritik Spinozas als Grundlage seiner Bibelwissenschaft." *Deutsche Literaturzeitung* 51 (1931): 2407–12.

Kügelgen, Anke von. *Averroes und die arabische Moderne: Ansätze zu einer Neubegründung des Rationalismus im Islam*. Leiden, Netherlands: Brill, 1994.

Kuhn, Helmut. "Naturrecht und Historismus." *Independent Journal of Philosophy* 2 (1978): 13–21.

Kuksewicz, Zdzislaw. "The Latin Averroism of the Late Thirteenth Century." In Niewöhner and L. Sturlese, *Averroismus*, 101–13.

Kymlicka, Will. *Politische Philosophie heute*. Frankfurt am Main: Campus, 1997.

Lachterman, David R. "Laying Down the Law: The Theological-Political Matrix of Spinoza's Physics." In Udoff, *Strauss's Thought*, 123–54.

Lambton, Ann. *State and Government in Medieval Islam*. Oxford: Oxford University Press, 1981.

Lameer, Joep. *Al-Fārābī and Aristotelian Syllogistics: Greek Theory and Islamic Practice*. Leiden, Netherlands: Brill, 1994.

Lampert, Laurence. *Leo Strauss and Nietzsche*. Chicago: University of Chicago Press, 1996.

Larmore, Charles. *The Morals of Modernity*. Cambridge: Cambridge University Press, 1996.

Lawrence, Frederick G. "Leo Strauss and the Fourth Wave of Modernity." In Novak, *Strauss and Judaism*, 131–53.

Leaman, Oliver. *Averroes and His Philosophy*. Oxford: Clarendon Press, 1988.

———. "Averroes' Commentary on Plato's *Republic*, and the Missing Politics." In *Across the Mediterranean Frontiers: Trade, Politics and Religion, 650–1450*. Selected Proceedings of the International Medieval Congress, University of Leeds, July 10–13, 1995 / July 8–11, 1996. Edited by Dionisius A. Agius and Ian Richard Netton, 195–203. Turnhout, Belgium: Brepols, 1997.

———. "Concept of Philosophy in Islam." In *Routledge Encyclopedia of Philosophy*, 5:5–9.

———. "Does the Interpretation of Islamic Philosophy Rest on a Mistake?" *International Journal for Middle East Studies* 12 (1980): 525–38.

———. "Introduction: The Jewish Philosophical Tradition in the Islamic Cultural World." In Nasr and Leaman, *History of Islamic Philosophy*, 673–76.

———. *An Introduction to Medieval Islamic Philosophy*. Cambridge: Cambridge University Press, 1992.

———. "Is Averroes an Averroist?" In Niewöhner and L. Sturlese, *Averroismus*, 9–22.

———. "Islamic Philosophy." In *Routledge Encyclopedia of Philosophy*, 5:13–16.

———. "Jewish Averroism." In Nasr and Leaman, *History of Islamic Philosophy*, 769–80.

———. "Jewish Averroism." In *Routledge Encyclopedia of Philosophy*, 1:598–602.

———. *Moses Maimonides*. London: Routledge, 1990.

Lerner, Ralph. "Beating the Neoplatonic Bushes." *Journal of Religion* 67 (1987): 510–17.

———. *Maimonides' Vorbilder menschlicher Vollkommenheit*. Munich: Carl Friedrich von Siemens Stiftung, 1996.

Lerner, Ralph, and Muhsin Mahdi, editors. *Medieval Political Philosophy: A Sourcebook*. Glencoe, IL: Free Press of Glencoe, 1963.

Levine, David Lawrence. "Without Malice but with Forethought: A Response to Burnyeat." In Deutsch and Nicgorski, *Strauss: Political Philosopher*, 353–72.

Levine, Peter. *Nietzsche and the Modern Crisis of the Humanities*. Albany: State University of New York Press, 1995.

Lewis, Bernard. *The Political Language of Islam*. Chicago: University of Chicago Press, 1988.

———. "Siyāsah." In *In Quest of an Islamic Humanism: Arabic and Islamic Studies in Memory of Mohamed al-Nowaihi*, edited by A. H. Green, 3–14. Cairo: American University in Cairo Press, 1984.

Lewy, Hans. *Chaldean Oracles and Theurgy*. Paris: Institut d'Études Augustiniennes, 1987.

Libera, Alain de. "Existe-t-il une noétique 'averroiste'? Note sur la réception latine d'Averroès au XIIIe et XIVe siècle." In Niewöhner and L. Sturlese, *Averroismus*, 51–80.

Lilla, Mark. "The Enemy of Liberalism." *New York Review of Books* 44, no. 8 (May 1997): 38–44.

Lisi, Francisco L. *Einheit und Vielheit des platonischen Nomosbegriffs: Eine Untersuchung zur Beziehung von Philosophie und Politik bei Platon*. Königstein, Germany: Hain, 1985.

Lowenthal, David. "The Case for Teleology." *Independent Journal of Philosophy* 2 (1978): 95–105.

———. "Comment on Colmo." *Interpretation* 18 (1990): 161–62.

———. "Leo Strauss's Studies in Platonic Political Philosophy." *Interpretation* 13 (1985): 297–320.

Madkour, Ibrahim. "Al-Fārābi." In Sharif, *A History of Muslim Philosophy*, 450–68.

Mahdi, Muhsin. "Alfarabi." In Strauss and Cropsey, *HPP*, 182–202.

———. "Alfarabi against Philoponus." *Journal of Near Eastern Studies* 26 (1967): 233–60.

———. *Alfarabi and the Foundation of Islamic Political Philosophy*. Chicago: University of Chicago Press, 2001.

———. "Alfarabi on Philosophy and Religion." *Philosophical Forum* N.S. 4 (1972): 5–25.

———. "The Editio Princeps of Fārābī's *Compendium Legum Platonis*." *Journal of Near Eastern Studies* 20 (1961): 1–24.

———. "Al-Fārābī's Imperfect State." Review of Walzer, *Al-Farabi on the Perfect State*. *Journal of the American Oriental Society* 110 (1990): 691–726.

———. "Islamic Philosophy in Contemporary Islamic Thought." In *God and Man in Contemporary Islamic Thought*, proceedings of the Philosophy Symposium of AUB 6.–10.2.1967, edited by Charles H. Malek. Beirut: American Univerity of Beirut, 1972.

———. "Man and His Universe in Medieval Arabic Philosophy." In *L'homme et son Univers au moyen Âge*, edited by Christian Wenin, 102–13. Louvain la Neuve, Belgium: Editions de l'Institut Supérieur de Philosophie, 1986.

———. "Remarks on Alfarabi's Attainment of Happiness." In Hourani, *Essays on Islamic Philosophy and Science*, 47–66.

———. "Remarks on Averroes' *Decisive Treatise*." In *Islamic Theology and Philosophy. Studies in Honor of George F. Hourani*, edited by Michael E. Marmura, 188–202. Albany: State University of New York Press, 1984.

———. "Remarks on 1001 Nights." *Interpretation* 3 (1973): 157–68.

———. Review of al-Fārābī, *Fuṣūl al-Madanī* ("Aphorisms of the Statesman"). *Journal of Near Eastern Studies* 23 (1964): 140–43.

———. "Science, Philosophy, and Religion in Alfarabi's *Enumeration of the Sciences*." In *The Cultural Context of Medieval Learning*, edited by J. E. Murdoch and E. D. Sylla, 113–47. Boston: Reidel, 1975.

Mahdi, Muhsin, and Owen Wright. "Al-Fārābī." In *Dictionary of Scientific Biography*, edited by Charles Gillispie, 4:523–26. New York: Charles Scribner's Sons, 1971.

Manser, G. M. "Das Verhältnis von Glaube und Wissen bei Averroës." In *Jahrbuch für Philosophie und spekulative Theologie*, 24:398–408, 25:9–34, 163–179. Paderborn, Germany: Schöningh, 1910, 1911.

Mansfield, Harvey C., Jr. "Reply to Pocock." *Political Theory* 3 (1975): 402–5.

———. "Strauss's Machiavelli." *Political Theory* 3 (1975): 372–84.

Margolióuth, D. "The Discussion between Abū Bishr Mattā and Abū Saʿīd al-Sīrāfī on the Merits of Logic and Grammar." *Journal of the Royal Asiatic Society*, n.s. 37 (1905): 79–112.

Markowski, Mieczyslaw H. "Die Grundzüge der Philosophie in Erfurt im 14. Jahrhundert." In Niewöhner and L. Sturlese, *Averroismus*, 187–200.

Marten, Rainer. "'Esoterik und Exoterik' oder 'Die philosophische Bestimmung wahrheitsfähiger Öffentlichkeit,' demonstriert an Platon und Aristoteles." In Holzhey and Zimmerli, *Esoterik und Exoterik der Philosophie*, 13–31.

McAllister, Ted V. *Revolt against Modernity: Leo Strauss, Eric Voegelin, and the Search for a Postliberal Order*. Lawrence: University of Kansas Press, 1996.

McDaniel, Robb. "The Nature of Inequality: Uncovering the Modern in Leo Strauss's Idealist Ethics." *Political Theory* 26 (1998): 317–45.

———. "The Philosopher's Jeremiad: Prophecy and Political Philosophy in Leo Strauss and Emmanuel Levinas." PhD dissertation, Vanderbilt University, 1998.

McGinnis, Jon. *Avicenna*. Oxford: Oxford University Press, 2010.

McShea, Robert J. "Political Philosophy, Human Nature, the Passions." *History of Politcal Thought* 7 (1986): 205–18.

Meier, Andreas. *Der politische Auftrag des Islam: Programme und Kritik zwischen Fundamentalismus und Reformen; Originalstimmen aus der islamischen Welt*. Wuppertal, Germany: Hammer, 1994.

Meier, Christian. *Die Entstehung des Politischen bei den Griechen*. Frankfurt: Suhrkamp, 1995.

Meier, Heinrich. *Carl Schmitt and Leo Strauss: The Hidden Dialog*. Translated by J. Harvey Lomax, foreword by Joseph Cropsey. Chicago: University of Chicago Press, 1995.

———. *Carl Schmitt, Leo Strauss und der "Begriff des Politischen": Zu einem Dialog unter Abwesenden*. Stuttgart: J. B. Metzler, 1988.

———. *Carl Schmitt, Leo Strauss und der "Begriff des Politischen": Zu einem Dialog unter Abwesenden*. Expanded ed. Stuttgart: J. B. Metzler, 1998.

———. *Die Denkbewegung von Leo Strauss: Die Geschichte der Philosophie und die Intention des Philosophen*. Stuttgart: J. B. Metzler, 1996.

———. *Die Lehre Carl Schmitts: Vier Kapitel zur Unterscheidung Politischer Theologie und Politischer Philosophie*. Stuttgart: J. B. Metzler, 1994.

———. "How Strauss Became Strauss." In *Reorientation: Leo Strauss in the 1930s*, edited by Martin D. Yaffe and Richard S. Ruderman, 13–32. New York: Palgrave Macmillan, 2014.

———. "Strauss, Leo." In *Metzler Philosophen Lexikon*, edited by Bernd Lutz, 860–65. Stuttgart: J. B. Metzler, 1988.

Mettler, Heinrich. "Lessing und Leibniz: Bemerkungen zur Exoterik anhand dreier Abschnitte aus 'Leibniz von den ewigen Strafen.'" In Holzhey and Zimmerli, *Esoterik und Exoterik der Philosophie*, 207–17.

Mitsis, Phillip. *Epicurus' Ethical Theory*. Ithaca, NY: Cornell University Press, 1988.

Mojsisch, Burkhard. "Averroistische Elemente in der Intellekttheorie Dietrichs von Freiburg." In Niewöhner and L. Sturlese, *Averroismus*, 180–86.

Montgomery, James E. "Leo Strauss and the Alethiometer." In *Renaissance Averroism and Its Aftermath: Arabic Philosophy in Early Modern Europe*, edited by Anna Akasoy and Guido Giglioni, 285–320. Dordrecht, Netherlands: Springer, 2013.

Morgan, Michael M. "Teaching Leo Strauss as a Jewish and General Philosopher." In *Jewish Philosophy and the Academy*, edited by Emil L. Fackenheim and Raphael Jospe, 174–88. Cranbury, NJ: Fairleigh Dickinson University Press, 1996.

Morris, James W. "The Philosopher-Prophet in Avicenna's Political Philosophy." In *The Political Aspects of Islamic Philosophy: Essays in Honor of Muhsin S. Mahdi*, edited by Charles Butterworth, 152–98. Cambridge, MA: Harvard University Press, 1992.

Morrisey, Will. "Review of Susan Orr, Jerusalem and Athens: Reason and Revelation in the Work of Leo Strauss." *Interpretation* 24 (1997): 243–47.

Motzkin, Aryeh Leo. "On the Interpretation of Maimonides." *Independent Journal of Philosophy* 2 (1978): 39–46.

Münkler, Herfried. "Carl Schmitt als Politischer Theologe." *Neue Politische Literatur* 41 (1996): 273–75.

Myers, Todd Eric. "Nature and the Divine: Classical Greek Philosophy and the Political in the Thought of Leo Strauss and Eric Voegelin." PhD dissertation, Louisiana State University, 1997.

Nagel, Tilman. "Kiṣaṣ al-anbiyāʾ." In *EI2*, 5:180–81. 1986.

———. *Staat und Glaubensgemeinschaft im Islam: Geschichte der politischen Ordnungsvorstellungen der Muslime*. Zürich: Artemis, 1981.

Najjār, Fauzī M. "Al-Fārābī on Political Science." *Muslim World* 48 (1958): 94–103.

———. "Fārābī's Political Philosophy and Shiʿism." *Studia Islamica* 14 (1961): 57–72.

———. "Political Philosophy in Islam." *The Islamic Quarterly* 20–22 (1978): 121–32.

———. "Siyasa in Islamic Political Philosophy." In *Islamic Theology and Philosophy: Studies in Honor of George F. Hourani*, edited by Michael E. Marmura, 92–110. Albany: State University of New York Press, 1984.

Namazi, Rasoul. *Leo Strauss and Islamic Political Thought*. Cambridge: Cambridge University Press, 2022.

Nasr, Seyyed Hossein. "Ibn Sīnā's 'Oriental Philosophy.'" In Nasr and Leaman, *History of Islamic Philosophy*, 247–51.

———, editor. *Ismāʿīlī Contributions to Islamic Culture*. Tehran: Imperial Iranian Academy of Philosophy, 1398 H/1977.

Nasr, Seyyed Hossein, and Oliver Leaman, editors. *History of Islamic Philosophy*. London: Routledge, 1996. 2 vols.

Naṣṣār, Naṣīf. *Mafhūm al-umma baina ad-dīn wa-t-tārīkh: Dirāsa fī madlūl al-umma fī at-turāth al-ʿarabī al-islāmī*. Beirut: Dār aṭ-Ṭalīʿa, 1992.

Netton, Ian Richard. "Al-Farabi, Abu Nasr (c. 870–950)." In *Routledge Encyclopedia of Philosophy*, 3:554–58.

———. *Al-Farabi and his School*. London: Routledge, 1992.

———. "Neoplatonism in Islamic Philosophy." In *Routledge Encyclopedia of Philosophy*, 6:804–8.

Neugebauer-Wölk, Monika, and Holger Zaunstöck, editors. *Aufklärung und Esoterik*. Hamburg: Meiner, 1999.

Neumann, Harry. "Civic Piety and Socratic Atheism: An Interpretation of Strauss's Socrates and Aristophanes." *Independent Journal of Philosophy* 2 (1978): 33–37.

———. "What Is Philosophy? An Interpretation of the Theological-Political Problem." *Independent Journal of Philosophy* 1 (1977): 31–38.
Neusner, Jacob. *Law as the Medium of Theology in Judaism*. n. p., 1997.
Niemeyer, Gerhart. "What Is Political Knowledge?" *Review of Politics* 23 (1961): 101–7.
Niewöhner, Friedrich. "Aufklärung mit Esoterik. Jüdisches Denken im 18. Jahrhundert." In Neugebauer-Wölk and Zaunstöck, *Aufklärung und Esoterik*, 355–63.
———. "Averroismus vor Averroes? Zu einer Theorie der doppelten Wahrheit im 10. Jahrhundert." *Mediaevalia Philosophica Polonorum* 32 (1994): 33–39.
———. "Der Aufklärer Maimonides." *Allgemeine Zeitschrift für Philosophie* 21 (1996): 25–39.
———. "Die zweifache Schrift der Weisen." *Die Zeit*, November 8, 1996.
———. "Einleitung zur deutschen Ausgabe." In Averroes, *KPP*, 7–17.
———. "Epikureer sind Atheisten: Zur Geschichte des Wortes apikuros in der jüdischen Philosophie." In *Atheismus im Mittelalter und in der Renaissance*, edited by Friedrich Niewöhner and Olaf Pluta, 11–22. Wiesbaden, Germany: Harrassowitz, 1999.
———. *Maimonides: Aufklärung und Toleranz im Mittelalter*. Wolfenbüttel, Germany: Lessing-Akademie, 1988.
———. "Platons Höhle wurde unterkellert: Leo Strauss wollte raus." *Frankfurter Allgemeine Zeitung*, November 4, 1997, L20.
———. *Veritas sive Varietas: Lessings Toleranzparabel und das Buch von den drei Betrügern*. Heidelberg: Schneider, 1988.
———. "Vom Lesen alter Bücher: Eine Kontroverse über den Philosophen Leo Strauss." *Frankfurter Allgemeine Zeitung*, November 27, 1985, 35.
Niewöhner, Friedrich, and Loris Sturlese, editors. *Averroismus im Mittelalter und in der Renaissance*. Zürich: Spur, 1994.
Nöldeke, Theodor. "Hatte Muhammad christliche Lehrer?" *Zeitschrift der Deutschen Morgenländischen Gesellschaft* 12 (1858): 699–708.
Nordmann, Ingborg, and Iris Pilling. *Hannah Arendt, Kurt Blumenfeld: ". . . in keinem Besitz verwurzelt": Die Korrespondenz*. Hamburg: Rotbuch-Verlag, 1995.
Novak, David, editor. *Leo Strauss and Judaism: Jerusalem and Athens Critically Revisited*. Lanham, MD: Rowan and Littlefield, 1996.
Orr, Susan. *Jerusalem and Athens: Reason and Revelation in the Work of Leo Strauss*. Lanham, MD: Rowan and Littlefield, 1995.
———. "Strauss, Reason, and Revelation: Unraveling the Essential Question." In Novak, *Strauss and Judaism*, 25–53.
Orwin, Alexander. *Redefining the Muslim Community: Ethnicity, Religion, and Politics in the Thought of Alfarabi*. Philadelphia: University of Pennsylvania Press, 2017.
Pavlin, James. "Sunni kalām and Theological Controversies." In Nasr and Leaman, *History of Islamic Philosophy*, 105–18.
Pangle, Thomas L. Introduction. In Strauss, *SPPP*, 1–26.
———. "Introduction to the Thought of Leo Strauss." In Strauss, *RCPR*, vii–xxxviii.
———. "On the Epistolary Dialogue between Leo Strauss and Eric Voegelin." In Deutsch and Nicgorski, *Leo Strauss: Political Philosopher*, 231–56.

———. "Platonic Political Science in Strauss and Voegelin." In Strauss and Voegelin, *FPP*, 321–47.

———. "The Platonism of Leo Strauss: A Reply to Harry Jaffa." *Claremont Review of Books* 4 (1985): 18–20.

Parens, Joshua. *Leo Strauss and the Recovery of Medieval Political Philosophy*. Rochester, NY: University of Rochester Press, 2016.

———. *Metaphysics as Rhetoric: Alfarabi's Summary of Plato's "Laws."* Albany: State University of New York Press, 1995.

Peltz, Christian. *Der Koran des Abū l-ʿAlāʾ*. Wiesbaden: Harrassowitz, 2013.

Peters, F. E. "The Greek and Syriac Background." In Nasr and Leaman, *History of Islamic Philosophy*, 40–51.

Pines, Shlomo. "Aristotle's Politics in Arabic Philosophy." *Israel Oriental Studies* 5 (1975): 150–60. Reprinted in *Studies in the History of Arabic Philosophy: The Collected Works of Shlomo Pines*, edited by Sara Stroumsa, 150–60 (Jerusalem: Hebrew University Magnes Press, 1996).

———. "Besprechung: Ventura, M.: La Philosophie de Saadia Gaon, Paris 1934 und ders.: Le Kalām et le Péripatétisme d'après le Kuzari, ebda 1934." *Orientalische Literaturzeitung*, no. 10 (1935): column 623.

———. "The Limitations of Human Knowledge according to Al-Farabi, Ibn Bajja and Maimonides." In *Studies in Medieval Jewish History and Literature*, edited by Isadore Twersky, 82–109. Cambridge, MA: Harvard University Press, 1979.

———. "On Leo Strauss." *Independent Journal of Philosophy* 5/6 (1988): 169–71.

———. "Philosophy." In *The Cambridge History of Islam*, edited by P. M. Holt, 780–823. Cambridge: Cambridge University Press, 1970.

———. "Shīʿite Terms and Conceptions in Judah Halevi's *Kuzari*." *Jerusalem Studies in Arabic and Islam* 2 (1980): 165–251.

———. "The Societies Providing for the Bare Necessities of Life according to Ibn Khaldūn and to the Philosophers." *Studia Islamica* 34 (1971): 125–38.

———. "Translator's Introduction: The Philosophic Sources of *The Guide of the Perplexed*." In Maimonides, *Guide*, lvii–cxxxiv.

Pippin, Robert B. "The Modern World of Leo Strauss." *Political Theory* 20 (1992): 448–72.

Platt, Michael. "Interpretation." *Interpretation* 5 (1975): 109–30.

Plessner, Martin. *Der OIKONOMIKOC des Neupythagoreers "Bryson."* Heidelberg: Winter, 1928.

———. "Nāmūs." In *EI1*, 3:911–14. 1936.

Pocock, J. G. A. "Prophet and Inquisitor; or, A Church Built upon Bayonets Cannot Stand: A Comment on Mansfield's 'Strauss's Machiavelli.'" *Political Theory* 3 (1975): 385–401.

Radtke, Bernd. "The Concept of wilāya in Early Sufism." In *Classical Persian Sufism from Its Origins to Rumi (700–1300)*, vol. 1 of *The Heritage of Sufism*, edited by Leonard Lewisohn, 483–96. London: Khaniqahi Nimatullahi Publications, 1993.

———. "How Can We Reach the Mystical Union? Ibn Ṭufayl and the Divine Spark." In Conrad, *World of Ibn Ṭufayl*, 165–94.

———. "Theologen und Mystiker in Ḫurāsān und Transoxanien." *Zeitschrift der Deutschen Morgenländischen Gesellschaft* 136 (1986): 536–69.

———. "Unio mystica und coniunctio: Mystisches Erleben und philosophische Erkenntnis im Islam." *Saeculum* 41 (1990): 53–61.

Rahman, Fazlur. "Law and Ethics in Islam." In Hovannisian, *Ethics in Islam*, 3–15.

———. *Prophecy in Islam: Philosophy and Orthodoxy*. London: Allen and Unwin, 1958.

Redner, Harry. *Malign Masters: Gentile, Heidegger, Lukács, Wittgenstein: Philosophy and Politics in the Twentieth Century*. New York: St. Martin's Press, 1997.

Reinert, Benedikt. *Die Lehre vom* tawakkul *in der klassischen Sufik*. Berlin: de Gruyter, 1968.

Renan, Ernest. *Averroès et l'Averroïsm*. Paris: Calmann and Lévi, 1861.

———. *Ibn Rushd wa-r-rushdiyya*. Translated into Arabic by ʿĀdel Zuʿaiter. Cairo: Dār at-Tanwīr, 1957.

Rescher, Nicholas. *Al-Fārābī: An Annotated Bibliography*. Pittsburgh: University of Pittsburgh Press, 1962.

Riedel, Manfred. "Metaphysik und Politik bei Aristoteles." *Philosophisches Jahrbuch* 77 (1970): 1–14.

———. "Political Language and Philosophy." *Independent Journal of Philosophy* 2 (1978): 107–12.

Ritter, Joachim. "'Politik' und 'Ethik' in der praktischen Philosophie des Aristoteles." *Philosophisches Jahrbuch* 74 (1966/7): 235–53.

Rosen, Stanley. *Hermeneutics as Politics*. Oxford: Oxford University Press, 1987.

———. "Human Order in a Hostile Universe." *Review of Politics* 58 (1996): 206–08.

———. "Politics or Transcendence? Responding to Historicism." In Strauss and Voegelin, *FPP*, 261–66.

Rosenblatt, Louis B. "A Reading of Leibniz." *Independent Journal of Philosophy* 2 (1978): 67–69.

Rosenthal, Erwin. "Averroes' Paraphrase on Plato's 'Politeia.'" *Journal of the Royal Asiatic Society* (1934): 737–44.

———. "Avicenna's Influence on Jewish Thought." In *Avicenna: Scientist and Philosopher*, edited by G. M. Wickens, 66–83. London: Luzac, 1952. Reprinted in E. Rosenthal, *Studia Semitica*, 1:290–307.

———. "The Concept of Eudaimonia in Medieval Islamic and Jewish Philosophy." In *Storia della filosofia antica e medievale*, 145–52. Florence: Sansoni, 1960. Reprinted in E. Rosenthal, *Studia Semitica*, 2:127–34.

———. "Maimonides' Conception of State and Society." In *Moses Maimonides*, edited by I. Epstein, 191–204. London: Soncino Press, 1935. Reprinted in E. Rosenthal, *Studia Semitica*, 1:275–89.

———. "The Place of Politics in the Philosophy of Al-Farabi." *Islamic Culture* 29 (1955): 157–78. Reprinted in E. Rosenthal, *Studia Semitica*, 2:93–114.

———. "The Place of Politics in the Philosophy of Ibn Bajja." *Islamic Culture* 25 (1951): 187–211. Reprinted in E. Rosenthal, *Studia Semitica*, 2:35–59.

———. "The Place of Politics in the Philosophy of Ibn Rushd." *Bulletin of the School of Oriental and African Studies* 15 (1953): 246–78. Reprinted in E. Rosenthal, *Studia Semitica*, 2:60–92.
———. *Political Thought in Medieval Islam*. Cambridge: Cambridge University Press, 1958.
———. "Some Aspects of Islamic Political Thought." *Islamic Culture* 22 (1948): 1–17. Reprinted in E. Rosenthal, *Studia Semitica*, 2:17–33.
———. "Some Observations on the Philosophical Theory of Prophecy in Islam." In *Mélanges Henri Massé*, edited by Ali-Akar Siassi, 343–52. Tehran: University of Tehran Press, 1963. Reprinted in E. Rosenthal, *Studia Semitica*, 2:135–44.
———. *Studia Semitica*. Cambridge: Cambridge University Press, 1971. 2 vols.
———. "Torah and 'Nómos' in Medieval Jewish Philosophy." In *Studies in Rationalism, Judaism and Universalism*, edited by R. Loewe, 215–30. London: Routledge, 1966. Reprinted in E. Rosenthal, 1:309–24.
Rosenthal, Franz. *Greek Philosophy in the Arab World*. Aldershot: Variorum, 1990.
———. "On the Knowledge of Plato's Philosophy in the Islamic World." *Islamic Culture* 14 (1940): 387–422 and 15 (1941): 396–98.
———. "Review of Erwin Rosenthal's 'Averroes' Commentary on Plato's Republic.'" *Muslim World* 47 (1957): 249–51.
———. "State and Religion according to Abū l-Ḥasan al-ʿĀmirī." *Islamic Quarterly* 3 (1956): 42–52.
Roth, Leon. *Spinoza, Descartes, and Maimonides*. Oxford: Clarendon Press, 1924.
Sabine, George H. "Review of Leo Strauss, Persecution and the Art of Writing." *Ethics* 63 (1953): 220–22.
Salkever, Stephen G. Review of Leo Strauss, *Studies in Platonic Political Philosophy*. *Political Theory* 13 (1985): 292–96.
Sandoz, Ellis. "Medieval Rationalism or Mystik Philosophy? Reflections on the Strauss-Voegelin Correspondence." In Strauss and Voegelin, *FPP*, 297–319.
Sandvoss, Ernst R. "Was ist Philosophie?" *Independent Journal of Philosophy* 1 (1977): 22–28.
Sankari, Farouk A. "Plato and al-Fārābī: A Comparison of Some Aspects of Their Political Philosophy." *Muslim World* 60 (1970): 218–25.
Saunders, Trevor J. Review of Leo Strauss, *The Argument and the Action of Plato's "Laws." Political Theory* 4 (1976): 239–42.
Scherer, Martin. "Die zweite Höhle: Frühe Schriften von Leo Strauss." *Süddeutsche Zeitung*, January 7, 1998.
Schimmel, Annemarie. *Mystical Dimensions of Islam*. Chapel Hill: University of North Carolina Press, 1975.
Schmidt-Biggemann, Wilhelm. *Theodizee und Tatsachen: Das philosophische Profil der deutschen Aufklärung*. Frankfurt am Main: Suhrkamp, 1988.
Schroeder, Frederic M., and Robert B. Todd, editor and translator. *Two Greek Aristotelian Commentators on the Intellect: The "De Intellectu" Attributed to Alexander of Aphrodisias and Themistius' Paraphrase of Aristotele "De Anima" 3.4–8*. Toronto: Pontifical Institute of Mediaeval Studies, 1990.

Seeskin, Kenneth. "Maimonides' Conception of Philosophy." In Novak, *Strauss and Judaism*, 87–110.

Shahjahan, Muhammad. "The Concept of Courage in the Philosophy of Al-Farabi." *Islamic Quarterly* 29 (1985): 234–39.

Sharif, M. M., editor. *A History of Muslim Philosophy*. Wiesbaden, Germany: Harrassowitz, 1963.

Shatz, David. "Prophecy." In *Routledge Encyclopedia of Philosophy*, 7:767–71.

Shell, Susan. "Meier on Strauss and Schmitt." *Review of Politics* 53, no. 1 (1991): 219–23.

———. "Taking Evil Seriously: Schmitt's 'Concept of the Political' and Strauss's 'True Politics.'" In Deutsch and Nicgorski, *Strauss: Political Philosopher*, 175–93.

Sherlock, Richard, and Roger Berrus. "The Problem of Religion in Liberalism." *Interpretation* 20 (1993): 285–30.

Sherwani, H. K. "Al-Fārābī's Political Theories." *Islamic Culture* 12 (1938): 288–305.

Sigmund, Paul. Review of Ralph Lerner's *Averroes on Plato's Republic*. *Political Theory* 3 (1975): 235–36.

Sim, May, editor. *The Crossroads of Norm and Nature: Essays on Aristotle's "Ethics" and "Metaphysics."* Lanham, MD: Rowan and Littlefield, 1995.

Smith, Steven B. "Leo Strauss: Between Athens and Jerusalem." In Deutsch and Nicgorski, *Strauss: Political Philosopher*, 81–105.

———. Review of Leo Strauss, *On Tyranny*. *Political Theory* 20 (1992): 690–93.

Soffer, Walter. "Modern Rationalism, Miracles, and Revelation: Strauss's Critique of Spinoza." In Deutsch and Nicgorski, *Strauss: Political Philosopher*, 143–73.

Söllner, Alfons. "Leo Strauss." In *Politische Philosophie des 20. Jahrhunderts*, edited by K. G. Ballestrem and H. Ottmann, 105–21. Munich: De Gruyter Oldenbourg, 1990.

———. "Leo Strauss: German Origin and American Impact." In Kielmansegg et al., *Hannah Arendt and Leo Strauss*, 121–38.

Spahn, Peter. "Oikos und Polis: Beobachtungen zum Prozess der Polisbildung bei Hesiod, Solon und Aischylos." *Historische Zeitschrift* 231 (1980): 529–64.

Spengler, Oswald. *Der Untergang des Abendlandes: Umrisse einer Morphologie der Weltgeschichte*. Munich: Beck, 1923. 10th ed., Munich, 1991.

Steenberghen, Fernand van. *Aristotle in the West: The Origins of Latin Aristotelianism*. Translated by Leonard Johnston. Louvain-la-Neuve, Belgium: Nauwelaerts, 1955.

———. *La philosophie au 13e siècle*. Louvain-la-Neuve, Belgium: Publications Universitaires, 1966.

Steiner, George. "Inscrutable and Tragic: Leo Strauss's Vision of the Jewish Destiny." *Times Literary Supplement* (November 1997): 4–5.

Steinschneider, Moritz. *Al-Fārābī (Alpharabius): Des arabischen Philosophen Leben und Schriften mit besonderer Rücksicht auf die Geschichte der griechischen Wissenschaft unter den Arabern*. St. Petersburg, 1869. Reprinted in Amsterdam: Philo Press, 1966.

———. *Die arabischen Übersetzungen aus dem Griechischen*. Graz, Austria: Akademische Druck- und Verlags-Anstalt, 1960.

———. *Die hebräischen Übersetzungen des Mittelalters, und die Juden als Dolmetscher*. Graz: Akademische Druck- und Verlags-Anstalt, 1956.

———. "Gauberi's 'entdeckte Geheimnisse': Eine Quelle für orientalische Sittenschilderung." *Zeitschrift der Deutschen Morgenländischen Gesellschaft* 19 (1865): 564

———. *Zur pseudepigraphischen Literatur des Mittelalters, insbesondere der geheimen Wissenschaften*. Berlin, 1862. Reprinted in Amsterdam: Philo Press, 1965.

Strohmaier, Gotthard. *Avicenna*. Munich: Beck, 1999.

———. "Doxography." In *EI3*. Published April 1, 2015, last updated July 19, 2021. http://dx.doi.org/10.1163/1573-3912_ei3_COM_26088.

Strothmann, R. "Taḳīya." In *EI1*, 4:680–81. 1934.

Stroumsa, Sarah. *Freethinkers of Medieval Islam: Ibn Al-Rawāndī, Abū Bakr Al-Rāzī and Their Impact on Islamic Thought*. Leiden, Netherlands: Brill, 1999.

Sturlese, Loris. "L'averroismo nella cultura filosofica tedesca medieval." In Niewöhner and L. Sturlese, *Averroismus*, 114–31.

Sturlese, Rita. "Averroè quantumque arabo et ignorante di lingua greca: Note sull'averroismo di Giordano Bruno." In Niewöhner and L. Sturlese, *Averroismus*, 319–50.

Sturm, Douglas. "Polities and Divinity: Three Approaches in American Political Science." *Thought* 52 (1977): 333–65.

Surmar, Bohumil. *Die Unterscheidung zwischen den wahren und falschen Propheten: Eine Untersuchung aufgrund der Lehre des Rabbi Moses Maimonides auf dem Hintergrund der rabbinischen Lehren, der griechischen und arabischen Philosophie und der Prophetologie des Islam*. Bern: Lang, 1997.

Tamer, Georges. "Markab turathī yaʿūd: Talkhīṣ Ibn Rushd li-kitāb Aflāṭūn fī s-siyāsa." *Dirasāt ʿArabīya* 34 (1998): 100–11.

———. "Religion als Instrument: Zum zweiten Band der Gesammelten Schriften Leo Strauss'." *Neue Zürcher Zeitung*, January 10/11, 1998.

Tanguay, Daniel. *Leo Strauss: An Intellectual Biography*. Translated by Christopher Nadon. New Haven, CT: Yale University Press, 2011.

Tarcov, Nathan. "On a Certain Critique of 'Straussianism.'" In Deutsch and Nicgorski, *Strauss: Political Philosopher*, 259–74.

Tarcov, Nathan, and Thomas Pangle. "Epilogue — Leo Strauss and His History of Political Philosophy." In Strauss, *HPP*, 907–38.

Tibawi, Abdul-Latif. "The Idea of Guidance in Islam from an Educational Point of View." *Islamic Quarterly* 3 (1956): 139–56.

Tibi, Bassam. *Der Wahre Imam: Der Islam von Muhammed bis zur Gegenwart*. Munich: Piper, 1996.

———. "Politisches Denken im klassischen und mittelalterlichen Islam zwischen Religio-Jurisprudenz (Fiqh) und hellenisierter Philosophie (Falsafa)." In *Pipers Handbuch der Politischen Ideen*, edited by Iring Fetscher and Herfried Münkler, 2:87–140. Munich: Piper, 1993.

Toulmin, Stephen. "The Evolution of Margaret Mead." *New York Review*, December 6, 1984.

Townsend, Daniel. "Leo Strauss and Islam." PhD dissertation, Deakin University, 2014.

Tucker, George Eliott. "Introduction." *Independent Journal of Philosophy* 1 (1977): 1–13.

Tworuschka, Udo, editor. *Gottes ist der Orient — Gottes ist der Okzident: Festschrift für Abdoljavad Falaturi zum 65. Gebutstag*. Vienna: Orientalisches Institut der Universität Wien, 1991.

Udoff, Alan, editor. *Leo Strauss's Thought: Toward a Critical Engagement*. Boulder, CO: Lynne Rienner, 1991.

Ullmann, Manfred. *Die Medizin im Islam*. Leiden, Netherlands: Brill, 1970.

———. *Die Natur- und Geheimwissenschaften im Islam*. Leiden, Netherlands: Brill, 1972.

Velásquez, Eduardo A. "The Moderate Enlightenment in America: Review of Ralph Lerner, *Revolutions Revisited: Two Faces of the Politics of Enlightenment*." *Review of Politics* 58 (1996): 157–61.

Villa, Dana R. "The Philosopher versus the Citizen: Arendt, Strauss, and Socrates." *Political Theory* 26 (1998): 147–72.

Walsh, David. "The Reason-Revelation Tension in Strauss and Voegelin." In *In Faith and Political Philosophy: The Correspondence between Leo Strauss and Eric Voegelin, 1934–1964*, edited by Peter Emberley and Barry Cooper, 349–78. University Park: Pennsylvania State University Press, 1993.

Walzer, Richard. "Aflāṭūn." In *EI2*, 1:234–36. 1960.

———. "Alfārābi's Theory of Prophecy and Divination." *Journal of Hellenic Studies* 77 (1957): 142–48.

———. "Arabische Übersetzungen aus dem Griechischen." *Miscellanea Medievalia* 9 (1962): 179–95.

———. "Aspects of Islamic Political Thought: Al-Fārābī and Ibn Xaldūn." *Oriens* 16 (1963): 40–60.

———. *Greek into Arabic: Essays on Islamic Philosophy*. Oxford: Cassirer, 1962.

Warren, Mark. "Nietzsche and Political Philosophy." *Political Theory* 13 (1985): 183–212.

Watt, William Montgomery. *Islamic Fundamentalism and Modernity*. London: Routledge, 1988.

———. *Islamic Philosophy and Theology*. Edinburgh: Edinburgh University Press, 1962.

Weber-Schäfer, Peter. *Einführung in die antike Politische Theorie: Erster Teil: Die Frühzeit*. Darmstadt, Germany: Wissenschaftliche Buchgesellschaft, 1992.

Wels, Henrik. "Zu einer Theorie der doppelten Wahrheit in dem 'Tractatus de aeternitate mundi' des Boethius von Dakien." In Niewöhner and L. Sturlese, *Averroismus*, 85–100.

Wensinck, A. J. "Rasūl." In *EI2*, 8:454–55. 1995.

Wielandt, Rotraud. *Offenbarung und Geschichte im Denken moderner Muslime*. Wiesbaden: Steiner, 1971.

Wilhelmsen, Frederick D. *Christianity and Political Philosophy*. Athens: University of Georgia Press, 1978.

Wiser, James L. "Reason and Revelation as Search and Response: A Comparison of Eric Voegelin and Leo Strauss." In *Faith and Political Philosophy: The Correspondence between Leo Strauss and Eric Voegelin, 1934–1964*, edited by Peter

Emberley and Barry Cooper, 237–48. University Park: Pennsylvania State University Press, 1993.

Wolfson, Harry A. "Additional Notes." *Hebrew Union College Annual* 3 (1926): 371–75.

———. "The Amphibolous Terms in Aristotle, Arabic Philosophy and Maimonides." *Harvard Theological Review* 31 (1938): 151–73.

———. "Note on Maimonides' Classification of the Sciences." *Jewish Quarterly Review* 26 (1935): 369–77.

———. *The Philosophy of Spinoza*. Cambridge, MA: Harvard University Press, 1934. 2 vols.

Wood, Gordon S. "The Fundamentalists and the Constitution." *New York Review of Books*, February 18, 1988.

Zaman, Muhammad Qasim. Review of Patricia Crone and Maritn Hinds, *God's Caliph: Religious Authority in the First Centuries of Islam*." *Islamic Quarterly* 34 (1998): 200–11.

Zimmerli, Walther Ch. "Esoterik und Exoterik in den Selbstdarstellungsbegriffen der Gegenwartsphilosophie: Eine historische Analyse in systematischer Absicht." In Holzhey and Zimmerli, *Esoterik und Exoterik der Philosophie*, 253–88.

Zuckert, Catherine. "Nietzsche's Reading of Plato." *Political Theory* 13 (1985): 213–38.

Index

Abū Bishr Mattā bin Yunis, 263n23
active intellect / intellectus agens, 50, 85–88, 93, 99–101, 183, 233n41, 236n51, 236n60, 237n61, 241n119
Adler, Cyrus, 40
Alexander of Aphrodisias, 50, 69
Althusser, Louis, 20
Al-ʿĀmirī, Abū l-Ḥasan, 52
Ammonius, 52
Anastaplo, George, 204n84
Anthropocentrism, 81
Aristophanes, 11
Aristotle, ix, xix–xx, 23, 29, 43, 50, 65, 68–69, 81, 93, 121, 166, 176–77, 212n18, 235n49, 254n62
Atheism, xv, xxi, 19, 27, 61, 78, 82–83, 103, 129–30, 162, 165, 171–72, 209n40
Averroes, xv, xxii–xxiii, 2, 23–24, 26, 28–37, 30–40, 53, 63, 68–69, 93, 95–96, 123–128, 156, 207n17, 209n40, 210n6, 239n99, 248n102, 249n122, 254n62
Averroism, 22, 36, 198n19, 207n18
Averroists, Latin, 161, 207n18
Avicenna, xv–xvi, xvii–xix, xxi–xxii, 2, 22–23, 40–44, 49–54, 55, 59, 72, 83–91, 94–98, 106, 156, 167, 191n5, 193n20, 211n11, 212n18, 218n47, 219n49, 219n50, 234n43, 236n58–60
Badawī, ʿAbd ar-Raḥmān, 212n18
Benjamin, Walter, 20
Berns, Laurence, 256n87
Bible, 4, 10, 34, 48, 67, 81–82, 129, 173, 198n19, 232n26
Bloom, Allen, 10, 14, 22, 202n61, 204n85
Burnyeat, Myles, 16–18

Christianity, 30, 175, 259n150, 262n20
Cohen, Hermann, 5, 25–26, 61, 63, 85, 233n35
Colmo, Christopher, 128, 140–41, 247n90
Cosmocentrism, 81

Dahriyya, xxiii
Descartes, René, 34–35
Deutsch, Kenneth L., 197n2
Dilthey, Wilhelm, 79
Diogenes Laertius, xix
Drury, Shadia, 18–20, 129, 197n2

Enlightenment, xvi, xxii, 11, 21, 26, 36, 40, 55, 60–62, 65, 79, 83, 118, 129, 152, 163, 171–73
Efros, Israel, 67
Epicurus, 26–29, 39
Epicureanism, 27, 207n11
eudaimonia, 28, 251n16. *See also* felicity

Falaquera, 67–68, 74, 226n63, 235n49
al-falsafa al-ʿamaliyya, 156, 181
al-falsafa al-madaniyya, 156, 181, 265n53
al-falsafa an-naẓariyya, 156
al-falsafa as-siyāsiyya, 156, 265n53
felicity, 51, 135–36, 139, 140–41, 148, 156–57, 162, 164, 180, 183–84, 251n16, 252n20, 252n22, 253n39. *See also* eudaimonia
al-Fārābī / Alfarabi, xv–xvi, xx–xxiv, 2, 4–8, 14, 19, 22–24, 43–44, 50–54, 63–69, 71–78, 84–85, 86–87, 90–91, 96–104, 105–9, 111–17, 133–43, 153, 156–62, 164–69, 176–85, 192n06, 193n20, 200n38, 201n44, 205n111, 213n22, 218n43, 230n126, 233n41, 240n112, 241n116, 241n120, 245n43, 253n39, 258n133, 260n164, 263n22–23, 265n51; philosophy and religion, 67, 116, 161, 178–80; *ar-raʾīs al-awwal*, 98; theory and praxis, 140, 184, 261n186

fiqh, 68, 117, 155, 255n63
Fradkin, Hillel, 4
first cause, 34, 99, 114, 176, 182
Fundamentalism, 175

Galen, 43, 69, 93
Green, Kenneth Hart, 3–4, 6
Guttmann, Julius, 118, 223n23

Habermas, Jürgen, 196n51
Halevi, Yehuda, 15, 109
happiness, 28–29, 30, 42, 70–71, 73–74, 101, 113, 116–17, 128, 135–37, 139, 162, 164–65, 179–81, 183, 225n52, 265n53. *See also* eudaimonia
hedonism, 27
Heidegger, Martin, 12–13, 40, 79, 83, 230n126, 232n30, 242n123
Hellenism, 262n14
Hobbes, Thomas, 10, 18, 40, 57–59, 222n15
Ḥunayn (Ḥunein) Ibn Isḥāq, xviii, 215n26, 215–16n27

Iamblichus, 52
Ibn ʿAdī, Yaḥyā, 34
Ibn Bāja, xxiii
Ibn Miskawayh, Abū ʿAlī, xviii, xx, 215
Ibn al-Qifṭī, 68–69
Ibn ar-Rāwandī, xxiii
ar-Rāzī, Abū Bakr, xxiii
Ibn Tibbon, Samuel, 63
Ibn Ṭufayl, xxiii, 86
Ibn Rushd, 34. *See also* Averroes
Ibn Sīnā. *See* Avicenna
al-ʿilm al-madanī, 181, 251n12, 255n63, 265n63
al-ʿilm al-insānī, 181
imagination, 6, 29–30, 32, 36, 93, 98–99, 138, 178–79
imam, 66, 95, 98, 100, 135, 140
Islam, xvi, 5, 39–40, 48, 53, 95–96, 100–1, 106–7, 141, 155, 175, 177, 218n44, 220n57, 234n45, 259n150

Jaffa, Harry, 11
John Philoponus, 52
Judaism, xxiii, 3, 4, 5, 7, 27, 34, 35, 40, 60, 61, 85, 95, 106, 198n19, 259n150

Kalām, 36, 68, 70, 76–77, 87, 113, 117, 227n74, 234n44, 265n43, 265n51
Kartheininger, Markus, 191n5
Kauffmann, Clemens, 13, 14
Kent, James Andrew, 20–21
al-Kindī, xxiii, 50
kitāb an-nawāmīs, xvii–xviii, xix, 193n20, 215n27. See also *nawāmīs Aflāṭūn*

law, divine/religious/revealed, xvi – xviii, xix, 2, 4 10, 12, 22, 33, 35, 39, 41–46, 50–52, 54, 59, 66, 70, 76, 77, 82–84, 88–89, 91, 94–95, 104, 105–24, 126–28, 130–31, 134–35, 139, 141, 155, 163, 171, 174–75, 177, 185, 191n5, 211n11, 212n18, 216n28, 218n43, 220n55, 223n20, 237n55, 240n91, 245n42, 246n43, 247n55, 249n101, 250n121, 255n59, 259n150
Lerner, Ralph, 213n21, 226n54, 226n56, 230n113
Lessing, Gotthold Ephraim, 15, 73
Liberalism, 56–58, 131, 223n15, 223n20
Locke, John, 18
Löwith, Karl, 131, 250n126

al-Maʿarrī, Abū l-ʿAlāʾ, xxiii
Machiavelli, Niccolò, 3, 16, 19–20, 29–30, 58, 80, 162
Mahdi, Muhsin, xix, 100, 102, 159, 201n44, 213n21, 241n108, 242n116
Maimonides, xvi, xix, xxi–xxii, 2–8, 10, 15, 18, 27, 34–37, 40, 61–64, 65–67, 69–72, 80, 84–87, 91, 94, 96–98, 102, 115–116, 123, 126, 135, 165, 167, 198n8, 200n38–39, 211n11, 224n30, 233n34, 234n41, 235n44, 236n46, 240n95, 246n43, 246n55
Marsilius of Padua, 162, 255n62
Marx, Karl, 20, 118
Massignon, Louis, 60
al-Māwardī, 155, 235–36n44
Meier, Heinrich, 12–15, 191n5, 211n11, 223n20

modernity, xxi, xxiv, 10–13, 17, 19–20, 22–24, 58–59, 61–62, 72, 79, 80–85, 102, 103, 118, 121, 130, 133, 153, 163, 171, 173, 175, 185, 223n15
Muhammad, xix, xx, 40, 49, 100, 177, 214n24, 218n43–45, 220n55, 235n44
Mūsā Ibn Maimūn. *See* Maimonides
mutakallimūn, 100

nabī. *See* prophet
Namazi, Rasoul, xix–xxi, 191n2, 194n31
nāmūs, xx, 43–44, 49, 212n18, 214n24–25
Nawāmīs Aflāṭūn, 44, 75, 106, 111
Nietzsche, Friedrich, xxiv, 1, 11, 20, 40, 60, 79–80, 118, 167, 196n49, 196n50
nomos, xvii, xx, 24, 52, 105–106, 108–113, 115, 129–130
nubuwwa. *See* prophecy

Olympiodorus, 52
Orr, Susan, 128, 232n18

Pangle, Thomas L., 8–9, 14, 203n82
Parens, Joshua, xxiv, 197n51, 230–31n122
Plato, xvi–xix, 2–4, 6–11, 14, 16, 18, 20, 23, 41–43, 49, 52–54, 56, 59, 63, 65, 68–69, 71–72, 74–79, 85, 90–93, 95, 97–98, 106–108, 112, 114, 117, 135, 138, 141, 156 – 157, 160–161, 163, 165, 167–168, 176, 184, 191n5, 192n12, 193n19, 202n61, 205n111, 210n6, 211n11, 212n18, 215n26, 217n40, 219n54, 227n59, 230n122, 232–33n26, 236n46, 239n76, 240n95, 243n4, 245n42, 250n121, 252n14, 253n21, 259n141; ideal state, xvi, 6, 53, 65, 73, 90–97, 104, 135, 182, 224n31; philosopher-king, 24, 74, 90–92, 94–99, 103–104, 113, 122, 130, 138, 166, 238n60, 240n95
Platonism, 10, 23–24, 73, 91–93, 166, 192n6, 197n51
Plotinus, 52, 93, 176, 218–19n47
Prometheus, 173
Prophecy, xvi–xx, xxiii, 2–4, 6–7, 10, 14, 22, 30, 40–44, 46–52, 54, 60, 62–63, 66, 70, 81, 83–104, 113, 140, 191n5, 211n11, 212n18, 215–16n27, 217n39, 218n44, 218n45, 220n55, 222n69, 235n44, 237n56, 240n95, 242n116, 242–43n119
prophet, xxi, 2, 4, 6, 10, 14, 24, 28–29, 32, 37, 40, 45–54, 59, 64, 66, 80, 84–104, 115–116, 125, 130, 134, 137, 140, 146, 155–156, 167, 177, 201n40, 204n83, 215n26, 216n29, 217n37, 217n39, 218n41, 218n43–45, 220n55, 234n41, 235n44, 237n56, 237n57, 238n60, 240n91, 240n95, 243n120, 263–64n21
providence, 7, 36, 62–64, 69–71, 77, 88, 116, 177, 227n67, 228n72, 241n101, 246n55
pseudo-Platonic *Book of Laws*, xvii, 222n69. See also *nawāmīs Aflāṭūn*
Pythagoras, 52, 220n55

Qurʾān, xxiii, 124, 217n39, 237n59, 250n121

rasāʾil ikhwān aṣ-ṣafāʾ, 66, 216n30
religion, critique of , 1–3, 10, 22–23, 25–31, 33–37, 55, 58, 61, 79–80, 105, 114–115, 174 – 175, 198n19, 207n10, 207n16, 233–34n26
revelation, xvi, xxii–xxiv, 2–5, 7, 10–14, 18, 24, 26, 31, 34, 39, 41, 43, 46–51, 54, 60–64, 66, 82, 84–90, 92–94, 96–98, 100–104, 105–107, 113–114, 118–122, 125–127, 129–131, 135, 144, 157, 172, 179, 183, 191n5, 198n19, 212n18, 232n18, 237n56, 242n112, 243n4
Rosenthal, Erwin I. J., 210n6, 239n76, 240n91, 245n42, 252n16
Rosenthal, Franz, 227n59
Rousseau, Jean-Jacques, 80

Schmitt, Carl, 143, 153, 222n4, 223n20
Scholem, Gershom, 191n4, 193n18
sharia (*sharīʿa*), xvi, xvii, xviii, xx, 24, 35, 39, 76–77, 105–106, 108, 111–115, 129–130, 135, 140, 155, 175, 212–13n18, 243n4, 245n42, 246n43, 248–49n99
siyāsa, xix, xx, 24, 134, 153, 154–158, 183, 212n18, 257n107

Socrates, xxii, 1, 8–14, 52, 61, 73, 92, 108, 122, 138, 145, 147–151, 165, 205n111, 220n55
Spinoza, Benedictus de, xv–xvi, 1–3, 5, 10, 22–23, 25–37, 39–40, 54, 59, 82, 114, 120–121, 198n19, 206n9
Sufism, 96

Theocracy, 31
Theocentrism, 81
Thomas Aquinas, 4, 255n62, 259n150
Torah, 27, 34, 64, 115, 126, 207n11
Townsend, Daniel, xxiv
Thrasymachus, 73, 108, 138, 153
at-Tirmidhī, al-Ḥakīm, 217n39, 218n45

umma, 181
utopia, 122

Voltaire, 126

waḥī, *See* revelation
Weimar Republic, 5–6, 13, 82

Xenophon, 3, 11, 16, 18

Zeus, xx, 111, 129
Zionism, 25